AFTER EMPIRE

ALSO BY DILIP HIRO

Non-fiction

Inside Central Asia: A Political and Cultural History of Uzbekistan, Turkmenistan, Kazakhstan, Kyrgyzstan, Tajikistan, Turkey and Iran *(2009)*

Blood of the Earth: The Battle for the World's Vanishing Oil Resources *(2007)*

The Timeline History of India *(2006)*

The Iranian Labyrinth: Journeys Through Theocratic Iran and Its Furies *(2005)*

Secrets and Lies: Operation "Iraqi Freedom" and After *(2004)*

The Essential Middle East: A Comprehensive Guide *(2003)*

Iraq: In the Eye of the Storm *(2003)*

War Without End: The Rise of Islamist Terrorism and Global Response *(2002)*

The Rough Guide History of India *(2002)*

Neighbors, Not Friends: Iraq and Iran After the Gulf Wars *(2001)*

Sharing the Promised Land: A Tale of Israelis and Palestinians *(1998)*

Dictionary of the Middle East *(1996)*

The Middle East *(1996)*

Between Marx and Muhammad: The Changing Face of Central Asia *(1995)*

Lebanon, Fire and Embers: A History of the Lebanese Civil War *(1993)*

Desert Shield to Desert Storm: The Second Gulf War *(1992)*

Black British, White British: A History of Race Relations in Britain *(1991)*

The Longest War: The Iran-Iraq Military Conflict *(1991)*

Holy Wars: The Rise of Islamic Fundamentalism *(1989)*

Iran: The Revolution Within *(1988)*

Iran Under the Ayatollahs *(1985)*

Inside the Middle East *(1982)*

Inside India Today *(1977)*

The Untouchables of India *(1975)*

Black British, White British *(1973)*

The Indian Family in Britain *(1969)*

Fiction

Three Plays *(1985)*

Interior, Exchange, Exterior *(poems, 1980)*

Apply, Apply, No Reply & A Clean Break *(two plays, 1978)*

To Anchor a Cloud *(play, 1972)*

A Triangular View *(novel, 1969)*

AFTER EMPIRE

THE BIRTH OF A MULTIPOLAR WORLD

DILIP HIRO

NATION BOOKS
New York

Published by Nation Books, A Member of the Perseus Books Group
116 East 16th Street, 8th Floor
New York, NY 10003
Nation Books is a copublishing venture of the Nation Institute and the Perseus Books Group.

Designed by Jeff Williams

Library of Congress Cataloging-in-Publication Data
Hiro, Dilip.
    After empire : the birth of a multipolar world / Dilip Hiro.
        p. cm.
    Includes bibliographical references and index.
    ISBN 978-1-56858-427-0 (alk. paper)
    1. World politics—2005-2015. I. Title.
D863.3.H57 2009
909.83'1—dc22

                                                                                    2009045919

10 9 8 7 6 5 4 3 2 1

CONTENTS

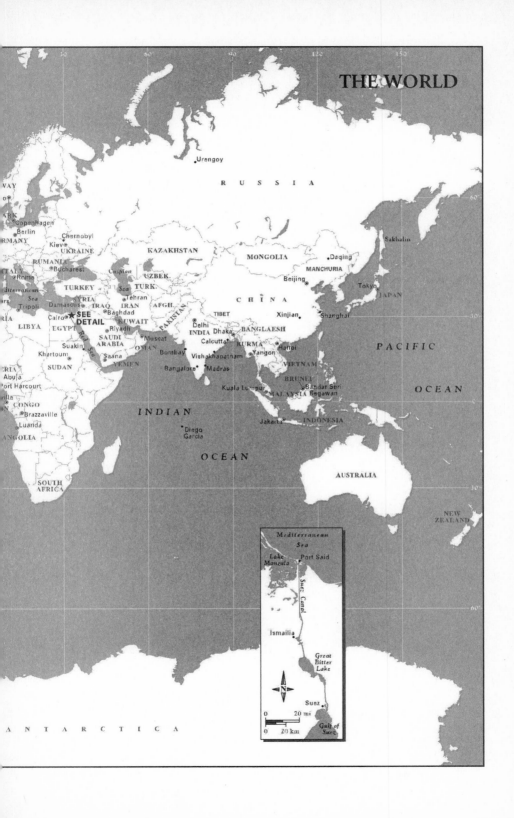

THE WORLD

•Urengoy

R U S S I A

Sakhalin

KAZAKHSTAN

MONGOLIA   MANCHURIA

•Daqing

Beijing•

Tokyo•

JAPAN

NORWAY
DENMARK
•Copenhagen
•Berlin
GERMANY
•Kiev
UKRAINE
RUMANIA
ITALY •Bucharest   Caspian
•Rome   Sea   UZBEK.
Mediterranean
Sea
•Tripoli   TURKEY   TURK.
ALGERIA   SYRIA   IRAQ IRAN AFGH.
LIBYA •Cairo ★SEE   •Baghdad
            DETAIL KUWAIT   PAKISTAN
EGYPT   •Riyadh
      Suakin Red   SAUDI   •Muscat
•Khartoum Sea   ARABIA OMAN
SUDAN   •Saana YEMEN
NIGERIA
•Abuja
Port Harcourt
Brazzaville
CONGO •Brazzaville
•Luanda
ANGOLA

•Damascus
•Tehran

TIBET

•Xinjian

•Shanghai

C H I N A

•Delhi
INDIA •Dhaka   BANGLAESH
•Calcutta   BURMA •Hanoi
•Bombay   •Vishakhapatnam •Yangon
•Bangalore •Madras   VIETNAM
                         BRUNEI
Kuala Lumpur•   •Bandar Seri
            MALAYSIA   Begawan

P A C I F I C

O C E A N

I N D I A N

•Diego
 Garcia

Jakarta•   INDONESIA

O C E A N

SOUTH
AFRICA

AUSTRALIA

NEW
ZEALAND

A N T A R C T I C A

Mediterranean
Sea

Lake   •Port Said
Manzala

Suez Canal

•Ismailia

Great
Bitter
Lake

N

•Suez

0   20 mi
0   20 km

Gulf of
Suez

PREFACE

When it comes to pomp and ceremony, dazzling color, and elaborate tradition, republics pale before monarchies. The annual opening of Congress in Washington appears drab when juxtaposed with the ceremonial unveiling of the new session of Parliament by the bejeweled and crowned Queen Elizabeth II. One of the greatest displays of imperial pageantry occurred on January 1, 1877, when Lord Lytton, viceroy of India, convened a durbar (imperial assembly) in a gigantic tented enclosure in Delhi, attended by 84,000 people, including 363 local kings, princes, and title holders in their fineries and diamond-studded turbans, to declare Queen Victoria the empress of India.

An equally historic occasion arose on January 1, 1992, in Washington, DC—the day after the collapse of the Soviet Union. If, by fluke, the protocol of the monarchical Britain had found its way into the contemporary United States by stealth, the world would have heard President George H. W. Bush declared the lord of the universe. Such a scenario had, of course, no chance of being realized. But that did not alter the fact on the ground. The United States of America no longer had a rival on the global scale. It was, quite simply, The Empire.

RISE AND FALL OF THE EMPIRES

Empires have a long history, and so do their trajectories. The earliest recorded empire-builder was Alexander the Great. A long-necked Macedonian, with deep-set eyes and a prominent nose, he died in 323 BCE, at the age of thirty-two. In terms of the amount of territory he conquered, he comes after Genghis

Khan (born Temujin, 1162–1227) and Tamerlane (aka Timur Beg, 1336–1405), both of them Mongol warriors. A sturdy man of medium height, haughty, slit-eyed, with scraggy, drooping beard and mustache, Genghis Khan ("Lord of the Universe" in Persian) was a military genius of exceptional ability. At 4.86 million square miles, the size of his empire remains unbeaten.

Today, however, it is Tamerlane, noted for his malevolent eyes and knotted cheeks, who looms large. Nearly six centuries after his death, he was resurrected by the post-Communist regime of Uzbekistan. Eager to establish a deep-rooted Uzbek identity, it declared Timur Beg the progenitor of the nation, even though he was not an ethnic Uzbek. Soon, his statues became as ubiquitous in the republic as Vladimir Lenin's were during the Soviet era.

More important, it was Tamerlane's great-great-great-grandson, Zahir Uddin Muhammad Babur (1483–1530), who founded the Mughal Empire in the Indian subcontinent—today's India, Pakistan, and Bangladesh. By happenstance, Babur's mother, Qultuq Nigar Khanum, was a descendant of Genghis Khan. So Babur shared the bloodlines of the world's greatest conquerors. A stout man, bearded and oval-faced, he coupled his exceptional military prowess with felicity with words, being equally at home with prose and poetry in Turkish, his mother tongue, and Persian, the literary language of the region. He left behind the *Babur Nama*, the earliest example of autobiographical writing by a ruler.

At its apogee the Mughal Empire was well ahead of the realms of the Ottoman Turks and the Persian Safavids. It began declining, as all empires eventually do, because its overlord, Emperor Aurangzeb, a lean, bearded man with austere looks, overextended his reach. Acquiring the title of *alamgir* ("lord of the universe"), he decreed that the coins in his mint be embossed "Emperor Aurangzeb Alamgir." A staunch Sunni, determined to defeat the Shiite rulers in southern India, he moved his military headquarters from Delhi to the south. "Mission accomplished," he proclaimed—as the northern Indian hinterland of his empire fractured.

The disintegrating Mughal Empire allowed the (English) East India Company—a commercial entity with its own army and navy—to conquer the subcontinent in stages by exploiting rivalries between the competing native rulers while funding its battles with the land revenue it collected. With the loss of Britain's American colonies in 1783, the center of its empire shifted to the Indian subcontinent.

The region fell to Britain in the mid-nineteenth century, with its government establishing direct control over it and Queen Victoria declaring herself empress of India. The possession of the vast, heavily populated subcontinent enabled Britain to claim that it ruled a quarter of the human race. Forging ahead of its competitors, France and the Netherlands, it gained the status of a superpower, with its pound sterling as the reserve currency. Britain's unassailable strength lay in its navy. Overall, it was the major seafaring nations in Europe—Belgium, Britain, France, the Netherlands, Portugal, and Spain—that sallied forth and built up overseas empires, big and small.

For the people of the subcontinent, the intrusion by Europeans, arriving by sea at first as merchants, was novel. Those who had subjugated the indigenous population before—the Afghan, Turkic, and Mughal warrior tribes from Central Asia—came overland through the Khyber Pass along the subcontinent's mountainous northwestern frontier. Over time these invaders got absorbed into the native population. This would not be the case with the British. They arrived by sea as fixed-term, contracted employees of the East India Company from a homeland with a distinct identity, to which they returned after their tour of duty. The company's establishment of trading posts at important Indian ports, followed by its piecemeal usurpation of political power in the hinterland, was unprecedented.

This approach was also deployed by imperial France in Indochina and North Africa and imperial Netherlands in Indonesia. As a category these overseas empires stood apart from the land empires established earlier by Genghis Khan, Tamerlane, and the Russian tsars, who either lacked naval forces or did not use them. By contrast, the United States gained entry into the imperialist club by deploying its navy against its Spanish counterpart in 1898 and seizing Cuba and the Philippines from Spain.

Later, air power would become the dominant element in large-scale conventional wars. By stationing warplanes on naval vessels, the United States would forge an extraordinarily powerful fighting machine. And by fabricating eleven aircraft carriers, it would leave other major powers, friendly or not, trailing far behind.

But, ultimately, wars are waged to capture and hold land. And if the occupying forces stay on for too long, they face resistance by the occupied. This applies to all major powers, however benign their declared intentions. The possession of aircraft carriers and a powerful air force has not enabled the

Pentagon to wage irregular warfare in densely populated countries or urban areas, or in a terrain unsuited to deploying mechanized firepower. Iraq and Afghanistan have highlighted the limits of America's military power.

In the political arena, the United States had earlier pioneered a softer version of imperialism—economic domination, with American corporations in cahoots with the indigenous elite. By so doing Washington exploited local resources without the expense and opprobrium of maintaining political-administrative control, which was an integral part of European imperialism. Nevertheless, a salient element common to both the political imperialism of Britain and the milder, yet equally exploitative, economic imperialism of America was the active participation by private individuals and companies to establish and then maintain the empire, with the imperial government providing the military umbrella.

Britain's break with political imperialism came in Iran, where economic imperialism became its template. Having won the contract to explore for oil, the company of a British prospector, William Knox d'Arcy, a colorful character addicted to betting on horses, struck petroleum in 1908 in Masjid-e Suleiman, the first commercially viable oil well in the Middle East. Since then the world has become heavily reliant on oil and gas to maintain or raise the living standards of the human race. And Western imperialism has become increasingly oriented toward exploiting the natural resources and cash crops of Asia, Africa, and South America. The decolonization of the European empires, and the political withdrawal of the United States from the Philippines after World War II, left Western economic domination intact. The prices of cotton and tea, for instance, continued to be determined in London, not in Bombay or Calcutta.

This book examines the world in its late imperial phase. The ideological certainties of the Cold War are gone, but so is the new dogma—aptly captured in the title of Francis Fukuyama's book *The End of History*—that cropped up as the Soviet Union collapsed. Top U.S. officials have used different terminology to describe America's sole superpower status, with U.S. Secretary of State Madeleine Albright calling the United States "the indispensable nation" and a senior aide to President George W. Bush declaring, "We are an empire now." But with the debacles in Iraq and Afghanistan glaringly obvious, and the U.S.-generated fiscal catastrophe wreaking havoc worldwide, U.S. policymakers are now floundering. One may now ask: What will the world look like, after The Empire?

During the Cold War, the United States found its capitalist mode of economic development challenged by the Soviet Union's socialist model of economic development in the recently independent countries of Asia and Africa, a group that came to be collectively called the Third World. With the demise of the Soviet Union, the People's Republic of China (PRC) has come to offer a viable alternative to the developing world. While its successful Communist revolution in 1949, wrought by an army of peasants, puzzled orthodox Marxists, its economic liberalization, starting three decades later, has befuddled Western experts. It has not led to the erosion of the monopoly over power that the Communist Party of China (CPC) has exercised since the founding of the PRC. Its staggering economic expansion in such a political setup presents a threat to the template imperial America has been exporting since World War II.

Though the Soviet Union is gone, its successor, Russia—accounting for nearly four-fifths of its territory and possessing vast reserves of hydrocarbons and strategic metals as well as a huge arsenal of nuclear weapons—remains a major power. On the other hand, the Kremlin no longer offers an alternative political-economic model to the non-Western world. In the regional context, both Iran and Venezuela—the first South American country to strike oil—stand out. The political and economic models they provide in their respective regions clash with the ones offered by the United States. In that sense, they constitute considerable "resistance" power.

In the 1960s Washington and other Western capitals subscribed to the thesis that Communist China and democratic India were engaged in a race whose outcome would settle the superiority of their competing social systems. Judged in those terms, China has won. But that does not diminish the power, present and potential, of India, home to one-sixth of humanity.

Equally important is the twenty-seven-member European Union, even though it is not a single political entity. It looms large on the economic horizon. The aggregate economies of its sixteen-member Eurozone come close to the GDP of the United States.

Since power is multifaceted, it is important to examine its soft side. The explosive growth in telecommunications along with a steep fall in rates has provided unprecedented opportunities to non-Western powers to challenge the dominance that America enjoyed in soft-power projection in the second half of the last century.

My thesis stands apart in several ways from that of others who have analyzed the emerging international order. *After Empire* does not revolve around

America. Nor is it dialectical—the United States versus China, the West against Asia, or democracies versus autocracies. The developments I describe in this volume have cumulatively led to an international order with multiple poles, cooperating and competing with one another, with no single pole being allowed to act as the hegemonic power. Quite simply, the age-old balance of power is back at work.

My narrative analysis strives to be realistic and nuanced, shorn of ideological bias or a soft corner for the United States.

A BIPOLAR WORLD AND AFTER

A glance at the past two decades shows a wide array of change—political, economic, and technological—with the demise of distance caused by the epochal arrival of the Internet. In diplomacy, the fall of the Berlin Wall in November 1989 was the political equivalent of an earthquake. It rearranged the contours of the international order. It proved to be the harbinger of the disintegration of the Soviet Union, one of two poles after World War II.

The rise of a bipolar world divided by ideology, and its existence for nearly two generations in the midst of the Cold War, had no parallels in global history. How the planet turned bipolar, providing an increasing number of freshly independent countries in Asia and Africa an option to choose either Western capitalist democracy or socialist authoritarianism—or to stay neutral—is the theme of Chapter 1.

The forty-five-year struggle between the competing blocs—maintained at the level of a cold war out of the dread of mutually assured destruction (MAD) threatened by the nuclear arsenals of the antagonists—ended with America's victory. The United States acquired, rightly, the sobriquet of "the Sole Superpower." In the constellation of 190-plus nations, it became the one and only sun. On the eve of the 2003 Iraq War, while accounting for only 5 percent of the world's population, it produced a quarter of the global GDP. Its 250,000 troops, posted abroad, guarded its seven hundred bases in 130 countries. This was the zenith of Pax Americana.

Rejoicing in the victory of market forces over Marxist doctrine, most Western intellectuals foresaw liberal, capitalist democracy becoming humanity's ultimate form of government—the end product of a long process of evolution, requiring mere management and mass education for its sustenance. In such an international order, American hegemony would remain unchallenged. And the age of imperial America would be secure for the foreseeable future.

Before long, though, events outside North America and Europe put an end to "the end of history" and its corollary of Washington's everlasting supremacy. The disparate challenges to America's global primacy stemmed as much from sharpening conflicts over natural resources, particularly oil and natural gas, as from ideological questioning of Western-style democracy and human rights as conceived and promoted primarily by American policymakers. At stake were also varied perceptions of national and imperial identities and history.

The end result was a revival of the pre–Cold War pattern of powers of different magnitude jostling for primary and secondary positions in the global hierarchy, with no single nation sitting at the apex of the pyramid. By now, the pyramid's pointed top has become jagged, with China and Russia steadily carving out niches for themselves near it.

While neither Beijing nor Moscow is striving to knock Washington off its still dominant position, they are no longer prepared to kowtow to the White House as the Kremlin did under President Boris Yeltsin in the 1990s. Instead, they are engaged in an adroit game of engagement and containment with America, cooperating on certain issues and competing on others.

While reinforcing its commercial links with Washington and accumulating U.S. Treasury bonds by the truckload, Beijing has emerged as the economic fountainhead of East Asia, home to a third of humanity. While cooperating with the United States to contain Islamic extremists in Afghanistan, the Kremlin had succeeded in reducing Washington's influence in the strategic, resources-rich Central Asia to a near cipher. In any case, American hegemony was not destined to be the exception. The trajectory of empires, rising to a peak and then declining, has remained unchanged since ancient times. Nonetheless, the credit for accelerating America's fall must go to President George W. Bush.

In overreacting to the September 11, 2001, terrorist attacks by starting two major wars, while reducing taxes at home, Bush did more damage to the United States than Osama bin Laden—a gangling Saudi fugitive with a shaggy beard and a white turban—could have imagined in his wildest dreams. Bush alienated not only vast swaths of the Muslim world, the non-Muslim parts of Asia and Africa, and Russia, but also Washington's traditional European allies. His reckless fiscal policies led to the financial tsunami of the century, which engulfed the globe. More important, it discredited the model of capitalism unveiled in the early 1980s by Bush's Republican predecessor, Ronald Reagan, to a degree that ardent socialists envied.

Chapter 2 summarizes Bush's follies—as well as the international achievements of President Bill Clinton during the period when America had its place in the sun. Exercising guardianship over defeated Russia, ruled by Yeltsin, was the Clinton White House's glaring foreign policy success.

Like a convert to a new faith, the impulsive Yeltsin jumped into the untried waters of laissez-faire capitalism headlong, throwing caution and discretion to the wind. Eventually, though, even he started to balk at the way the White House tried to micromanage the Kremlin and the disdain with which his American overlord, Clinton, treated Russia's feelings about Serbia and Serbians, culturally akin to Russians, the Orthodox Church and the Cyrillic script being the strong threads binding them.

A late realization that, though defeated in the Cold War, Russia had a vast arsenal of nuclear weapons put some spine into the wayward Yeltsin. This process was bolstered by his foreign minister during 1996–1998, Yevgeny Primakov. By successfully checkmating the United States at the United Nations Security Council on the issue of Iraq's weapons of mass destruction in 1998, Primakov, backed by China, gave the international community a foretaste of a multipolar world. He showed that the title of Sole Superpower did not entitle America to hijack the UN Security Council at will.

With the advent of Vladimir Putin—a lean-faced, muscular judo expert—in the Kremlin, Russia fully recovered its lost confidence and clout, thanks to his strong personality and leadership style as well as soaring oil prices, which hit $147 a barrel in July 2008, funneling $1 billion a day into the Russian treasury.

Chapter 3 traces the chronicle of the Russian Federation under Yeltsin and Putin. The link to Chapter 4 is provided by hydrocarbons—with Iran, the pioneering petroleum state in the Persian Gulf region, sharing space with Venezuela, the first South American country to find oil. Oil has played a critical role in shaping both states. While Shiite Islam and turbaned mullahs in black cloaks have been a crucial element in Iran's history, generals in medal-covered, starched uniforms have been leading characters in the annals of Venezuela. After all, Simon Bolivar, the liberator of Venezuela and five other South American republics from the yoke of imperial Spain, was a general. Such a past helps to bring into focus the ascent of Hugo Chavez, a former military officer whose earthy humor, issuing from his well-formed mouth in a jowled face, is as repulsive to U.S. politicians as it is attractive to the poor in Venezuela.

What grates the elite in his republic most are his mixed Amerindian, African, and Spanish origins.

The Chavez phenomenon is symptomatic of the rising political consciousness of the peoples of Amerindian and African antecedents who have taken to using the ballot to win power at the expense of white settlers favored by Washington. Equally threatening to the United States is the continuing, viable existence of the Islamic Republic of Iran. By holding regular elections for parliament and president, its regime shows the rest of the world—particularly the autocratic monarchs of the oil-rich Gulf states—that the relationship between Islam and representative government is symbiotic.

A much greater and more fundamental challenge to the concept and practice of Western democracy comes from the People's Republic of China, the globe's most populous nation and its third largest economy, after America and Japan. Chapter 5 outlines the chronicle of China since World War II. Like the earlier superpowers, America and the Soviet Union, the ascent of the PRC to great-power status has been fitful rather than linear. My narrative covers the period from the rule of Mao Zedong—a chubby-faced, stocky man seldom without his tunic—to Hu Jintao—a bespectacled figure, neatly coiffured, in a business suit—through Deng Xiaoping and Jiang Zemin. It traces the evolution of the Communist Party of China from a vanguard revolutionary party representing the interests of the toiling masses to a governing party representing the vast majority of the people, including capitalists. What the CPC has retained is its Leninist party structure and its monopoly of power.

My text provides earlier examples of China blazing a unique trail of its own. Contradicting Karl Marx's thesis that only the industrial proletariat in urban areas could be the vanguard of class revolution, Mao transformed peasants in an overwhelmingly agrarian China into a revolutionary army to smash the traditional class structure. By combining an armed struggle against the imperialism of Japan occupying parts of China with furthering socialism, Mao led a movement that had no precedence. (His example would later be followed by Ho Chi Minh in Vietnam.) Neither the Bolshevik nor the French revolution was anti-imperialist. And the anti-imperialist American revolution left property and class relations untouched.

The PRC's admission to the World Trade Organization (WTO) in 2001 accelerated its integration into the global capitalist order. This was viewed by most Western China-watchers as paving the way for the PRC to turn into a multiparty democracy. They took their cue from Taiwan, South Korea, and

Singapore, which, at their inception as independent states, were ruled by authoritarian leaders. But as their economies expanded, they morphed into multiparty democratic entities. My narrative shows that their expectations about the PRC were misplaced, and explains why.

As a leading WTO member, with its exports amounting to more than a third of its GDP, the PRC could not escape the consequences of the economic slump that afflicted the United States in 2008 and spread across the globe. But its control of the critical banking sector has protected it from the worst fallout of the fiscal morass. This was also the case with India, a founding member of the WTO but, in stark contrast to China, a vigorous, multiparty democracy. The reason for feeling the heat but not getting burned by the financial meltdown was the same as with the PRC: government control of the banking industry. Nearly three-quarters of the banking in India is nationalized.

Chapter 6 outlines the economic and political chronicle of India. It traces India's gradual colonization by the British, starting in the mid-eighteenth century with the East India Company, and leads to the present day, when the country is a leader in information and communications technology. While it deserves its much-flaunted title of the "world's largest democracy"—with its many political parties, an independent judiciary, and lively media—it suffers from certain major weaknesses. Principal among these are the absence of a strong government at the center and the presence of rampant corruption, mind-numbing red tape, and a scandalously skewed distribution of wealth, with seven out of ten Indians living below $2 a day. It has no chance of ever catching up with the PRC. Yet its possession of nuclear bombs and its advanced missile and space programs entitle it to be considered a major power in this survey.

The continuing progress—not to say viability—of a multiethnic, multilingual Republic of India remains an unstated inspiration for the architects of the twenty-seven-member European Union. But the two cases are widely varied. The salient difference is that the Indian subcontinent was welded into a single administrative-political unit by imperial Britain. The task that befell the democratic successors to the departed Britons on the eve of the independence and partition of the subcontinent was to keep administering an existing entity with a long history. But melding more than two dozen European nations with diverse histories and perceptions, dating back many centuries, into a single identity is a truly Herculean assignment. It is beyond the capabilities of even the most adroit politicians and statesmen. So it has proved—with the fairly modest 2007 Reform/Lisbon Treaty yet to be ratified by its recalcitrant member, Ireland—a salient point made in Chapter 7.

When viewed from the setting of 1950, the year the complex process began with the joint management of the state-owned coal and steel industries of France and West Germany, the progress of economic—and other—integration of Europe has been impressive. But in the absence of a federal or confederal structure, neither of which is on the horizon, the European Union will remain a hobbled giant.

The jump in EU membership came with the disintegration of the Soviet bloc in 1990. With that, a whole clutch of countries became eligible for admission since they met the condition of being ruled by a government elected in a free and fair poll. That remains the bottom-line definition of democracy, to which are added the concept of separation of the executive, legislative, and judicial organs of the state. However, in the case of constitutional monarchies (such as Britain) or indirectly elected presidents (as in Germany), the legislative and executive arms are combined.

There are other variants of democracy, according to Chapter 8, not least the Islamic version as practiced in Iran. This chapter also explains how China's leaders perceive democracy and how in their view the PRC is making progress in that field. Equally important are the concepts of freedom and human rights: Whereas Western leaders keep stressing political rights, many of their non-Western counterparts emphasize economic, cultural, and social rights. Preeminent among the latter have been the Chinese.

It was at the instigation of PRC leaders that the scholars of the Chinese Academy of Social Sciences (CASS) delved into the concept of power in all its manifestations. CASS came up with a formula to quantify comprehensive national power (CNP). Consisting of sixty-four indexes, the all-encompassing CNP statistic takes into account "soft power," as defined by Joseph Nye of Harvard University. Chapter 9 outlines the challenges to the soft power of America, particularly outside Europe, by examining the role of television news channels, cinema, and such prestigious projects as hosting the Olympics and undertaking space exploration.

The impact of globalization and ongoing nonviolent competition in the field of soft power does not preclude the world's hot spots bursting into flames. This is the subject of Chapter 10. The future flashpoints between the major powers belong to one of the following categories: (a) perceived threat to national security, (b) control of disputed territories, (c) competition for vital resources such as oil and natural gas, and (d) currency and trade. Washington's insistence on erecting anti-missile defense facilities in Eastern Europe is a prime candidate for causing a clash between the United States and Russia. Equally, the Iranian regime's fear of being toppled by the United States has the potential to go critical.

Taiwan's status leads the list in category b. Besides Taiwan, the United States will be the main antagonist of the PRC. That will also be the case when the normal commercial competition for hydrocarbons between Washington and Beijing escalates to deploying force to gain possession of oil and gas fields. This was the root cause of the conflict between America and Japan, leading to the Japanese attack on Pearl Harbor in 1941.

Less dramatic yet no less important is the spat between Washington and Beijing about currency and commerce. Many American politicians as well as some Obama administration officials are accusing the PRC of manipulating its currency, the yuan, to boost its exports and accumulate U.S. dollars to be used as a political lever in the future. If the American administration were to declare officially that China was manipulating the currency and take compensatory measures, such as imposing tariffs on Chinese imports, then Beijing would retaliate by unloading its vast portfolio of U.S. Treasury bonds. That would send tremors through the capital markets worldwide.

The concluding chapter provides a sketch of how a multipolar world will look and function in a post-empire era. Imagine a group of knights in armor fencing with one another, each one trying to get the better of his immediate challenger while being ready to help a fellow knight in distress, the common aim of all of them being to ensure that none of them emerges as the unchallenged champion to demand and receive tribute from the rest. In that ceaseless jousting, the knights will go on changing their partners and adversaries to achieve the overarching objective of keeping the field free of an overlord—a privilege enjoyed until recently by America.

The epilogue takes the narrative to October 2009. It is not indexed.

I am indebted to my editor, Carl Bromley, for his unflagging interest and support.

DILIP HIRO
London
October 2009

CHAPTER 1

RISE AND FALL
OF THE BIPOLAR WORLD

Global history after World War II was dominated by two superpowers—the United States and the Soviet Union—engaged in a cold war, which included competing for loyalties of the uncommitted countries, collectively called the Third World. This era, likely to go down in the world chronicle as unique, lasted for four and a half decades.

The essence of that struggle was aptly encapsulated by President Harry Truman in 1950 and the Soviet leader Nikita Khrushchev a decade later. "In a shrinking world . . . it is not an adequate objective to seek to check the Kremlin design, for the absence of order among nations is becoming less and less tolerable," said Truman. "This fact imposes on us, in our own interests, the responsibility for world leadership." As expected, Khrushchev viewed the growing list of independent nations in Asia and Africa differently. "The renovation of the world along the principles of freedom, democracy and socialism, in which we are now taking part, is a great historical process," he declared. "The success of national liberation movement, due in large measure to the victories of socialism, in turn strengthens the international position of socialism in the struggle against imperialism."[1]

Divided by contrasting ideologies yet coexisting in a "balance of terror" due to the deployment of fearsome nuclear arsenals, in the end both overextended their reach, thereby inducing their decline—the Soviet Union in Afghanistan in the 1980s and the United States in Iraq two decades later.

Tracing the rise of these superpowers shows that their ascent to the pinnacle was fitful—jagged rather than smooth. America came into its own because

it joined World War II, but only after it was attacked by Japan. And during
the second half of the twentieth century, it was seriously challenged by the
Kremlin. The Soviet Union offered an alternative civilization free of the profit
motive driving the capitalist system. Its rapid industrialization and impressive
literacy gains appealed to the leaders of the rising Third World of independent
Asian and African countries.

AMERICA RISES TO THE FORE

In 1900 America had the second largest European population after tsarist Russia. But it was an imperial weakling. Though the U.S. Navy's fleet carried out
exercises in the Pacific in 1907, President Teddy Roosevelt recognized it as a
junior partner to the British Navy—"the guarantor of the peace in the world,"
where the gold-based British pound was the reserve currency. A decade and a
half later, on the eve of World War I (1914–1918), America had become the
world's largest manufacturer on earth, though it exported only 5 percent of its
GDP. The United Kingdom, in comparison, exported 25 percent of its GDP,
typical of an imperial power of its time.

America entered World War I in April 1917 on the strict understanding that
any postwar peace settlement would concede its demand for an open door to
trade and investment in Europe and its overseas markets, while accommodating the European victors' territorial ambitions. Its entry facilitated the Allied victory: with two-thirds of the globe's oil output of 1.38 million barrels per
day, it supplied three-fourths of the petroleum needs of the Allies until the
end of the war in November 1918.

But after the war Britain and France stuck to their old policies of exclusion. When, for example, new oil fields were discovered in northern Iraq,
British and French oil companies tried to exclude American petroleum companies. Washington pressed the case of its oil corporations vigorously. It succeeded. Two U.S. oil companies became part of the consortium in 1931 to
explore the gigantic Kirkuk oil field.

In the preceding decade, American companies had started penetrating the
markets of Europe and its areas of influence, turning the United States into a
global commercial power.[2] Yet this did not turn them or their government
into unqualified champions of free trade. At the first indication of a serious
economic challenge from abroad, Washington resorted to protectionism with

its Emergency Tariff Act of 1921, followed by the Fordney-McCumber Act of 1922. Earlier, in 1920, the Senate had blocked Wilson's move to join the League of Nations.

There was little, then, to suggest that the twentieth century would be dubbed "the American Century." Most U.S. politicians were ill at ease with the outside world. And American morale collapsed in the wake of the stock market crash on October 24, 1929. On that day the Dow Jones Industrial Average nosedived by 22.6 percent, with 13 million shares changing hands, resulting in losses of $5 billion, or, in today's terms, $680 billion. In another fire sale of 16.4 million shares that followed, the market lost a further $14 billion.[3]

U.S. lawmakers raised further tariff barriers by adopting the Smoot-Hawley Tariff Act of 1930, and European governments reciprocated. World trade declined by a staggering 60 percent between 1929 and 1932. The economic downslide continued in the United States. Between 1929 and 1933, America's farm output fell by half, and industrial capacity stagnated at 40 percent. More than 9,000 banks, two-fifths of the total, went bust, with losses of $2.5 billion—today's $340 billion—to depositors and shareholders. The fall in money supply led to deflation of 24 percent. Unemployment soared eightfold to 25 percent, with 12.8 million jobless.[4] Even those in work were on short time and short wages. By the time the presidential election in November 1932 had led to the victory of Franklin Delano Roosevelt—winning 57 percent of the vote and all but six states—the stock market had lost 89 percent of its value from its peak on September 3, 1929.

The situation was so bleak that in 1931 more than 100,000 Americans applied to the New York–based trade mission of the Soviet Union (which then lacked full diplomatic relations with the United States) to emigrate. But only 10,000 were accepted—chiefly engineers, factory workers, teachers, and artists.[5]

The Great Depression engendered an acute crisis of confidence that persisted throughout the 1930s, with many thoughtful Americans questioning their social system based on laissez-faire capitalism. In that environment, the New Deal acted as a palliative. In Roosevelt's words, it imposed "practical control over blind economic forces and blindly selfish men" through governmental intervention in managing the economy.

During 1933–1937 the money supply grew, and the GDP rose by 10 percent a year, three times the normal rate. It gave Roosevelt enough confidence to declare in his second inaugural speech in 1937, "We have always known that heedless self-interest was bad morals; we know now it is bad economics [too]."[6] But the economic gains of his first administration vanished when Roosevelt reversed his policies. In order to balance the budget, he slashed public spending, cutting the Works Progress Administration by half, and upped taxes. And by raising the reserve requirements for banks, he reduced money supply and caused deflation. Recession returned in 1937–1938.

WORLD WAR II LIFTS AMERICA

The American economy only started to recover with the onset of World War II. The destruction caused by total war in occupied Europe forced the rest of the continent to place orders in the United States. Once Washington joined the fray in December 1941, the draft wiped out mass unemployment. And the fiscal stimulus needed to wage war finally lifted America from the Great Depression. The wartime demands of the Allies, which now included the Soviet Union, accelerated the nation's economic growth. Little wonder that between 1939 and 1945, the GDP of the United States rose by an average of 9 percent.[7]

Washington's entry into the war on the Allied side ensured the defeat of the Axis Powers. At 410,000 dead, America's human loss was minimal compared to other participants. The war also left the United States in possession of nearly two-thirds of the globe's gold reserves and more than half of its industry.[8] In stark contrast, the conflict left the victorious European imperialist powers—Britain, France, and the Netherlands—exhausted and nearly bankrupt. The collapse of the British, French, and Dutch forces in southeast Asia in the face of the Japanese invasion destroyed the image of the white man's invincibility in the eyes of the local peoples. Therefore it became an uphill task for the European imperial powers to reestablish their rule over their colonies in Asia. This led to political decolonization in Asia—a process advocated by both America and the Soviet Union. They emerged as the two true victors of World War II, which ended in Europe in May 1945 and three months later in Asia, after the Pentagon had dropped two atom bombs on Japan, killing nearly 200,000 people.

Victory in the war coupled with their booming economy at home made Americans and their politicians regain faith in their way of life and economic system after a decade of despair. In their newfound euphoria they came to believe that their way of life would now appeal to all those who lived beyond America's shores.

Intent on avoiding the recession that had followed World War I, the United States took a lead in complementing the postwar international body, named the United Nations—a virtual successor to the League of Nations—with economic institutions. The Allied nations that gathered at Bretton Woods, New Hampshire, in July 1944 agreed to establish the International Bank for Reconstruction and Development (later renamed the World Bank) to provide soft loans and the International Monetary Fund (IMF) to cover short-term imbalances in international trade to stabilize exchange rates. It also decided to hammer out a General Agreement on Tariffs and Trade (GATT). It declared the U.S. dollar, pegged to gold at $35 an ounce, as the international reserve currency. Washington would use its control of the World Bank and the IMF as an effective weapon in the Cold War with Moscow, denying credits and loans to the regime it disapproved.

In the postwar years Washington's Marshall Plan revived the economies in Western Europe. By deciding to station U.S. warships in the Mediterranean, and giving military aid to Greece and Turkey in 1947, President Truman signaled the arrival of America as a superpower. The next year, following the political coup in Czechoslovakia—with the Czech Communist Party engineering the exit of its non-Communist partners in the coalition government while the military remained neutral—Washington increased its defense budget, raising the size of its peacetime volunteer army to a record 660,000 soldiers. With the creation of the North Atlantic Treaty Organization (NATO) in 1949, the United States became the accepted leader of the West.

This set the scene for the postwar White House to popularize Americana through "soft power"—consumer goods, flashy cars, and large, well-furnished houses displayed in Hollywood movies, as well as the multifarious ideas of liberty.

The Soviet Union and Eastern Europe spurned the offer of U.S. bounty. With the founding of the People's Republic of China in 1949, Communism emerged as a strong rival to U.S.-led capitalism.

A military challenge to America came in June 1950, when Communist North Korea attacked South Korea. Truman rallied the Western allies and, because of the Soviet boycott of the UN Security Council, got a UN mandate to reverse the North Korean invasion. But when the U.S.-led forces of the UN expelled the North Koreans from the south within months, Truman ordered them to advance into North Korea. They almost reached the Chinese border. This led the PRC to intervene on a massive scale. By the spring of 1951 the war was stalemated around the line partitioning the Korean peninsula into two halves.

The Korean War, which claimed more than 36,500 American lives, proved so unpopular that Truman's approval rating plunged to 22 percent in 1952—a record until 2008, when it was broken by President George W. Bush with his approval rating down to 20 percent.

Truman's Republican successor, (Retired) General Dwight Eisenhower, who won the presidential contest on a promise to end the Korean War, proved adroit enough to note that there was a point beyond which his fellow citizens were unwilling to make sacrifices to advance Pax Americana. He therefore opted for clandestine intervention abroad with the assistance of the local vested interests. Out of this strategy emerged the successful coups engineered by the Central Intelligence Agency in Iran and Guatemala in 1953 and 1954, respectively. It was hardly surprising, therefore, to find that U.S. foreign aid was 95 percent military. By now, in the heat of the Cold War, any differences between Republicans and Democrats on foreign policy disappeared.

The bipartisan stance on external affairs in Washington reached its apogee in Vietnam in the next decade under Democratic presidents. John F. Kennedy sent military advisers to South Vietnam in 1963, and two years later Lyndon Johnson dispatched combat troops. The decade-long war consumed the lives of nearly 3 million Vietnamese—in the North and the South—and almost 40,000 Americans. Like Mao Zedong in China before him, Vietnamese Communist leader Ho Chi Minh produced an indomitable force by combining anti-imperialism—directed first against France and then America—with socialism.

The Pentagon's military intervention in the Vietnamese civil war, which caused deep divisions in American society, took the shine off America. The subsequent expense, peaking at 9 percent of the nation's GDP, led to high inflation and burgeoning budget deficits. As gold reserves at the U.S. Bullion Depository at Fort Knox, Kentucky, fell, currency traders staged dollar raids, exchanging dollars for gold bars at the Bretton Woods rate of $35 per ounce, to test the American Treasury's resolve. President Richard Nixon faced an acute dilemma.

The only way to dissuade foreigners from seeking Fort Knox gold was to raise interest rates, which would have caused recession. So in 1971 Nixon coupled his package of wage and price controls, tax cuts, and higher tariffs with taking the dollar off the gold standard. He thus followed in the footsteps of Britain, the earlier superpower. It had unpegged the British pound from gold four decades ago, the first sign of declining economic muscle.

In their long battle with the Americans, the Vietnamese received moral and material assistance from neighboring Communist China as well as the Soviet Union, one of the two superpowers. The Kremlin acquired that status in August 1949, when it tested its first atom bomb and ended Washington's monopoly on nuclear arms.

RISE OF THE SOVIET UNION

Moscow achieved parity with Washington in the scale of destruction it could cause with a single weapon just six decades after tsarist Russia entered the industrial age in a meaningful way. Its annual iron and steel output stood at 4 million tons on the eve of World War I. In that conflict, the tsar sided with Britain, France, and Japan against Germany, the Austro-Hungarian Empire, and the Ottoman Empire.

The protracted bloodiness of the conflict, which erupted on August 1, 1914, led to a revolution in Russia on February 27, 1917. The abdication of Tsar Nicholas II on March 2 was followed by the official inauguration of the provisional government, led first by Prince Gregory Lvov and then Alexander Kerensky of the Social Revolutionary Party. The Kerensky government found itself assaulted from the right and the left. Compared to the right, the left was well organized under the Bolshevik faction of the Russian Social-Democratic Labor Party led by Vladimir I. Lenin, then in exile.

In the background was the bloody combat between the Allies and the Central Powers, which had necessitated the deployment of half a million Russian troops in the Caucasus to frustrate the Ottoman plans for a major offensive. The war created such acute political and economic crises that the Kerensky government became weak and vulnerable. Sensing this, Lenin concluded that the time had come to deliver a coup de grâce to the system.

Bolsheviks seized power in the capital, Petrograd (now St. Petersburg), on November 7, 1917—or October 25, according to the Julian calendar then in vogue in Russia—when their forces overthrew the provisional government. Within hours of the revolution, power passed to the 650 delegates of the Second All-Russian Congress of the Soviets of Workers', Peasants' and Soldiers'

Deputies, which assembled in the capital. They elected the Council of People's Commissars, the new Soviet government, headed by Lenin.

Thus ended the short-lived democratic experiment in Russia. There was no time for the cardinal principles of Western democracy—separation of powers, independent judiciary, and free press—to strike roots in Russian soil. The country moved from one narrowly based dictatorship of the monarch to another—dictatorship of the proletariat—from the autocratic rule of the small exploiter minority to the authoritarian rule of the large exploited majority, with state power vested with the Bolsheviks.

Bolshevik Communists believed that their program of investing the working population of peasants, workers, and soldiers with power while suppressing the exploiting bourgeoisie had a universal appeal, beyond the bounds of nation and country. Their belief chimed with the sentiment of Benjamin Franklin at the time of the American Revolution of 1776: "The cause of America is the cause of all mankind." In Franklin's case, the mission was to transfer sovereignty from the hereditary monarch to citizens of a republic who would invest their democratically chosen representatives with the authority to rule for a fixed period of time. Two and a half centuries later, hereditary monarchs were still thriving, with the one in Saudi Arabia sitting atop a quarter of the reserves of the world's petroleum, a mineral more precious than gold and the one that opened a new chapter in civilization.

By mid-1918 Russia was in the midst of a civil war, with the Bolshevik Red Army being opposed by regular and irregular armed men called the White Guards, local nationalist elements, and Russia's erstwhile Allies in World War I, including Britain, France, America, and Japan. The civil war ended with the Bolshevik victory in 1920. Two years later came the formation of the Union of Soviet Socialist Republics (USSR). After Lenin's death in 1924, his successor, Joseph V. Stalin, mercilessly purged the party of his rivals and launched the first Five Year Plan in 1928.

A series of five-year plans converted privately owned agricultural land into cooperative and state farms, achieved almost universal literacy, and brought about rapid industrialization while consolidating the power of the Communist Party of the Soviet Union. These achievements would prove crucial in mobilizing the USSR during World War II and producing a literate, highly motivated, and disciplined force—a contrast from the demoralized army of illiterate serfs who were drafted to fight in World War I by the tsarist regime.

Stalin at first stayed out of World War II, which erupted in September 1939; he described it as a fight between imperialists. That changed when Nazi Germany, having overrun continental Europe (except its ally Italy and the Iberian Peninsula), invaded the Soviet Union in June 1941. This was a classical example of an imperialist power overextending itself.

Nazi Germany's invasion of the Soviet Union transformed the imperialists' war into the "people's war," according to Stalin. The subsequent welcoming of the dictatorial Soviet Union into the democratic camp of Britain and America was yet another historic instance of the formation of an opportunistic alliance to achieve a balance of power.

Adolf Hitler's aggression enabled Stalin to merge successfully the Bolshevik revolution with Russian nationalism and help unify nearly 140 ethnic groups living in the Soviet Union. Nazi Germany ended up deploying three-quarters of all its troops on the Eastern Front, which resulted in nearly 70 percent of total German casualties in more land combat than the rest of the war theaters combined.[9] Moscow's reward for routing the lethal German military came in February 1945 at the Yalta Conference, where the United States and the USSR carved out their respective spheres of influence.

The acquisition of the atom bomb in 1949 conferred on the Soviet Union the title of a superpower—an ascent that had been far from smooth. The war consumed 23 million Soviet lives and destroyed a quarter of the Union's physical assets. Yet Stalin, determined not to abandon the cardinal principle of self-reliance in peacetime, spurned the offer of financial aid from Washington in the form of the Marshall Plan. By the time Stalin died in 1953, the Soviet Union, unaided by outsiders, had achieved high growth rates comparable to those of postwar West Germany and Japan, which had received generous funds from Washington for reconstruction.

In 1955 the Soviet union signed a Treaty of Friendship, Cooperation and Mutual Assistance with Albania, Bulgaria, Czechoslovakia, East Germany, Hungary, and Romania to form the Warsaw Pact as a counterforce to NATO. At the end of that decade, the Kremlin had the second largest navy. It beat the United States in launching Sputnik into outer space in 1957, thus demonstrating to the world that science and technology advanced faster and better under socialism than capitalism.

In the increasingly independent Third World, many leaders found the Soviet model of development compatible with the state-centered and justice-centered ideals they cherished during their decades of struggle against European imperialism. It was a path to modernity and industrialization without the continued subservience to Western corporations that had operated in their lands under the umbrella of a European imperial power.

Those nationalist leaders from Asia and Africa who had visited the Soviet Union before World War II were impressed by the progress it had made in the two decades after the Bolshevik Revolution and the civil war. The Indian nationalist leader Jawaharlal Nehru, an intellectual and historian of high caliber, was an admirer. He praised "the tremendous flowering of science" in the Soviet Union and "the application of that science to the betterment of human beings who live in those vast territories."[10] Another salient feature that impressed Nehru and other nationalist Afro-Asian leaders was the welcome absence of profit motive in the centrally planned, rapid industrialization of the Soviet Union.

Under the rubric of fighting Communism, Washington got involved in the Vietnamese civil war between North Vietnam and South Vietnam, from 1963 onward. The long war caused widespread protest in the United States, with middle-class men, resistant to the draft, at the forefront. While the American nation became bitterly split, its prestige fell drastically in the Third World. The budget deficits, inflation, and weakening U.S. dollar forced Nixon to devalue the dollar.

A further humiliation awaited the United States when, following the victory of the North Vietnamese forces over the South Vietnamese in April 1975, American diplomats had to flee the embassy in Saigon (Ho Chi Minh City) by helicopter. America's standing in the Third World plunged.

That debacle taught Washington to use force only in extremis, to safeguard its vital interests. It would be a decade later when the Kremlin would draw a similar lesson from its ill-considered 1979 military intervention in Afghanistan, which violated the superpower détente, formalized in the 1972 Anti-Ballistic Missile Treaty and the 1975 Helsinki "Final Act," making international borders in Europe inviolable. The Kremlin overextended itself at a time when its economy was declining, and when China under Deng Xiaoping changed tracks from socialism to state capitalism, which weakened the Soviet Union in its ideological rivalry with America.

After assuming power in March 1985, Mikhail Gorbachev tried to salvage the situation by initiating perestroika (i.e., restructuring) and glasnost (i.e., transparency) at home and completing the withdrawal of Soviet troops from Afghanistan by February 1989. Seven months later, at the UN General Assembly in New York, he made a grand gesture, calling for the "demilitarization of international relations." He announced the immediate withdrawal of six Soviet tank divisions from East Germany, Czechoslovakia, and Hungary. That voluntary step led to the fall of the twenty-eight-year-old Berlin Wall in November, with German reunification following almost a year later.

Gorbachev and President Bush agreed to end the Cold War "with no winners and no losers." That led to the dissolution of the Warsaw Pact in July 1991. Five months later the Soviet Union disintegrated, and Washington felt free to disregard its understanding of "no winners, no losers." On January 28, 1992, in his State of the Union address, George H. W. Bush said, "By the grace of God, America won the Cold War." The United States readily donned the mantle of the victor and pressed its advantage.

CHAPTER 2

AMERICA'S PLACE IN THE SUN—ECLIPSED BY WARS AND A FISCAL MELTDOWN

What is exceptional about the term "the New World Order" is the speed with which its meaning changed. When Indian prime minister Rajiv Gandhi uttered the phrase for the first time in November 1988, after his meeting with Soviet leader Mikhail Gorbachev, it meant a globe characterized by "nonviolence and the principles of peaceful coexistence." Within two years, President George H. W. Bush had appropriated the term and declared that its future depended on Washington and Moscow responding to Iraq's aggression against Kuwait, which occurred in August 1990. As the Pentagon prepared to advance into Iraqi-occupied Kuwait in January 1991, Gorbachev appealed to Bush to give President Saddam Hussein a last chance to withdraw—but to no avail. Later, having triumphed in the First Gulf War, Bush stated that in the New World Order, America would be "obligated" to lead the world community to "an unprecedented degree."

In practice, it meant turning the United Nations into a handmaiden of the State Department and having Washington's version of democracy and human rights adopted as the agenda of the UN Security Council. The White House succeeded in this mission to a large extent for almost a decade.

Sometimes unexpected events occurred dramatically in the course of implementing this policy. If these were captured in searing or gruesome television images—highlighting an unacceptable price to be paid for extending Washington's power and influence to unfamiliar corners of the globe—public opinion in America turned sour. That forced top U.S. decision makers to reverse course. Such was the case in Somalia, but not in Haiti or Iraq.

Molded largely by Mark Bowden's book *Blackhawk Down* and the subsequent Hollywood movie by the same name, the lingering impression that Somalia has left on the American public is that eighteen U.S. soldiers lost their lives in pursuit of a Good Samaritan mission in a faraway place, trying to catch the archetypical bad guy, Muhammad Farrah Aideed, a Somali warlord.

The truth is startlingly different. In his conversations with a London-based Arab journalist, Osama bin Laden revealed that it was Al Qaida–affiliated Arabs operating in Mogadishu—not Aideed's militia—who had downed the two Blackhawk helicopters.[1] They had honed their skills by targeting Soviet helicopters in Afghanistan during the mid-1980s with the U.S.-made, shoulder-held, ground-to-air missiles supplied by the CIA ex gratia.

Somalia was, however, a small fish compared to post-Soviet Russia. The self-appointed task of taming the old Russian bear into the civilized ways of the capitalist world was, by any measure, gigantic. In the end, the zeal with which the Clinton administration pursued this aim—disregarding some of the basic tenets of the sovereignty of nations—destroyed whatever legitimacy a seriously ill Boris Yeltsin had at the beginning of his second term in 1996. A sycophant of America and all things American at the start, he found Washington's relentless pressure humiliating. To recover some of the esteem he had lost among Russians as a result of his craven behavior, and to show them that he was not irretrievably spineless, he started making defiant statements toward the end of his second term. In the case of Russia, therefore, the Clinton administration overshot the mark and turned its overall performance into a mixed bag—just as Bush had in Iraq after expelling the Iraqi forces from Kuwait.

IRAQ: A MIXED BAG

Iraqi president Saddam Hussein's brutal invasion of Kuwait in 1990 appalled the popular imagination in America. Bush's rallying of twenty-eight nations to reverse Iraq's occupation of Kuwait, sanctified by the UN Security Council, succeeded in its objective in March 1991. The Iraqi army was routed in Kuwait and expelled. Bush then tried to push a strictly American agenda for postwar Iraq through the Security Council.

Backed by Britain, the United States proposed a resolution at the council to aid Kurds in northern Iraq—repressed under Saddam's rule partly because they fought alongside the Iranians during the 1980–1988 Iran-Iraq War—under Chapter VII of the UN Charter, which had been invoked in all previous resolutions on Iraq's invasion of Kuwait. China protested, referring to the UN Charter's Article 2, paragraph 1: "The organization is based on the principle of the sovereign equality of all its Members." It failed to see how Chapter VII—"Action with respect to threats to the peace, breaches of the peace, and acts of aggression"—could apply to the fate of the Kurdish minority in Iraq. Arguing that the draft resolution interfered in the domestic affairs of a sovereign state, China threatened to veto it. Washington relented.

So the preamble to Security Council Resolution 688 referred to the UN Charter's Article 2, paragraph 7: "Nothing contained in the present Charter shall authorize the United Nations to intervene in matters which are essentially within the domestic jurisdiction of any state, or shall require the Members to submit such matters to settlement under the present Charter; but this principle shall not prejudice the application of enforcement measurements under Chapter VII."

Even then China abstained. So did India, then a nonpermanent member of the council.[2] The central governments in Beijing and Delhi—with ethnic minorities along their borders agitating for independence—rightly viewed this resolution as a dangerous precedent threatening the unity of their meganations. The joint stand taken by China and India showed that when it came to safeguarding the territorial integrity of a country, there was no difference between a democracy and an autocracy. With three other council members opposing, the resolution secured ten votes, one more than the minimum required.

After condemning the repression of the civilian population in many parts of Iraq, "including most recently in Kurdish-populated areas," Resolution 688 demanded that the Iraqi government should allow access by international organizations to those needing assistance. Led by Washington, the council's three Western permanent members declared that Resolution 688 entitled them to send troops to northern Iraq and establish safe encampments to provide supplies for Kurdish refugees. Baghdad's protest that this was blatant interference in its internal affairs fell on deaf ears.

Under Operation Provide Comfort, the United States, backed by Britain and France, set up a safe haven in a 3,600-square-mile "security zone" adjoining the Iraqi-Turkish border and deployed 16,000 troops. In June they barred the Baghdad government from flying its aircraft beyond the Thirty-sixth Parallel by declaring it an "Air Exclusion Zone," thus depriving Iraq of sovereignty over part of its air space.

But the matter did not rest there. Intent on overthrowing Saddam Hussein's regime, the policymakers in Washington highlighted the regime's campaign in the southern marshes to flush out Shiite fugitives in the summer of 1992. At the UN Security Council, they called on Max van der Stoel, the UN Special Rapporteur on human rights in Iraq, to submit his findings on the condition in the marshes. China, India, Zimbabwe, and Ecuador objected. They argued that the Security Council was concerned with international security and peace, *not* human rights, a subject covered by the UN Human Rights Commission.

To spike the critics' charge that he was exploiting a major foreign policy decision for partisan ends while accepting the Republican Party's renomination as its presidential candidate, Bush drafted British Prime Minister John Major to state that America, Britain, and France had decided to impose an air exclusion zone for Iraqi planes below the Thirty-second Parallel to safeguard the Shiites in the marshes. Saddam Hussein refrained from ordering his military to attack the patrolling Western aircraft. That would have given Bush an opportunity to flex his military muscle and boost his electoral chances.[3] By getting away with his latest move, unchallenged, Bush deprived Iraq of sovereignty over two-fifths of its air space. That whetted his appetite.

He then extended his misuse of the UN Security Council to Somalia.

SOMALIA: A STEP TOO FAR

The amalgamation of the British colony of Somaliland and the Italian protectorate of Somalia, on the eve of their independence in July 1960, led to the formation of the Somali Republic, popularly known as Somalia. A strategic country on the Horn of Africa, independent Somalia inherited deeply embedded clan and regional loyalties.

A military coup in 1969 brought Major General Muhammad Siad Barre to power. He tilted toward the Soviet Union, which had been supplying arms to the republic since its inception. But in 1977 he switched sides and joined the U.S.-led camp. In exchange for generous economic and military aid by the

Reagan administration (1981–1989), he allowed the Pentagon the use of air and naval facilities at Somalia's ports of Berbera and Mogadishu for a decade.

When the anti-Barre guerrilla groups began gaining control over northern and central Somalia, Barre became more authoritarian and repressive. He reinforced ties with Washington by granting American oil companies exploratory and production rights in nearly two-thirds of the republic. He was overthrown in January 1991 by the militia of the United Somali Congress (USC) led by General Aideed. The USC captured the capital, Mogadishu.

Soon the USC split, with the faction led by Aideed controlling southern Mogadishu, including its seaport and airport, and his rival Ali Mahdi Muhammad administering central Mogadishu and its northern suburbs. The fighting between the warring factions prevented farmers from planting and harvesting crops. That led to a famine in parts of the country. A UN-mediated cease-fire reduced the extent of the fighting, but Mogadishu remained bitterly divided.

Keen to maintain U.S. oil corporations' interests in Somalia, the Bush administration activated the UN Security Council to intervene militarily in the Somali civil war. Resolution 751, passed in April 1992, led to the creation of UNOSOM I (United Nations Operations in Somalia I) to oversee the UN's arms embargo against Somalia and restore order.

Washington's move upset not just the Somali warlords but also the public. The arrival of predominantly Western troops revived Somalis' fear of a return of European imperialism. They were opposed to foreign intervention under any garb. They noted the link between American oil companies and government when they saw Bush's special envoy using the headquarters of Phillips-Conoco, an American oil company, as his base. The warlords showed scant respect for UNOSOM I troops, who were authorized to use force only in self-defense.

In the face of such opposition, Bush should have turned to the Organization of African Unity (OAU), whose charter included mediation between warring parties, to settle the Somali crisis. He did not. Instead, he pressed the UN Security Council to further his foreign policy in the Horn of Africa. He succeeded. In November 1992 the council decided to establish the United Task Force (UNITAF) under Chapter VII of the UN Charter. It was authorized to use "all necessary means" to establish a secure environment for "humanitarian operations" in Somalia. This would prove to be the thin end of the wedge.

Supplying three-quarters of the 34,000-strong force, the Pentagon led the UNITAF, with Pakistan providing the second largest contingent. It arrived in

Somalia in early 1993 under the auspices of Operation Restore Hope. Initially, the heavily armed UNITAF succeeded in imposing an uneasy peace on the fractious clans and transported supplies to the famine-stricken areas.

Meeting in Addis Ababa, Ethiopia, the warring factions reached an agreement in March to end hostilities and form a transitional National Council to function as the central authority for two years. But the accord would soon unravel.

Following the bipartisan approach to foreign policy, Democratic President Clinton stayed on the path created by his Republican predecessor. At his administration's behest, the UN Security Council decided in March 1993 to set up UNOSOM II to support the new Somali accord at Addis Ababa and initiate nation building, including disarming various militias, restoring law and order, and helping the people to set up a representative government—a grossly overambitious mission.

Initially, Somalis welcomed the rations that U.S.-led forces distributed. But soon word spread that the Americans had come to convert Somalis to Christianity, a dismaying prospect that reminded the locals of earlier attempts by the Italian rulers at proselytizing. The Americans traced the origins of this rumor to Aideed's camp.

The arduous task of disarming the militias fell to the Pakistanis. In June 1993, a Somali militia killed twenty-four Pakistani soldiers in an ambush. The next day, at Washington's behest, the UN Security Council Resolution 837 called for the apprehension of those responsible for the killings—the militia of Aideed. Soon the U.S. Navy acted on its own by announcing a $25,000 award for Aideed's arrest.

The frequent gun battles between Aideed's militia and the Pakistanis led to civilian casualties, which alienated the locals from UNOSOM II. That helped militia leaders to present UNOSOM II forces as evil, foreign interlopers. This environment won recruits for Al Qaida (Arabic for "The Base"), led by bin Laden, based in neighboring Sudan since April 1991. Al Qaida recruits used Islam as a rallying cry against UNOSOM II. The Pentagon acted as it always has—by raising the military stakes. What was worse was that after getting the UN involved militarily in a bitter civil strife, Washington began acting unilaterally at the same time. By August 1993, it had deployed its Special Forces, such as Rangers and Delta, to operate *outside UN control.* Thus Clinton did what Bush had done before: He bent the UN Security

Council to his will as far as he could while retaining, and using, the power to act unilaterally.

In early October, the Americans launched a concerted attack on Aideed's forces. In the fighting, two U.S. Blackhawk helicopters were shot down, and three others damaged, by shoulder-held missiles and rocket-propelled grenades. Several wounded Americans remained trapped at the crash sites all night. At daylight, a large force of the U.S. Tenth Mountain Division, backed by Malaysian and Pakistani troops, riding more than a hundred vehicles, tanks, and armored personnel carriers, with an air cover of helicopters, battled Aideed's militia. They rescued the American survivors at one site. But they were unable to reach the second, where a single survivor was being protected by two American snipers. They were overrun by Aideed's fighters.

By the time the Battle of Mogadishu was over, some 500 to 1,000 Somali militia and civilians were dead—as were eighteen Americans, including the two snipers. Their corpses were dragged through the streets as the locals cheered—an event captured by TV cameras. The news clips disgusted American viewers. Public opinion turned sharply against U.S. participation in the Somali civil war—an intervention that had gone largely unnoticed by ordinary Americans so far. It would have been unwise of Bush—who made his first million as an oil man—to explain to his fellow Americans that he was risking U.S. blood and treasure to protect the interests of petroleum corporations. Clinton had found no reason to backtrack.

When Washington blamed Aideed for the loss of the Blackhawk helicopters, he denied the charge. Rightly so. Three years later, at his Afghan hideout, bin Laden would own up to the responsibility for downing the helicopters.

Responding to popular pressure at home, Clinton set the deadline of March 31, 1994, for total American withdrawal from Somalia. (While Somalis welcomed the news, bin Laden and his followers were dismayed to see their prime quarry depart.) Other nations announced their exit. Accepting the fait accompli, the UN Security Council redefined UNOSOM II's mission as peacemaking and reconstruction with a deadline of March 1995.

In sum, it was a chastened recognition by the United States and others that the Washington-led strategy of coercion and force had failed in Somalia. In comparison, the U.S. administration fared better in its familiar backyard— in Haiti.

HAITI: A FAMILIAR STOMPING GROUND

Though an independent republic since 1804, Haiti has always existed in the shadow of the United States.

After occupying it from 1915 until nearly two decades later, the United States maintained a strong influence in Haiti until 1947. Ten years later, backed by the army, Doctor François Duvalier (aka Papa Doc) was elected president. He retained the high office through fraudulent elections until his death in 1971. His son Jean-Claude Duvalier (aka Baby Doc) succeeded him as an ill-formed dictator at the age of nineteen.

When the Militia of National Security Volunteers—the infamous secret police, known as Tonton Macoutes, meaning Uncle Gunnysack[4]—proved inadequate to curb rising popular unrest, and the military commanders withdrew their support from him in 1986, Jean-Claude Duvalier turned to the U.S. embassy in Port-au-Prince. It helped him to flee, and he ended up in France.

Mounting violence on the eve of the 1987 presidential poll led the military to postpone the election. In the subsequent poll in late 1990, to the surprise of many, Jean Bertrand Aristide, a slightly built former Catholic priest popular among the poor, won the presidency with 67 percent of the vote. But his rule lasted only seven months. He was overthrown by the military commanders in September 1991 and replaced by their nominee, Joseph Netette, with real power resting with General Raoul Cedras.

Aristide spent his exile first in Venezuela and then in the United States, where he gained support for his cause. He caught the attention of the White House.

Clinton had the option of urging the Organization of American States (OAS) or the Caribbean Community (CARICOM) to defuse Haiti's crisis. Or he could have interfered directly in Haiti's affairs, as Washington had done repeatedly in the past—or taken unilateral military action as Reagan and Bush had done in the respective cases of Grenada and Panama in 1983 and 1989. But Clinton chose to pursue the grand strategy of using the UN Security Council as an instrument of U.S. foreign policy. At his urging, the council imposed nominal economic sanctions against Haiti and then intensified them in the spring of 1994. They hurt common people rather than the military junta and its hangers-on.

Finally, Washington succeeded in getting the Security Council to adopt Resolution 940 in July 1994 to authorize a U.S.-led multinational force "to uphold democracy" by restoring Aristide. China voiced opposition. It argued that "up-holding democracy" was not the business of the UN Security Council and that Haiti's internal politics did not affect international peace and security. Brazil, then representing Latin America at the council, agreed. They were backed by Mexico, whose UN ambassador, Victor Olea, condemned the resolution for setting "an extremely dangerous precedent in international relations."

The practice of an open vote, rather than secret ballot, at the Security Council, which makes its non-Western members vulnerable to U.S. pressure, militates against free choice. In the end, pressured by Washington, Brazil abstained. China did the same. While Latin American and Caribbean countries chafed at the UN Security Council's unprecedented stance, the White House was jubilant. Clinton had succeeded in putting the UN stamp on Washington's stance on democracy and human rights—in gross violation of Paragraph 7 of Article 2 of the UN Charter.

Haitians forecast bloodshed when the UN-authorized, U.S.-led forces arrived to dislodge the military rulers. Luckily, that did not happen—because of the unexpected intervention by Jimmy Carter, the former U.S. president. He succeeded in persuading the military junta to step down but remain in Haiti, unharmed. So the U.S.-led "invasion" of Haiti injured no one. As a face-saving formula, Haiti's generals allowed the Pentagon's forces to land at Port-au-Prince in September as "peacekeepers."

On resuming his presidency, Aristide disbanded the army and established an armed civilian police force. He completed his term in office in February 1996, treating his three years in exile as part of his presidential term.[5]

While Haiti was a centuries-old stomping ground for America, Russia was a virgin field. Yet as the victor in the Cold War, the United States felt confident of transforming post-Communist Russia into its image.

POST-SOVIET RUSSIA: THE BIG PRIZE

The sweeping changes that Russia's president Boris Yeltsin announced after the failed coup by hardliners in August 1991 endeared him to Washington. They included the dissolution of the Communist Party. And following his declaration that Russia needed "a reformist breakthrough," the two-tier parliament—the Congress of People's Deputies and the smaller Supreme Soviet composed of the representatives of the constituent regions—authorized him to restructure the economic system by decree over the next year. He initiated the process on January 2, 1992, by decontrolling retail and wholesale prices in one grand sweep.

Yeltsin's abrupt, albeit constitutionally dubious, dissolution of the Soviet Union in December 1991 gained him further appreciation from Bush. He got the red-carpet treatment during his visit to Washington in June 1992. He and his American host declared that their countries had entered "a new era of friendship and partnership."

The much flaunted "partnership" would turn out to be grossly unequal. Whereas Russia underwent political and financial turmoil during the last decade of the twentieth century, with the ruble plunging sharply in 1998, the United States experienced unprecedented economic growth for almost eight years. Its salient features were minimal inflation, high productivity, low unemployment, and a thriving stock market, and the transformation of the huge U.S. federal budget deficit of the 1980s into notable surpluses.

The basic outline of the Moscow-Washington "friendship and partnership" was stated in April 1992 by the Eighty-first American Assembly of the leading lights of government, business, media, and academia. It resolved that the U.S.-led allies should "deeply and swiftly engage in the process of transforming the political and economic orders of the former Soviet republics."[6] Thus, public and private institutions in America assigned themselves the task of re-creating Russia as a capitalist, democratic entity, with the State Department supervising the transition.

Under the generic title of "advisers," hundreds of American specialists fanned out across the Russian Federation in government ministries (particularly economic and finance), large enterprises, media, think tanks, universities, political parties, and trade unions, and acted as watchdogs against black market corruption. They were funded generously by the federal government, foundations, and university endowments. In addition, American individuals bankrolled their favorites among Russia's politicians, tutored senior Russian bureaucrats, helped draft Russia's laws and Yeltsin's decrees, and even participated in rewriting textbooks.

Disastrously, instead of adopting a separate, step-by-step approach in prices, money supply, and denationalization, the American experts prescribed sweeping across-the-board action in all economic areas at once. It was tantamount to a physician making his patient swallow all of the medicine at one sitting.

Many of the American advisers had a vested interest in pushing this reckless agenda. They were linked to top Wall Street investment banks, which picked up lucrative fees and commissions in privatizing gigantic Russian assets.

The advisers' overall economic objectives were to abolish consumer and welfare subsidies, dismantle the public sector consisting of over 17,000 major and medium-sized state-owned enterprises, and expose domestic producers to the imports of highly developed foreign competitors, with minimal intervention by the state following a strict monetarist policy of budgetary austerity.

Initially, restrained by diplomatic protocol, American officials were discreet in their utterances about post-Communist Russia, leaving nonofficials to do the plain talking. Zbigniew Brzezinski, a former U.S. national security adviser, for instance, declared in autumn 1992 that Russia's "economic and even political destiny . . . is now increasingly passing into de facto Western receivership."[7] More outspoken was the statement in an anonymous letter circulating in Washington, published by the Moscow-based *New Times* in June 1993: "The key to [Russia's] democratic recovery is no longer in its hand. It is in ours."[8] Later, the Clinton administration too lost its inhibitions.

Russia's parliament, reflecting popular sentiment, often clashed with Yeltsin. Such was the case when, in December 1992, he recommended that Acting Prime Minister Yegor Gaidar, a champion of "radical abolitionism" and shock therapy—offering short-term hardship for higher living standards later—be confirmed in his job. Parliament refused. It opted for a safe pair of hands, conservative Viktor Chernomyrdin. In the subsequent tussle between Vice President Alexander Rutskoi, a proponent of gradualist reform, and Gaidar, Washington vociferously backed Gaidar.

With the collapse of the Kremlin's competing economic system, America's belief in its capitalist system rose to hubris. It reinforced its grip over the IMF and the World Bank, both based in America's capital city. Out of this grew the "Washington Consensus": Reduce government's role in the economy, curtail state spending and subsidies, abolish price controls, slash administrative bureaucracy, privatize public sector enterprises, open doors to foreign investment, reduce tariffs, float currency exchange rates in the free market, and let the financial system regulate itself or be regulated lightly.

The Washington Consensus became the mantra of the IMF and the World Bank. It was to be applied not only to the former members of the Warsaw Pact but also to those countries firmly in the American camp during the Cold

War—such as Mexico in 1994. The wholesale application of the Washington Consensus to post-Soviet Russia led to hyperinflation in 1992–1993, reducing the life savings of most Russians to a pittance, driving tens of millions into poverty, and creating a vast chasm between the indigent many and the affluent few.

Urging Yeltsin to "stay the course," the Clinton White House decried his critics as "fake" reformists. It tied its financial aid to the acceptance of its prescriptions of economic liberalization but failed to deliver. Its blatant interference in Russia's internal affairs was inversely proportional to what it provided the Kremlin: a niggardly 7 percent of total U.S. foreign aid. By contrast, the European Union, whose aid to Moscow was eleven times higher than America's, refrained from commenting on Russia's domestic issues.[9]

Suffering Russians protested. Reflecting the popular mood, the parliament moved to impeach Yeltsin in March 1993. Yeltsin made an unsuccessful attempt to shut it down. The Clinton administration intervened, denouncing the parliament as "a citadel of Red-Brown reaction," the terms "Red" and "Brown" referring respectively to Communists and nationalists. By so doing it undermined the concepts of separation of power, a representative legislature, and a legitimate opposition. So much for furthering democracy around the globe.

Encouraged by Washington's partisanship, Yeltsin overstepped his authority on September 21 and signed a decree dissolving the two houses of Parliament. He called an election in mid-December for a two-tier Federal Assembly, composed of the Duma, representing voters at large, and the Federation Council, representing the eighty-nine regions (i.e., provinces). The first task of the 450-member Duma—half of its members elected on a party list, with a threshold of 5 percent, and the other half from single-member constituencies—with a tenure of two years, would be to draft a new constitution.

Yeltsin's decree was challenged not only by the chairman of the Supreme Soviet, Ruslan Khasbulatov, but also by his vice president, Rutskoi. The Supreme Soviet removed Yeltsin from office and appointed Khasbulatov president; the Congress of People's Deputies backed the move.

Efforts to reconcile the two sides over the next ten days failed. The parliamentarians hunkered down in their ten-story building known as the White House. Tension rose. Street fights broke out between pro- and anti-Yeltsin crowds. On October 4, 1993, armored vehicles, ordered by Yeltsin, smashed the barricades protecting the Russian White House. Then tanks fired at the upper floors of the building, which emptied. The commandos stormed the premise and arrested many parliamentarians, as well as Khasbulatov and Rutskoi.[10] Yeltsin's coup against the popularly elected parliament left 187 people dead.

The bloody episode, which shocked and dismayed the Russian people as well as true democrats in the rest of the world, won the applause of Washington. Repudiating its sermon that the rule of law and the sanctity of a constitution were the building blocks of democracy, the Clinton administration stuck to its stance of backing Yeltsin, right or wrong. Sheer opportunism trumped principles.

A further trampling of democratic tenets and practice was in the offing. Instead of waiting for the still-to-be-elected Federal Assembly to draft a new constitution, as he had decreed, Yeltsin accomplished the task unilaterally. He put the document to referendum on December 12, the day elections to the Duma were held.

Unsurprisingly, the new constitution enhanced the president's power at the expense of the legislature, giving him the authority to appoint the government, dismiss the prime minister, and, in certain circumstances (such as the parliament's refusal to endorse his prime ministerial nominee three times in two weeks), to dissolve the parliament. It was this constitution, which created a strong executive authority, that would later draw the ire of most Western analysts during the presidency of Vladimir Putin.

Nearly three out of five Russians approved the constitution, a convincing majority showing its preference for a strong executive with a robust leader in charge, but nine of the eighteen republics and ten regions refused to adopt it. On the other hand, voters overwhelmingly rejected Yeltsin's policies, with seven out of eight casting their ballots against the pro-Yeltsin candidates in the parliamentary poll. They opted largely either for the recently launched Communist Party of the Russian Federation or the ultranationalist Liberal Democratic Party (LDP) of Vladimir Zhirinovsky. Securing a quarter of the popular vote, the LDP became the largest single group in the state Duma.

Russian voters thus demonstrated their opposition to Washington's intrusion into their country's internal affairs. Ignoring this clear, democratic message, the Clinton administration continued its intervention, treating Russia as a defeated country rather than America's friend and partner.

Partly to withstand Zhirinovsky's pressure in the Duma, and partly to divert public attention away from the faltering economy, where by 1994 the withholding of wages and pensions had become routine, Yeltsin resorted to force to reverse the independence of Chechnya (the Chechen Republic). He did so after rejecting the offer of mediation by Khasbulatov, a Chechen who was pardoned by the new Duma and released.

In December 1994, Russian troops rolled into Grozny, the capital of the breakaway republic. They met stiff resistance from armed Chechen nationalists. The Kremlin increased the troop level to 70,000. By April 1995, nearly 25,000 Chechen civilians and 1,500 Russians were dead.

While the bloodshed turned the public opinion in Russia against the war, the Clinton team hailed Yeltsin as the "Abraham Lincoln of Russia."[11] The comparison was ludicrous. Chechnya was a tiny entity, 5,900 square miles in area with a population of 1 million, while Russia, spread over 6.5 million square miles, contained 150 million people.

THE SERBIAN FACTOR

No such historical parallel had come in handy for the Clinton administration when the secession of Slovenia and Croatia from the Socialist Federal Republic of Yugoslavia in 1991 created a dilemma for Bosnia-Herzegovina (henceforth Bosnia). Composed of ethnic Serbs, Croats, and predominantly Muslim Bosnians, Bosnia had to decide whether to stay with the rest of the federation (backed by most ethnic Serbs) or declare independence (favored by most Bosnians and Croats).

A referendum in February–March 1992, boycotted by Serbs, unanimously backed independence. This led to civil war. Intervening on the side of Bosnians and Croats, NATO staged its first-ever air strikes in April 1994—against the Serbs in Bosnia. Yeltsin denounced NATO for doing so without consulting him.

Russians felt affinity with ethnic Serbs based on their common Cyrillic script and the Orthodox Church. Ultranationalists in the Duma were vocal in their support for Serbia. And Serbs, led by President Slobodan Milosevic, a staunch Serb ultranationalist, looked to the Kremlin to be their protector. But the Serbs' aggressive actions against Bosnians and Croats created a dilemma for Yeltsin, who was eager to defuse the crisis peacefully to underscore his ability to succeed in the international arena where all others had failed.

Ignoring Yeltsin's pleas, the Serb leaders refused to abandon their offensives against non-Serbs. This crippled his leverage. On the other hand, with NATO's intervention against the Serbs escalating, the anti-American and anti-Western feelings in Russia had risen so sharply that Yeltsin could not afford to be seen yielding to NATO's pressure. The net result was a steep decline in the influence of pro-Western advisers in the Kremlin.

NATO's air war against the Serbs, coupled with coordinated ground offensives by the Bosnians and Croats, compelled Milosevic to sue for peace. Much to the relief of Russia and other European nations, an agreement signed in Dayton, Ohio, in November 1995 ended the war, which claimed nearly 100,000 lives.

The critical role of NATO in ending the civil war in Bosnia encouraged hawks in the Clinton White House to advocate extending NATO eastward in violation of Bush's promise to Gorbachev not to expand NATO beyond the reunited Germany. In the absence of a strong counterargument, the hawks carried the day.

The news of this development, conveyed to Yeltsin through back channels, dismayed him. He knew that NATO's enlargement was deeply unpopular among Russians and that it would fatally damage his already weak chances of reelection in June. He appealed to Clinton to postpone his decision on the subject. Clinton obliged.

U.S. Intrusion in the Presidential Poll

Omens were unpromising for Yeltsin's reelection. The continuing fall in the GDP since 1992 had reduced its size by nearly 45 percent by the time the election campaign warmed up in the early spring of 1996. Little wonder that to secure 1 million signatures to qualify Yeltsin as a candidate, railway and metal workers were pressured to sign the nominating petition while collecting their wages.[12]

The Clinton team went into high gear to bolster Yeltsin's electoral chances. It facilitated the dispatch of electioneering experts to Moscow to advise Yeltsin's campaign committee. U.S. ambassador Thomas Pickering appealed to Grigory Yavlinsky, a serious liberal candidate, to withdraw his bid. Prodded by Washington, the IMF offered Russia a $10.2 billion loan, the second largest sum it had ever sanctioned, far exceeding the total of what it had lent Moscow during the past three years. On April 20, Yeltsin chaired a meeting with the representatives of the Group of Seven (G7) to discuss "nuclear security," a subject of rarefied interest. Its sole purpose, according to U.S. Deputy Secretary of State Strobe Talbott, was to give Yeltsin a pre-election boost.

The TV channels owned by billionaire Vladimir Gusinsky and Boris Berezovsky mounted a pro-Yeltsin public relations blitz that Soviet propagandists would have envied. Yeltsin's TV ads were prepared in consultation with Oglivy & Mather, a top-notch Madison Avenue public relations company, and individual American specialists. Consequently, his campaign surpassed the legal expenditure limit for electioneering—a serious infringement of the law conveniently overlooked by the authorities.

Even then, it was only in the second run, in July 1996, that Yeltsin beat his Communist rival Gennady Zyuganov.

PAYBACK TIME FOR YELTSIN

Indebted to Washington for the invaluable service it had rendered to ensure his second term as president, Yeltsin was in a pliant mood. Clinton lost little time in demanding a payback. On the eve of the November 1996 congressional elections, he announced his intention to enlarge NATO.

Yeltsin had his doubts about the necessity of such an act. But he lacked the will, moral or political, to resist the White House.

At the NATO summit in May 1997 in Paris, Yeltsin reluctantly signed the NATO-Russia Founding Act. It gave Russia the status of a consultant in NATO's deliberations in return for the impending NATO expansion into the former members of the Warsaw Pact. Barely six weeks later, urged by Washington, NATO invited the Czech Republic, Hungary, and Poland to apply for membership, which they would gain in March 1999.

Having successfully twisted Yeltsin's arm on NATO, Clinton tried to cheer up the Russian leader. He successfully lobbied to upgrade Russia to full membership of the G7, where it had been allowed to participate in political discussions since 1994.

Russia attended the G7 finance ministers' gathering in London in February 1998 to discuss the six-month-old financial crisis of the "tiger economies" of Thailand, Indonesia, and South Korea. Who could have predicted then that within six months it would be Russia's financial meltdown that would engage G7 leaders? The Kremlin's crisis was caused by a slump in oil prices that resulted from the Asian meltdown spreading to Hong Kong, Malaysia, and the Philippines and lowering demand for the commodity.

There was another important reason for the crisis. After Yeltsin's reelection, his overconfident government permitted nonresident portfolio investors to convert rubles into hard currencies. This led to a fall in the foreign reserves of Russia's central bank, Bank Rossii. That in turn encouraged foreigners to withdraw funds from Russian currency and securities, forcing Bank Rossii to spend its dollar reserves to defend the exchange rate of 5.3 to 7.1 rubles to 1 U.S. dollar. The trend started in autumn 1997. On January 1, 1998, the central bank introduced the new ruble, equaling 1,000 old rubles. But this had no impact on steadying the fall in the confidence of the Russian currency.

Ignoring the slump in the financial markets, visiting Vice President Al Gore declared in March 1998, "Optimism prevails universally among those who are familiar with what is going on in Russia."[13]

While foreigners unloaded rubles and Russian securities, oil prices continued to fall. The double whammy forced Bank Rossii to stop upholding the ruble-dollar rate on August 17, 1998. It widened the dollar exchange band to 6.0 to 9.5 rubles and said that the ruble-denominated debt would be restructured in a manner to be announced later. It declared a ninety-day moratorium on the payment of some obligations, including certain debts and currency contracts. With only $18.4 billion in reserves, Bank Rossii ended up defaulting on its outstanding loans of $40 billion. Western banks and investors lost $80 to 100 billion, the biggest single loss until then.[14] By the end of the year, the floating ruble lost 71 percent of its value against the greenback, falling to 21 rubles to a dollar.

The latest fiscal crisis impoverished that class of Russians who had come up in the aftermath of the Soviet collapse. It took the shine off the American-style capitalism the Yeltsin government had welcomed with open arms.

The following spring Washington would deliver another blow to Yeltsin's standing among his people—in Serbia. After witnessing, approvingly, the Socialist Federal Republic of Yugoslavia shrinking to a rump of Serbia and Montenegro, the West's attention turned to Serbia, where the Muslim-majority province of Kosovo complained of persecution by the central government of President Milosevic.

CLINTON'S CIRCUMVENTION OF THE UN

Anticipating a Russian veto at the UN Security Council for a resolution authorizing military action against Serbia for repressing the rebel forces in Kosovo, Clinton sidestepped the international body. He decided to use the

enlarged NATO for the purpose. With that, the doctrine of "liberal interven-
tionism," deployed without UN cover, lost its international legality. It became
what it always was—a doctrine to further the interests of the West as determined largely by the United States backed by Britain.

When NATO started bombing Serbia on March 24, 1999, Yeltsin froze relations with it. He instructed former prime minister Chernomyrdin to defuse
the crisis. He invited Clinton to meet him aboard a Russian submarine in the
Mediterranean. Clinton ignored the gesture. As NATO continued bombing
Serbia, targeting its economic infrastructure, the popular standing of America among Russians plummeted. To his discredit, the UN secretary-general,
Kofi Annan, did not protest NATO's military strikes made without the sanction of the UN Security Council. Anxious to secure a second term as the UN's
highest official, he kept quiet so as not to displease Washington.

In Serbia, unable to withstand the daily bombings, Milosevic accepted
NATO's terms on June 12, after seventy-eight days of air strikes. This brought
relief to the Russian people and politicians. But it was not enough for the
Washington-Moscow ties to return to the status quo. The damage done to
that relationship by the Clinton administration's circumvention of the UN to
pulverize a close ally of the Kremlin proved irreparable. Soon thereafter Yeltsin
sent a public message to that effect. Meeting on the sidelines of the annual
summit of the Shanghai Conference Organization (SCO) in the Kyrgyz capital of Bishkek in August 1999, he joined his Chinese counterpart, Jiang Zemin,
to outline an "anti-NATO" pact. This was the beginning of a bond that would
grow stronger by the year.

The renewed military campaign against Chechnya by the newly appointed
prime minister, Vladimir Putin, a former KGB officer, in October—unveiling
the Second Chechen War—met with criticism by Clinton. He warned that the
Kremlin would "pay a heavy price" for its tactics of targeting civilians, and
face international isolation.

Aware that the parliamentary elections were only two months away, Yeltsin
fired a robust salvo. "It seems Mr. Clinton has forgotten Russia is a great power
that possesses a nuclear arsenal," he said.[15] Overly sensitive to electoral politics at home and abroad, Clinton decided not to hit back.

Once the poll established the pro-Putin parties in the lead in the Duma,
Talbott flew to Moscow to reassure Yeltsin that the United States did not want
to spoil relations with the Kremlin even on Chechnya. When, on the last day
of 1999, Yeltsin decided to retire early as president and name Putin as acting

president, the Clinton White House praised Putin as "one of the leading reformers" with whom it could do business. It turned a blind eye to Putin's
blood-drenched "liberation" of Grozny in the Second Chechen War.

Putin's success in the presidential election in March 2000 provided Clinton with an opportunity to claim "a genuine democratic transition" in Russia. He hailed the event as a glowing evidence of the correctness of his
general policy toward Moscow. Subsequent developments in Russia would
prove him wrong. In any case, this was the last time the Russian people or
politicians would show any interest in the White House's comments on their
domestic affairs.

Though the Republican Party won the presidency in November 2000, the
new occupant of the White House, George W. Bush, did not visualize de-
tracting from his predecessor's stance on Russia and Eastern Europe. That
meant expanding NATO eastward and making Eastern Europe part of the U.S.
missile defense system. On the other hand, the terrorist attacks ten months
later, being the first on mainland United States since its inception, opened a
new chapter in Washington's foreign policy in general.

AMERICA'S POST–9/11 SPURT

The terrorist suicide strikes by hijacked aircraft on the World Trade Center
(WTC) in New York and the Pentagon in Washington on September 11, 2001,
led to the deaths of 3,000 people, the leveling of the WTC's two 110-story tow-
ers, and a partial destruction of the Pentagon. They shook the world.

Among other things, the attacks transformed the lackadaisical presidency
of George W. Bush, who had crawled to the high office on a minority popular vote. He wrapped himself up in the Stars and Stripes and donned the mantle of a war president. Taking advantage of the traumatized state of the nation,
he extended the reach of the executive branch to a degree not seen in recent
memory. He brushed aside the generous offer of allies to contribute to his
self-declared "war on terror," expected to be overlong and arduous.

Then, disastrously, in midstream, he diverted the Pentagon's high-tech war
machine from Afghanistan to Iraq as the second chapter of a seemingly endless warfare. Lacking solid information that Iraq, a country with a battered
army and economy, was a direct threat to America, his administration con-
cocted evidence by means that, if done by an individual or a private company,
would have landed the perpetrator behind bars for many years.

The only bright spot of the Iraq saga was the actual invasion, brilliantly planned and meticulously executed. The rest was a series of blunders. It did greater damage to the economy and standing of America than Al Qaida leaders could have imagined achieving in their wildest dreams.

As the trajectory of every imperial power since the Roman Empire shows, a great power brings about its decline by overextending its reach. That is what the United States, the erstwhile sole superpower, did by invading Iraq in 2003.

In retrospect, given the almost universal sympathy the United States received, including from Iran's Supreme Leader Ayatollah Ali Khamanei, because of the terrorist attacks, the immediate period after 9/11 was America's finest hour.

On September 12, 2001, the UN Security Council passed Resolution 1368, which called on "all States to work together urgently to bring to justice the perpetrators, organizers and sponsors of the terrorist attacks." Since it had become known by then that Al Qaida was responsible for the air assaults, it was the first time that the Council had adopted a resolution that applied not to a state or states but to individuals or groups.

Bush declared an open-ended "war on terror." He combined this with a plan to re-form the Greater Middle East—comprising the Arab Middle East, Iran, and Afghanistan—in the image of America. U.S. Defense Secretary Donald Rumsfeld (2001–2006) summed up the policy. "We have two choices," he said. "Either we change the way we live, or we change the way they [those in the Greater Middle East] live. We choose the latter."[16] His chief strategist, Douglas Feith, would later declare that America's aim was to "transform" not just the Middle East but the "broader world of Islam generally"—and that meant a further thirty-six non-Arab, Muslim-majority countries.

In the end, though, the Bush team changed the way Americans live, not the lives of Arabs or Muslims in general. It created the Department of Homeland Security and enforced the USA PATRIOT (Uniting and Strengthening America by Providing Appropriate Tools Required to Intercept and Obstruct Terrorism) Act. This law greatly enhanced the government's powers of searching, wiretapping, Internet eavesdropping, surveillance, policing, and detention, and it curtailed civil liberties.

BUSH'S CALAMITOUS LEADERSHIP

Unluckily for America and the rest of the world, the mantle of waging an endless war on terror fell on a politician least equipped for it. He was deficient in all the major qualities that cumulatively produce inspiring leadership: intelligence, articulation, charisma, self-knowledge, a steep learning curve, insatiable curiosity, logical thinking, imagination, flexibility, ability to understand and express nuances, and open-mindedness. His eight years in the White House revealed him to be inarticulate, blinkered, and narcissistic— an arrogant man who disdained nuance and never owned up to his faults and mistakes, readily shifting the blame to others for his failings.

Naïvely, he kept a list of Al Qaida's top leaders, and as they were killed or captured, he ticked them off in the belief that eliminating them would decimate a hydra-headed organization. He failed to understand that his policy of invading Muslim countries like Afghanistan and Iraq was unwittingly acting as a recruiting agent for the jihadist movement.

Bereft of intellectual curiosity, he announced that he did not read newspapers and retired to bed by 10 PM. Any news that was worthy of his ears—he added—was conveyed to him by his chief of staff (then Andrew Card) and national security adviser (then Condoleezza Rice). Knowing his aversion to bad news, they indulged his weakness. Thus Bush created his own *virtual* reality. His incuriosity coupled with arrogance enabled him to excise the most disastrous reality from his psyche and let him pile up blunder upon blunder.

His attention span was notoriously short. Logical thinking and nuanced expression were alien to him. His extempore speeches revealed his true measure. His off-the-cuff remarks about the Iraqi insurgents to the American generals in Iraq in 2004 were typical. "Kick ass!" he railed. "We must be tougher than hell! . . . There is a series of moments and this is one of them. Our will is being tested, but we are resolute. We have a better way. Stay strong! Stay the course! Kill them! Be confident! Prevail! We're going to wipe them out!"[17]

None of this would have surprised the team of American experts who calculated the IQs of the U.S. presidents since George Washington using a complex procedure. They found that Bush scored poorly on "openness to experience, cognitive proclivity that encompasses unusual receptiveness to aesthetics, actions, ideas and values," a factor closely associated with intelligence. Compared to Bill Clinton (182), John F. Kennedy (182), Abraham Lincoln (195), and Thomas Jefferson (199), Bush's score was zero.[18]

Bush preferred to trim brush or cycle around his Crawford ranch than compose arguments for launching preventive wars. He delegated this task to such second-rate, neoconservative intellectuals as Feith; Paul Wolfowitz, deputy secretary of defense under Rumsfeld; and Richard Perle, chairman of the quasi-official Defense Policy Advisory Committee during the first Bush administration. They were all associated with the Project for the New American Centenary (PNAC) and its neoimperialist stance.[19]

Bush defied the basics of waging a war. When a government declares war, it calls on its citizens to tighten their belts and pay more taxes to fund the armed conflict. Defying logic and precedence, Bush actually cut taxes on the rich and let Americans believe that despite the war on terror—expected to be long and hard—they would go on living as before. In the absence of the draft (which existed during the Vietnam War), ordinary Americans did not feel directly affected by this conflict. But Bush could not mask for long the ill effect of waging two wars. He inherited a federal budget surplus of $120 billion for fiscal 2001 (October 2000–September 2001) from Clinton and left behind a budget deficit of $1.2 trillion (October 2008–September 2009). During his presidency, the trade deficit reached record levels. The two deficits contributed to creating the most acute fiscal crisis since the Great Depression.

In the immediate aftermath of 9/11, the European Union promised full cooperation. And once it became clear that the terrorist acts had originated abroad, NATO activated its Article 5: An attack on one member is an attack on all. But when NATO members offered combat troops to punish the Taliban government in Afghanistan, which had provided haven to bin Laden, the Saudi mastermind behind the Al Qaida attacks, Bush summarily rejected the overture. America was more than capable of punishing its enemies on its own, he said, underscoring his preference for unilateralism.

So it proved. The Pentagon's military campaign, beginning October 7 and conducted by General Tommy Franks, commander of the CENTCOM (Central Command, covering twenty-five countries in Asia and Africa), led to the flight of the Taliban from Kabul five weeks later. But the war was far from over. Bin Laden and his contingent escaped across the Afghan border into the autonomous tribal belt of Pakistan to fight another day. Still, Bush pressured Rumsfeld to expedite plans to invade Iraq as part of the ongoing war on terror. General Franks began transferring Special Forces teams and other specialists to the Gulf region immediately.

His victory in Afghanistan encouraged Bush to withdraw the United States from its 1972 Anti-Ballistic Missile Treaty with Russia, which limited anti-ballistic missile (ABM) systems used to defend attacks by missile-delivered nuclear weapons. On December 31, he notified the Kremlin accordingly, giving it a six-month advance notice as required by the treaty. This was a further example of Bush's unilateralism that would reach its peak in the invasion of Iraq.

CHASING THE MIRAGE OF IRAQ'S WMD

In his State of the Union speech on January 29, 2002, Bush called North Korea, Iran, and Iraq an "axis of evil," asserting that these countries were pursuing projects for producing weapons of mass destruction.

Among these three, Bush had been particularly focused on Iraq since taking office. At the first National Security Council (NSC) meeting on January 30, 2001, the first item on the agenda was Iraq. The next NSC meeting on February 1 was devoted exclusively to that country. Advocating "going after Saddam," Rumsfeld said, "Imagine what the region would look like without Saddam and with a regime that's aligned with US interests. *It would change everything in the region and beyond*. It would demonstrate what US policy is all about" (emphasis added). In short, sheer power politics. Rumsfeld then talked about post-Saddam Iraq—the Kurds in the north, the oil fields, and the reconstruction of the country's economy.[20]

On February 16, Bush signed a secret National Security directive establishing aims and objectives of the war on Iraq.[21] From then on, the Bush White House resorted to deliberate misinterpretations, spins, and fabrications of the material purportedly supplied by the CIA, which was often reprocessed by the Office of Special Plans (OSP) set up by Rumsfeld, under William Luti. An undersecretary of defense, Luti was a former aide to hawkish Vice President Dick Cheney and a longtime advocate of an invasion of Iraq. Cheney resorted to visiting the CIA headquarters in Langley, Virginia, and bullying its personnel to prepare a case that Iraq's president was pursuing WMD programs and that he was in league with Al Qaida. This was done to seek congressional backing for war on Iraq.

Suppressing information and doctoring facts were not limited to collecting and analyzing intelligence on foreign countries. Almost a year after the invasion of Iraq, sixty leading scientists—a third of them Nobel Laureates—accused the White House of "systematically distorting" scientific facts to fit its policy aims on the environment, health, biomedical research, and nuclear weaponry.[22]

In the case of the Iraq War, unknown to Congress and the general public, its first phase started several weeks *before* the congressional vote investing

Bush with war powers in mid-October. It was on August 29 that, following a meeting with Bush at his Crawford ranch, Rumsfeld ordered Operation Southern Focus, authorizing the Pentagon to hit Iraqi targets *not* involved in attacking the U.S.-UK warplanes enforcing the no-fly zone in the south below the Thirty-third Parallel since 1992. That is, the air campaign part of the Iraq War preceded the ground invasion by almost seven months. It is worth recalling that in the 1991 Gulf War, the Pentagon-led forces had conducted thirty-nine days of nonstop bombing before undertaking a ground offensive that lasted barely four days.

Prominent among those who were alarmed by Bush's move was Al Gore, former U.S. vice president. "President Bush is telling us that the most urgent requirement of the moment—right now—is not to redouble our efforts against Al Qaida and bin Laden [still at large] . . . but instead to shift our focus and concentrate on immediately launching a new war against Saddam Hussein," he said in late September 2002. "And he is proclaiming a new, uniquely American right to preemptively attack whomsoever he may deem represents a potential future threat."[23] Gore was referring to the Bush Doctrine as outlined in *The National Security Strategy of the United States*, a thirty-three-page document published on September 20. It replaced the doctrine of containment and deterrence, which Washington had followed in its dealings with its adversaries since World War II, with preventive war—euphemistically called "anticipatory self-defense" by its proponents.[24]

The preventive war doctrine was the brainchild of Wolfowitz. He had originally conceived it in 1992 as undersecretary of defense for policy under Bush Senior soon after the collapse of the Soviet Union. Based on the contentious assertion that it was not multilateral organizations like the UN that brought about stability but a superpower like America, Wolfowitz's policy paper proposed that the United States should disengage from its formal alliances and use its military power worldwide to prevent the emergence of any potential future rival and stop the spread of nuclear arms. If the United States found itself considering use of force to prevent the development or use of WMDs by another nation, its options should include "pre-emptive action." Any future alliances will be "ad hoc assemblies, often not lasting beyond the crisis being confronted, and in many cases carrying only a general agreement over the objectives to be accomplished."[25] Bush Senior rejected the document, as it clashed with his aim to co-opt the recently defeated Soviet Russia into the new international order.

A decade later, *The National Security Strategy of the United States* issued by his son read like the declaration of a Roman emperor or a Napoleon I or John Bull—the portly, arrogant symbol of the sprawling British Empire. This version of Pax Americana came in a long line of past empires wherein the imperialist power, believing in its inherently superior values, has preached the doctrine of "civilizing" the "natives" while dominating them—a theme captured aptly in Rudyard Kipling's poem "The White Man's Burden." Under the rubric of a freedom agenda, the Bush administration burdened itself with transforming the Greater Middle East by "liberating" its citizens by force and installing a Washington-approved democratic model as a means to forestalling terrorist attacks on American targets in the future.

Rumsfeld and Wolfowitz had imbibed the thesis of the book *The Arab Mind* by Raphael Patai, a Hungarian-Israeli-American academic: The only thing Arabs understood was force—followed by pride and saving face. Out of this seed arose the strategy of "Shock and Awe," which Rumsfeld would implement in Iraq with the backing of Bush and Cheney, whose chief intellectual adviser, Bernard Lewis, believed that in the Arab world "nothing matters more than resolute will and force."

In their missionary zeal, none of the American policymakers sought answers to the following basic questions: Are the many countries in the Greater Middle East to be considered as one homogeneous mass simply because they are Muslim and Arab or Iranian, and are governed by autocratic or semiautocratic rulers? Or do the reasons for the absence of democracy in the region vary from country to country? Is the Greater Middle East ready for a radical switch-over to American-style democracy? And how do the intellectuals in the region assess the current situation?[26]

U.S. officials' lack of curiosity went hand in hand with absolute confidence in the efficacy and lethal power of the Pentagon: sheer power politics, as aptly summarized by Rumsfeld at the first NSC meeting in January 2001. Such thinking was inherent in the operative term "war on terror." It rested on two pillars. One, there was a unified multinational foe out there just as there was during the Cold War under the umbrella of the Warsaw Pact. Two, the strategic response to this enemy had to be military.

The first assumption was wrong. There were various jihadist groups in the world, with each of them following a specific aim. While the Palestinian Hamas was intent on ending the Israeli occupation by all means, including violence, the Lashkar-e Taiba (Army of the Pure) in Pakistan aimed to liberate Kashmiri

Muslims from the yoke of the Indian government. They were not under the command and control of Al Qaida leaders. As for the response to this threat, unlike the countries of the Warsaw Pact, the enemy now consisted of many nonstate entities. So diplomacy and economic competition were out—but not ideology, or the wielding of soft power.

The deployment of an overwhelming force became the sole strategy of the Bush White House to such an extent that in Iraq's case there was no coherent postwar plan. This catastrophic void came about as a result of two factors. One was Rumsfeld's aversion toward nation-building; he was given the sole authority for waging the war and dealing with its consequences. The other was the blatantly wrong analogy of equating Saddam Hussein with Adolf Hitler and thus viewing the invasion of Iraq with a World War II perspective.

Saddam tried to model himself not on Hitler but on Joseph Stalin, who accelerated the industrialization of his country and used terror as a modus operandi of his government. And visualizing postinvasion Iraq as postwar Germany or Japan was equally wrong. Both Germany and Japan signed total surrender documents. Saddam did not surrender; he went underground. Nor did any general from the Iraqi defense ministry. Also, in Japan, where the administrative infrastructure remained intact, Emperor Hirohito ordered his government to cooperate fully with the occupying forces of America. By contrast, in 2003 the Pentagon smashed the state machinery in Iraq.

Gore's prescient warning that diverting the Pentagon's resources from the unfinished war in Afghanistan to invade Iraq would seriously damage America's ability to win the war against terrorism and lead the international community was drowned out by the fearsome scenarios painted by the White House. Saddam was exploring ways of using unmanned aerial vehicles loaded with chemical or biological weapons for missions targeting America, claimed Bush on October 7, 2002, the first anniversary of the Afghanistan War. Furthermore, he revealed that U.S. satellite photographs had shown Iraq rebuilding facilities at the former nuclear program sites.

Trusting Bush's word, on October 10 and 11 Congress gave him war powers by a comfortable majority, including the possibility of waging war without UN approval. Outside Congress, the mainstream press—print and broadcasting—shed its customary healthy skepticism that is the hallmark of good journalism. Even the *New York Times* and the *Washington Post* ran front-page stories based on the say-so of Ahmad Chalabi, an exiled Iraqi leader who had been sentenced to twenty-two years' imprisonment by a Jordanian court for his shady foreign exchange dealings as a leading banker in Amman.[27]

Neither Congress nor the media noticed that war with Iraq was not debated at the level of the principals—state secretary, defense secretary, treasury secretary, CIA director, and attorney general—or the NSC, with the pros and cons aired fully and ending with a vote. That the United States would attack Iraq was treated as a given. The only subjects to be discussed were when and how to make it short and efficient.

In November, while UN inspectors, readmitted into Iraq under a strict new inspection regime, began searching for WMD, the CENTCOM established a forward base at Saliyah Camp near the Qatari capital of Doha. The high point of the Bush administration's attempt to establish Iraq's guilt—irrespective of the UN's failure to find any WMD in Iraq—came on February 5 at the UN Security Council. U.S. Secretary of State Colin Powell presented Washington's case against Iraq.

All the salient "facts" of Powell's presentation turned out to be false. For instance, the "poison factory" allegedly operated in the Kurdish area of Iraq by Abu Mussab Zarqawi, a senior assistant to bin Laden, was no more than "a derelict dump" according to C. J. Chivers of the *New York Times*. The contrast between the allegations and the actuality could not have been starker. Alleged: precursor chemicals, 3,307 tons; Tabun and Sarin nerve agents, unspecified amounts; VX nerve agent, 1.6 tons; Anthrax spores raw material, 25,500 liters; Aflotoxins and Ricin, unspecified amounts; and Botulinum toxin. Actual: one vial of ten-year-old Strain B of Botulinum toxin in an Iraqi scientist's domestic refrigerator. Instead of up to 18 mobile bioweapons laboratories, only 2 suspected, harmless mobile laboratories turned up. There were supposed to be 30,000 bombs, rockets, and shells for poison agents, up to 20 Al Hussein surface-to-surface missiles with a range of 410 miles (650 kilometers), and an unspecified number of L29 unmanned aerial vehicles. None materialized.[28]

Ignoring antiwar demonstrations in 600 towns and cities in fifty-five countries, including 150 in America, which involved 15 to 20 million protestors, on February 15, 2003, and the ongoing, unhindered UN inspections in Iraq, the Bush administration, backed by Britain's Prime Minister Tony Blair, introduced a draft resolution at the UN Security Council. It sought authorization for military action against Iraq for failing to cooperate fully. It gained the support of only Bulgaria and Spain. Among those who opposed war on Iraq were not just Russia and China but also France and Germany. And even though Spanish Prime Minister Jose Maria Aznar conferred with Bush and Blair on the Portuguese island of Terceira in the Azores on March 16, he refused to send a single combat soldier to join the invading Anglo-American forces.

By mounting an illegal invasion of Iraq, the "good" war in Afghanistan, launched in self-defense, would turn "bad," with America and its NATO allies facing a resurgent Taliban seven years after the Pentagon's Afghanistan campaign. By then, hundreds of thousands of Iraqi civilians were dead, one-fifth of the 25 million Iraqis were displaced internally or driven into exile, and the Bush administration had inadvertently bolstered its earlier adversaries in Afghanistan, Iran, and Lebanon and spawned fresh ones in Iraq and Pakistan. Any lingering doubts about the illegality of the Iraq War were dissipated when Kofi Annan, in an interview with the BBC World Service on September 15, 2004, called it "illegal."[29]

MOMENT OF GLORY BEFORE THE FALL

As military campaigns go, the Pentagon's Operation Iraqi Freedom, launched on March 20, 2003, will go down in history as an outstanding triumph. In retrospect, though, it would turn out to be the point at which the American Imperium began sliding downwards.

Within four weeks, the 300,000 strong Anglo-American ground forces (seven-eighth American), equipped with 920 tanks, 900 warplanes and combat helicopters, and 50 unmanned aerial vehicles, and backed by 6 aircraft carrier groups, put to flight Iraq's 389,000 troops, who lacked air cover.

The nonstop bombing—involving 23,000 precision-guided missiles, 750 cruise missiles, and 1,570 cluster bombs—for four weeks caused an estimated damage of $100 billion to Iraq's civilian and military infrastructure. (Following the standard practice of making an inventory of the damage to the civilian and military infrastructure of a defeated nation, the Pentagon would have made an estimate for its records, but that figure has not yet been revealed.) This amount was five times the sum the U.S. Congress would later sanction for Iraq's postinvasion reconstruction.[30]

While the hot war cost Washington $45 billion, the continuing turmoil in Iraq pushed the total to $666 billion by the fifth anniversary of its full-fledged invasion in March 2008. Besides 140,000 American troops, there were 163,000 nonmilitary personnel working on the Pentagon's contracts, and U.S. tax-payers were spending $5,000 *per second* in Iraq.[31] By then nearly 4,000 American soldiers were dead—as were 250,000 to 650,000 Iraqis, with an estimated 150,000 killed in Shiite-Sunni warfare between February 2006 and early 2008.

Though, for all practical purposes, the Pentagon-led invasion of Iraq was over by April 16, 2003, it was not until May 1 that Bush announced a formal end to "major operations" aboard a warship near San Diego with a banner in the background proclaiming "Mission Accomplished."

This mission had gone beyond the overthrow of Saddam Hussein's regime. It had shattered the highly centralized state apparatus, letting the mobs in Baghdad loot and burn 156 public buildings, except the Oil Ministry, which was diligently guarded by American troops.[32]

Soon after, Paul Bremer, head of the Coalition Provisional Authority, the proconsul of Washington, completed the destructive process by disbanding the military and police as well as intelligence agencies. He also dismissed all civil servants and academics, who had been required by Saddam's regime to become members of the governing Baath Party (officially, Arab Baath Socialist Party). This was the culmination of the Bush administration's "year zero" strategy for Iraq.

As the dictatorial head of the secular Baath Party, Saddam had brutally suppressed Islamists, whether Sunni or Shiite. Following his overthrow, the Shiite religious network, which had functioned surreptitiously during the Baathist rule, surfaced quickly to provide essential public services to the community.

As early as April 23, the American public got a dramatic exposure to Iraqis' religiosity on TV. On that day almost 1.5 million Shiites, men and women, gathered in Karbala, the burial place of Imam Hussein, to commemorate the fortieth day of mourning of Imam Hussein's death in 681 CE, a memorial banned by the ruling Baathists for nearly thirty years. Many of the pious carried whips of mortification—such as thick cat-o'-nine-tails made from chains—to flagellate themselves. The mourners shouted, "No, no to America; yes, yes to Islam."[33] Later, most of these pious Shiites would form the bulk of a million-strong demonstrations in Baghdad, sponsored by Muqtada al Sadr, a young Shiite religious leader, to demand the departure of the American forces.

The publication of the *Comprehensive Report by the Special Adviser to the DCI* [Director of Central Intelligence] *on Iraq's WMD* by Charles Duelfer on

October 6, 2004, drove the final nail in the coffin of the rationale for invading and occupying Iraq. The 1,000-page document summarized the results of fifteen months' search by 1,200 inspectors supplied by the CIA, and the earlier UN inspections from June 1991 to December 1998 and from November 2002 to March 18, 2003. The total cost of these inspections and the administrative oversight amounted to $900 million. The report concluded finally and irrevocably that Iraq destroyed stockpiles of illicit weapons within months of the end of the 1991 Gulf War, and that Iraq was not actively seeking to produce WMD.[34]

The indignation and humiliation caused by the occupation of their country by an infidel army, the wanton destruction of Iraq's social and economic infrastructure, and the loss of power enjoyed by the Sunni minority since 1638, dating back to the Ottoman Empire, brought about an alliance of local and foreign jihadists, Sunni tribal leaders, disgruntled former Baathists, and disbanded soldiers, policemen, and intelligence personnel. What helped cement this alliance was the torture of Iraqi detainees by the American guards at Abu Ghraib prison near Baghdad, which was exposed by CBS's *60 Minutes* a few days before the first anniversary of Bush's "Mission Accomplished" declaration. The airing of the revolting pictures of Iraqi prisoners' abuse and torture was followed by the publication of more pictures and documents by the award-winning Seymour Hersh in the *New Yorker*.[35] The official explanation of a few "bad apples" among the lower ranks of the Pentagon, some of whom were convicted, failed to demolish the widespread belief that the atrocious behavior by the guards at Abu Ghraib flowed from authorization given at the very top.

This belief crystallized into indisputable fact on December 12, 2008. On that day the Senate Armed Services Committee released its unclassified, twenty-nine-page report on the subject—the result of eighteen months' work and seventy interviews. It laid bare the trail of the memos and instructions leading to Rumsfeld. He ruled that the SERE (Survival, Evasion, Resistance, Escape) techniques aimed to teach elite American soldiers how to endure torture should be "reverse engineered." The SERE program was developed during the Cold War, with Pentagon trainers exposing airmen and others likely to be captured in war to Soviet-style tactics: disrupted sleep, exposure to extreme heat and cold, hours in uncomfortable stress positions, and water boarding, in which the detainee's face is covered with cloth and water is poured from above to create a feeling of suffocation. The senators discovered memos requesting permission for torture including "wet towel treatment or water boarding." Approval of torture—"enhanced interrogation," in Orwellian double-speak—was sought and granted at the highest level. Among the techniques was "making a prisoner wear a dog leash and perform dog tricks."[36] However, Rumsfeld worked within the parameters set by the commander in chief. On February 7, 2002, Bush signed a secret determination that "Common article 3 of Geneva Conventions," which would have afforded minimum standards for humane treatment, did not apply to Al Qaida or Taliban detainees.

For most people outside America, the Abu Ghraib prisoner scandal was a moral tipping point, the final step in transforming Iraq's foreign liberators into its oppressors. The episode also marked a tipping point for public opinion in the United States. In the Internet era, with instant, worldwide transmission of the Abu Ghraib images, described by Rumsfeld as "blatantly sadistic, cruel, and inhumane," Americans were directly exposed to the dark side of the armed occupation of a racially, culturally, and historically different nation.

Such turning points could also be found in the history of imperial Britain and France. In the late 1950s, British popular support for the war in Kenya to crush the Mau Mau nationalist guerrilla struggle fell after the exposure of a fatal beating at the Hola detention camp. And a leaked report from the International Committee of the Red Cross on torture in Algiers at about the same time proved to be the tipping point in French public backing for the war of occupation in Algeria.

The resistance against the American occupation in Iraq stiffened. The result was a bloody mayhem that, following the assuming of power by religious Shiite leaders through the ballot, threatened to turn into a full-fledged civil war between Sunnis and Shiites in 2007.

AMERICA'S DOWNHILL SLIDE

Bush's scenario of the violent overthrow of Saddam's dictatorship unleashing a secular, democratic wave in the Middle East failed to materialize. His team was disabused of its naïve assumptions by none other than some of the official documents. For instance, a report by the U.S. Defense Science Board's Task Force on Strategic Communication (in the global war on terrorism), published in November 2004, concluded that "there is no yearning-to-be-liberated-by-the-U.S. groundswell among Muslim societies," and that "Muslims do not 'hate our freedom,' but rather they hate our policies."[37]

Unwilling to face reality, the Bush administration suppressed the National Intelligence Estimate (NIE) entitled, "Trends in Global Terrorism: Implications for the US," completed in April 2006. Its existence came to light only when the *New York Times* leaked it five months later. It highlighted the "centrality" of the U.S. invasion of Iraq in fomenting terrorist cells and attacks globally. The invasion and subsequent developments had helped to spread radical Islam by providing a focal point for anti-Americanism. It had created "a new class of terrorists" who are "self-generating" and who can create terror cells capable of mounting an attack without much outside help. Earlier, based on this as yet secret report, General Michael Hayden, deputy director of National Intelligence (later CIA director), said, "New jihadist and networks and cells, sometimes united by nothing more than their anti-western agendas, are increasingly likely to emerge. If this trend continues, threats to the U.S. at home and abroad will become more diverse and that could lead to increasing attacks everywhere."[38] In short, the invasion of Iraq, mounted as part of the ongoing "war on terror," ended up increasing terrorism rather than eliminating it.

Ironically, in the process of making the planet safe, Bush found himself labeled as a menace to international amity. An opinion poll by the leading newspapers of Britain, Canada, Israel, and Mexico in 2006 showed that 75 percent considered Bush as "a great or moderate danger to world peace," higher than North Korea's Kim Jong Il's 69 percent.[39] What about advancing the "freedom agenda" by overthrowing Saddam's dictatorial regime and letting secular, democratic forces in the region take charge? Contrary to the Bush team's expectations, when given a free choice, voters favored Islamist parties that were anti-Washington and pro-Tehran—even in U.S.-occupied Iraq.

THE "FREEDOM AGENDA" TURNED UPSIDE DOWN

The Palestinian territories provided a stark example. Believing that Clinton had invested too much time and energy to forge an agreement between Israeli Prime Minister Ehud Barak and Yasser Arafat, president of the Palestinian Authority and chairman of the secular Fatah Movement, Bush opted for "benign neglect" of the world's longest running dispute. Refusing to meet Arafat, he called on the Palestinians to reject his corrupt and inept government. Arafat died of a mysterious disease in November 2004 and was succeeded by Mahmoud Abbas, a favorite of Washington.

In January 2006, in a free and fair parliamentary election, Palestinians rewarded Fatah's rival, Hamas, with a landslide victory. "There is something healthy about a system that does that," Bush said, congratulating the Palestinian voters for rejecting "the old guard." But when it was explained to him that Hamas was the acronym of *Harkat al Muqawamma al Islami*—meaning Movement of Islamic Resistance—he did a swift turnaround. He refused to recognize the Hamas government and proceeded to impose sanctions against it. But Hamas's victory was only the latest manifestation of the success of political Islam in the region's electoral politics.

Islamist parties or individuals performed well in the pioneering local government contests in Saudi Arabia in early 2005 and parliamentary elections in Egypt, Lebanon, and Iraq later in the year. The reasons for this phenomenon varied; the Middle East is *not* a single homogeneous mass.

Once Iraq was incorporated into the (Sunni) Ottoman Empire in 1638, Shiites were persecuted and discriminated against. This continued after the dissolution of the Ottoman Empire. King Faisal, installed by the British, was Sunni, and so were the leaders of the Baath Party, which seized power in 1968.

Mosque and religion became the last resort of Iraqi Shiites. Their religious hierarchy quietly set up a clandestine network during the Baathist rule. The Pentagon-led invasion created a massive political-administrative vacuum. It was immediately filled by the hitherto underground network of the Shiite religious establishment and backed by the militias of the Shiite religious parties.

As for Sunnis, the dominant minority for centuries, the thirteen-year-long UN economic sanctions, starting in 1990, hurt them as much as they did non-Sunnis. Continued impoverishment led Sunni masses to turn to Islam. So, unsurprisingly, once Sunnis decided to participate in the electoral process, most of them favored the Iraqi Islamic Party–dominated Iraqi Accord Front.

The exiled Iraqi leaders' view, eagerly accepted by the Bush team, that Iraqis were predominantly secular was unsubstantiated. Public opinion polls were banned by Saddam's regime. The Baath Party was secular in the sense that one of its three founders, Michel Aflaq, the ideological guru of Saddam, was a Christian. Far more reliable was the confidential poll conducted in July 2004 for the International Republican Institute (IRI), an offshoot of the U.S. Republican Party. It was leaked. Seven out of ten respondents said that the Sharia—i.e., Islamic canon—should be the "sole basis" of Iraqi laws, and the same proportion preferred a "religious state," with only 23 percent preferring a secular state.

The elections to the Transitional Assembly in January 2005, and the subsequent parliament elected in December under the new constitution, confirmed the veracity of the IRI survey. In the December general election the Shiite United Iraqi Alliance, the brainchild of Grand Ayatollah Ali Sistani, won almost four-fifths of the seats that should have gone to the majority Shiite community. Likewise, the Iraqi Accord Front garnered 80 percent of the places that minority Sunnis could claim. In contrast, the secular Iraqi National List secured only 9 percent of the seats and the secular Kurdistan Alliance 17 percent.

For all practical purposes, the postinvasion constitution had turned Iraq into an Islamic republic. An article in it states that the Sharia is the fundamental source of Iraqi legislation. Another article says that no Iraqi law shall violate the undisputed principles of Islam. Prime Minister Nouri al Maliki and his predecessor Ibrahim Jaafari were leaders of the Islamic Daawa (i.e., Call) Party committed to establishing an Islamic regime in Iraq. On major issues of the state, they both consulted Shiites' supreme religious leader, Sistani. These developments, and the emergence of strong ethnic and sectarian identities in Iraq followed by bloody intersectarian violence, provided a powerful argument to the authoritarian and semiauthoritarian regimes in the Arab Middle East to resist political liberalization. In their disapproval of America's invasion and occupation of Iraq, the rulers were in tune with popular sentiment. The Annual Arab Public Opinion Poll by the University of Maryland and Zogby International, involving 4,000 respondents from Egypt, Jordan, Lebanon, Morocco, Saudi Arabia, and the United Arab Emirates, showed that 81 percent believed that Iraqis are worse off now than before the invasion.[40]

As for the home base of the "liberator" of Iraq—Bush—it slowly dawned on the American people that he had expended huge public treasure and blood to put religious Shiites in power in Baghdad and generate a low-intensity war between embittered Sunnis and newly empowered Shiites.

In the Palestinian territories, there was no question of a Sunni-Shiite divide, as all Palestinians are Sunni. So the reasons for the rise of Hamas in these territories occupied by Israel since 1967 were different. The ruling Fatah Movement suffered from tensions between local leaders and those who had spent many years abroad before returning after the 1993 Oslo Accords. The leadership of Hamas was almost wholly local.

Since the Palestinian state was not fully formed, the ranks were able to exercise direct pressure on the leadership. As the governing party since 1994, which had proved corrupt and inept in administering the Palestinian entity, Fatah saw its standing wane. Arafat's demise deprived it of its most valuable political asset. By contrast, Hamas had a history of providing free social services to the needy long before the Oslo Accord and was not tainted with corruption and cronyism.

By imposing sanctions against the democratically elected Hamas government, the Bush administration undermined its much-hyped "freedom agenda." Most people in the Arab and Muslim world concluded that Washington was committed not to democracy per se but only if it produced results that furthered its interests. They noted too that it was only after failing to find WMD in occupied Iraq, or prove linkage between Saddam's regime and Al Qaida, that the Bush team had started trumpeting its democratic crusade in the region. And, tellingly, after electoral politics pushed up Islamist parties to the fore, its ardor for a "freedom agenda" cooled.

AMERICA'S MORAL AUTHORITY PLUNGES

Over the years, Americans became aware of the gross human rights violations the Bush government had committed. It had resorted to "extraordinary renditions" by hooded intelligence agents in unmarked aircraft, used clandestine "black site" prisons in countries infamous for torturing detainees, practiced "reverse rendition" of the suspects found to be innocent by abandoning them blindfolded at obscure frontiers, and conducted "robust/enhanced interrogation" by keeping suspects on dog leashes and bombarding them with intolerable sounds, including meows from cat food commercials and Eminem rapping about America.

Besides the widely known Guantánamo Bay detention center in the U.S.-controlled enclave in Cuba; the five known prisons in Iraq, holding 15,800 people without charge; and another fifteen "facilities" in Afghanistan with 600 inmates, there was a long list of "black sites" in Asia, Africa, and Europe. The host countries included Egypt (six sites), Pakistan (six sites), Morocco, Syria, Uzbekistan, Romania, and Poland. In addition, the Pentagon had used seventeen ships as floating prisons.[41] These "black sites" sprang up soon after Bush signed a secret authorization to the effect within a week of 9/11—on September 17, 2001.

The torture tactics had proved counterproductive as far as "high value" suspects were concerned. Unable to withstand the torture, the suspects often gave false and even dangerously misleading intelligence that, when followed up, damaged America's national security rather than enhanced it.

At these sites, several detainees were killed during interrogation. Many more committed suicide. The subject was aired frequently, and the mistreatment of the detainees condemned widely, by Western media and nongovernmental organizations—but rarely by any important Western government publicly. (In contrast, the deaths of dozens who died in the torture cells of Egypt, Pakistan, Morocco, Uzbekistan, and elsewhere went unreported.) This influenced public opinion in Europe. A survey by the Washington-based Pew Research Center in 2006 showed that since 1999 a favorable view of America fell in all major European countries: Britain, from 85 percent to 56 percent; France, 62 percent to 39 percent; Germany, 67 percent to 37 percent; and Spain, 50 percent to 23 percent.[42]

In Europe there was also a growing awareness of the deteriorating quality of life in America. In a country of 300 million, 45 million lacked health insurance. One out of a hundred adults was in jail. In the thirty-member Organization of Economic Cooperation and Development of industrialized nations, the United States ranked twenty-fourth in math skills. Because of the deficient U.S. educational system, two out of three American voters could not name the different branches of government, and one out of five believed that it was the sun that revolved round the earth.[43]

The Pew Research Center's Global Attitudes Survey of 45,000 people in forty-seven nations in 2007 provided a wide-ranging measure of America and Bush in the world. In forty-three countries, majorities wanted the American troops withdrawn from Iraq "as soon as possible," including 56 percent in the United States. While 80 percent of Americans viewed their country favorably, only 21 percent of Egyptians or Jordanians did so—down to 9 percent among

Turks. Among those who were repelled by the Bush administration's insularity and arrogance were 83 percent of Canadians and a majority of Japanese and South Koreans. Overall, a positive view of America had fallen in twenty-six of the thirty-three countries that were covered by a similar survey in 2002. "The trouble in Iraq and the mistreatment of prisoners at Abu Ghraib in Iraq and Guantánamo are a driving force behind much of anti-Americanism, " the survey report concluded.[44]

Another global index of America's growing unpopularity could be gleaned from the voting pattern of the UN General Assembly. In 1995, more than half of the resolutions backed by Washington were adopted by the General Assembly. In 2006, the proportion had fallen below a quarter.[45]

These polls were conducted in 2006–2007, when Iraq was embroiled in low-intensity civil war. It was triggered by Al Qaida activists' escalating suicide and vehicle-borne attacks on Shiites, capped by the bombing of the sacred shrine of Imam Hassan al Askari in Samarra in February 2006. In retaliation, militias representing Shiites resorted to abducting and killing Sunnis across Baghdad. Intersectarian violence intensified. Mixed neighborhoods in the capital, cleansed of the minority sect, were then fortified with miles of blast walls of concrete.

RISE OF IEDS

Instead of showcasing America's muscle and glory, the wars in Afghanistan and Iraq demonstrated the limitations of the world's most lethal, highest-tech military machine, the unreliability of U.S. intelligence, and the incompetence of the White House. The Pentagon found itself engaged in an asymmetrical conflict in Iraq, where, in the words of General Brent Scowcroft, national security adviser to two American presidents, the United States was "being wrestled to a draw by opponents who are not even an organized state adversary."

In the emerging asymmetrical warfare, the Improvised Explosive Devices (IEDs) played a preeminent role. An IED is a bomb constructed and deployed in ways other than in conventional military action. Since an IED builder improvises with the materials at hand, the supply of these weapons is limitless. They fall into three categories: package, vehicle-borne, and human-borne. The package IED is generally placed, hidden, on the curb of a road to be detonated when vehicles or pedestrians pass, and is called a roadside bomb. It may be partially comprised of conventional military explosives, such as an artillery round, attached to a detonating mechanism.

There was an exponential growth in the deployment of IEDs in Iraq, with 2,500 IED explosions *a month* in 2006.[46] By 2007, IEDs had caused two-fifths of the total deaths of U.S. troops. A generously funded Joint IED Defeat Organization at the Pentagon was engaged in urgent research and a development program to devise means of countering IEDs—with little success so far.

During fiscal year 2007, the Iraq War emptied Washington's treasury by more than $150 billion, and there was the further expense of the conflict in Afghanistan. They contributed a hefty proportion of the federal budget deficit of $454.8 billion in fiscal 2008 (October 2007–September 2008).[47] Bush's reckless fiscal policies of funding two wars while cutting taxes had turned the United States into the biggest debtor on the planet by 2005. It was a humiliating fall for a country that only six decades earlier was the world's biggest creditor. With no end to the wars in sight, the United States became increasingly dependent on foreign countries to close its fiscal gap by buying U.S. Treasury bonds, maturing in two, five, ten, or thirty years.

Washington's financial power received a severe blow in August 2007, when the sub-prime mortgage crisis hit the markets. It started a process that shook the foundations of American-style capitalism on a scale not seen since the Great Crash of 1929. "We have a sub-prime financial system, not a sub-prime mortgage system." This statement from Nouriel Roubini, a prescient economics professor at New York University, would be borne out as the crisis unfolded in ever grimmer phases.[48] His calculations would show credit losses peaking at $3.6 trillion for U.S. institutions, half of them by banks and broker-dealers, with the American banking system's capital of $1.4 trillion having a shortfall of $400 billion.[49]

THE RISE AND RISE OF SYNTHETIC CREDIT

What was once hailed as financial wizardry by mathematical geniuses, fresh from the Massachusetts Institute of Technology and other centers of higher learning, recruited by Wall Street—guaranteeing rising profits with falling risks—would be dismissed later as one more attempt by alchemists to turn dross into gold. In today's globalized world, however, these whiz kids, backed by their avaricious bosses, brought disaster far beyond the shores of their country.

Unlike military coups, fiscal bankruptcies or collapses do not occur overnight. They are a long time in the making. Such was the case with the financial meltdown, which started slowly in August 2007 in the United States and gathered fearsome momentum in September 2008 to engulf the globe. It led to the decimation of the giants of the U.S. fiscal world, dizzying gyrations of stock markets, and the sharpest and widest economic collapse in living memory—job losses in millions, catastrophic falls in retail trade and durable goods like cars and personal computers, and steep cuts in travel.

The seeds for the catastrophe were sown by Bush. He turned the surplus budget of fiscal 2001 into a deficit of $158 billion the following year. He left behind a budget with a shortfall of nearly 9 percent of the GDP of $13.8 trillion. (It is worth noting that the limit for the budget deficit for the members of the sixteen-strong Eurozone is 3 percent of the GDP.) The national debt ballooned from $5.7 trillion in 2001 to $10.6 trillion in November 2008. It amounted to 74 percent of the GDP—almost twice the size of Britain's (38.3 percent) and four times China's (18.4 percent).

During Bush's presidency, consumers went on a spending binge because of cheap money. Following 9/11, the Federal Reserve Board halved the interest rate in a series of cuts to 1.75 percent within three months. The rate-slashing continued until June 2003, three months into the Iraq War—dipping to 1 percent, the lowest figure for nearly half a century. It stayed there for a whole year. With annual inflation running at about 3 percent during 2001–2004, net interest rates were negative. Money and credit were available for free, engendering a feeling of euphoria.

Easy credit spiked house prices to double-digit annual growth. It enabled home owners to use real estate as a virtual ATM. With bank deposits earning virtually no interest, the national savings rate plunged to almost zero in 2007, down from 12 percent a quarter century ago. Indeed, consumers spent $106 for every $100 they earned.

Such profligacy led to a widening gap between imports and exports, increasing the foreign trade account deficit. Between 2005 and 2006, the U.S. trade deficit rose from $711 billion to $764 billion—its fifth consecutive record—and soaked up 70 percent of the rest of the world's trade surpluses. The Bush administration closed the gap by borrowing other countries' dollars. By pushing up its foreign debt to a dangerous height, and turning the dollar into a volatile currency, it drove the U.S. financial system to a breaking point.

Earlier, in November 1999, the Republication-majority Congress had repealed the Glass-Steagall Act of 1933 and replaced it with the Gramm-Leach-Bliley Act. The new law abrogated the distinction between depository and investment banks as mandated by the 1933 Act. It allowed the depository banks to operate in deregulated financial markets in which distinction between loans, deposits, securities, and other financial instruments was blurred. So these banks began operating as investment banks and started underwriting and trading in such new-fangled financial instruments as mortgage-backed securities and collateralized debt obligations (CDOs).

Under the Glass-Steagall Act, depository banks were well regulated. Required to maintain capital reserves at a certain level, they were barred from taking too much risk. In the late 1980s, alarmed at the low capitalization at major banks, the authorities imposed tighter rules on capitalization in the United States and elsewhere. The process continued until the mid-1990s. This squeeze made bank executives envious of how poorly capitalized mortgage companies were thriving.

The key to mortgage lenders' prosperity was securitization: assembling pools of mortgages and then selling investors shares in the regular repayments received from borrowers.[50] Securitization made the original lender blasé about the borrowers' ability to repay. These mortgage packages were later blended with bonds of varying credit-worthiness. The subsequent loan packages changed hands in the form of increasingly esoteric financial instruments.

The interlinked and overlapping loans became so complex and sophisticated that no one could work out who owned what underlying loan or the worth of these loans. In accounting, loans or mortgages appear as assets. And assets are listed at their current values, which change daily. When loans go bad, or company shares owned by a bank fall steeply, the assets decline, and make the bank's balance sheet look shaky. That in turn makes the bank reluctant to lend to customers or other banks. A bank is required to maintain a certain percentage of assets in cash. In Hong Kong it is 14 percent, in China 13–14 percent, and in America 8 percent.

The property mortgaging sector has evolved since the 1930s. Besides regulating the stock market through the Securities and Exchange Act of 1934, mandating the minimum wage, giving subsidies to farmers, and unleashing a massive public works program, President Franklin Roosevelt's New Deal tackled the home ownership issue head-on. It made the Savings and Loan associations, or banks—dating back to the nineteenth century as community-based establishments for savings and mortgages—the chief instrument to widen home possession.

To keep these banks liquid, Washington founded the Federal National Mortgage Association, popularly called Fannie Mae, in 1938. (When it was privatized in 1968, it became a hybrid, with capital supplied by shareholders but underwriting done by the federal government.) It, and the Federal Home Loan Mortgage Corporation, known as Freddie Mac—established in 1970 to compete with Fannie Mae—purchased mortgages from banks and other lenders to free the latters' cash to be used for fresh loans. Both Freddie Mac and Fannie Mae remained Government Sponsored Enterprises (GSE). So they could raise funds more cheaply than their competitors and offer loans at lower interest rates than others for home purchase. However, the deposits in their accounts were not guaranteed by the federal government, as stated in the law.

Initially, these GSEs remained solvent by transferring a package of mortgages to a trust. Consider the case of a trust owning properties worth $10 million, with the borrowers paying it 5 percent interest. So it would have an annual income of $500,000 received in twelve installments. If a pension investment fund bought a 10 percent certificate of this trust for $1 million, it earned $50,000 a year. The downside was that property mortgages had different maturity dates, and that their credit-worthiness varied between super-safe AAA bonds with low returns and junk CCC bonds with high returns and short maturity periods.

An innovation, called the Collateralized Mortgage Obligations (CMO), emerged in 1983 during the early days of the presidency of Republican Ronald Reagan, who, as a free marketeer, advanced deregulation, starting with the airlines in 1981. The CMO was a composite product designed by a Freddie Mac team and Larry Fink. It had three layers. The top 70 percent, consisting of super-prime mortgages, had a low return but first claim on all cash flow; the middle 20 percent, consisting of prime mortgages, had a higher return but secondary claim on the income; and the bottom 10 percent, made up of subprime mortgages, had the highest return but was also the first to take losses. Over time, the bottom layer would acquire the title of "toxic waste." (A subprime mortgage resulted when a lender provided cash to a person with poor or no credit history while requiring him or her to make repayments at above-normal levels.) So, overall, here was a financial product with bond-like yields that catered to demands across a wide range of risk.

The CMOs became popular even as some of them came to acquire more than a hundred layers. Though the CMOs lost their luster in 1994 after a sudden interest rise of 0.5 percent, which lowered the return on all fixed-income assets, the construction of a composite product was extended to debts of all types, including commercial mortgages, corporate loans, high yield takeover loans, and emerging market loans. The resulting instrument was named Collateralized Debt Obligation (CDO)—a synthetic security backed by a variety of debts.

Like the CMO, the CDO was a derivative, deriving its value from other financial instruments. And like its predecessor, it was often split into three tranches: the senior tranche, containing assets with the credit rating of AAA; the mezzanine, containing assets with AA to BB rating; and the bottom unrated equity tranche. As with the CMO, the lowest layer offered the highest return while being the first to bear losses, thus earning the sobriquet of "toxic waste." But unlike the CMOs, the CDOs were guaranteed by credit insurance against loan repayment defaults. With that provision in place, the CDOs were set firmly on a path of exponential growth. By 1997, they had emerged as the fastest growing sector of the synthetic securities market. Most of the large banks and asset managers founded their own CDOs.

In 1998, Brooksley Born, chairwoman of the Commodity Futures Trading Commission, sought to extend its regulatory reach into derivates. But she was overruled by Alan Greenspan, chairman of the Federal Reserve Board since 1987, and Treasury Secretary Robert Rubin.[51]

Once the formula devised by David X. Li of Gaussian Cupola models in 2001 enabled traders to price CDOs quickly, their popularity soared—globally. This was one more example among many others where America, foremost in productivity and market efficiency, dazzled the rest of the world with its innovations in the fiscal area. The international derivatives market mushroomed from $106 trillion in 2002 to $531 trillion on the eve of the global fiscal meltdown in September 2008.

By 2001, hedge funds were gaining popularity as well. Though devised originally by Alfred Winslow Jones in 1949, they became a regular feature of the financial markets only in the 1960s. A hedge fund is an investment vehicle that is allowed by U.S. regulators to invest not only in stocks and bonds but also in debt, currencies, commodities, and derivatives. It tries to counter potential losses by hedging its investments, often by short selling. "Short selling" is the term used when an investor executes an order to sell a financial instrument, such as shares, through his or her broker without owning it. The brokering firm borrows these shares from its own inventory or from the market. The actual transfer of the shares occurs within the settlement period, which varies between three and five working days from the trading date. Such investors become short sellers. They watch the share price, and when, in their opinion, it has declined sufficiently, they buy these shares at the reduced price, replenish the brokering firm's inventory, and pocket the profit. Conversely, if the share price rises and they find themselves having to buy shares at that level, they lose. Nowadays, however, many investment funds use other methods as well as short selling to increase return.[52]

Since hedge funds are open only to a limited category of rich or professional investors and are barred from advertising or soliciting, the regulators exempt them from the rules about liquidity, derivative contracts, management fees, leveraging, and short selling. They tend to specialize. By the early 1990s, they accounted for three-fifths of large global investments. Later they also became dominant in the markets for derivatives with high-yield ratings. Between 1990 and 2001, hedge funds' assets grew nearly fourteenfold, to $537 billion. Five years later, the figure leaped to $1.1 trillion, involving about 9,000 hedge funds.[53] So far the attempts by the U.S. Securities and Exchange Commission (SEC) to get hedge funds to register and be subject to tighter regulations have failed. Their managers do not reveal their trading strategy or performance to anyone except their clients.

Besides hedge funds, certain other financial instruments are not properly regulated: money market funds,[54] derivative contracts, and Structured Investment Vehicles (SIVs), shadow CDOs in the form of limited partnerships that collect packages of bank loans or other securities. Altogether they constitute a shadow banking system (or shadow fiscal system). Because of their growing popularity, the size of the shadow banking system ballooned. This caused unease.

But when the U.S. Senate Banking Committee held hearings on derivative contracts in 2003, Greenspan described them as "an extraordinarily useful vehicle to transfer risk from those who should not be taking it to those who are willing to and are capable of doing so." Therefore, he added, "We think it would be a mistake to more deeply regulate the [derivative] contracts."[55]

Greenspan's word prevailed—not that of Warren Buffett, the richest man in America then and known as an investment wizard. In his 2003 letter to the shareholders of his Berkshire Hathaway Assurance Corporation, he called derivatives "financial weapons of mass destruction," and added that "they are easy to get in but hell to get out." Later he would explain that, by spinning a "web of mutual dependence" among various financial institutions, derivative contracts kept the investors entangled for years, creating real hazards once those assets started to decline.[56]

The availability of credit insurance for CDOs encouraged investors—insurance companies, investment banks, investment trusts, money market funds, mutual funds, pension funds, private banks, SIVs, and unit trusts—to take increasingly higher risks in an endless pursuit of higher and higher returns. Some CDO managers assembled risky tranches of several existing CDOs to produce a $(CDO)^2$—with the widest possible range of highest-to-lowest risk-rated tranches. It was tantamount to building a fifty-story skyscraper on a foundation of rubble. Following the Gramm-Leach-Bliley Act of 1999, cash-rich depository banks joined the list of investors in CDOs.

By then, yet another financial innovation had taken hold: the Credit Default Swap (CDS). This arrangement allowed the transfer of third-party risk from one party to the other. One party in the CDS was a lender who faced credit risk from a third party. The counterparty insured this risk in exchange for regular periodic payments—an insurance premium, in essence. If the third party defaulted, then the insurer purchased from the insured the defaulted asset by paying out the principal and the remaining interest on the debt. But, unlike traditional insurers, the sellers of CDSs did not have to be regulated entities, and they were not required to maintain any reserves to pay off CDS buyers. Also, CDS contracts were valued on a daily basis, making them volatile, which was not the case with traditional insurance contracts.

However, the CDS was particularly helpful to those American mega-banks that wanted to expand abroad. For a premium, along with the interest due on a loan that a foreign bank had given, the American bank provided the non-American company a guarantee against any loan repayment default. The arrangement was beneficial to both parties. Having insured itself against a default on its loan, the non-American bank felt free to lend that amount to some other borrower, thus increasing the size of its capital. And the American company received the interest on the original loan plus its premium. Small wonder that between 2001 and mid-2008, the notional value of global CDSs shot up fifty-five-fold—to $55 trillion, a sum equal to the GDPs of all the nations of the world.[57]

The CDSs would end up playing a major role in the downfall of such financial stalwarts as Merrill Lynch, Lehman Brothers Holdings, and American International Group. In the absence of regulation for CDSs, these financial corporations did not set aside cash in case there was default on the insured loans. They blithely took it for granted that none or very few of these loans would go bad. But when their overly optimistic assumption went awry, it did so with such vengeance that it jeopardized the very existence of the company.

In America the first decade of the twenty-first century witnessed sharp cuts in federal interest rates in the wake of the collapse of high-tech shares in July 2000, after the high-tech-heavy NASDAQ Composite had surpassed 5,000 on March 9, 2000, barely four months after crossing 3,000. The Federal Reserve reduced the rate from 6.5 percent in May 2000 to 3.5 percent in August 2001. Further slashing after 9/11 depressed the rate to 1 percent in June 2003. The GDP picked up. But the Federal Reserve stayed put at 1 percent for one year. Then, to counter inflation, it upped interest rates seventeen times in succession to 5.25 percent in June 2006.

In some instances the returns on CDOs were 2 percent to 3 percent higher than corporate bonds with the same credit rating. In the fiscal world the credit ratings agencies perform a vital role. Until the mid-1990s the leading ratings agencies—Standard & Poor's, Moody's, and Fitch Ratings—had relied exclusively on income from investors who bought their researches and analyses. Their bias-free assessment of the financial health ranged from the bonds issued by state and city governments to complex mortgages.

Since assessing complex CDOs yielded higher fees than traditional debt, ratings agencies became more interested in the newfangled financial instruments—and more profit-oriented, particularly when privately owned firms like Moody's went public in 2000. That made them friendly toward the issuers of debt. They began operating closely with the corporations whose debts they assessed for hefty fees. While Moody's doubled its income between 2002 and 2006, with its stock price tripling, the ultimate losers were the buyers of debt it had rated.[58]

Just before its collapse on September 15, 2008, Lehman Brothers carried an A2 rating by Moody's. That placed it in the investment-grade range. And the day before the U.S. government moved to save AIG from bankruptcy, its senior unsecured debt had Moody's rating of Aa3, which is higher than A2.[59] The depth to which greed had penetrated the ratings agencies was captured by a

Standard and Poor's employee in an internal e-mail thus: "It [the debt] could be structured by cows and we would rate it."[60]

It was revealed later that when Countrywide Financial, the topmost mortgage lender, complained that Moody's assessment of a pool of securities underwritten by it was "too tough," Moody's management upgraded the rating the next day.[61]

It was not until July 2008, a year into the sub-prime crisis, that the SEC published a report saying that ratings agencies brazenly flouted conflict-of-interest guidelines and prioritized profit making. In the absence of adequate staff and time to process a vastly increased volume of work, the agencies continued to issue half-baked ratings.[62] In short, instead of acting as watchdogs, their core role, the ratings agencies got lured by the greed gripping the U.S. fiscal system and turned into lapdogs.

With the global CDO issuance in 2006 hitting a record $521 billion, the cumulative international CDO market ballooned to $2 trillion. Given the increasingly globalized economies, when the virus of unfathomable derivatives landed the U.S. fiscal system into a sickbed, all the important banking systems suffered grievously—except those in India and China. In India 70 percent of the banking system was nationalized, and the capital ratio was 12 to 13 percent. Above all, unlike Greenspan, the governor of the Reserve Bank of India, Yagan V. Reddy, "basically believed that if bankers were given the opportunity to sin, they would sin."[63]

Almost two out of five financial instruments comprising CDOs were backed by house mortgages, with nearly half of them being sub-prime. This had happened because many mortgage companies or brokers had lured low-income people to buy adjustable rate mortgages (ARM), with low initial payments rising later to higher figures. Some of these buyers were "ninja"—no income, no job, no assets. Among those who recommended sub-prime and adjustable rate mortgages was none other than Greenspan.

Yet contrary to the popular perception that mortgage companies opened up the money spigot to help African-Americans and Hispanics to become home owners, 40 percent of the mortgages were for second homes or for buy-to-rent arrangements taken out by well-to-do, predominantly white Americans.[64]

Galloping interest rates in 2005–2006 led to higher installments that the holders of sub-prime or adjustable rate mortgages were required to pay. Many of them could not. The result was high default rates. Also, steeper borrowing costs reduced demand. The first-time buyers, essential to maintain the upward trend in the real estate market, vanished. The property bubble burst. House prices started declining. Defaults shot up, and foreclosures in 2007 were 75 percent above the previous year's figure.

Some of the originators of the sub-prime or adjustable rate mortgages were owned or controlled by such leading financial institutions as Merrill Lynch and GE Capital, part of General Electric, a top U.S. corporation that had purchased WMC Mortgage, a sub-prime lending business, in 2004. During that year, the SEC let securities firms raise their leverage from 12:1 to 33:1. In other words, a mere 3 percent decline in asset values could wipe out a company. That is how securities companies became both too big and too fragile.

Because of the deregulation mania that gripped the United States from 1981 onward, lending in the nonregulated sectors rose from 20 percent to 75 percent in the next quarter century.[65] During that period while the national GDP doubled, credit increased fourfold. The contribution of the financial sector to the GDP rose from 5 percent to 8 percent partly because of the comparative decline in the contribution made by the manufacturing industry being transferred overseas, chiefly to China—a trend that accelerated after China's admission to the World Trade Organization in 2001.

In any case, the financial sector is the bodyguard of the real economy. Damage to it leads directly to debilitation of the output in goods and services. It was the stock market crash in October 1929 that caused the Great Depression of the 1930s. Conversely, when the fiscal industry is thriving, its euphoria permeates society at large.

While the credit spigot was gushing with cash and the "Spend! Spend!" party was in full swing, a spoiler materialized in the person of Nouriel Roubini. In his speech on September 7, 2006, he outlined his study of the economic crises in Mexico (1994), Thailand-Indonesia-Malaysia-South Korea (1997–1998), Russia and Brazil (1998), and Argentina (2000). He noticed common weaknesses: huge current account deficits, covering the shortfalls by borrowing from abroad, thus acquiring a large exposure; poor banking systems marred by excessive borrowing and reckless lending; and weak corporate governance. Applying these criteria—objectively—he predicted the next country to join the list: the United States.[66] His 2006 estimate of the cost of the housing crisis at $1 trillion to $1.3 trillion would later be backed by the venerated IMF. With such outstanding and accurate forecasts to his credit, the epithet of "Oracle," conferred on Greenspan by his admirers, ought to be transferred to Roubini.

What actually followed Roubini's prediction was much worse. For starters, the United States was not just another country; it was the foremost economy in the world, and the dollar was the international reserve currency. Second, the sub-prime mortgage crisis converged with the collapse of the inflated credit created by synthetic devices such as the CDOs, for which no buyers could be found. Third, the bursting of the housing bubble came along with the drying up of liquidity in the banking sector. As a result, the global capital traffic got disrupted, leading to a series of currency crises. With the fall of most currencies outside the United States because of the international investors' switch from them to the dollar, the safest currency, American institutions repatriated their dollars, thus strengthening the U.S. currency but making American exports expensive.

FINANCIAL TSUNAMI OF THE CENTURY

The first signs of trouble appeared in early 2007. The bearish real estate market and the rising delinquencies by sub-prime borrowers affected construction companies and mortgage lenders. In April, New Century Financial filed for Chapter 11 bankruptcy protection after it was forced by its backers to repurchase billions of dollars worth of bad loans. Two months later, the venerable Bear Stearns, the fifth largest U.S. investment bank, liquidated its assets in one of its hedge funds, which had made large bets on the sub-prime market, at the cost of $1.6 billion. Then its second hedge fund failed. Finally, on July 31, 2008, these two funds filed for Chapter 15 bankruptcy.

Fearing a terrifying storm ahead, Moody's started lowering the ratings of large swaths of debt. That unnerved the capital market. The downgraded fiscal entities attempted to meet their debts and raise their capital by selling assets. That depressed asset prices, reducing the troubled companies' assets even further.

The warning by Ben Bernanke, chairman of the Federal Reserve since 2006, that the crisis in the U.S. sub-prime lending market could cost up to $100 billion would turn out to be a gross underestimate—a measure of the blinkered view of top financial officials. Later, the IMF would put the aggregate losses by the banks, including failed mortgage loans, devalued mortgage-backed securities, and bad debts, at $1.4 trillion.

A top Bear Stearns executive's statement on August 3, 2007, that credit markets were in the worst turmoil he had witnessed in twenty-two years marked the second phase of the deepening crisis.

The contagion spread to Europe. On August 9, French bank BNP Paribas suspended three investment funds worth € 2 billion (£1.4 billion). It explained that the turmoil in the U.S. sub-prime mortgage sector had made it impossible for it to evaluate the assets in the funds because the market for these CDOs had vanished.

These events highlighted the weakness of the U.S.-led Western global financial system and regulatory framework. Widespread criticism of the high ratings given to bundles of debt that included sub-prime mortgages by the Wall Street–based ratings agencies ensued. And rightly so.

They were not the only ones infected by the burgeoning greed. The mania to make more and higher profits than before spread from Wall Street to the City of London, second in size in the global fiscal markets. At both financial hubs, investment bankers earned high salaries and bonuses, around 60 percent of their salaries, by playing with other parties' borrowed capital. To stuff their pockets with still more cash, they took higher and higher risks.

Year 2008 started with Countrywide Financial being sold to Bank of America for a mere $4.1 billion. When Bear Stearns's share price nosedived from $36 to $2 within two working days, it was sold to J. P. Morgan Chase on March 17—but only after the intervention of the Bush administration. It offered a guarantee of $29 billion against Bear Stearns's mortgage liabilities, thus making the rest of the bank worth buying. The event shook the market, with the share price of Lehman Brothers Holdings, another vital pillar of Wall Street, falling by nearly half in a day.

The intervention by the Bush White House, steeped into the ideology of free markets, would have been unthinkable even a month earlier. But Bernanke and Treasury Secretary Henry Paulson, former head of Goldman Sachs, the number one investment bank on Wall Street, warned the president that the collapse of Bear Stearns could lead to a "chaotic unwinding" of the U.S. financial system.[67]

The American markets inferred that ideology had given way to pragmatism at the White House, and that it had decided to uphold the principle of "Too big to fail" rather than apply the free marketeers' mantra of "moral hazard": let companies face the consequences of their directors' actions.

To counter the downward slide, the Federal Reserve lowered interest rates, and Congress passed a $150 billion economic stimulus package. These measures proved inadequate. The plunge continued. In July, Los Angeles–based IndyMac Bank, the largest Savings and Loan bank in the area, became the latest high-profile casualty—the fourth largest bank failure in American history. By August 2008—marking a year of the sub-prime mortgage crisis—the total market value of the top ten U.S. investment banks had fallen by $221 billion.

This was just the proverbial tip of the iceberg. In early September, Fannie Mae and Freddie Mac, the leading Government Sponsored Enterprises (GSE), found themselves in trouble. They possessed or guaranteed nearly half of the $12 trillion worth of home mortgages in America. Because of the escalating de-fault rate and collapsing housing market, they had more than $5 trillion in mortgage-backed securities and debt, and not enough assets. They faced bank-ruptcy. Though the federal government was not legally bound to shore them up, it had no option but to throw them a lifeline. Their failure would have had a global impact. Foreigners held GSE bonds—treating them on a par with U.S. Treasury bonds—to the tune of $1.5 trillion, with China's investment of $340 billion in the lead, followed by Japan.[68]

On September 7, the Bush administration placed Fannie and Freddie into "conservatorship" of the Federal Housing Finance Agency, with the U.S. Trea-sury committed to investing up to $200 billion in preferred stock and ex-tending credit through 2009 to keep these GSEs solvent. In plain English, the Bush White House nationalized Fannie and Freddie, the most sweeping U.S. government intervention in private financial markets in decades. The Bush administration took this giant step to avoid international fiscal meltdown. Yet the dreaded cataclysm would be triggered by yet another record-breaking event—soon.

It happened on September 15. The 158-year-old Lehman Brothers filed for Chapter 11 bankruptcy protection, listing its liabilities at $768 billion (includ-ing $155 billion in unsecured bonds) and assets of $639 billion. Besides the sub-prime residential mortgages, Lehman also held a big chunk of toxic com-mercial real estate. Lehman Brothers and its several subsidiaries provided ser-vices in investment banking; equity and fixed-income sales, research, and trading; investment management; private equity; and private banking.

For reasons not disclosed at the time, the federal government failed to res-cue Lehman Brothers. (It was not until December 1 that Bernanke explained that the collateral provided by the company was insufficient.) That shocked the capital and stock markets. Their fear turned into panic as they realized that Washington was reverting to the principle of "moral hazard."

Lehman Brothers's filing of the biggest bankruptcy in U.S. annals sent tremors in the markets throughout the globe, turning Wall Street's trauma into a worldwide fiscal crisis. The Dow Jones Industrial Average plunged 504 points, or 4.4 percent, to 10,917, the sharpest points drop since the New York Stock Exchange reopened after 9/11. Confidence fell precipitately as asset prices nosedived. The remaining credit channels ran dry.

As a result of Lehman Brothers's chaotic bankruptcy, which followed the last-minute breakdown of its talks with two serious buyers, the holders of the commercial papers issued by Lehman lost money. A commercial paper is an IOU used by banks and large corporations to raise loans, often unsecured, for periods not exceeding nine months to meet urgent needs like payroll. It is sold at a discount from its face value, and the interest is lower than the ongoing banks' rates. On maturity it is almost invariably rolled over. Its chief buyers are money market funds, which, being super-safe, qualify as virtual cash investments. The total outstanding commercial paper at the end of 2007 in America amounted to a staggering $1.78 trillion.[69]

Lehman Brothers's $155 billion in unsecured bonds were held by many investors worldwide. Following its bankruptcy, the price of this commercial paper plunged by 85 percent. That affected money markets. Investors withdrew $400 billion from money market funds. One such fund, Putnam, which had loaded up on Lehman debt, found its assets falling below the dollars deposited by its investors. This led to a run on money market funds, halting the purchase of commercial paper. Deprived of this cash inflow, the issuers of commercial paper had no choice but to draw down their credit lines. That in turn put paid to interbank lending—a short-term arrangement that enables banks to manage liquidity and maintain their capital reserves at the mandatory level. As a result, the premiums over and above the safest rate of interest shot up to record levels. The circulation of credit, on which the economy of an industrialized nation depends, seized up.[70]

The next gigantic U.S. financial institution to be stricken severely by the Credit Default Swaps was American International Group (AIG), a New York–based insurance and financial services corporation. The globe's eighteenth largest company, it did business around the world. Its exposure to a lot of bad loans, and its unrealistic valuation of mortgage-backed securities, led to a 95 percent decline in its share value. On September 16, the Federal Reserve Bank lent AIG $85 billion in exchange for a nearly 80 percent stake in its equity—the biggest cash injection into a private company by the federal government so far.[71]

Two days earlier, the directors of Merrill Lynch—the investment bank whose logo of a "prancing bull," captured in shining bronze, greets visitors to Wall Street—had sold the company to the Bank of America after a year of huge losses linked to sub-prime mortgages and their derivatives.

By the end of that week in September, the panic in the capital markets had spread to the stock markets around the world, from Sao Paolo to Shanghai, creating a global financial meltdown. It radically recast Wall Street on September 21. The remaining two giant investment banks, Goldman Sachs and Morgan Stanley, converted their legal status from investment banks to deposit-taking bank holding companies. That allowed them access to aid from the Federal Reserve in return for a greatly increased level of government supervision. Thus ended the era of investment banking dominated by five Leviathans.

That did not mean depository banks were immune. On September 25 came the largest bank failure in American history. Following a run during which Washington Mutual's customers withdrew $16.7 billion in ten days, the bank went into receivership. This was a fresh reminder, if one was needed, that in the final analysis, depository banks depend on the trust of ordinary citizens, and that they will fail if they lose it.

When faced with these gigantic busts, Paulson handled the deepening crisis on a case-by-case basis. He asked for $700 billion of public funds to buy up private banks' toxic assets. That is, he failed to see the woods for the trees. It would be left to British Prime Minister Gordon Brown, who had been finance minister for a decade, to diagnose the malady correctly—dwindling faith in the banks—and administer the right medicine forthwith.

On September 29, when the House of Representatives turned down the bill centered around Paulson's plan to buy bad mortgage debt from banks so they could resume lending to each other again, the Dow Jones Industrial Average crashed. It lost a record 777.68 points, far above the 684.81 point loss on the first trading day after 9/11.

Gloom spread across the Atlantic. Bank shares nosedived. Credit froze.

EUROPE AND ELSEWHERE

Irrespective of their political hue, European governments acted swiftly to contain the contagion originating in New York. Faced with the collapse in the share price of Fortis Bank, the biggest private employer in Belgium, the governments of Belgium, Luxembourg, and the Netherlands nationalized it on September 28. The next day, Bradford and Bingley Bank became state property in Britain at £41.3 billion. The German government bailed out the commercial property loan giant Hypo Real Estate on October 5 at the cost of €50 billion. It went on to guarantee the savers' deposits to the full, which led others to follow suit. None of these measures slowed the freefalls in the continent's financial sectors. In London, HBOS and Lloyds Bank suffered a 40 percent loss in share values on October 7. A systemic collapse appeared imminent.

Early the next day Brown's government unveiled a plan to force the eight biggest British banks to raise their capitalization levels with its assistance, and offered £200 billion as short-term loans to banks and a further £250 billion of loan guarantees to support interbank lending to revive liquidity in money markets.

At a special European summit on Sunday, October 12, major European countries decided to emulate Brown's example and inject hundreds of billions of euros into banks while guaranteeing their debts. Simultaneously, the central banks of America, Britain, the European Union, Sweden, Switzerland, and Canada cut interest rates by 0.5 percent—and China by 0.27 percent. The following day, Britain announced the infusion of £37 billion ($64 billion) into Royal Bank of Scotland Group (RBS), Lloyds, and HBOS, to avert a banking meltdown. Thus the state ended up owning 60 percent of RBS and 40 percent of HBOS.[72]

Among those who applauded Brown for his speed was Paul Krugman, the Nobel prize–winning economist and a *New York Times* columnist. In reality, Brown acted in the nick of time. Both RBS and HBOS were only "hours away from being unable to open for business [on Monday, October 13]," according to a revelation made later by Sir John Gieve, deputy governor of the Bank of England.[73]

In Washington, Paulson got the message. He said that he would use the bailout money to buy equity stakes in banks rather than their toxic waste securities. Once Congress had passed the $700 billion bailout—titled Troubled Asset Relief Program (TARP)—on October 7, the Treasury pumped $250 billion into the top nine banks on October 14 and bought minority shares. That, in theory, entitled the U.S. government to have an input into the banks' decision making at the top.

This was hardly surprising. Paulson, a former head of the largest American investment bank, was cast in the same mold as Greenspan—except that a thundering admission from the renowned "Oracle" was in the offing.

"THE MAESTRO" EATS HUMBLE PIE

"I made a mistake in presuming that the self-interests of organizations, specifically banks and others, were such that they were best capable of protecting their own shareholders and their equity in the firms," said Greenspan in his testimony to the Committee on Oversight and Government Reform of the 110th Congress on October 23, 2008. "I discovered a flaw in the model that I perceived is the critical functioning structure that defines how the world works."

Chairman Henry Waxman said, "In other words, you found that your view of the world, your ideology, was not right, it was not working." Greenspan replied, "Absolutely, precisely." That is, Greenspan admitted that he was wrong to trust free markets to regulate the financial system without stronger government oversight.[74]

In his prepared statement, Greenspan described the financial crisis as a "once-in-a-century credit tsunami." He said that the bankers' disregard for shareholders' equity had left him "in a state of shocked disbelief." Rightly so. Barely a week earlier, it was revealed that Wall Street financial employees would receive bonuses of $70 billion![75]

This was a "once in a lifetime" turnaround by the high priest of free markets, idolized by many as "Maestro."[76] In a speech at Georgetown University a year earlier, Greenspan had argued that the problem was not that the derivative contracts failed, but that the people using them got greedy. It was the lack of integrity among the derivative traders that had created the crisis: Those selling derivatives were not as reliable "as the pharmacist who fills the prescriptions ordered by your physician."

The roots of Greenspan's faith in the rationality of bankers and derivative traders could be traced to the worldview of his icon, Ayn Rand (aka, Alisa

Rosenbaum, died 1982), as laid out in her philosophical novel *Atlas Shrugged* (1957). A proponent of freewheeling capitalism, and an opponent of trade unions and egalitarianism, she placed her faith in "rational self-interest," which is fleshed out in her novel. So too is her Mammon-loving belief: "Until and unless you discover that money is the root of all good, you ask for your own destruction."[77]

The truth was that it was not the first time in living memory that U.S. bankers had displayed gross irresponsibility and greed. The Savings and Loan crisis of the late 1980s, when Greenspan was head of the Federal Reserve, was caused by the Savings and Loan banks offering high interest rates to depositors to attract funds and then gambling with them. The subsequent crisis involved the failure of 747 S&L banks. Of the total cost of $160 billion to resolve it, all but $35 billion was paid by the federal government. As a result of this drainage of money, the average annual new house construction during 1986–1991 almost halved to 1 million, the lowest figure since World War II.[78]

Another important facet of the S&L saga was that the U.S. government took over the ailing banks, fired the boards of directors and top managers, got rid of bad assets, turned them into healthy companies, and sold them to private investors. Contrary to the prevalent belief in America that government is a poor manager of companies, the federal authorities hired honest, efficient bankers who performed superbly. In essence, the U.S. government nationalized banks and transformed them into profit-making firms. But at no point did the dreaded N-word appear anywhere. The nationalized banks were called "bridge banks."[79] It was ironic for a nation and its leaders priding themselves on their pragmatism to be too ideological to accept that nationalization is one of several tools to be deployed to defuse a severe crisis. That remains the case even now.

Instead of plodding through the turgid prose of the 1,000-plus-page *Atlas Shrugged*, Greenspan should have imbibed the lucid text of the 210-page *The Great Crash 1929* (published in 1955) by John Kenneth Galbraith, an economist of towering intellect. His study of the bubbles of freebooting capitalism from the tulip bulb craze in the Netherlands in the 1630s to the stock market crash of 1929 in America showed that a capitalist system functioning on the free-market paradigm was cyclical and unstable and needed to be regulated by the state. Galbraith explained how the arrival of new technology—railroads, radio broadcasting, and so forth—engendered an overly optimistic glow, raised expectations of higher returns on capital, and led to excessive exposure to risk, fraudulent dealings, and ultimate bust. The enlarged business activity encouraged speculation and enterprise in the fiscal sector. Out of this emerged innovative ways of money supply and freshly designed financial instruments to enable more and more companies to garner a piece of the booming pie.

In the current case, the new dawn in technology was ushered in by the Internet and its allies—search engines and e-mail. With one stroke, they made massive information available in a jiffy, and abolished distance. They boosted productivity in the United States and elsewhere. In the fiscal arena it was the introduction and massive adoption of the newfangled financial instruments, principally the CDO and the CDS, capped by a formula devised in 2001 to evaluate CDOs quickly.

Galbraith died in 2006. Had he been alive in August 2008, he would have been bemused to note Greenspan claiming that "the past decade has seen mounting global forces [the international version of Adam Smith's invisible hand] quietly displacing government control of economic affairs."[80] Here was Greenspan's economic parallel to Francis Fukuyama's "end of history." Under the infallible guidance of the Maestro, the United States experienced almost unbroken growth for nearly a decade. Therefore, the boom and bust cycles, built into in the DNA of modern capitalism, are dead. Q.E.D.

The latest fiscal meltdown, originating in Wall Street, led to attacks on American-style capitalism not just by the usual suspects but by Washington's European allies.

No Lament for the Free Market's Demise

Prominent among the European leaders who criticized America's unbridled capitalism was conservative French President Nicolas Sarkozy, the rotating president of the European Union (July–December 2008). A fresh convert to "regulated capitalism," Sarkozy railed against the "dictatorship of the market." Describing the laissez-faire ideology of the United States practiced during the sub-prime crisis as "simplistic and dangerous," he said, "A certain idea of globalization is drawing to a close with the end of financial capitalism that imposed its logic on the whole economy. The idea that markets are always right was a crazy idea."[81] He was happy to be seen reading the French translation of *Das Kapital* by Karl Marx.

The book, first published in 1867, became a best seller in Germany. Its finance minister, Peter Steinbruck, predicted confidently that as a result of the fiscal meltdown, the United States would lose its role as a "financial superpower." Not to be left behind, his Italian counterpart, Giulio Tremonti, another conservative, pointed out that earlier in the year he had published a book highlighting the downside of globalization.

The leaders of those Asian countries that, a decade earlier, had to follow the IMF's diktat of curtailing public spending and letting the banks plagued by bad loans fail to receive its aid were now full of schadenfreude. They alluded to the derogatory terms used by IMF officials in private—"the lazy Latinos," "the crony capitalism of Asians"—and noted with ill-disguised scorn how the same IMF functionaries had kept their lips sealed as the United States and other Western countries did what the IMF had forbidden Asians to do. Now, to the IMF's deep embarrassment, the balance sheet of the Federal Reserve had rocketed from $800 billion to $1.8 trillion within a few months because of Washington's massive intervention in the private financial sector.

Stung by these barbs from Asian leaders, Sarkozy and Brown aired the idea of improved surveillance of complex financial markets to prevent excesses in the future, with a global regulator compelling banks and hedge funds to shed their traditional opacity, and the establishment of an international organization to oversee the credit rating agencies. Bush disagreed. "We must recognize that government intervention is not a cure-all," he said. "History has shown that the greater threat to economic prosperity is not too little government involvement in the market—but too much."[82] He apparently missed the point that the cataclysmic fiscal crisis was caused by lack of supervision over the burgeoning shadow banking. Worse, even where government regulation existed, it was applied lightly, or not at all.

On his appointment as chairman of the SEC in 2001, Harvey Pitt promised a "kinder, gentler" agency. But facing a backlash from the scam related to the 2002 collapse of Enron Corporation, Bush decided to replace him with William Donaldson in 2003. When he started acting as the investors' advocate, as is the SEC's brief, he was denounced for being "too aggressive" by Wall Street. So out he went in 2005. In came Christopher Cox, who resumed the "softly, softly" approach, preferring civil fines and deferred prosecution agreements instead of criminal proceedings for fraud. The cases of prosecution for stock fraud plummeted from 437 in 2001 to 133 in the first eleven months of 2008. Between 2000 and 2007, FBI prosecutions fell from 69 to 9.[83]

Three days after Cox had assured the markets that Bear Stearns was solvent, the investment bank went bust. Following the December 2008 bankruptcy of Bernard L. Madoff Investment Securities LLC, involving a loss of $65 billion, the biggest fraud in history, Cox was obliged to admit the agency's "multiple failures" over the past ten years to investigate credible allegations of wrongdoing by Madoff.

Such dereliction of duty was a contrast to the speed with which Sarkozy acted to rally worldwide cooperation to tackle the unprecedented fiscal tsunami. The leaders of twenty economically important countries—the G20—assembled in Washington on November 15. Besides the G8, the other participant countries and multinational organizations were Argentina, Australia, Brazil, China, India, Indonesia, Mexico, Saudi Arabia, South Africa, South Korea, Turkey, and the European Union. They appointed working groups to tackle forty-seven regulatory and economic issues and report to the next G20 summit in London in April 2009.

According to Sarkozy, "Europe for the first time expressed its serious determination. Never ever had the Americans been willing to negotiate the kinds of radical regulatory changes that were on the table in Washington." He went on to proclaim the end of the era of American hegemony in world finance. "America is the Number 1 power in the world," he declared. "Is it the only power? No, it isn't. We are in a new world."[84]

Unsurprisingly, Bush had a different take on the summit. The leaders had reaffirmed the importance of free markets, free trade, and the primacy of national regulation, he declared. It was virtually impossible for him to escape from his world of make-believe. When asked to comment on the financial meltdown toward the end of his tenure, when hundreds of thousands of Americans were losing jobs and homes, Bush said, "I quipped in Texas that Wall Street got drunk, and we got a hangover."[85] Thus he provided the world with an updated example of Nero fiddling while Rome burned.

By then, however, it was the words of Barack Obama, the winner of the presidential race on November 4, that counted.

EXIT THE MOST UNPOPULAR U.S. PRESIDENT

A CBS News poll in December showed Bush's approval rating sinking to 20 percent, a record low.[86] The inexorable slide in his popularity started in August 2005 with his catastrophic response to Hurricane Katrina. While the furious hurricane drowned New Orleans, he continued his vacation at his Crawford ranch unperturbed. That was the moment when the scales fell off the eyes of most Americans. They increasingly saw a raft of his failures—from the catastrophic invasion of Iraq to the default on global warming to ballooning budget and trade deficits. Since they could not eject him from the White House, they reduced the Republican Party to a minority in both houses of Congress in 2006.

For once Bush registered reality. He replaced Rumsfeld with Robert Gates, a former CIA director, known for his pragmatic moderation. A revision of the war strategy in Iraq followed. Out of that emerged the much hyped "surge," the title given to the addition of 30,000 combat troops. The subsequent decline in the violence from the summer of 2007 occurred as a result of several factors. The prime reason was the Pentagon's establishment of the generously funded Awakening Councils and their recruitment of 94,000 Sunni militants—each receiving a monthly salary of $300—who had become disillusioned by the gratuitous violence of Al Qaida in Mesopotamia. Its victims were not only Shiites but also those fellow Sunnis who did not unquestioningly obey its diktats.

At the strategic level, mirroring Bush's invasion of Iraq while cutting taxes and failing to devise a coherent postwar plan, Al Qaida in Mesopotamia tried to defy logic and precedence. The first and foremost condition for an insurgency to triumph is to have the sympathy of the population at large. This is what Communist insurgents in Vietnam had when battling the French and American armies during the third quarter of the last century. It was also the case with the nationalist militants in Algeria fighting imperialist France in the 1950s. But blinded by their theological orthodoxy, Al Qaida in Mesopotamia waged a bloody campaign against Shiites, who formed 60 percent of the Iraqi population, decrying them as "snakeheads," attacking their religious gatherings and processions, and bombing their holy shrines.[87] Little wonder that Al Qaida in Mesopotamia met the same fate as the Communist guerrillas in the British colony of Malaya who mounted their insurgency in 1948. They were almost invariably ethnic Chinese, a minority. Therefore their violent campaign became the exception to the five major insurgencies launched after World War II and resulted in failure in 1960. So in Iraq, sooner or later, with or without the "surge," Al Qaida in Mesopotamia, caught in the cul-de-sac of its narrow, bigoted view of Islam, was bound to fail, letting its bigger, more lethal, alien enemy, the United States, claim success.

In global terms, the Internet provided the audience an unprecedented chance to express their opinion of Bush. At his last press conference in Baghdad on December 14, 2008, he became the target of a dramatic gesture by Muntazar al Zaidi, an Iraqi journalist. "This is farewell kiss, you dog," Zaidi shouted as he aimed his shoe at Bush standing next to Iraqi Prime Minister Nouri al Maliki. "This is from the widows, the orphans and those who were killed in Iraq," he cried as he hurled his second shoe. Bush dodged both times. Iraqi security guards and U.S. Secret Service agents dragged Zaidi away. The event, broadcast on television, became an instant international story. In the online game "Sock & Awe," which let players throw brown loafers at Bush, 46 million cyber shoes struck the presidential head in the first three days.[88]

The only positive thing that could be said about Bush was that his disastrous policies paved the way for the electoral victory of Democratic candidate Barack Obama, the African-American senator from Illinois. Obama won 52.9 percent of the popular vote of 131 million, and 365 electoral college ballots, and his Republican rival, Senator John McCain, 45.7 percent of the ballots, and 173 electoral college votes. McCain's defeat marked the end of the Reaganite phase of capitalism, which stressed deregulation of markets, in the United States.

What helped Obama make his mark during the Democratic primaries was his unqualified opposition to the Iraq War combined with his robust criticism of Bush for diverting resources from Afghanistan prematurely to invade Iraq. But by the time the race for the White House got in stride after Labor Day in 2008, the downturn in the economy became the number one concern of voters, highlighted not only by news headlines but also by a growing loss of jobs and escalating price of gasoline, which exceeded $4 a gallon. His proposal for increasing taxes on the affluent was well received by the vast majority of Americans, who noted that under Bush's watch the average chief executive officer of a corporation earned 350 times the salary of the average worker.

The *New York Times*/CBS News poll conducted a week before election day showed that 89 percent viewed the U.S. economy negatively. Moreover, six out of seven Americans thought that the United States was "pretty seriously on the wrong track." And rightly so.[89] Their country was suffering from multiple deficits: fiscal, trade, energy, and geopolitical. In the geopolitical arena, the three-member "Axis of Evil"—Iraq, North Korea, and Iran—stood out.

Once North Korea found itself named as a member of the Axis of Evil in January 2002, it became belligerent. After withdrawing from the nuclear Non-Proliferation Treaty (NPT), it accelerated its nuclear weapons program and tested an atom bomb in October 2006. That forced Bush to reverse his hard-line stance toward Pyongyang. His envoy returned to the six-party talks—China, Japan, North Korea, Russia, South Korea, and the United States—on Pyongyang's nuclear program. In the end, as a result of hard bargaining, in return for North Korea dismantling its nuclear arms program, Bush agreed to remove it from the terrorist list and provide it with much needed fuel oil for its electricity generating plants.

Washington's relentless threats against Iran for its ongoing nuclear program had not worked. If anything, they encouraged Tehran to accelerate its program. The limp economic sanctions imposed on Iran through the UN Security Council had only a marginal impact on the regime, which saw its oil income soar with escalating prices until mid-2008.

Elsewhere in relation to the Middle East, the launching of the Middle East conference in Annapolis, Maryland, in November 2007, with the aim of realizing the creation of a viable, independent Palestine by the end of 2008, proved sterile. Nothing illustrated the steep fall of America's esteem in the region better than the stance of President Hosni Mubarak of Egypt, a close ally of Washington and the second largest beneficiary of U.S. foreign aid. Defying the State Department's policy of isolating Hamas, the radical Palestinian organization, Egypt acted as an intermediary between it and its rival, Fatah, to reconcile them. Furthermore, it helped Hamas, controlling the Gaza Strip since June 2007, to withstand the economic siege imposed on it by Israel, which had the backing of Washington. It turned a blind eye to the opening of up to six hundred tunnels between the border town of Rafah and Egypt along its twelve-kilometer border with the Gaza Strip. The emboldened Hamas government brought the smuggling business of the tunnels into the open by charging their operators $3,000 a year and taking part of the smuggled fuel.

As such, the conclusion of "Global Trends 2025: A World Transformed," the report by the U.S. National Intelligence Council released in November 2008, that by 2025 America would no longer be able to "call the shots" alone seemed superfluous. This was already the case.

A glaring example of Washington's impotence came three months earlier—in the Caucasian republic of Georgia. Late on August 7, Georgia mounted a ground and air-based attack against Tskhinvali, the capital of the breakaway region of South Ossetia, killing up to four hundred people. The Kremlin reacted by dispatching troops into South Ossetia and mounting bombing raids into Georgia. The next day the Abkhazian and Russian soldiers opened a second front by attacking the Kodori Gorge, held by Georgia, and invaded western Georgia. Russia's navy blocked the Georgian coast. Following five days' intense combat, the Russians and their local allies expelled the Georgian forces from South Ossetia. The Russian troops occupied the Georgia towns of Poti and Gori.

"Bullying and intimidation are not acceptable ways to conduct foreign policy in the 21st century," said Bush.[90] The irony of that statement was lost on him. In any case, his administration did not go beyond verbal condemnation of Russia's overwhelming military response to Georgia's attempt to regain control of the breakaway provinces of South Ossetia and Abkhazia.

When asked whether the Kremlin had overreacted in Georgia, a republic of a mere 4 million, Russian Prime Minister Vladimir Putin replied, "What did you expect us to do? Respond with a catapult? We punched the aggressor in the face, as all the military text books prescribe."[91] This was vintage Putin, given to using salty language. Nonetheless, his underlying confidence stemmed from the soaring income from Russian oil and gas.

Chapter 3

Return of the Russian Bear

B y the time Vladimir Putin stepped down as president after serving two terms in 2008, Russia had come a long way from its nightmares of the 1990s. It had reestablished itself as a great power, possessing nearly half of the deployed global arsenal of 11,400 nuclear weapons, and the third largest foreign currency and gold reserves in the world.

Equally important, Russia emerged as the indispensable source of energy for the rest of Europe. Dependence on Russia's oil varied from 14 percent of its consumption for France to 81 percent for Hungary. Reliance on Russian natural gas ranged from a quarter of its demand for Italy to 100 percent for Finland. Overall, Russia supplied more than two-fifths of the gas imports of the twenty-seven-nation European Union. That proportion will rise to a half by 2030 with the exhaustion of the North Sea gas deposits.

The growing economic and diplomatic confidence of Russia, stemming from Putin's firm style of governance and the escalating prices of hydrocarbons, brought it into conflict with the intransigent administration of U.S. President George W. Bush, who had become addicted to his unilateralist ways after 9/11.

Though Putin was widely credited with strengthening the spine of Mother Russia, there were earlier signs of the Kremlin reestablishing its identity by loosening its apron strings with the White House, particularly in external affairs. The politician who initiated this shift was Yevgeny Primakov. He served as foreign minister from January 1996 until his promotion to prime minister in September 1998.

During this period the Clinton administration had kept up its strategy of using the UN Security Council to advance its policy on Iraq. Its ultimate aim was the overthrow of President Saddam Hussein's regime, irrespective of the extent of its cooperation with UN inspectors charged with locating and destroying Iraq's facilities for producing weapons of mass destruction. In early 1998 at the Security Council, Primakov rallied China and France against Washington and forced it to withdraw its draft resolution authorizing military action against Iraq. By so doing, he gave a preview of a multipolar world, where a superpower is successfully stymied by an alliance of great powers.

As prime minister, Primakov swiftly rectified the abuses of freewheeling capitalism. Yeltsin and his backers among the billionaire oligarchs saw his rising popularity and aspirations for the presidency as a threat to their interests. So Primakov got the sack—a step that was quietly applauded by the Clinton administration.

GREAT TRANSITION = GREAT DEPRESSION

What to Americans was Russia's "Great Transition" to capitalist democracy was for most Russians the Great Depression, more severe than its American version. They viewed their economic collapse as an import from America, stamped "Made in U.S.A."

Contrary to the popular perception in the West, it was Mikhail Gorbachev—not Boris Yeltsin—who started reforming the Soviet-style command economy. Within two years of assuming the supreme office in March 1985, he permitted state enterprises to trade their surplus output freely. Then, in certain cases, he allowed state ownership to be transferred to the employees and management of an enterprise and let it function in the freshly created cooperative sector outside the government-directed Five Year Plan. Several thousand enterprises joined the cooperative sector. With the ending of central trading monopolies in 1988, the constituent republics established their own trade organizations. This opened up possibilities for enterprising Russians to enter the privately run import-export market. Gorbachev also opened the door slightly to foreign investment. He could not advance economic reform further chiefly because the state planning apparatus lacked the tools to collect proper information to reallocate resources to meet popular needs.

Under his policy of glasnost (transparency) and perestroika (restructuring), censorship became lax and then ceased. The May 1989 elections to the Congress of People's Deputies were fairly free and produced an animated legislature where lively debate thrived. Next, the Communist Party of the Soviet Union (CPSU) disavowed its "leading role," meaning monopoly of power. This, and the abolition of censorship, produced an avalanche of complaints and grievances by a multiethnic nation that had been muzzled for nearly three generations. It led to political turmoil that neither Gorbachev nor the CPSU was equipped to tackle adroitly.

As described earlier (in Chapter 1), there was no tradition of gradual change in Russia. Yeltsin confirmed this—with a bang. Lacking any understanding of economics or the functioning of the world beyond the former Soviet Union, and surrounded by charlatans and lackeys, he signed a series of decrees that fueled hyperinflation. The 2,520 percent inflation in 1992 wiped out Russians' savings. Withholding of wages and pensions became commonplace in 1993–1994. The GDP shrank every year from 1992 to 1996, the cumulative total being almost half. Real earnings fell by more than half.[1] Russians' anguished despair was aptly captured in the often-repeated one-liner: "Everything they [Communists] told us about communism was false—but everything they told us about capitalism is true."[2]

Yeltsin's plan to sponsor a two-party system by getting Viktor Chernomyrdin to assemble all pro-Yeltsin groups under the umbrella of his party, Our Home Is Russia, as a center-right bloc, with Duma speaker Ivan Rybkin leading a "loyal" center-left coalition, failed to materialize.

As victims of Yeltsin's catastrophic economic management, voters strongly disapproved of his policies in the December 1995 parliamentary poll, the first held under the 1993 constitution. Russia's Democratic Choice, the renamed party of Yegor Gaidar, an ardent proponent of economic shock therapy, failed to cross the 5 percent threshold. By contrast, gaining nearly a quarter of the vote, the re-formed Communist Party of Russian Federation (CPRF) was well ahead of others. Allied with the Agrarian Party, representing the interests of collective farms, it held 177 seats. The ultranationalist Liberal Democratic Party of Vladimir Zhirinovsky controlled 51 seats. However, the slim majority that the anti-Yeltsin opposition mustered fell short of the two-thirds total needed to overturn the president's veto or amend the constitution.

"People's Capitalism" Delivers
Mafia Capitalism

Outside electoral politics, a far-reaching, privatization-related development had taken place. The State Property Management Committee, charged with denationalization, opted for a voucher scheme, meant to usher in "people's capitalism," and implemented it during 1992–1994. By dividing Russia's fixed and floating assets by its population in September 1992, the Committee came up with a voucher with the face value of 10,000 rubles. Because of hyperinflation, however, a voucher soon fetched less than 4,000 rubles, falling to 1,500 rubles in the black market—just enough to buy a pair of shoes. So instead of using vouchers to purchase shares in enterprises listed for privatization, most voucher holders sold them to unscrupulous entrepreneurs—well versed in sharp practices learned earlier in underhand currency dealings that started in the last days of Gorbachev's rule—for a bottle of cheap vodka, or to the managers of mutual funds, often members of the former Soviet political or industrial elite. Thus millions of vouchers ended up with a few hundred crooked yet influential Russians. They gained control of most of the 7,000 major businesses and a further 10,000 medium and large enterprises that were denationalized by the end of 1994.[3]

Next came the second round of privatization leading to further concentration of wealth. Faced with a deep budget deficit in 1995, the Kremlin adopted banker Vladimir Potanin's plan to raise loans from private banks by "leasing" them shares in large state-owned companies in hydrocarbons, telecom, metals, and the media as collateral. It implemented the scheme in the autumn of 1995 through auctions. By limiting the bidding to the favored insiders, the government got a raw deal, with the lenders "leasing" valuable equity at bargain-basement prices. Under the agreed terms, if the Kremlin failed to repay the loans by September 1996, the "lease" would expire, and the ownership of the shares would pass automatically to the lender. As expected, the government failed to meet the deadline. And the lenders, flush with untold wealth, appeared on the Russian scene as "oligarchs."

They acquired assets in hydrocarbons, manufacturing, public buildings, transport, banking, telecom, military equipment, and the media. Prominent among the oligarchs were Boris Berezovsky, with major stakes in leading banks and TV channels and oil; Mikhail Khodorkovsky, an oil and gas tycoon;

Vladimir Gusinsky, owner of a national television channel, NTV; Mikhail Fridman, a billionaire banker and oilman; Alexander Smolensky, the founder of one of the largest private banks; and Roman Abramovich, with assets in hydrocarbons.[4] They became so influential that they routinely evaded taxes through subterfuge with impunity, a strategy that would later redound against them. For the present, though, they were hell-bent to ensure that Yeltsin remained president of Russia.

Yeltsin's prospect of reelection looked uncertain. Despite strong backing from Washington and local oligarchs for his candidacy, he left little to chance. He appointed electoral officials who were partisan. Overruling his generals, he announced the end of the military draft by 2000, a popular move. He increased pensions by 50 percent.

His most serious rival was Gennadi Zyuganov, chairman of the CPRF, actively supported by former Vice President Alexander Rutskoi. His manifesto included strengthening Parliament at the expense of the president and a critical review of privatization. Pointedly, he called for a medical committee to assess the health of the candidates, thus highlighting Yeltsin's chronic heart problems.

In the first round on June 16, Yeltsin secured 35.3 percent of the vote, and Zyuganov 32.0 percent, each of them well ahead of the rest. A week before the final round on July 3, Yeltsin suffered his fourth heart attack. He was rushed to a sanitarium while his aides attributed his absence from the public eye to a "head cold." When, two days later, he struggled to hold a prearranged meeting with retired general Alexander Lebed to discuss Chechnya, the attending medical staff were removed from the news footage. On the polling day, aided by his wife, he staggered a few yards to the ballot box brought to the sanitarium.

He garnered 53.8 percent of the vote and forty-six regions, and Zyuganov 40.3 percent of the ballots and forty-three regions.

Yeltsin's reelection reinforced the power of the oligarchs who had contributed their vast resources to ensure his success. They became more brazen in avoiding taxes. In this enterprise they were assisted by the general corruption that prevailed in the government bureaucracy and judicial system.

Once Yeltsin had been corralled into accepting NATO's eastward expansion in May 1997, Clinton awarded him with a seat at the G7 table nine months later. The timing proved inauspicious.

THE FIRST GLIMMER OF A MULTIPOLAR WORLD

By February 1998, Clinton's micromanagement of UN inspections of Iraq's WMD program to further his domestic agenda had become so blatant that Russian Foreign Minister Primakov could no longer stomach it. He persuaded Yeltsin to cease bending his knee to Clinton. The president was well aware of Primakov's expertise on the Middle East. He started his career as an Arabic-speaking correspondent of the Soviet news agency, TASS, in the region and came to know most Arab leaders, including Saddam Hussein, personally. And after the Soviet breakup, he served as director of Russia's Foreign Intelligence Service for four years.

The leaders of China and France too found Washington's behavior unacceptable. At the UN Security Council, Primakov particularly welcomed Beijing's willingness to work closely with him to counter Clinton's belligerence toward Saddam Hussein's regime, which had been the target of five CIA-directed coup attempts, the last one in June 1996.

In early 1998, tensions at the UN Security Council reached a climax. The U.S. ambassador to the UN, Bill Richardson, said that if the Council decided to ease or lift sanctions against Iraq before it had implemented "all relevant" Council resolutions, the United States would veto the resolution. Russia, along with China and France, contested this unilateral interpretation of the Council resolutions. The Kremlin issued a counterthreat: It would veto the U.S. resolution, backed by Britain, authorizing use of force against Iraq if it failed to offer "full and unconditional access" to UN inspectors. This was so uncharacteristic of the timorous Russia that the Clinton administration had got accustomed to that the United States backed off. It withdrew its draft resolution.[5]

Russia's remarkable checkmating of America at the Security Council was a milestone in international diplomacy. Unsurprisingly, it was glossed over in the American and British media. It marked the end of Washington's unchallenged supremacy at the UN for almost a decade. It was the first, and welcome, glimmer of the emergence of a multipolar world.

The success of Kofi Annan, the UN secretary general, in meeting Saddam Hussein in Baghdad and getting him to resolve the standoff peacefully, in late February 1998, signified a victory of diplomacy over saber-rattling. Its enthusiastic welcome by Russia along with China and France contrasted sharply with the ill-grace with which America and Britain accepted it reluctantly.

The Kremlin's remarkable foreign policy coup left a mark on the White House. It concluded, rightly, that when it came to safeguarding its vital interests, Russia would not shy away from wielding its veto at the UN Security Council—just as the United States had done scores of times. That realization would lead the Clinton administration to circumvent the Security Council when dealing with Serbia a year later.

For the present, Russia's moment of diplomatic glory had no impact on its lackluster economic performance.

POLITICAL FALLOUT OF THE RUBLE MELTDOWN

Despite substantial input by American and European investors into its economy, Russia continued to limp along. Its tax-collecting system was rickety, its commercial law inchoate, and its judicial system corrupt. The nonpayment of taxes by the hydrocarbon and other sectors increased the federal budget deficit, with public revenue covering only half the expenditure. The government covered the shortfall by issuing junk bonds with high yields, ranging from 18 percent to 65 percent, and short-term maturity. Local banks and foreign investors lapped them up.

However, when the second Yeltsin administration allowed nonresident portfolio investors to convert rubles into hard currencies, they started moving out of rubles, draining the foreign exchange reserves of Bank Rossii, the central bank of Russia. That set in motion a vicious cycle. The fall in oil prices made matters worse. On January 1, 1998, the central bank introduced the new ruble, equaling 1,000 old rubles, hoping it would steady the nerves of the currency market. It did not.

On August 17, 1998, Bank Rossii ceased supporting the ruble in foreign exchange markets. Its default on contracts worth $40 billion favored Russians at the foreigners' expense. But it failed to stop hundreds of banks going bust, as depositors rushed to withdraw their savings.

A political storm followed. On August 21, the Duma passed a nonbinding resolution (248 to 32 votes) calling on Yeltsin to resign. The next day Yeltsin sacked his young reformist prime minister, Sergei Kiriyenko. But the Duma refused to endorse his nominee, Viktor Chernomyrdin, as his successor.

The tug of war between the executive and legislative branches pushed the ruble further down. On August 26, Bank Rossii stopped ruble-dollar trading altogether. Setting diplomatic protocol aside, Clinton flew to Moscow. On September 2, Bank Rossii abandoned the floating peg policy, letting the ruble find its own level unaided. That day, bolstered by his meeting with Clinton in the Kremlin, Yeltsin warned of a systemic crisis if the Duma did not endorse his nominee for prime minister.

Communist deputies responded by threatening to pass an impeachment motion against Yeltsin. That would have barred him from dissolving Parliament, his ultimate weapon. A compromise ensued. Yeltsin proposed Primakov as premier. He was left of center in the political spectrum and favored a broad-based cabinet and regulation of the mafia capitalism that had devastated most Russians. He got 317 votes, with 63 opposing.

While Primakov was in tune with the parliament and public opinion, he was viewed suspiciously by the Clinton administration, the unspoken warden of the Russian Federation. It had known him as a proponent of multilateralism in world affairs who visualized Russia, China, and India forming a strategic triad as a counterforce to the United States.

Primakov led the government at a time when the seven-year-long depression had reduced Russia's GDP to half its size in 1991. Quality of life had fallen steeply. The murder rate soared to 30 per 1,000—fifteen times the figure for Western Europe, Eastern Europe, China, Japan, and Israel. The death rate rose by a third, with the nation diminishing in size annually by 500,000, while the birthrate declined by 40 percent.[6] Life expectancy, at sixty-five, fell behind China's, at seventy-two.

Primakov formed a broad-based government, with nearly half of the ministers being reformist, with the rest centrists or left of center. It brought much-needed relief to civil servants, troops, and miners, owed back wages of over $4 billion, by printing more money. By so doing it avoided issuing junk bonds, a prime source of the fiscal trouble. It regulated the financial sector and encouraged output along the lines of the anti-Depression reforms of U.S. President Franklin Roosevelt.

But Clinton, a latter-day Democrat who had imbibed the free markets and monetarism of Milton Friedman, disapproved of Primakov's bold steps. At his behest, the IMF refused to release the $13 billion package it had promised Moscow in July 1998, a third of which was earmarked to wipe out wage arrears. But the moderate, pragmatic steps by the new government reassured foreign investors, slowed capital flight, and facilitated restructuring of Russia's foreign debt of $150 billion.

In the event, the grossly devalued ruble aided Moscow. By making imports very expensive, it boosted local industry. Also, it made Russian oil and gas cheap in terms of dollars, the currency in which hydrocarbons are traded internationally. The upswing in oil prices from 1999 onward helped the Kremlin further. That reassured Russian policymakers that there was economic life after the IMF.

To Primakov's delight, the opinion polls showed that two out of three Russians approved of his government. He had emerged as the most trusted politician because of his pragmatic competence, intelligence, and honesty. He surpassed Yeltsin in popularity.

Meanwhile, the process of impeaching Yeltsin, which had started with the Duma appointing a committee to that effect in May 1998, gathered pace. The five counts for impeaching Yeltsin included signing an illegal agreement to dissolve the Soviet Union in 1991, abetting murder during the assault on the parliament in 1993, and mounting an unnecessary war in Chechnya. The voting in the chamber would take place a year later.

These serious charges were a contrast to the ones leveled at Clinton following the revelation of his sexual relationship with Monica Lewinsky, a White House intern, in January 1998: perjury and obstruction of justice. The Lewinsky episode dragged on for more than a year. While the Republican-majority House of Representatives impeached Clinton, the Senate failed to muster the two-thirds majority to dismiss him. Throughout this riveting episode the Clinton team monitored closely the progress in Yeltsin's impeachment case.

Emulating Clinton, who ordered a bombing blitz against Iraq on the eve of the impeachment vote in the House of Representatives on December 19, 1998, to divert public attention, Yeltsin decided to do something dramatic. His chance came on March 24, 1999. That day NATO unleashed its bombing campaign against Serbia for repressing the rebel forces in the Muslim-majority province of Kosovo. Yeltsin suspended relations with NATO. He dispatched several warships to the Mediterranean. But NATO kept up its incessant bombing, thus highlighting inter alia Yeltsin's impotence.

As the Duma prepared to vote on his impeachment on May 15, Yeltsin summarily fired Primakov. This pleased the Clinton team, which considered him an unreconstructed socialist. By contrast, Primakov's dismissal stunned parliamentarians and the public. Undeterred, the Duma pressed ahead with the impeachment vote. The charge that Yeltsin exceeded his powers by sending the military into Chechnya carried the most votes, 283—just 17 short of the required two-thirds majority to dismiss him.

Yeltsin survived the most serious crisis in his checkered career by the skin of his teeth.

"Barbarians in the Sky"

The purpose of NATO's air strikes and missile attacks on Serbia's economic infrastructure was to "degrade" President Slobodan Milosevic's capabilities. What many neutral observers found objectionable was that NATO had launched military action without the approval of the UN or the fifty-six-member Organization for Security and Cooperation in Europe (OSCE)—a UN-sanctioned body dealing with conflict prevention and crisis management. As a result, Russians' view of America altered radically. Most of them saw Americans as "barbarians in the sky."[7] When, following Milosevic's acceptance of NATO's terms, the air strikes ended, there was a palpable sigh of relief in the Kremlin and outside.

But for all practical purposes, the Serbian episode ended Yeltsin's honeymoon with the White House. Even though Primakov no longer held any official position, his imprint on the Kremlin's foreign policy had remained intact. The evidence came in August 1999, when Yeltsin cosigned an "anti-NATO" statement with Chinese President Jiang Zemin at the Shanghai Conference Organization summit in Bishkek, Kyrgyzstan. That month, Yeltsin once again fired his prime minister, Sergei Stepashin. His next choice fell on Vladimir Vladimirovich Putin (born 1952), head of FSB (*Federalnaya Sluzhba Bezopasnosti*), the internal security service, for the past year. Having won the Duma's endorsement, Putin lost little time to display his firm style of governance. The invasion and occupation of Dagestan by 2,000 Islamist guerrillas from the adjoining independent Chechen republic of Ichkeria in early August provided him the opportunity.

But a month later, after the Russian troops' successful counterattack in Dagestan, apartment blocks in Moscow and two southern towns were bombed, killing three hundred. The Kremlin blamed Chechen terrorists without providing evidence. But the Russian public was so outraged that few bothered to demand proof. The net effect of the explosions was a surge for Putin's iron-fist policy toward the Chechen rebels.

Putin took charge of military operations. In early October the Russian forces entered Chechnya in large numbers. Within two months, they captured northern and central Chechnya and encircled the capital, Grozny. In the process they inflicted heavy casualties not only on the armed rebels but also on civilians. As they approached Grozny, they called on the residents to flee or be treated as enemies.

When Washington criticized Moscow's targeting of civilians, Yeltsin issued a strong riposte, calling Russia "a great power." His stance helped Putin's freshly founded party, Unity, to win almost as many seats (eight-four) as the Communist Party (ninety) in the Duma poll on December 19, forging ahead of Primakov's centrist Fatherland–All Russia (forty-five). The Union of Right-Wing Forces, with thirty-two seats, backed Putin. Overall, the opposition was less numerous in the new Duma than before, with the pro-Putin factions in the majority.

On December 31, Yeltsin resigned prematurely. Putin became the acting president, thus enhancing his chances of success in the electoral contest to be held within three months. By putting his nominee in the presidential seat Yeltsin assured himself of immunity from prosecution—a prospect he could not count on from an as yet undecided winner of the electoral race. Putin obliged with alacrity. His first presidential decree made Yeltsin immune from criminal prosecution.

Whereas well-informed democrats in Russia were suspicious of Putin, a shadowy figure, and considered his sudden elevation a virtual coup plotted and executed within the walls of the Kremlin, the Clinton White House hailed him as one of the foremost reformers. Russia's capture of Grozny, reduced to rubble, in February 2000, improved Putin's electoral chances.

Physically, intellectually, and temperamentally, Putin was a stark contrast to his predecessor. A corpulent creature, frequently ill, Yeltsin had been a typical party apparatchik before his break with Gorbachev. Surrounded by sycophants and hangers-on, and addicted to excessive drinking despite acute heart problems, he had lurched from one crisis to the next and operated without any coherent vision or strategy.

Putin began his career as an operative in the KGB's foreign espionage department. It demanded high standards of intelligence, integrity, cunning, and fealty for its members, and trained recruits rigorously to spurn the allurements that came with postings in Western cities. A fluent German speaker, he served in Dresden, East Germany, from 1985 to 1990. After the Soviet breakup, he headed the Committee for External Relations of the mayor in St. Petersburg, his birthplace. His thesis for his graduate degree in economics dealt with the economics of natural resources like oil and gas. It gave him a firm grounding in a subject that would loom large during his presidency. Next, he was transferred to the Kremlin's presidential property department, the successor to the assets of the Soviet-era Communist Party. After supervising the Kremlin's links with the regions, he moved to the FSB as its head.

He came across as an energetic, youthful, articulate figure. But that was not enough to ensure his electoral victory. The powerful oligarchs, keen to keep their wealth and influence, backed him to the hilt. They figured that, being a strong character, he would deliver on his word and let them function as they had under Yeltsin. Since the highly influential state-run TV channels backed Putin, he had an advantage over his rivals. Yet he won only about 52.5 percent of the ballots in March 2000, thus narrowly avoiding a second run, with his nearest rival, Gennadi Zyuganov, scoring 29 percent. The credible claims of doctoring of the ballot count were ignored.

Putin inherited a Russia where nearly three out of four Russians existed either below or near the poverty line. With the national GDP of $200 billion in 1999, the per capita GDP was merely $1,330. The average life expectancy of a Russian male had fallen below sixty years, and Bank Rossii had only $12 billion in foreign reserves.[8]

PUTIN'S FIRST TERM

Under Putin, the economy expanded steadily. His sober, agile, and businesslike persona imbued the Kremlin with a radically different aura from Yeltsin's. He judged the popular mood correctly. Citizens were yearning for security, which they had enjoyed during most of the Soviet rule, even if it meant diminution of their civil rights and freedoms.

His rule became associated with rising living standards, with average monthly wages rising ninefold to 13,800 rubles. An average annual growth of 7.6 percent pushed the per capita GDP to nearly $9,000 during his eight years in office.[9] While the hydrocarbon boom was the main engine behind the torrid economic expansion, Putin's style of governance brought social and political stability and restored the pride that Russians had acquired during the era of a bipolar world.

He used his first term to consolidate his position at home. He advanced the process of centralizing power initiated by Yeltsin. He abrogated the election of regional governors, tightened the regulation of political parties and NGOs, and minimized parliamentary opposition by changing the electoral system completely to proportional representation. He curbed the influence of the oligarchs and warned them off politics, while taking unpopular steps early on.

Putin backed the "reformist" policies of his new economics minister, German Gref. The minister adopted a 13 percent flat tax for personal income and corporate earnings, and abolished the graduated tax structure, a long-established norm in capitalist countries. That meant slashing company profit tax by more than half from the previous 30 percent. He made up the loss in revenue by reducing housing and utility subsidies. He also diluted labor protection rights.

Abroad, Putin went out of his way to court the White House. During his brief period as acting president, he thawed relations with NATO and revived meetings of the NATO-Russia Permanent Joint Council.

He hoped the gesture would make President George W. Bush heed his misgivings about the Pentagon's plans for installing missile defense components in Eastern Europe adjoining Russia. At the G8 summit in Genoa, Italy, in July 2001, he appealed to Bush to abandon his missile project, arguing that expanding NATO was creating insecurity on the fringes of Europe. As an alternative he proposed creating "a single security and defense space" in Europe by replacing NATO or letting Russia join it as a full member. Bush ignored the proposal.[10]

Following the terrorist attacks on New York and Washington, in September, Putin offered full cooperation in Bush's war on "terror," meaning extremist Islamists, who had been Moscow's bane in Chechnya long before 9/11. The Kremlin offered access to Russian airspace for humanitarian missions, participation in some search and rescue operations, and arms supplies to anti-Taliban forces—and sharing of intelligence gathered by the Russian espionage apparatus based in Tajikistan sharing 720 miles (1,150 kilometers) of border with Afghanistan. Furthermore, Putin let the leaders of the Central Asian republics—part of a defense alliance with Russia, called the Collective Security Treaty Organization—decide the extent of their cooperation with Washington. Uzbekistan and Kyrgyzstan leased military bases to the Pentagon.

Earlier, encouraged by Moscow's friendship with America, the 2001 National Energy Policy document issued by the White House had noted approvingly that Russia had increased its output in older oil fields, and that new fields were being developed, including those with U.S. and other non-Russian investments.

HIGH ON HYDROCARBONS

In the wake of the Soviet Union's dissolution and the subsequent economic upheaval, Russia's oil output dropped from 9.33 million barrels per day (bpd) in 1991 to 8 million bpd the next year. As a precursor to abolishing the Ministry of Oil Industry, the Kremlin set up Rosneft ("Ros" for Rossiya and "Neft," meaning oil), which began functioning in April 1993. Then ten oil companies and refineries were spun off from Rosneft to form as many vertically integrated firms. Following acquisitions, the total shrank to five.

Of these the four that mattered most—Lukoil, Yukos, Sibneft (Siberian Oil), and Tyumen (later TNK)—were cornered by tycoons Khodorkovsky, Berezovsky, Fridman, and Abramovich. The depleted Rosneft, owning only three refineries and several run-down oil fields, was transformed into a joint stock company in 1995.

The production slide, stemming from rapid changes in ownership and management, continued until 1998, when oil output fell to a little over 6 million bpd.

Gas production too followed a similar trajectory. Soon after its founding in 1992, Gazprom, which replaced the Ministry of Gas Industry, became a joint stock company. It was privatized in 1994, with the state holding 40 percent of its shares, and a further 15 percent sold to employees and management at a discount. By allocating 1 percent of its equity to foreigners in 1996 as Global Depository Receipts and raising $2.5 billion in bond sales the following year, it found a footing in Western capital markets. They would later finance its ambitious expansion plans. In 2000, Gazprom accounted for 93 percent of Russia's gas production of 545 billion cubic meters, which was one-tenth lower than the 1991 figure. Gazprom and Lukoil together possessed two-fifths of Russia's oil reserves of 72 billion barrels and almost all of its gas reserves, the highest in the world. Western technology applied to Russia's new oil fields, as a result of the 2002 U.S.-Russian Energy Dialogue, helped bring the 2004 output to the 1991 level. But the problem of depleted Russian oil fields did not lend itself to a feasible solution.

In any event, overall Russia's laws were designed to favor local companies and discourage foreign investment in its energy sector. The Kremlin was not alone in this. Washington too pursued this line, as would become clear when it vetoed a Chinese petroleum corporation acquiring a U.S. oil corporation in 2005.

An expert on Russia's natural resources, Putin realized that its sale to private companies at give-away prices during Yeltsin's presidency was hurtful to national interests. He devised the grand strategy of enabling large state-owned enterprises to earn massive profits for the government to achieve its social and political goals. Therefore he decided to reverse the privatization process—particularly in the energy sector, "the inner sanctum of the Russian economy." He deployed Roseneft, Lukoil, and Gazprom to achieve this aim, bolstering them to become giant corporations, which posted the highest gas output in the world, and displacing America as the second largest oil producer in 2005. Consuming only 2.9 million bpd at home, Russia had 6.8 million bpd available for export, second only to Saudi Arabia's 8.7 million bpd.

Putin's policy of squeezing out indigenous and Western private companies from the energy sector played well with the public. His popularity rubbed off on the United Russia party, with which he was closely associated. In the December 2003 Duma election, it won 223 seats—with the Communist Party (52) a distant second, followed by the Liberal Democratic Party (36). In the March 2004 presidential poll Putin was reelected with 71.3 percent of the vote, and his nearest rival Nikolay Kharitonov, the candidate of the Agrarian Party allied with the Communists, mustered less than a fifth of his total. Putin's star was on the rise, and so was Russia's, as it began wielding the powerful hydrocarbon weapon.

CONCEPT OF SOVEREIGN DEMOCRACY

An increasingly confident Putin proved flexible at home. When the people protested against his plan to substitute subsidized housing and medicine and free transportation with cash, he withdrew the scheme. His decision had partly to do with the "color revolutions" in Georgia and Ukraine within a year, followed by the Tulip Revolution in Kyrgyzstan. The Rose Revolution in Georgia in November 2003 led to the fall of its government, which was unable to withstand the pressure from peaceful demonstrations at home and Western powers abroad. The event was noted by the Kremlin—nothing more.

But what happened in Ukraine next year alarmed the Putin government. The peaceful demonstrations against the victory of the pro-Moscow candidate,

Viktor Yanukovich, in the November 2004 presidential race, marred by rigging, led to a standoff. The protestors, carrying orange flags, were backed by NATO members. The decision by the Supreme Court to hold another vote led to the defeat of Yanukovich by his pro-West rival, Viktor Yushchenko, thus bringing the Orange Revolution to a successful conclusion. While the Western media never investigated the originators and planners of the meticulously organized demonstrations and the participants' occupation of the main square in Kiev, Russian foreign intelligence discovered the hand of pro-West non-Ukrainians, who had mounted similar campaigns in Serbia and Slovakia before.[11]

The events in Kyrgyzstan in March 2005 alarmed Russia even more. Peaceful protest at rigged parliamentary elections led to two-thirds of the country falling into the hands of the opposition and the overthrow of President Askar Akayev. He fled to Moscow. The involvement of Western NGOs in the episode, to be called the Tulip Revolution, was far from covert.[12]

Russian leaders viewed these developments as part of Washington's dual-track policy of encircling Russia. Encroachment on Russia's backyard and placement of pro-Western leaders in power were to be complemented by the installation of American missiles and a radar system in Eastern Europe. The Russians decided to meet the challenge militarily and ideologically. They had no intention of challenging the concept of letting citizens choose their governing representatives through the ballot. What they needed to do was to come up with a model of democracy with Russian or Slavic characteristics. While committed to regular elections, this version was to be antithetical to the phenomenon of a grassroots upsurge overthrowing a government.

The task to define such a model fell to Vladislav Surkov. A former businessman and public relations chief of a leading private bank and the ORT television channel, Surkov became Putin's first deputy chief of staff in 1999.[13] During Putin's second term in office, he acquired the role of an ideologue. Defining sovereignty as a political synonym of competitiveness, he labeled the Russian version as "sovereign democracy." In practical terms, sovereignty meant economic independence, military power, and strong cultural identity. This was a reprise of the ideology summarized by Count Sergei Semenovich Uvarov (1786–1855), the longest serving president of the Academy of Sciences during the rule of Tsar Nicholas I: "Orthodoxy, Sovereignty, Nationalism." The term "orthodoxy" applied to the Russian Orthodox Church.

In present-day Russia, sovereign democracy is shorthand for the two salient statements in the preamble to the constitution drafted primarily by Yeltsin: the regime in Moscow is democratic, and its democratic credentials can only be verified by Russians. Any attempt by foreigners to examine it would be tantamount to interference in Russia's domestic affairs. Also, "sovereignty" means that non-Russian values and standards are not applicable.

Western analysts preferred the term "managed democracy." They described how Putin had transformed independent media, particularly television, into a sycophantic tool of the state either directly or through Gazprom Media, a subsidiary of Gazprom; imprisoned his leading opponents or forced them into exile; and made the judiciary play second fiddle to the executive. This model of democracy rested on the centralized control of internal security forces, enlarged state monopolies, and electronic mass media, they explained.

Yet, to the surprise and disappointment of Western commentators, most Russians favored "managed democracy." Successive polls showed 70 percent favoring Putin and a strong executive authority. And by stepping down after two consecutive terms as president, Putin wrong-footed those who had wagered that he would get the Russian parliament to amend the constitution and run for president for the third term and beyond.

In any case, the political system needed to be in tune with the national identity, which crystallized during Putin's presidency.

POST-SOVIET RUSSIAN IDENTITY

Religion emerged as an important part of the new Russian identity. The following and influence of the Russian Orthodox Church (ROC) rose steeply in the post-Soviet era, particularly during Putin's years in the Kremlin. Unlike Yeltsin, whose devotion to the church was less than sincere, Putin is a devout Russian Orthodox. He attends religious services regularly, which only four out of ten Russians do.[14] But since the majority of Russians trust the ROC, it is a source of moral and spiritual legitimacy to the regime, even though, constitutionally, church and state remain apart.

Today there are up to 500 Orthodox Church publications and 3,500 church Web sites. The first Orthodox Church media festival in 2004 in Moscow attracted four hundred journalists. "Church has become part of public ritual," said Nikolai Uskov, editor of the Russian edition of GQ magazine. "Glamorous people must believe, go to church, have icons, and go on to pilgrimages to [holy] places in Russia."[15]

The ROC is an important element in differentiating Russians from Europeans. Polls show that 70 percent of Russians do not consider themselves European, and nearly half view the European Union as a threat to Russia's economic independence.[16] In area, the Russian Federation's European region is only one-sixth of the total.

It is worth noting that following the mutual excommunication of the patriarch of Constantinople (now Istanbul), Michael Cerularius, and Pope Leo IX in 1054, the gap between the Western Roman Catholic Church led by the pope in Rome, with Latin as the official language, and the Orthodox Eastern Church, headed by the patriarch in Byzantine Constantinople, with Greek as the official language, became unbridgeable. The Orthodox churches, noted for their rich liturgical practices and devotional use of icons, remain different from Roman Catholic or Protestant churches.[17] More important, the Orthodox Church did not go through a reformation. It did not split as the Roman Catholic Church did in 1517, leading to the rise of Protestantism, with the resulting conflict between the two churches shaping the history of Europe until the Treaty of Westphalia in 1648.

ROC leaders agree with the Putin government that Russian civilization is different from Europe's. Taking up the theme, Surkov argues that Russians and Westerners view the world differently. "Russian cultural consciousness is clearly holistic [and] intuitive and opposed to [the] mechanistic [and] reductionist," he notes. "Synthesis prevails over analysis, idealism over pragmatism, images over logic, intuition over reasoning, general over particular. This does not mean that the Russians lack analytical thinking and people in the western countries intuition. The issue here is the ratio."[18] That, according to Surkov, leads to "the aspiration for the political wholeness through the centralization of power functions . . . idealization of the goals, pursued by the political struggle . . . [and] personification of political institutions. All these phenomena exist in other political cultures, however, their presence in our political culture exceeds the average level."[19]

Along with this theoretical underpinning went a reassessment of the Soviet past and the Yeltsin era. "No return to the 1990s" became the slogan not just of the United Russia party, led by Putin, but also of all other parties and factions. The pro-American and pro-EU politicians and lobbies, which thrived under Yeltsin, vanished.

Besides strident state propaganda and the rewriting of history books, what destroyed the influence of the United States in Russia was the Pentagon's illegal invasion of Iraq in 2003. Putin was indignant when Bush ignored his pleas to give UN inspectors a chance to finish their task and not rush into invading Iraq. The steadily rising prices of Russia's oil and gas exports raised his confidence. He captured the popular mood in Russia when in his State of the Nation address on April 25, 2005, he said, "Above all it must be acknowledged that the collapse of the Soviet Union was the geopolitical catastrophe of the century."[20] Yet, shorn of its non-Russian territories of the Soviet and Tsarist eras, Russia held the promise of a comeback on its own by exploiting its vast oil and gas reserves.

EXPLODING OIL PRICES

Russia's swelling oil and gas income shored up its foreign reserves to $315 billion in 2006. The Russian Stabilization Fund, consisting of export duty on oil and a surcharge on its output above the $27 a barrel mark, overshot its initial target of 500 billion rubles (about $20 billion) within a year of its founding in 2004. Its size was large enough to cover the deficits of the federal budget and the Pension Fund—and enable Bank Rossii to start repaying foreign debts before they were due.[21]

Oddly, soaring hydrocarbon riches went hand in hand with the prosecution of the country's richest man, Mikhail Khodorkovsky, head of the oil company Yukos, who was arrested on charges of fraud and tax evasion in October 2003. Seeing Russia's foremost tycoon in the dock pleased the public, which viewed the oligarchs as avaricious thieves. Khodorkovsky was found guilty as charged and sentenced to nine years' imprisonment in 2005.

The Kremlin's critics perceived its action as a vendetta against Khodorkovsky for funding the opposition parties in the 2003 parliamentary election. However, the prosecutor alleged that the accused had tried to bribe Duma members to block amendments to the law to tax windfall profits and close offshore, tax-evasion loopholes. During Yeltsin's presidency, his billionaire backers bribed Duma members at critical moments to achieve the results Yeltsin wanted. So Khodorkovsky did nothing worse than indulge in a practice that had a precedent. But the profound difference this time was that Khodorkovsky was acting as an independent operator against the will of the Kremlin. Such an enterprise needed to be crushed at all costs, the Putin team seemed to have decided.

A separate case of tax evasion was lodged against Yukos in July 2004, along with a $7 billion claim for back taxes. Yukos had allegedly reduced its tax liability from the standard 30 percent to 11 percent by using Russia's underdeveloped areas, which offered tax concessions, as its main base. The court case caused a sharp decline in Yukos's share price. The government auctioned its assets to recover back taxes. Most of these ended up with Rosneft, and the rest with Gazprom, before Yukos was declared bankrupt in August 2006.

Flush with cash, Gazprom acquired a 75 percent stake in Sibneft from Abramovich for $13 billion in 2005. Pressured by the Kremlin to renegotiate the lucrative Production Sharing Agreement that Royal Dutch Shell had signed in 1993–1994, it sold half of its Sakhalin-2 oil and gas development project to Gazprom for $7 billion.

The fivefold increase in petroleum prices between 1998 and the spring of 2006, and a corresponding rise in related gas prices in 2005–2006, made Gazprom the world's third largest corporation by market value after Exxon Mobil and General Electric. Employing 430,000 people, it owned not only 155,000 kilometers (95,000 miles) of pipelines but—through its subsidiaries—assets in newspapers and TV channels, banking (Gazenergoprombank), insurance, agriculture, and construction. As the country's largest urban and rural landowner, it constructed roads and hospitals, thus emulating the state-owed Petroleos de Venezuela (PdVSA). It accounted for 8 percent of the national GDP and a quarter of the federal government's tax income.

In theory, Gazprom was like any other corporation with its investors, directors, and annual general meetings. In practice, its decisions were made by Putin and his small coterie in informal meetings and passed on to Dmitry Medvedev, the company's chairman since 2000, who also happened to be deputy prime minister and a former Kremlin chief of staff. Later government ministers would be appointed as directors of Gazprom as well as Rosneft.

The burgeoning revenue from hydrocarbons enabled Putin and his successor Medvedev to build up Russia's lagging industry and military. It also allowed them to deploy state-controlled Gazprom, Lukoil, and Rosneft to advance Russia's geopolitical interests. This was not a novel strategy. Knowingly or otherwise, Putin followed in the footsteps of the United States. Exploiting America's position as the largest oil producer in the world for more than half a century, the U.S. government, working in tandem with petroleum companies, had wielded the oil weapon to further its national interests. It used this lever to gain American companies access to Europe and the Middle East after World War I. That resulted inter alia in the American oil giants' monopolizing the hydrocarbon industry in Saudi Arabia. Summing up the situation, a top State Department official wrote in August 1945: "A review of the diplomatic history of the past 35 years will show that petroleum has historically played a larger part in the external relations of the United States than any other commodity."[22] Following the 1956 Suez War, Washington refused to help Britain and France with sorely needed oil supplies until and unless they had withdrawn from the occupied territories of Egypt. They relented.

RUSSIA'S CATCH-UP

At home, the Kremlin started using its hydrocarbon revenue to revive Russia's industry. It consolidated the aerospace companies into a state-controlled conglomerate, United Aircraft, with plans to make it the world's number three producer of civilian aircraft. In 2007 it decided to reconstitute the civilian assets of the Russian Federal Atomic Energy Agency (Rosatom) into a single holding company, Atomprom. The plan was to consolidate many disparate state agencies dealing with nuclear power to create a complete-cycle corporation from uranium mining to generating electricity and building new power plants. The number of nuclear reactors was to rise from thirteen to forty.[23] Abroad, Atomprom was to compete with General Electric, Toshiba, Aviva of France, and Mitsubishi Heavy Industries. To accelerate high-tech innovation, the Kremlin set up Nanotechnology Corporation and Russian Technologies Corporation. At the same time it listed forty-two "strategic" sectors—oil and gas, aerospace, aviation, nonferrous mining, arms production, fishing, TV and radio channels and mass circulation newspapers, telecom, etc.—where foreign investment was to be restricted. The Kremlin also decided to invest part of its hydrocarbon wealth to upgrade its depleted military machine and project a sharper military profile abroad.

With Bush continuing to reject his argument that implanting elements of Washington's anti-missile system in Eastern Europe would destroy the existing nuclear balance, ultimately enabling the Pentagon to launch a nuclear first strike against Russia,[24] Putin ordered the resumption of long-range air patrols, involving nuclear bombs, that had ended with the Soviet Union's collapse.[25] His April 2008 proposal for a joint American-Russian missile defense against Middle Eastern states, comprising radar sites in southern Russia, failed to elicit a positive response from Bush.

In September 2008 the Kremlin carried out its largest military exercise since 1992 across all eleven time zones of its territory. It involved tens of thousands of soldiers, thousands of vehicles, and squadrons of warplanes. It ended with the firing of three inter-continental ballistic missiles (ICBMs), carrying multiple warheads, one of them spanning a record 7,200 miles (11,400 kilometers).[26]

In his first address to the nation as president on November 4, Medvedev warned that radio-electronic equipment located in Russia's western region would jam the elements of the U.S. missile defense system. Also the Kremlin planned to use its sophisticated radio jamming equipment, helped by its Baltic fleet in the port of Baltiysk, to sabotage the Pentagon's missile defense system and place short-range missiles in Kaliningrad that, during the Soviet times, hosted powerful SS-20s, capable of massive destruction in Europe.

Later that month, following the annual EU-Russian summit in Nice, French President Nicolas Sarkozy, then also holding the European Union's rotating presidency, said, "Deployment of a [U.S.] missile defense system [in Europe] would bring nothing to security in Europe. It would complicate things."[27] Equally welcome to Medvedev was Sarkozy's statement that "we would meet in mid-2009 to lay the foundation of what could possibly be a future pan-European security system."[28]

Russia got the ball rolling at the OSCE meeting in Helsinki in early December. Its foreign minister, Sergey Lavrov, proposed that the OSCE, with its membership covering North America, Europe, and Central Asia, be upgraded into a multilateral security organization by a mutually agreed treaty. The legally binding treaty should be built on the following principles: respect for international law, acceptance of the UN Charter, commitment not to use force, guarantees that no single nation or group of nations takes a dominant role in Europe's security, and arms control. During the debate that followed, various ideas were offered on what the new treaty should contain.

But Bush remained uncompromising. So later that month the Kremlin stated that over the next three years it would build seventy ICBMs as well as short-range missiles, three hundred tanks, fourteen warships, and fifty warplanes, and make up its deficiency in drones and high-precision bombs.[29] It was on track to set up its own GLONASS (Global Navigation Satellite System) as a rival to America's GPS, Global Positioning System, a crucial element in modern warfare.

Alarmed at Bush's executive order in October 2006 tacitly asserting a U.S. right to space weapons, and continued opposition to the Russian-Chinese efforts to secure an international ban on space weapons, Medvedev announced that Russia would build a space defense system, upgrade current ICBMs to protect them from space-based components of the American anti-missile defense system, and set up a "guaranteed nuclear deterrent system," including a fleet of submarines, armed with cruise missiles, by 2020.[30] Moscow had woken up to the fact that more than half of the $52.4 billion spent on nuclear weapons and programs by the Pentagon in the previous fiscal year had been used to upgrade, operate, and sustain its nuclear arsenal.[31]

Medvedev's statement was a clear signal that Moscow was preparing for an all-out nuclear war with the United States in the future if the latter did not revert to respecting the doctrine of spheres of influence that was agreed and implemented by America, the Soviet Union, and Britain at the 1945 Yalta Conference. The White House argued that the doctrine of the spheres of influence died with the end of the Cold War. If so, then Russia would encroach on Latin America, the traditional backyard of the United States, came the retort from the Kremlin. "Latin America is becoming an obvious link in the chain making a multi-polar world," Putin said in September 2008. "We will allocate more and more attention to this vector of our economics and foreign policy."[32]

A DISTINCT FOREIGN POLICY

Putin succeeded in restoring Moscow's influence in Central Asia. Reacting against Washington's relentless pressure for democratization and free markets, irrespective of social or economic consequences, Central Asian leaders adopted the "managed democracy" of the Russian variety. They noticed, approvingly, how this version delivered a Russian parliament in December 2007 with the ruling United Russia party garnering 70 percent of the seats—followed by the election of forty-two-year-old Medvedev, anointed by Putin, as president, securing 71 percent of the ballots.

All five Central Asian republics, except Turkmenistan, were members of the Moscow-led Collective Security Treaty Organization (CSTO), which also included Armenia and Belarus. In a significant move in February 2009, the CSTO decided to establish a joint Rapid Reaction Force of 10,000 under a central command, including Russian paratroopers, to replace the existing contingent of 3,000, which lacked a central command. The members of this force will take over the Manas base in Kyrgyzstan when it is vacated by the Pentagon in August 2009.

Putin also made strides in regaining the influence that Moscow used to have in the Arab Middle East and North Africa before 1991. He went on to befriend Saudi Arabia, an arch foe of the Soviet Union. In October 2003, he became the first head of a non-Muslim country to address the fifty-seven-member Islamic Conference Organization (ICO), headquartered in Jeddah, Saudi Arabia. He pointed out that Islam's presence on Russian soil preceded Christianity's. Overlooking the Russian army's brutality in Chechnya, the ICO gave observer status to Russia, even though only one out of its seven citizens is Muslim. That led to the founding of the Russia-Muslim World Strategic Vision Group in Moscow.[33] It held its annual conferences in different capitals of the Muslim world. Putin changed his terminology. Instead of branding Chechen rebels as "Muslim fundamentalist terrorists," he started calling them "terrorists linked to international networks of criminals, drug and arms traffickers."

Part of the rationale behind the Kremlin's opposition to the U.S. invasion of Iraq was that it would boost radical Islamism and terrorism, which would affect Russia, since Muslims are the largest non-Russian ethnic group. The anti-American sentiment that mushroomed in the Muslim world in the wake of that invasion emboldened Putin to speak his mind about Washington's policies. During his trip to Ankara in December 2004, he compared America to the nineteenth-century European imperialist, "a strict uncle in a pith helmet instructing others how to live their lives" and punishing the protestors with a "missilebomb truncheon."[34]

After the surprise victory of Hamas in the parliamentary poll of Palestinians in January 2006, Putin broke ranks with the United States and the European Union when they demanded that the Hamas government recognize Israel, renounce violence, and accept the previous Israeli-Palestinian agreements. Hamas refused. So America and the European Union did not recognize it. In contrast, Putin invited Hamas leaders to Moscow.

During his March 2006 visit to Algiers, Putin wrote off the $4.7 billion Algeria owed to the Soviet Union and agreed to sell $7.5 billion worth of weapons to Algeria. A year later, in the course of his trip to Riyadh, he offered to sell arms and nuclear power plants to the Saudi kingdom.

Reviving their strategic links with the former Soviet Union, Syria and Libya offered Russia the use of their naval facilities in, respectively, Tartus and Benghazi, with the Libyan leader Muammar al Qaddafi stating in October 2008 that such an arrangement would be a guarantee of nonaggression by the Pentagon. Both countries started negotiating with the Kremlin, which announced that its navy planned to station warships permanently in friendly countries.

Russia's geopolitical partnership with Iran has been a sore point with the State Department. Other points of friction have also arisen between Moscow and Washington, especially in the Balkans.

STANDING UP TO AMERICA

The Kremlin had started distancing itself from the White House during the latter part of the Yeltsin's presidency, but Putin took the process to its logical conclusion. He stood up to America when the need arose—as it did in the spring of 2006, when Vice President Dick Cheney criticized Russia for misusing its gas supplies to Ukraine for political ends under the guise of a price dispute.

Putin used his annual State of the Nation speech to Parliament on May 10 to give a robust response to Cheney. Noting that the U.S. defense budget was twenty-five times Russia's and that America had turned itself into a castle, he remarked, "As they say, 'Comrade Wolf knows whom to eat. He eats without listening and he is clearly not going to listen to anyone.'" By "Comrade Wolf," he clearly meant "Uncle Sam." He added, "Where is all the pathos about protecting human rights and democracy when it comes to the need to pursue their own interests?"[35] In short, while Washington had no qualms about advancing its interests by all means, it was criticizing Moscow for pursuing its own interests.

On the eve of the G8 summit in St. Petersburg on July 16, 2006, Putin argued in his media interviews that Western criticism of Russia's energy policies, foreign affairs, and embrace of democracy sprang from "outdated Cold War competition and even misguided colonial era arrogance."

"If we go back 100 years and look through the newspapers, we see what arguments the colonial powers of that time advanced to justify their expansion into Africa and Asia," he told a French channel, TF-1. "They cited the arguments such as playing a civilizing role, the particular role of the white man, the need to civilize 'primitive peoples.'

"If we replace the term 'civilizing role' with 'democratization,' then we can transpose practically word for word what the newspapers were writing 100 years ago to today's world and the arguments we hear from some of our colleagues on issues such as democratization and the need to ensure democratic freedoms."[36]

Putin's views were in tune with the popular opinion at home. A poll taken during the run-up to the G8 summit in St. Petersburg had revealed that 58 percent of Russians regarded America as an "unfriendly country."

At the Forty-third Munich Trans-Atlantic conference on security policy in February 2007, Putin mounted a frontal attack on a unipolar world order. "However one might embellish this term [unipolar world], at the end of day it describes a scenario in which there is one center of authority, one center of force, one center of decision-making," he said. "It is a world in which there is one master, one sovereign. And this is pernicious, not only for all those who are in the system, but also for the sovereign itself, because it destroys itself from within. And this certainly has nothing in common with democracy. Because democracy is the power of the majority in the light of the interests and opinions of the minority." (Almost two years later, French President Nicolas Sarkozy said, "Let's be clear about this: There is no longer just one country that says what we should do and think. We will not accept a return to a single way of thought.")[37]

The Russian president deplored the propensity to solve problems militarily. "Today we are witnessing an almost unrestrained hyper-use of force—military force—in international relations, a force that is plunging the world into an abyss of permanent conflicts," he said.

> We are seeing a greater and greater disdain for the basic principles of international law. One country, the United States, has overstepped its national boundaries in every way. This is visible in the economic, political, cultural and educational policies it imposes on other nations. . . . This is very dangerous. Nobody feels secure any more because nobody can hide behind international law. This is nourishing an arms race with countries seeking to obtain nuclear weapons. . . . We're witnessing the untrammeled

use of military in international affairs. . . . Why is it necessary to bomb and to shoot at every opportunity?[38]

Putin's speech, delivered to an audience that included Robert Gates, the newly appointed U.S. defense secretary, made international headlines. Gates dismissed it as "the blunt talk of an old spy." It had no impact on Washington's foreign and defense policies, with their plans for ten interceptor missiles near Redzikowo in Poland and a radar base near Prague firmly in place. Washington reiterated that the reason for installing this system was to counter the threat posed by rogue states like Iran. It ignored the Kremlin's argument that Iran did not have nuclear weapons or the means of delivery to hit Eastern Europe. If the threat was real, then the most suitable location for the anti-missile defense system was either in Azerbaijan or southern Russia.

Encountering a tin ear at the White House, the Kremlin issued its foreign policy document in April 2007. "The myth about the uni-polar world fell apart once and for all in Iraq," it stated. "A strong, more self-confident Russia has become an integral part of positive changes in the world." It stressed the centrality of national sovereignty and the primacy of the UN in resolving disputes.[39] Meanwhile, Moscow considered upgrading its nuclear missile arsenal, putting more missiles on mobile launchers, and moving its fleet of nuclear submarines to the North Pole, where they would be virtually undetectable.

While maintaining its status as a great power by virtue of its arsenal of nuclear weapons, Russia had acquired a potent nonmilitary weapon by making most of Europe dependent on its natural gas supplies.

THE BEAR'S PAW ON THE GAS SPIGOT

Western Europe's dependence on Siberian gas started in the wake of the 1973–1974 oil shock, when Europeans searched for alternatives to petroleum. Moscow started supplying gas to West Germany in 1975 on a small scale through transnational pipelines. Following the 1979–1981 oil shock, West Germany and its neighbors decided to raise their intake of Soviet gas by building additional pipelines. Washington objected. It banned the export of U.S. equipment to erect the pipeline and then tried to ban the export of any European equipment containing American technology. Western Europeans protested. Finally, the two sides reached an agreement in 1985. Western Europeans agreed to limit their imports of Soviet gas to 30 percent of their need and help develop Norway's gas industry.

Since then, Europeans' dependence on the gas supplied by Gazprom has increased enormously. The European countries wholly or largely dependent on supplies by Gazprom include Austria, Belarus, Bosnia, Bulgaria, the Czech Republic, Estonia, Finland, Georgia, Hungary, Latvia, Lithuania, Macedonia, Moldova, Poland, Slovakia, and Turkey. Germany receives almost half of its gas supplies from Gazprom, and France and Italy nearly a quarter each. The European Union as a whole receives about 25 percent of its gas consumption from Gazprom. Plans are well advanced to build a $12 billion North European Gas Pipeline to bring Siberian gas to Vyborg and then to the German port of Greifswald via the Baltic Sea.

This has strengthened Moscow's geopolitical leverage. When Ukraine failed to meet Gazprom's demand for a higher price for the gas being sold to it below the market rates, Gazprom shut off supplies on January 1, 2006, freezing Ukrainians and hurting their industry. Ukraine relented.

The Kremlin asserted that Gazprom's decisions were purely commercial, and that it did not use its product as a political tool. After Moscow's war with Georgia in August 2008, Putin pointed out that Russia did not cut off its gas supplies to Georgia during or after the fighting. But that did not mask the reality: European Union members were vulnerable to gas blackmail. One of the main, albeit unstated, reasons for the muted response to Russia's disproportionate military response to Georgia was undoubtedly Europeans' crippling dependence on natural gas from Gazprom.

As the European Union's most populous member, and the world's fourth largest economy, Germany matters more than any other constituent of the European Union. And Moscow had forged strong ties with Berlin—as it had in the tsarist era, when Germans were preeminent in developing industry in Russia. Now German industrialists were as keen to ship machinery and high-tech equipment to post-Communist Russia as Germans were to import Russian gas. Between 2000 and 2007, Germany's exports to Russia increased fourfold, to €28.2 billion, and almost matched the imports of Russian gas and other commodities in value.[40]

It is a truism that commerce affects diplomacy. Among the European Union's Big Five, Britain, the least dependent on Russian gas, was the most hawkish on the Georgian-Russian war, lining up with Washington. All others—France, Germany, Italy, and Spain—refused to condemn Russia. The European Union's collective judgment, delivered by its then president, Sarkozy, was that the war was not an open-and-shut case. By taking a neutral stand, Sarkozy persuaded Prime Minister Putin, the real power in Moscow, to halt the Russian military's march on the Georgian capital, Tbilisi.

Whatever the rights or wrongs of the Georgian-Russian war, it had a negative impact on Russia's standing in the capital markets.

GLOBAL FINANCIAL CRISIS

With the first hint of a fiscal crisis on Wall Street in August 2007, many hedge fund managers started liquidating their assets in stocks and investing the cash into oil, gold, and other commodities. Their move was also a hedge against the dollar, which had been declining for the past two years.

The resulting steep rise in commodity prices benefited Russia, a leading exporter of hydrocarbons and metals. In July 2008, oil hit a record of $147 a barrel. Russia's foreign exchange ballooned to a record $597.50 billion on August 8, 2008—the day Russia responded to Georgia's military move in South Ossetia.

Moscow's excessive military response unnerved foreign investors. Between the Kremlin's move and Lehman Brothers's bankruptcy on September 15, 2008, they withdrew nearly $57 billion from Russia. After that, the pace accelerated. It depressed both Moscow-based stock exchanges—the Moscow Interbank Currency Exchange (Micex) market, where trading is done in five currencies, and the RTS, with its exclusively ruble settlements.

Dominated by Russian and foreign investment funds, RTS and Micex suffered heavily. By the end of the year they plunged 72 percent and 67 percent respectively. But unlike in the United States, where a third of Americans were investors in stock markets, largely through mutual funds, the proportion among Russians was only 3 percent. Medvedev traced the debacle in the Russian stock markets to the contagion originating in America. Echoing his French counterpart, Sarkozy, he announced the end of the era when "one economy and one country dominated [the world]."[41]

Despite repeated minor devaluations of the ruble, Bank Rossii's effort to hold the currency within its prescribed range cost it a quarter of its foreign reserves of nearly $600 billion by the end of 2008. Nonetheless, the year registered 6 percent growth in the GDP. To aid the banking and fiscal sector, the government set aside over $200 billion to be distributed by the state-run VEB Bank

(Vneshekonombank), which was instructed to deny loans to those receiving funds from other sources.[42]

The crisis provided the Kremlin with an opportunity to favor state-owned companies and those private corporations that had cooperated with it in the past while punishing those that had not. It intended to gain more financial control over weakened industries particularly in natural resources, com-modities, and telecom—and thereby further reverse the radical economic changes that followed the dissolution of the Soviet Union. Whether such a transformation wrought by Putin's government would help the Kremlin tackle the problems of rampant corruption, inflation at 13 percent, and rickety health services, not to mention the declining population and flawed judicial system, remained to be seen.

In his inaugural address in May 2008, Medvedev, former chairman of the board of trustees of the Association of Russian Lawyers, had called for a na-tional program for "a true respect of the law" and the dissipation of "legal ni-hilism," which he defined as "corruption in the power bodies." The task he had set for his presidency covered not just the traditional bribe-taking by those in authority but also the subverting of judicial independence by the politi-cians in power. This was indeed a tall order for a government that found it-self on its back foot diplomatically, from the war with Georgia, and economically, as a result of a two-thirds fall in oil prices within five months of their peak in July.

The price plunge left unchanged, however, the rising importance of petro-leum in civilian life as well the military. The quadrupling of oil consumption per American soldier that had occurred between World War II and the 1991 Gulf War quadrupled again between the 1991 conflict and the U.S.-led inva-sion of Iraq a dozen years later.[43]

Historically, the introduction of a tank in 1916 to replace the cavalry radi-cally changed the strategy of warfare. Britain, a leading combatant in World War I, stood to gain. It had ready access to petroleum then being extracted in Iran, the first country in the region to strike oil on a commercial scale. Oil would emerge as the dominant factor to shape not just the economy of Iran, then called Persia, but also its politics. This would be the case also with Venezuela, which, with its successful find of petroleum in 1913, broke the oil monopoly in the Western Hemisphere enjoyed by the United States and Canada since 1858.

CHAPTER 4

IRAN AND VENEZUELA

OIL FUELS DEFIANCE

As a civilization with a six-thousand-year history, Iranians, like Chinese, have a strong sense of themselves and their history. The Persian Empire of the past spanned large areas in the Middle East and Central Asia and clashed with the competing realms of the tsars and the Ottoman Turks. In the modern era, Iran, the core of the Persian Empire, acquired the distinction of being one of the only two Muslim countries that were not colonized either by the Ottoman Turks or by any European nation—the other being Afghanistan.

Little wonder that Iranian nationalism could not accommodate for long the economic imperialism that London came to exercise through the British-owned Anglo-Persian Oil Company (APOC). That company discovered the first commercially viable oil field in the Middle East—at Masjid-e Suleiman—in 1908. Its reserves of more than one billion barrels proved a boon to APOC. It enabled Winston Churchill, the first lord admiral, to build a fleet of oil-fuelled warships to rival the German navy and play an important role in winning World War I. A generation later, commercial oil was found on the Arabian Peninsula, first in Bahrain and then in Kuwait and Saudi Arabia.

Besides imperial Britain, with its empire in the Indian subcontinent and protectorates in the Arabian Peninsula, the other country that had a strong influence on Iran was Russia. In the era before the Bolshevik Revolution, the shahs of Iran were in the habit of borrowing heavily from the tsars to maintain their profligate, royal style. That gave Russia considerable leverage over

Iran. But with the rising importance of oil in Iran, Britain became the un-
contested Big Brother to the shah of Iran.

The refusal of Reza Shah Pahlavi to declare war against Germany even after
Adolf Hitler had invaded the Soviet Union in June 1941 led to his forced abdication in favor of his son, Muhammad Reza, who joined the Allies. Once
World War II ended in the victory of the Allies, who advocated freedom and
independence for all nations, it created an environment in which Iranian nationalism bloomed. It aimed to free Iran from the clutches of the Anglo-
Iranian Oil Company, the renamed APOC.

IRAN'S PIONEERING STEPS

Iran became the first country in the region to emulate the example of Mexico (in 1938) and nationalize its oil industry in 1951, establishing the National
Iranian Oil Company (NIOC). That led to an acute crisis, resulting in the
flight of Muhammad Reza Shah Pahlavi and his restitution following a coup
engineered by the U.S. Central Intelligence Agency, its first such undertaking.
A Western consortium led by American oil corporations took over the management of Iran's oil industry .

In 1960, Iran was one of the six founder members of the Organization of
Oil Exporting Countries (OPEC), with all except Venezuela being in the Gulf
region. Pursuing OPEC's self-reliant policies, the NIOC took over the operations and ownership of the Western oil consortium in July 1973.

After the quadrupling of oil prices in 1973–1974, the Gulf monarchies followed the lead of Iran and nationalized the Western oil companies in their
countries. From then on, state-owned petroleum corporations in oil-bearing
countries became so dominant that by the beginning of the twenty-first century they possessed 87 percent of the world's oil reserves. The remainder, owned
by the Western oil giants, were mostly in North America and Western Europe.

During the 1978–1979 revolutionary movement, it was the strike by oil
workers, starting on December 5, 1978, that deprived the government of three-
quarters of its revenue and made the fall of the pro-Western shah inevitable.
That paved the way for the establishment of an Islamic Republic under the
leadership of Ayatollah Ruhollah Khomeini in February 1979. His unique
achievement was that he succeeded in blending Iranian nationalism with
Islam, and he proved its immense power by toppling a Washington-backed

secular regime that, commanding an armed force of 440,000 soldiers, had appeared rock solid.

Another pioneering idea of Iran was the buyback formula in the oil industry. It stemmed from Article 43 (8) of Iran's constitution, which specified "prevention of foreign economic domination of the country's economy." That meant a ban on giving ownership of land or territorial seabed to foreign entities. This innovative arrangement allowed Iran to pay the guest company in oil and gas to the extent of enabling it an annual rate of return of 15–18 percent on its investment within four to five years. It would be adopted by many other oil-bearing states. Iran's nationalism thus came to benefit a large group of countries at the expense of the Western oil giants—once known as the Seven Sisters, five of them American.[1]

When, violating his promise, President Jimmy Carter decided to let the exiled shah into America in October 1979, the popular mood in Iran turned virulently anti-American. The tension that had existed all along between Iranian nationalism, encompassing Shiite Islam, and the deification of all things American, including secularism and gross materialism, came to the fore and escalated into popular hostility toward the United States.

Urged by Khomeini to intensify a campaign against America, a group of militant students seized the sprawling U.S. Embassy in Tehran and held fifty-three diplomats hostage to be traded for the shah, who had been charged by the Islamic regime with committing crimes against the nation. Carter froze Iran's assets in America, broke off diplomatic ties, and imposed economic sanctions against Tehran.[2]

The loss of Iran, which, along with Israel and Saudi Arabia, had formed a tripod on which Washington's regional policy had rested for the past three decades, was a terrible blow to the United States. In an effort to replace that leg of the tripod, the Carter administration turned eastward and tried to embrace Pakistan closely—an enterprise that was helped by the Soviet Union's military intervention in Afghanistan in December 1979.

Khomeini called Washington's severance of ties a "second revolution," with its focus against America, "the Mother of Corruption"—the first revolution having been against the shah, "a Child of the Mother of Corruption." It aimed to purge American influence that had permeated all facets of life in Iran, except the mosque, as well as Iran's foreign policy, which had led the shah to forge strong diplomatic, economic, and intelligence links with Israel.

The Khomeini regime's breaking of ties with Israel, and handing over of its mission in Tehran to the Palestine Liberation Organization (PLO), went down well not only with his religious followers but also with the young secular left-ists who had backed the revolutionary movement. It was welcomed too by those Arabs who had felt betrayed by Egyptian President Anwar Sadat's bilat-eral peace with Israel in March 1979 at the expense of Arab unity and without the resolution of the Palestinian problem.

Carter's failure to secure the release of the American hostages held by Iran was one of the two main reasons why he lost the 1980 presidential contest to Ronald Reagan, the other being the economic recession caused by a sharp hike in oil prices before and after the Iranian revolution. It was as yet another pi-oneering achievement of Iran, being the first instance where the policies of a Third World leader had an impact on the domestic politics of America.

The release of the American hostages came at the end of the Carter presi-dency in January 1981. His successor, Reagan, promised noninterference in Iran's domestic affairs and lifted economic sanctions against Tehran. These pledges would prove fragile.

Since then, by implementing wrong or misguided policies in the region— from intervening in the Lebanese civil war on the Christian side in 1982 to in-vading Iraq under false pretences in 2003—the White House has fanned anti-U.S. sentiment in the Middle East. Its uncritical support for Israel and its failure to resolve the Israeli-Palestinian conflict have tarnished its image in the region. The 2008 Arab Public Opinion Poll—covering Egypt, Jordan, Lebanon, Morocco, Saudi Arabia, and the United Arab Emirates—by the University of Maryland and Zogby International showed that 50 percent thought that bro-kering a fair Arab-Israeli peace would improve the image of America in the Middle East and North Africa.[3] Conversely, the unresolved Israeli-Palestinian strife has increased support for Tehran's opposition to the American-Israeli alliance in the region.

Periodic attempts at halfhearted reconciliation notwithstanding, the Is-lamic Republic and the United States have been pursuing hostile agendas.

A CONTINUING TUG-OF-WAR

When Iraq, ruled by President Saddam Hussein, attacked Iran in September 1980, the Carter administration put the aggressor and the victim on the same footing and declared itself neutral, secretly hoping for the downfall of the fledgling Khomeini regime. It never happened. The Reagan White House confirmed Carter's neutrality in public but began aiding Iraq covertly with war intelligence on Iran, gathered by its satellites and channeled through Saudi Arabia.

Revolutionary Iran's attempts to ignite republican upsurge in the six Arab Gulf monarchies failed. But it gained support among the Shiites in Lebanon, mired in a civil war between pro-Western, Christian-dominated groups and anti-Western, Muslim-dominated factions, including the PLO. Israel's invasion of Lebanon in June 1982 to expel the PLO from Beirut complicated the situation. It led to the posting of a multinational force, led by the United States, to oversee the evacuation of PLO fighters from Beirut in September.

The Lebanese civil war continued, with the Muslim-dominated camp gaining an upper hand. To reverse the trend, America and France intervened with warplanes and warships on the side of the Christian-dominated Lebanese army in September 1983. This angered the army's local adversaries. On October 23, truck bombing of the U.S. and French military headquarters left 241 American and 59 French troops dead.

In January 1984, suspecting Tehran's hand behind the killings, Washington placed Iran on the list of nations that support international terrorism, thus subjecting it to strict export controls. When the Congress voted for an embargo on all imports from Iran in October 1987, Reagan signed it into law.

By then, Washington had discarded any pretense of neutrality in the Iran-Iraq War, dispatching its navy to the Gulf in support of Iraq's allies, Kuwait and Saudi Arabia. While the ostensible purpose was to escort tankers carrying Kuwaiti oil through the Gulf to foreign destinations, this was an undisguised U.S. tilt toward Baghdad. It was also a move to offset the odium surrounding the Irangate scandal, which was exposed in November 1986. Contrary to its public policy, the United States had clandestinely supplied arms to Iran in exchange for its aid in securing the release of the American hostages held in Lebanon by pro-Iran Shiite groups. The prime mover behind this deal was Israel. Aware that the Iranian military, equipped before the revolution almost exclusively with U.S.-made arms, was in dire need of such weapons and parts, and keen to prolong the war between two anti-Zionist states, Israel deployed one of its leading arms merchant to initiate the process with some "rogue" officials in Reagan's administration. Khomeini had no qualms about securing desperately needed weapons from any source. Realizing that the war had become a unifying force, enabling him to consolidate the Islamic revolution, he wanted to prosecute it as long as he could.

But the U.S. Navy's overt intervention in the conflict, with one of its warships shooting down an Iran Air airbus, carrying 290 people, in July 1988, forced Khomeini to rethink his stance. Also Iraq's widespread use of chemical weapons to regain its territories demoralized the Iranian troops. These developments led Khomeini to accept a year-old UN-brokered cease-fire in August 1988, thus ending the longest conventional war of the twentieth century. He died ten months later.

History took a momentous turn in December 1991, when the Soviet Union disintegrated. With that, its former oil-rich constituents—Azerbaijan and Kazakhstan—became accessible to Western petroleum corporations. As in the past, they needed to follow the broad guidelines laid out by the White House, which remained hostile to Iran.

Washington succeeded in getting the NIOC excluded from the hydrocarbon industry of Azerbaijan, also making sure that none of the pipelines originating in Azerbaijan passed through Iran. In March 1995, President Bill Clinton issued an executive order barring American individuals or companies from working in Iran's oil and gas industry. On April 30 (Remembrance Day in Israel), Clinton announced at the World Jewish Congress meeting in New York that he was banning trade with Iran forthwith. That put a stop to U.S. oil corporations buying $4 billion worth of Iranian crude annually and processing or selling it abroad and to American companies exporting $326 million worth of goods—mainly corn, rice, and oil industry equipment—to Iran.[4] In 1996, the Clinton administration launched its Persian-language program aired by Radio Free Iran in Prague. It ignored Tehran's protest that this was a violation of the 1981 agreement regarding noninterference in Iran's internal affairs.

A BRIEF THAW

The election of Muhammad Khatami, a moderate politician, as president of Iran in 1997 opened a window of opportunity for reconciliation. In a TV interview in January 1998, he said that the period when American diplomats were taken hostage in Tehran was over and that the rule of law must be respected domestically and internationally. His proposal for an exchange of cultural, academic, and sports delegations was accepted by Washington.

But it was not until March 2000 that U.S. Secretary of State Madeleine Albright admitted publicly that Washington had created a climate of mistrust with Iran by "playing a significant role" in the 1953 coup against Iran's democratically elected prime minister, Muhammad Mussadiq, and by providing long-standing support for the dictatorial shah. She regretted the past "shortsightedness" in America's policy.[5]

In October, an American spokesman called for talks between the two governments regarding Iran's support for international terrorism, its program to acquire nuclear weapons, and its opposition to the Middle East peace process. There was no mention of Iran's agenda: to discuss Washington's unremitting drive to dominate the Persian Gulf region and flood it with its weapons, its strategic alliance with Israel, and the unfreezing of Iran's assets of $10–12 billion in American banks.

Nearly a year later, Iran's leaders were quick to condemn the 9/11 attacks on New York and Metropolitan Washington and called on the international community to "take measures to eradicate such crimes." Addressing the Friday prayer congregation in Tehran, Supreme Leader Ayatollah Ali Khamanei said, "Mass killing is a catastrophe wherever it happens and whoever the perpetrators. It is condemned without distinction."[6]

On the eve of America's military campaign against the Taliban on October 7, President George W. Bush sent a confidential memorandum to Iran through the Swiss embassy (charged with representing America's interests), assuring it that the Pentagon would not use Iranian air space. The next day Iran replied that it would rescue any U.S. personnel in distress in its territory, thus implying its de facto membership in the coalition. That day the Bush administration petitioned a federal judge to throw out a $10 billion suit against Iran by the 1979 American hostages. It later transpired that Iran had allowed 165,000 tons of U.S. food aid for the Afghan people to be unloaded at an Iranian airport and shipped through its territory into Afghanistan.[7]

Moreover, Tehran clandestinely shared with Washington its intelligence on the fanatically anti-Shiite Taliban and Al Qaida's Osama bin Laden through back channels. Ever since the Taliban's capture of Kabul in September 1996, Iran, collaborating with Russia, had provided weapons, fuel, technical assistance, and military advisers to the anti-Taliban Northern Alliance based in northern

Afghanistan adjoining Tajikistan. Now Iran instructed the ethnic Tajik warlord Ismail Khan, based in the eastern Iranian city of Mashhad, to coordinate his attack on western Afghanistan with the Pentagon. He did so. The spontaneous jubilation of Kabul's residents that followed the overnight departure of the Taliban from the capital on November 12–13 highlighted the unpopularity of the oppressive Taliban regime, a point repeatedly made by Iran since 1997.

In December 2001, Iran's foreign minister, Kamal Kharrazi, worked actively with U.S. diplomats at a conference near Bonn, Germany, to install Hamid Karzai as leader of the interim government in post-Taliban Afghanistan. Tehran awaited a quid pro quo from Washington—thawing of relations as a start.

Instead, Iran's leaders heard their country described as a member of Bush's "axis of evil" along with Iraq and North Korea in his State of the Union address on January 29, 2002. "Our second goal is to prevent regimes that sponsor terror from threatening America or our friends and allies with weapons of mass destruction. . . . North Korea is a regime arming with missiles and weapons of mass destruction, while starving its citizens. Iran aggressively pursues these weapons and exports terror. . . . Iraq continues to flaunt its hostility toward America and to support terror. . . . States like these, and their terrorist allies, constitute an axis of evil, arming to threaten the peace of the world."[8] This shocked Iranian leaders. They felt angry and betrayed.

They held their breath as the Pentagon prepared to invade Iraq, ruled by Saddam, a bête noire of Iran. His overthrow removed a potentially grave threat to Iran, which was the first victim of his aggression in 1980. They saw Saddam's bronze statue toppled in downtown Baghdad on April 9, 2003.

Three weeks later, Tim Guldimann, the Swiss ambassador in Tehran, faxed Iran's groundbreaking offer to the State Department, explaining in his cover note that it had been seen by Khatami as well as Ali Khamanei. It listed the agendas of both sides, including Iran's nuclear program, for discussion without preconditions and included a list of working groups and road maps.[9]

The hawkish U.S. Vice President Dick Cheney and his aides calculated that the Iranians' offer stemmed from fear and weakness. If so, that enhanced Washington's leverage in its talks, with the Iranians holding weak cards. The timing, therefore, favored the Bush team. Instead of grabbing the offer, Washington said, "We don't talk to Evil." It figured, wrongly, that its removal of Saddam by force would unleash a liberal democratic wave in the region, which would reinforce its bargaining power and isolate Iran. Drunk on the rhetoric of Bush's premature and misleading declaration of "Mission Accomplished," it passed up a real opportunity to resolve a generation-old dispute.

IRAN ON THE UPSWING

What the Bush team did not realize was that, by overthrowing Saddam Hussein's strong centralized regime, it destroyed the zero-sum equation that had existed between Iraq and Iran, which had belonged to competing camps during the Cold War. The 1958 coup against the pro-British Iraqi king, Faisal II, by the Arab nationalist officers friendly with Moscow pitted Baghdad against Tehran, where the pro-American Muhammad Reza Shah Pahlavi had been reinstalled after a CIA coup five years earlier.

The intense rivalry between the neighbors continued during the post-shah period in Iran, even though the Khomeini regime's break with Washington did not lead to its alignment with Moscow. The theocratic nature of Tehran's new government was antithetical to the secular administration of Saddam. So the zero-sum equation between Iran and Iraq remained intact—until Saddam's disastrous invasion of Kuwait in August 1990, followed by the dissolution of the Soviet Union in the following year.

As international pressure against Iraq escalated, Saddam made reluctant peace with Iran, ceding the small Iranian territory Baghdad still held, to secure his battle front in the occupied Kuwait. Yet his deep hatred of Iran and Iranians remained. He wanted Iran's leaders to fear him. The International Atomic Energy Agency (IAEA) inspectors' discovery of Iraq's advanced plans for nuclear arms, following its defeat in the 1991 Gulf War, alarmed Iran.

That was the most probable trigger for the Iranian government to initiate a nuclear weapons program—clandestinely, so as not to violate the nuclear Non-Proliferation Treaty (NPT) it had signed during the shah's rule. Saddam's cat-and-mouse game with UN inspectors for years on end confirmed Tehran's fears that he had a supersecret nuclear project going. Even his senior generals thought so. It was only on the eve of the Pentagon-led invasion of Iraq in March 2003 that Saddam told them that he had no "supersecret" weapon, a confession that led to a large-scale defection of senior officers. The reports of Saddam's disclosure and his generals' defections went a long way to reassure Iran's leaders. And that seemingly led to their abandoning the nuclear arms program, which, in any case, had not progressed beyond theoretical work on the designs of an atom bomb and a warhead.[10]

According to Washington's National Intelligence Estimates released in December 2007, the Iranians ceased the development of nuclear weapons in the autumn of 2003. This conclusion was based on information stored in the laptop of a senior Iranian technician, recruited by the CIA until his arrest in mid-2004. These documents showed theoretical calculations and schematic designs for an atom bomb and a warhead, but provided no proof of actual work in progress.[11] Having damaged their professional reputation on Iraq, CIA and other intelligence officials were cagey about latching on to circumstantial evidence and crying wolf.

At least American intelligence officials had the sagacity to examine their past and learn from it. That could not be said of George W. Bush. He had not bothered to examine what even his father had done earlier in the case of Iraq, and to draw pertinent conclusions.

WAGES OF IGNORING HISTORY

Following the expulsion of the occupying Iraqi forces from Kuwait in February 1991, Bush Senior, leading a coalition of twenty-eight nations, called on Iraqis to rise up against Saddam. The Kurds in the north responded, and so did the Shiites in the south. Bush Senior came to the rescue of the Iraqi Kurds under the guise of the UN Security Council Resolution 688 concerning "the repression of the Iraqi civilian population." By contrast, he allowed Saddam's forces to deploy helicopter gunships to mow down the Shiite rebels in the south. Why?

He and his top aides understood that Saddam's overthrow would end the classic Iraqi-Iranian zero-sum equation. Once the long-suffering Shiite majority in Iraq was in the driver's seat in post-Saddam Iraq, it would ally with the predominantly Shiite Iran.

That is precisely what happened twelve years later. Out of the ashes of Saddam's regime arose a Shiite-dominated government. The U.S.-led overthrow of Iran's enemies to the east (in Afghanistan) and the west (in Iraq) inadvertently prepared the ground for Iran to assume the regionally dominant role its leaders consider logical.

Iran has the largest population in the region, is four times the size of Iraq, shares land and water borders with nine countries, and has a coast that runs along the whole Persian Gulf as well as part of the Arabian Sea, not to mention the landlocked Caspian Sea. It also has the second largest reserves of oil as well as natural gas in the world.

Diplomatically, Iran was riding a wave of political Islam in the Arab world, from Iraq to Egypt via the Palestinian territories. Though the reasons for the rise of Islamist parties varied from country to country, they had one thing in common: most of their citizens lauded the Islamic Republic of Iran for standing up to the U.S.-Israeli partnership.

Tehran was at the center of the Iran-Syria-Hizbullah-Hamas alliance that had succeeded in blocking the implementation of the American-Israeli plans. The opinion polls in the region after Hamas's victory in the Palestinian elections in January 2006 and the Israeli-Hizbullah war in August showed Hassan Nasarallah of Hizbullah, Prime Minister Ismail Haniyeh of Hamas, and President Mahmoud Ahmadinejad of Iran leading the popularity league table. The first-ever municipal elections held in Saudi Arabia on a limited franchise in 2005 resulted in Islamist candidates winning handsomely. And the general elections in Kuwait, held after its liberation by the United States in 1991 on a franchise covering only one-fifth of its citizens, repeatedly ended with Islamists forming either a majority in the parliament or the largest group.[12]

Such political orientation on the Arabian Peninsula and Levant boosted the confidence of the Iranian regime. Its ardent supporters tended to define themselves in opposition to America, which they perceived as a font of global arrogance out of which flowed inequity.

Celebrating the twenty-ninth anniversary of the seizure of the U.S. embassy in Tehran on November 4, 2008 (which happened to be presidential election day in America), Khamanei said that Iran's hatred for America ran deep and that differences between the two went beyond "a few political issues."[13] Referring to Washington's interference in Iran's internal affairs, he demanded an apology. Khamanei's hard line stemmed partly from the strategic partnership that Iran built up with post-Communist Russia.

RELATIONS WITH RUSSIA

Following Khomeini's death in 1989, Iran inked a fifteen-year, $15 billion trade and investment agreement with Moscow, which contained arms transfer and military assistance components of $2 to $4 billion. The following year Iran started receiving MiG-29 fighter jets. Then followed the delivery of three Kilo class submarines.[14]

It was in that context that Russia agreed in principle in 1992 to rehabilitate and finish a civilian nuclear power plant started by the shah at Haleyle, twelve kilometers (seven miles) south of Bushehr port. The initial $800 million contract with the Kremlin to rebuild two 1,000-megawatt, light-water, nuclear-fueled generators, with Iranian participation, was changed to a turnkey agreement in 1998.

In desperate need of foreign exchange, Yeltsin's government rebuffed Washington's pressure to cancel the contract. Nuclear technology was one of its most successful exports, and it had made inroads in several Asian countries, including China and India. It reassured the Clinton administration that its reactors could not be used to produce weapons-grade plutonium, reminding it that along with South Korea it had agreed to supply two similar reactors to North Korea, at a cost of $4.6 billion.

Despite Russia's repeated reassurances to the contrary, America and Israel insisted that Iran, possessing its own uranium ore, was bent on producing nuclear weapons. So they put as many hurdles in Iran's way as they could to gain time to devise, jointly, appropriate response capabilities and doctrines.

While asserting its commitment to prevent proliferation of nuclear weapons, Moscow repeatedly declared that there was no evidence that Iran was working on a nuclear arms program. It felt vindicated when Washington's December 2007 National Intelligence Estimates on the subject concluded that Iranians ceased the development of nuclear weapons in the fall of 2003. A fortnight later, Russia shipped nuclear fuel to Iran under IAEA supervision and seal for the civilian power plant near Bushehr.

During his visit to Tehran in October 2007, President Vladimir Putin referred to the ongoing cooperation between his country and Iran on space, aviation, and energy issues. "Russia is the only country that is helping Iran to realize its nuclear program in a peaceful way," he said.[15]

After several delays and hiccups, Russian and Iranian engineers started testing the nuclear plant using simulated fuel rods of lead, instead of nuclear fuel, on February 25, 2009, with a plan to commission the power station fully by the end of the year.

Earlier, as a result of Iran's failure to provide a full account of its nuclear program to the International Atomic Energy Agency (IAEA), its case had been referred to the UN Security Council. The Council demanded that Iran should suspend enrichment of uranium. Tehran ignored the demand. In December 2006, in exchange for Washington dropping its opposition to Russia's supplying the Bushehr power plant with nuclear fuel, the Kremlin agreed to support a U.S.-sponsored resolution for minor economic sanctions against Iran—under Article 41 of the UN Charter's Chapter VII. This article specifies "measures *not* involving the use of armed force," and it is Article 42 that allows the use of "air, sea or land forces" to maintain or restore international peace and security. A second Security Council resolution in March 2007 reiterated the earlier one. And a third resolution in March 2008 extended the financial sanctions to a few more individuals and organizations. In October 2008, Russia, backed by China, refused to consider any further economic penalties on Iran, which continued to enrich uranium, as was its right under the NPT. The Kremlin calculated, rightly, that if Iran was pushed too hard, it would follow the example of North Korea, quit the NPT and expel IAEA inspectors—an eventuality it wanted to avoid at all costs.

Meanwhile, commercial and military ties between the two neighbors strengthened. Tehran increased its purchases of advanced Russian weaponry, including S-300 surface-to-air, anti-aircraft missiles that can track and hit an aircraft a hundred miles away, according to Esmail Kosari, deputy head of the parliament's committee for Foreign Affairs and National Security.[16] In the economic field, Iran worked closely with the Kremlin to forge an international organization of natural gas producers. At its initiative a Gas Exporting Countries Forum (GECF) was formed in 2001, with its liaison office in Doha, Qatar, to exchange information among its members. At their seventh annual meeting in December 2008 in Moscow, presided over by Putin, GECF's fourteen members decided to adopt a charter. It included ways of "influencing" global prices for gas and coordinating investment plans to dissuade members from flooding the market.[17] The official denials notwithstanding, the GECF is set to become a gas cartel like its oil counterpart OPEC.

MULTIFARIOUS CHALLENGE TO AMERICA

Iran's natural gas reserves are so abundant that, at its current annual output of 112 billion cubic meters, it will take 450 years to exhaust them. At the production rate of 4.4 million bpd in 2007, its petroleum reserves will last until

2095. These hydrocarbon riches make the Islamic Republic particularly attractive to energy-hungry China. In December 2007, the China National Petrochemical Corporation, known as Sinopec, signed a $2 billion contract to develop Iran's Yadavaran oil field.[18]

Iran's annual oil income soared to $65 billion in 2007, enabling it to fulfill its promises of aid to the Hamid Karzai administration in Afghanistan ($560 million) and the Nouri al Maliki government in Iraq ($1 billion). Iran was the first country to offer aid to the Hamas authorities in Gaza when they were sanctioned by America and the European Union. It has continued to help the cash-strapped regime in Damascus. The funds to Hizbullah in Lebanon flow both from the official coffers as well as from generously endowed religious foundations in Iran.

Though no match for the military might of the United States or its technology and industry, Iran poses a threat to Washington's interests in a region that holds three-fifths of the world's oil deposits and two-fifths of its gas reserves. It provides an alternative to royal autocracies in the Gulf with a republican model based on the tenets of Islam, which enjoin a representative government. The Islamic Republic's continued existence as a viable, even thriving, political entity poses a threat to Washington's plans to export secular liberal democracy to the region. Iran shows how nationalism, Islam, and representative government can work in harmony and remain viable in a world of competing versions of democracy.

Its continued ability to defend itself with its own resources—it fought a long war with Iraq without borrowing a penny abroad—tarnishes the image of the Muslim monarchies in the region, which, despite their oil and gas riches, cling to the coattails of the Pentagon for their security, both external and internal. It demonstrates to the hereditary rulers in the Arabian Peninsula that it is perfectly possible—indeed desirable—to come together in a regional alliance and provide security to all its members without relying on an outside power.

The threat that Iran poses to Washington's hegemony in the planet's most strategic region is serious and a challenge to America's status as the self-appointed policeman of the globe. Another country that has made an adroit use of its oil income and poses a serious challenge to U.S. hegemony in the Western hemisphere is Venezuela under President Hugo Chavez.

Iran and Venezuela were the first in their respective regions to strike oil on a commercial scale, with Venezuela's pioneering oil field operated by Royal

Dutch Shell in 1913. As members of OPEC, Iran and Venezuela advocate hard-line policies, including replacing the greenback with the euro as the currency in which petroleum is traded internationally. In mid-2006, they agreed to joint production of a dozen products, from oil to automobiles, with Iran's Petropars company pledging to invest $4 billion in Venezuela's hydrocarbon industry. A year later, Iranian-designed cars and tractors were coming off the assembly lines in Venezuela. Direct flights between Tehran and Caracas helped rein-force ties.

VENEZUELA, THE RISE OF AN OIL STATE

During the 1920s, dominated by the presidency of General Juan Vincente Gomez, infamous for his generous tax concessions to foreign companies in re-turn for kickbacks, Venezuela's petroleum output increased tenfold, to 380,000 bpd. It became the globe's second largest oil producer after the United States. Petroleum accounted for three-quarters of its export earnings. As the main en-gine of development, oil, extracted mainly by two foreign corporations—one American and the other British—became intertwined with Venezuela's ex-ternal policy and internal politics, as was the case also with Iran.

Even since Venezuela's independence from Spain in 1811, the generals have frequently mounted coups to usurp supreme power. Gomez, who first seized the presidency in 1908, staged his third coup in 1931. It was only after his final exit from politics four years later that the civilian governments tried to re-dress the imbalance in Venezuela's relationship with foreign oil corporations. They succeeded. The Petroleum Law of 1943 required these firms to pay half of their profits, *before* the deduction of foreign taxes, as local corporation tax.

A decade-long civilian rule ended with a coup by a revolutionary military junta in 1945. It appointed Rómulo Betancourt, the founder of the left-of-center Democratic Action Party, as president. His strict enforcement of the Petroleum Law inspired the rulers in the Persian Gulf region to follow suit. And his declaration of universal suffrage paved the way for all adult citizens to elect the president.

His bold move did not secure a firm footing for a democratic setup, though. His successor, Rómulo Gallegos, who won three-quarters of all votes, was overthrown by General Marcos Pérez Jiménez in 1948. After letting a couple of his nominees act as presidents, Perez Jiménez ordered an election in 1952, which he contested. When the early results showed him losing, he stopped the counting and declared himself president. Yet his fanatical anti-Communism and cozying up with foreign oil companies won him the Legion of Merit in 1954 from President Dwight Eisenhower. (A year earlier, Eisenhower had ordered the CIA to overthrow the democratically elected government of Muhammad Mussadiq in Iran.)

During Pérez Jiménez's rule, petroleum output doubled by 1957. But, the bulk of the oil income was siphoned off by the privileged elite, leaving little to benefit the masses. Support for the brutal dictator petered out even within the officer corps of the navy and air force. Though a coup by air force officers in January 1958 failed, it led to a popular uprising, triggered by the clandestine Patriotic Front of politicians allied with disaffected military officers. The Front overthrew Pérez Jiménez.

On his return from exile, Betancourt was elected president by popular vote. His inauguration in early 1959 would mark the end of military putsches in Venezuela, with the Democratic Action Party and the right-of-center Social Christian Party dominating electoral politics, often deploying patronage and fraud. Under his watch, Venezuela became a founder-member of OPEC in 1960.

Contrary to the general perception that it was OPEC's decision during the October 1973 Arab-Israeli War to stop oil supplies to the Western countries backing Israel, and reduce its overall output, it was the Organization of Arab Oil Exporting Countries (OAPEC), formed in 1968 with its headquarters in Kuwait, that made that decision. So the non-Arab members of OPEC—Iran and Venezuela—continued their exports as before to America and the Netherlands, deemed hostile by OAPEC.[19]

Just as the rise of Ayatollah Khomeini in Iran was related, in the final analysis, to the vagaries of a country's overdependence on its oil resources, so too was the emergence in Venezuela of Hugo Chavez, the bête noire of Washington in Latin America. The mid-1970s splurge in revenue created by the quadrupling of oil prices shaped the economic—as well as political—histories of both countries.

Iran's Muhammad Reza Shah Pahlavi unleashed an overambitious program of industrialization and construction, vowing to make Iran the fourth most powerful nation after America, the Soviet Union, and Japan. Iran's GDP rose by 34 percent in 1974 and by 42 percent in 1975. The overheated economy induced massive migration of villagers to urban centers and fueled inflation. When the government curtailed spending and controlled prices, recession followed. It caused popular discontent. In the absence of secular opposition, brutally suppressed by the shah, it fell to the mosque and its leaders, who could not be silenced, to voice the grievances of the disaffected masses.

That is where Iran's history diverged from that of Venezuela, with its tradition of military officers intervening in the political process. After all, Simón Bolívar (1783–1830), who liberated six South American countries from Spanish rule during the second decade of the nineteenth century,[20] was a general.

In Venezuela, the benefits of the dramatic spike in oil prices accrued to the presidency of Carlos Andres Pérez (1974–1979). Following the example of the Gulf monarchies, which nationalized the Western oil corporations operating in their countries since the 1930s, Pérez placed the hydrocarbon industry in the public sector. To great popular applause, the state-owned Petroleos de Venezuela, S.A. (PdVSA) took over 11,000 oil wells, eleven refineries, fourteen tankers, and port terminals as well as pipelines after the government had compensated the foreign corporations adequately.[21]

Like the shah of Iran, Pérez embarked on many long-term industrial projects. To finance them, his government took out short-term loans. Many ministries and public institutions borrowed without congressional approval. Given the endemic government corruption and mismanagement, a lot of money disappeared into the pockets of senior civil servants.

During the election campaign of 1978, the opposition Social Christian Party's candidate, Luis Herrera, raised an effective slogan, "Where is the money?" He won. But instead of cutting state expenditure as promised, he increased it. This reversal was related to the events in Iran. The Islamic revolution of 1979 followed by the Iran-Iraq War in 1980 led to the trebling of the price of oil to $39 a barrel.

But the record-high cost of oil depressed demand for it, leading to a steep price decline. Venezuela's currency, the bolivar, pegged to the U.S. dollar, came under pressure. Herrera bit the bullet and devalued it in February 1983. Recession followed. The GDP fell by 6 percent, as unemployment doubled to 14 percent. The external debt, at $34.2 billion, stood at double the figure for 1978. Penury and hardship became widespread.

It was then that the seeds of disaffection with the post-Betancourt era began to grow roots. Prominent among those who accelerated the process was Hugo Chavez, a twenty-seven-year-old army captain appointed an in-structor at the nation's military academy in 1981. He hero-worshiped Bolívar, a Caracas-born general. Bolívar's statues abound in Venezuela, and his name graces highways, public buildings, and stadiums. Two years later, Chavez set up the clandestine Revolutionary Bolivarian Movement-200 (MBR-200) in the military.

THE MAKING OF THE BOLIVARIAN REVOLUTION

As a military instructor, Chavez imbued politically promising cadets with the anti-imperialist ideology of Bolívar, who had strived to create a united, inde-pendent Latin America. By the time Chavez's cadets had graduated in 1985, he had many MBR-200 Bolivarian cells in the military.

Meanwhile, the economy had deteriorated further under the presidency of Herrera's successor, Jamie Lusinchi of the Democratic Action Party. Oil prices fell below $10 a barrel in 1986. His repeated devaluation of the bolivar fueled inflation and budget deficits. His attempt to alleviate the situation by raising salaries and controlling prices failed. So voters looked forward to the return of Carlos Andres Pérez as president, hoping he would re-create the booming Venezuela of the mid-1970s. This was not to be.

Having denounced the IMF as "a neutron bomb that killed people but left buildings standing" during his election campaign, Pérez turned to it for a $4.5 billion loan within weeks of assuming office in early February 1989. It came with the strings of the "Washington Consensus" firmly attached. The subse-quent shock therapy—encapsulated in the immediate doubling of gasoline price and bus fares—caused massive rioting and looting in Caracas and else-where on February 27, 1989.

Pérez declared an emergency, imposed martial law, and called out the troops to restore order. By the time they and the armed police had succeeded in their mission, three days later, an estimated 500 to 1,500 people were dead. The brutal episode, called the Caracacazo (meaning "Caracas smashed"), left the nation traumatized and the Betancourt-era democratic model severely devalued. The ranks of the clandestine MBR-200 swelled.

Sporadic rioting and looting broke out throughout the next year, with the army being ordered to shoot the unarmed rioters. Pérez's deregulation of the banking sector led to the collapse of more than half of the banks from embezzlement and fraud, with scores of bankers fleeing with depositors' funds. The gap between the affluent few and the indigent many grew wider. Kleptocracy thrived.

Under lieutenant-colonel Chavez's leadership, the MBR-200 movement gained recruits from within the presidential honor guard at the official Miraflores Palace. On the night of February 3–4, 1992, MBR-200 rebels struck. They captured the Miraflores Palace. But Pérez escaped through the underground garage and went on the air in the middle of the night. This demoralized the rebels. The loyalist troops arrested Chavez, but he was allowed to appeal on TV to the remaining resisting rebels outside the capital to surrender. Overnight, he became the face of the rebellion.

Nine months later, while Chavez languished in a prison, his associates attempted to seize power again. They failed—but only after they had broadcast a videotape of Chavez announcing the government's downfall. Then the wheel of fortune turned. In May 1993, the Supreme Court found Pérez guilty of misappropriating 250 million bolivars from the president's discretionary fund. After his dismissal by the National Assembly, he spent two years in jail.

Following the trauma of the Caracacazo in 1989, two failed coup attempts, and the president's impeachment, voters turned to the healing figure of the seventy-eight-year-old Rafael Caldera in the presidential race. He won by a narrow majority as the leader of a new party, National Convergence, which he had formed after leaving the Social Christian Party.[22] Caldera's victory ended the duopoly on power the two main parties had enjoyed for three and a half decades. Within weeks of his inauguration in February 1994, Caldera dismissed the charges against Chavez and other coup leaders who had not been tried.

FROM PUTSCH TO POLITICS

Chavez and his comrades set up the left-of-center Movement for the Fifth Republic (MVR).[23] The main features of its Bolivarian ideology were anti-imperialism, meaning political and economic sovereignty; participatory democracy; economic self-sufficiency; equitable distribution of oil revenue; and elimination of corruption. Once its leaders registered MVR as a political party with the National Electoral Council in July 1997, it became the electoral front of the semiclandestine MBR-200.

Starting with a mere 11 percent backing in the opinion polls in early 1998, Chavez gained popularity with his vow to lead a nonviolent revolution of the underprivileged: He would radically change the status quo by getting an elected constituent assembly to rewrite the constitution. The collapse of oil prices to below $10 a barrel, creating a huge budget deficit and hyperinflation of 800 percent, helped his cause. He won 56 percent of the vote—almost twice as much as Caldera and well ahead of his rival Romer Salas of the Social Christian Party, with 40 percent.

Street dancing and jubilation by the poor at large contrasted with the silent despair that descended on the upscale neighborhoods of Caracas and other urban centers. The rich and well-off, almost always of pure Spanish descent, despised Chavez—a dark-skinned son of schoolteachers, born in a mud hut near a provincial town, with mixed Amerindian, African, and Spanish blood. In the continental context, Chavez's rise in Venezuela would be a harbinger of a profound change in South America, with the Amerindian, African, and mixed-race communities asserting their collective strength through the ballot to end the traditional white settler monopoly over power since the colonization of the continent by Spain.

On assuming the presidency in February 1999, Chavez and his oil minister, Rafael Ramirez, convinced other OPEC members and four non-OPEC countries—Mexico, Norway, Oman, and Russia—to cut output. They did, and prices rose.

Chavez was reelected in July 2000 with a higher vote than before under a new constitution—containing fresh provisions for presidential recall and the public defender to oversee the actions of the president and the National Assembly—passed by a thumping majority in a referendum. His government initiated land reform, made education free up to university level, and introduced a publicly funded health care system.

As chairman of OPEC, Chavez visited UN-sanctioned Baghdad during his tour of the capitals of all OPEC states to invite Saddam Hussein to an OPEC summit in Caracas on the organization's fortieth founding anniversary in September. His defiance of the Clinton administration's warning about visiting Baghdad set the tone of his foreign policy. Most OPEC leaders attended the summit, which decided to maintain the $22–28 price range for an oil barrel.[24]

Venezuela agreed to supply twelve Caribbean and Central American countries with oil at $20 a barrel, giving them fifteen years to pay with 2 percent interest. Chavez thus gained the diplomatic backing of the Caribbean and Central American states to the detriment of Washington, which, since the days of the Monroe Doctrine of 1823, has treated this region and South America as its backyard.

After World War II, the CIA carried out successful coups against Jacobo Arbenz in 1954 in Guatemala and Salvador Allende in 1973 when they attempted land reform. Washington violated the sovereignty of Cuba in 1961 with its failed Bay of Pigs campaign, of the Dominican Republic in 1965 by overthrowing President Juan Bosch, of Grenada in 1983 by toppling the popularly elected prime minister Maurice Bishop, and of Panama in 1989 by overthrowing its ruler, General Manuel Noriega.

The steady recovery of oil prices raised Venezuela's GDP growth to 4 percent by the end of 2001, while slashing its inflation to 12 percent, the lowest rate in fifteen years. The fact that his country continued to be the fourth largest supplier of oil to the United States, after Canada, Mexico, and Saudi Arabia, emboldened Chavez to challenge and insult U.S. President George W. Bush with impunity. He got away with calling him Mr. Danger,[25] a drunk, and a fool.

Unlike Fidel Castro, who ruled an offshore island, Chavez was the elected leader of an oil-rich country on South America's mainland. And since Chavez was not an orthodox Communist like Castro, Washington could not paint him in detestable colors. Nor could he be decried as an atheist, since he was a practicing Catholic who argued that Jesus Christ was the first socialist. He could not be dismissed as a dictator. He played by the rules of representative democracy. He came to power through the ballot, held frequent referendums on matters of import, and accepted the voters' verdict even when it went against his wishes—as in the 2007 referendum on the sixty-one changes to the constitution, including the one abolishing the two-term limit on the presidency.

LOCKING HORNS WITH MR. DANGER

Chavez's relations with the Bush administration soured when Washington welcomed his arrest and overthrow in a coup by dissident generals and opposition media tycoons on April 12, 2002—an operation that failed two days later. This happened partly because a million people from the poor neighborhoods of Caracas demanded his release and partly because all other Latin

American capitals refused to recognize the post-Chavez government. Whereas the inhabitants of the barrios of the capital had demonstrated and rioted before, most notably in 1989, this was the first time that they succeeded in changing the fate of their country through direct action.

The episode damaged Washington's standing in the Western hemisphere. It showed that the Bush administration's commitment to democracy was skin-deep. It stood out as the only government in the Western hemisphere to applaud the toppling of a democratically elected leader by the military.

To the White House's consternation, the popular, progressive policies of Chavez were presenting a viable alternative to the American free-market package offered to Central and South American countries. It felt a need to quash the Bolivarian revolution as it had done to similar movements in the past—from those of Arbenz in the early 1950s, Bosch in the mid-1960s, Allende in the early 1970s, and the Sandinistas in Nicaragua in the 1980s.

Used to having its way in its backyard, the United States was unwilling to give up. It instigated Chavez's opponents to strike again—this time nonviolently. Responding to the anti-Chavez leaders' calls for a general strike in December 2002, the union officials of the PdVSA brought production almost to a halt. Chavez assumed total control and replaced the old guard with loyalists. The strike petered out as 2003 unrolled. In 2004, the PdVSA's output returned to the prestrike level. Venezuela reverted to being the globe's fourth largest oil exporter after Saudi Arabia, Russia, and Iran.

In June 2005, under his newly unveiled PetroCaribe Initiative, Chavez offered petroleum at discount rates to fifteen states in the region. The benefiting countries' support for Venezuela was on display at the fourth summit of the thirty-four-strong Organization of American States (OAS) at Mar Del Plata, near Buenos Aires, in November.

Chavez stole the show both at the summit table and at the soccer stadium filled with 25,000 supporters. Appearing alongside Argentine soccer idol Diego Maradona, Chavez described the stadium as "the grave site of the Free Trade Area of the Americas" (FTAA). Having announced a $10 billion antipoverty program in the rest of the Americas, Bush arrived in Mar Del Plata confident to witness the signing of the neoliberal FTAA, which aimed to turn the Americas into a free-trade zone dominated by the United States. It did not happen.[26]

Chavez provided a striking contrast to Bush. While Bush was obtuse and set in his ways, Chavez was endowed with an acute, yet supple, mind. Above all, unlike Bush, he learned from his mistakes and was flexible while not losing sight of the ultimate objective. Whereas Bush was fond of offering short quips, Chavez entertained his audience with long speeches filled with robust humor, which went down well with his underprivileged audience.

Instead of merely attacking Washington's move on trade, Chavez had come up with an alternative. He used the signing of the People's Trade Agreement with Cuba to exchange the supply of Cuban doctors and teachers with Venezuela's sale of 96,000 bpd of oil at a discount in December 2004 to launch *Alternativa Bolivariana para los Pueblos de Nuestra América* (Bolivarian Alternative for the People of Our America, or ALBA, meaning "dawn" in Spanish). ALBA aimed higher than economic integration of Latin America and the Caribbean, its ultimate goal being sociopolitical integration.

At Mar Del Plata, Bush, though conversant in Spanish, often found himself out of the loop at the conference. Disappointed, he departed before the end, letting a cocky Chavez declare, "The great loser today was George W. Bush."[27] By now Chavez had learned to frame the issues facing Latin America in a Joan of Arc fashion, portraying himself to be fighting for his native continent.

His message of anti-imperialism and resistance to the Washington Census reverberated through more and more countries in Latin America and the Caribbean. Venezuela under his rule provided an appealing alternative to the centuries-old, Washington-dominated model just as Iran did in the Middle East with a working model of Islam married to democracy.

Chavez did not have to work hard to prove his case against the Washington Consensus. Between 1960 and 1980, the per capita income in South America increased by 82 percent. But after the introduction of the "free-market revolution" in 1980, the per capita income over the next twenty-five years rose by a mere 10 percent.[28]

Under Chavez's watch, the GDP growth rose from 4 percent in 2001 to 10.3 percent in 2006, with the poverty rate declining to 33 percent from 43 percent in 1999.[29] Remarkably, by some calculations, the private sector in 2006 accounted for a larger share of the GDP than before Chavez's presidency.

Chavez remained tuned to the needs of underprivileged Venezuelans. In 2006 his government deposited $10 billion into a fund for social programs, called Bolivarianism, up from $8 billion in 2005. The program involved introducing free health care to seven out of ten Venezuelans, provided largely by 20,000 Cuban doctors; launching a mass literacy campaign; distributing subsidized food and medicine to three out of five Venezuelans; and funding eye surgery for a quarter million people. Its overall aim was to reduce poverty to below 30 percent, a target it met.[30]

In his drive to alleviate poverty, Chavez broke new ground, much to the embarrassment of the Bush administration: He lent a hand to assist the poor in the United States. His government offered to ship 12 million gallons of heating oil to low-income families in Massachusetts through CITGO, the Houston-based subsidiary of PdVSA—a scheme arranged by local congressman William Delahunt. The fuel was sold at 40 percent below market prices to deserving families during winter. The scheme was applied to twenty-three states and covered 200,000 households. It cost $100 million a year.[31]

What the Bush White House found even more galling was to realize that during Chavez's seven-plus years of presidency, Venezuela's foreign aid exceeded the nearly $2 billion the United States allocated for its development programs and drug war in Latin America.[32] Because of the 500 percent rise in oil prices during that period, Caracas could afford to give $16 billion in foreign aid or subsidies to more than thirty countries, ranging from Indonesia to Argentina to Cuba, while simultaneously shoring up its own foreign exchange reserves. By purchasing $2.5 billion of Argentina's debt, Chavez enabled left-leaning Argentine President Nestor Kirchner to clear the IMF loan of $9.8 billion. Venezuela's subsidies included free eye surgeries for poor Mexican Amerindians and Nicaraguans.

Chavez's ALBA project took off. Bolivia joined it in April 2006, followed by Nicaragua, Honduras, and Ecuador. Along with three Caribbean countries, total ALBA membership rose to eight. With the election of Mauricio Funes of the Farabundo Marti National Liberation Front as president of El Salvador in March 2009, ALBA will most likely acquire its ninth member.

Chavez assisted not only President Evo Morales of Bolivia but also the freshly elected President Daniel Ortega in Nicaragua. And his friendship with Cuba and its leaders, Fidel and Raul Castro, remained strong. In a riposte aimed at Bush, he went on to describe these countries forming "the Axis of Good."[33]

Chavez's policies received a popular mandate when he got reelected in December 2006, winning 61 percent of the vote, with his sole rival, Manuel Rosales of the Democratic Action Party, trailing at 38 percent.

Driven by Bolívar's Dreams

Chavez inherited a nation that was a founder-member of the eleven-strong Latin American Integration Association (ALADI, *Asociación Latinoamericana de Integración*), established in 1980. It was a free-trade zone but limited only to goods. It did not require coordination of policies by the member-states. Since then it has become an umbrella under which subregional organizations have emerged to create a common economic area.

Prominent among these is the *Mercado Comun del Sur* (Mercosur, Common Market of the South), formed by Argentine, Brazil, Paraguay, and Uruguay in 1994 to promote free movement of goods, people, and currencies. It was badly damaged by Argentina's fiscal crisis of 2001. Since then it has acquired Bolivia, Chile, Colombia, Ecuador, and Peru as associate members.

In 2006 the Chavez government signed an agreement for Mercosur membership. With the ratification of the pact by three of the four parliaments of Mercosur members by 2009, Venezuela was on track to participate in its parliament in 2010.[34]

Chavez's proposal to establish a Bank of the South as a Latin American version of the IMF was accepted when leaders of twelve South American nations decided in May 2008 to form the Union of South American Nations (*Unión de Naciones Suramericanas*, UNASUR) by combining Mercosur and the four-member Andean Community, formed in 1969. They agreed to give judicial and political dimensions to the union—as the European Union had done before. The European Union was to be the model for UNASUR. Its headquarters will be in Quito, Ecuador, and its bank, the Bank of the South, in Caracas.

These leaders also planned to create a military coordinating component to be called *Conselho Sul-Americano de Defensa* (Council of South American Defense, CSD) with an increasingly NATO-like structure. Brazilian defense minister Nelson Jobim described the basic tenets of the CSD as an integrated alliance without an operating field capability. The CSD will coordinate military technology and resources on South America's mainland. Chavez is a strong backer of the CSD and visualizes it as a powerful tool to block the Pentagon's military forays into South America.

Nothing illustrates the sea change on the continent better than the policies of former trade union leader Luyiz Inacio Lula da Silva, president of

Brazil, the giant of South America in area, population, and GDP. In December 2008 he chaired the meeting of thirty-one countries of Latin America and the Caribbean at the Brazilian tourist resort of Sauipe, which—for once—excluded the United States and the European Union, but included Cuba. Condemning America and the European Union for causing the fiscal turmoil that was "roiling" the region, the assembled leaders demanded a role in creating a solution.[35]

Instead of going to the World Economic Forum at Davos, Switzerland, as he had done in the past, Da Silva appeared at the Eighth World Social Forum, attended by representatives of fifty-nine countries, in Belem at the mouth of the Amazon River. Also present were the presidents of Bolivia, Ecuador, Paraguay, and Venezuela. The Forum's theme, appropriately, was "Another world is possible." Da Silva attacked North American and European bankers for their casino mentality, which had brought about the global fiscal meltdown.[36] At the Forum there was a strong presence of Amerindians, who spoke eloquently and confidently.

THE "NATIVES" DISCOVER POWER OF THE BALLOT

Hugo Chavez's electoral victory in 2006 symbolized more than the effectiveness of his type of leadership. The earlier electoral success of Evo Morales, an Amerindian, signified that after centuries of second-class citizenship at the bottom of the heap topped by European immigrants, the descendants of Amerindians and African slaves had begun wielding their franchise to seize power from white settlers.

Having won the presidency, Morales held a referendum on the new constitution in January 2009. In contrast to the old version, which formalized subjugation of indigenous people, the latest document reserved seats for Amerindians in Parliament and bureaucracy. It won 60 percent of the vote.[37] This was a remarkable achievement for Amerindians, who were deprived of the franchise until the mid-1950s and were even barred from crossing the plaza in front of the presidential palace in La Paz.

Besides Venezuela and Bolivia, the rise of "the natives" became manifest in Colombia, Peru, and Paraguay and was set to continue no matter what happened to Chavez. That alarmed the United States, the traditional ally of the privileged white settlers in the Western hemisphere, more than the insults hurled at Bush by Chavez at home and abroad.

"Yesterday, ladies and gentlemen, from this rostrum, the president of the United States, the gentleman to whom I refer as the Devil, came here, talking as if he owned the world," Chavez said, addressing the UN General Assembly in September 2006. He added that he could smell the sulfur the Devil had left behind at the podium where he stood. At the end of his speech, he received the loudest and longest applause, exceeding four minutes, which was eventually cut off by UN officials.[38]

Chavez possessed an uncanny talent for displaying realpolitik behind closed doors and entertaining ribaldry in public. His knowledge was impressive. In a single speech he would move seamlessly from Bolívar to Bertolt Brecht, Castro to Christ, and Karl Marx to Miguel de Unamuno, a Spanish philosopher.

In its dealings with Chavez, the Bush White House was at a disadvantage. Venezuela was the fourth largest source of imported oil for America, and many refineries in the United States were designed specifically to refine heavy Venezuelan oil.

In South America, Chavez continued to outshine Bush. He upstaged Bush's tour of five Latin American states regarded friendly to Washington in March 2007 by simultaneously undertaking a tour of Argentina, Bolivia, and other countries. The local and regional media covered Chavez's foreign visits more fully than Bush's.

The Bush administration's attempt to show Chavez evolving into a dictator failed when in 2007 he immediately accepted the voters' wafer-thin rejection of the constitutional amendments, including the one removing the two-term limit on serving as president, he had presented them.

While sounding confident and defiant, Chavez remained alert to the prospect of an invasion by the Pentagon to effect "regime change" in Caracas. Leaving nothing to chance, he introduced a program to give weapons training to 500,000 civilians to be armed ultimately with Kalashnikovs, either purchased from Russia or manufactured at home under license. To dissuade the United States from attacking Venezuela, its oil minister Ramirez warned that in that eventuality, PdVSA would stop its exports, thus spiking already high oil prices, and would take its petroleum away from the United States and sell it elsewhere.

CHAVEZ TURNS TO MOSCOW

After his reelection in 2006, Chavez adopted the policy that Putin had been pursuing since his reelection in 2004—pressuring, successfully, Western oil companies to rewrite the contracts that Russia had signed during the disastrous mid-1990s. Chavez decreed that by May 1, International Workers' Day, the PdVSA should acquire a minimum stake of 60 percent in the projects in the Orinoco River basin (370 miles by 43 miles) and invite the current Western oil corporations operating there to remain as minority stakeholders. The foreign companies were to get their compensation in oil instead of cash—thus following the example of Iran, which had pioneered this method of payment in the late 1980s. In the Orinoco region of Venezuela foreign oil companies were upgrading tarlike crude into more sellable petroleum and thus compensating the declining output of the older fields containing conventional oil.

On May 1, 2007, amid jubilant scenes, all six foreign petroleum corporations ceded operational control to oil employees of PdVSA, wearing trademark red shirts emblazoned with "Yes to Nationalization," with Exxon doing so under protest.[39]

Faced with Chavez's undiminished truculence and his relentless drive to undermine Washington's influence in the continent, the Bush administration needed to react. It did. Having alleged earlier that Venezuela was not cooperating with its war on drugs and having stopped the sale of spare parts for the U.S.-made F-16 fighter jets, it extended the ban. In May 2006, alleging noncooperation by Caracas in its fight against terrorism, it embargoed weapons sales to Venezuela altogether.

The Pentagon's ban on the sale of spare parts for U.S.-supplied warplanes led Chavez to turn to the Kremlin for arms. During his visit to Moscow in July he placed $1 billion worth of orders for twenty-four Sukhoi-30 fighter jets, fifteen armed helicopters, and 100,000 Kalashnikov assault rifles to replace old Belgian FALs, and received a license to produce Kalashnikovs in Venezuela. Further orders for Russian arms followed.

By 2007, Venezuela had become the second largest buyer of Russian weaponry, after Algeria. During his next visit to Moscow, besides ordering more fighter jets, armed helicopters, and assault rifles, Chavez finalized a $1 billion deal to purchase five diesel submarines to defend Venezuela's oil-rich undersea shelf and thwart any possible future economic embargo imposed by Washington.

In Minsk, Belarus, he put the final touches to the purchase of an air defense system with long-range radar and missiles. The goal of strengthening Venezuela's military defenses was to deter imperialist aggression, he explained. Through these defense and other contracts, Chavez was aiming to crystallize forces opposed to Washington.

Visiting Moscow for the sixth time in July 2008, Chavez signed an arms deal worth $1 billion, including twenty S-300 Tor-M1 anti-aircraft missiles capable of tracking and hitting an aircraft a hundred miles away, three diesel-powered submarines, and Ilyushin warplanes. Russia's Lukoil and TNK-BP Oil signed contracts with PdVSA to explore oil reserves in Orinoco Valley, while Gazprom agreed to explore the area for gas. Chavez called for a strategic partnership with Russia to defend Venezuela against the aggressive threats of Washington. In March 2009, he invited Russia's strategic bombers to use La Orchila Island's airfield.[40]

Just as the rocketing prices of oil during the first half of 2008 boosted Chavez's ego and rhetoric, the subsequent plunge in the cost of petroleum in the second half of the year had a contrary effect. Venezuela ended its $100 million program to help poor households in almost half of the states of America. His government had to curtail its expenditure on social welfare while battling to bring down inflation of 30 percent and fight endemic corruption, which ranked Venezuela 138th out of 163 countries.

Yet, urged by Chavez, 54.6 percent of the voters backed the abolition of the term limit on the president—as well as governors and mayors—in a referendum in February 2009, thus exceeding their opponents by almost 1 million ballots.

At OPEC meetings, Venezuela advocated deep cuts in production in line with the depressed demand caused by the global recession, which originated in the United States. While the low price of oil worried the Chavez government, he and other radicals in Latin America were full of schadenfreude to see the much-hyped "Washington Consensus" meet its doom and shake the foundations of Reaganite capitalism.

A firm believer in advance thinking, Chavez had begun planning for the day when the United States decided not to import Venezuelan crude—and turned to China. In August 2006, during his fourth visit to China since 1999,

Chavez revealed that Venezuela's oil exports to China would treble in three years to 500,000 bpd. He described Beijing's support as politically and morally significant. In this case, geopolitics trumped economics. While shipping crude oil to a destination thirty tanker days away was not economical, Chavez was eager to shift his oil customer base away from the United States, while China was keen to diversify its purchases from the Middle East.

Along with a joint refinery project to handle Venezuelan oil in China, Chinese companies have contracted to build a dozen oil drilling platforms, supply eighteen oil tankers, and collaborate with PdVSA to explore new oilfields in Venezuela. To shorten the distance between Venezuela and China the oil tankers have to travel, their petroleum companies considered laying a pipeline to the Pacific through Colombia. During Chinese Vice President Xi Jinping's tour of South America in early 2009, the China Development Bank agreed to loan PdVSA $6 billion for the oil to be supplied over the next twenty years.[41]

Ever since China became an oil importing republic in 1993, it has been scouring the world to secure petroleum supplies. So it was only too pleased to sign oil contracts with Venezuela.

CHAPTER 5

CHINA

THE PEACEFUL RISE OF A GIANT

The stratospheric rise of China from a war-ridden, backward country in 1949 to a roaring economic and diplomatic giant within six decades is unparalleled in world history. By the time the Chinese celebrate the centenary of the People's Republic of China (PRC) in 2049, its GDP will be the highest on this planet. China would thus revert to the position it held until 1820, when it accounted for one-third of the global GDP.

Today, measured by the Purchasing Power Parity, China's GDP is only behind America's. Its foreign reserves of $1.9 trillion are more than three times those of the sixteen-nation Eurozone. As the largest holder of U.S. Treasury bonds (maturing in five, ten, or thirty years), it has become the "indispensable nation" for the Federal Reserve Bank. During his two and a half years as Treasury secretary until January 2009, Henry Paulson visited China more than seventy times to encourage the greenback's sagging value through the soaking up of U.S. debt, and later to help weather the financial tempest.[1] His most critical trip occurred soon after September 2007, when, against the sliding value of the dollar, Cheng Swei, vice chairman of the Standing Committee of the National People's Congress (i.e., Parliament), said that China would invest outside U.S. dollar financial instruments. Beijing refrained from doing so, and in return the Bush administration stopped criticizing the PRC on trade and currency policies.[2]

In doctrinal terms, what the American and other advocates of the free market find galling is that China has accomplished an economic miracle under a command economy. All but one of the thirty-five most highly valued companies on the Shanghai Stock Exchange are wholly or partly state-owned. And the valuation of some is staggering.

On being listed on the Shanghai Stock Exchange in November 2007, the market value of the state-run PetroChina surged to nearly $1 trillion—worth more than the combined market values of Exxon Mobil (originating in Standard Oil, established in 1870) and General Electric, the topmost American corporation. In the list of the twenty most valued companies in the world in 2007, China, with eight, surpassed the United States, with seven.

Astoundingly, it has taken China a mere three decades to achieve the level of industrialization that Western nations did in two *centuries*. During that period, China, with only one-fifth of the global population, doubled the world's workforce and lifted 300 million peasants into urban modernity, with two-thirds going into industry and the rest into construction. They produced more than half of the planet's garments and footwear.

Over the past quarter century, the average economic growth has been 9 percent, per capita incomes have risen sixfold, and 400 million—all of the 300 million in towns plus another 100 million in villages—have been lifted out of poverty.[3]

The poll by the Pew Global Attitudes Project in April 2008, covering a sample of 3,312 disproportionately urban Chinese, showed that 86 percent were satisfied with their country's direction, up from 48 percent in 2002—and 25 percent and 32 percent ahead of the figures for Australia and Russia, the second and third in the league table. And 82 percent were content with the national economy, 30 points above the 2002 statistic. By contrast, only 23 percent of Americans were satisfied with their country's direction, and only 20 percent with the national economy.[4]

Chinese leaders describe the dazzling economic advance of their country as an unprecedented example of a "peaceful rise" of a nation in modern times. "Peaceful" is the operative word. The rise of all great powers in recent history—Britain, Russia, America, Japan, and Germany—resulted from violent expansion, colonization of foreign lands and peoples, and exploitation of natives and their resources, often forcefully.

In sharp contrast to the steep decline in America's favorable image abroad, China experienced a contrary trend. The Pew Research Center's survey of forty-seven countries during April and May 2007, with a sample of 45,000, showed that China's influence abroad was widely seen as growing faster than America's and having a more beneficial impact on African states than did the United States. In most African states, the favorable view of China outweighed the unfavorable by more than 70 percent to 9 percent. The corresponding figures for other major powers in the continent were Russia (60:26), India (46:43), America (42:39), and Japan (29:67).[5]

AN UPWARD PATH WITH WIGGLES

As with earlier great powers, the ascent of China has been wiggly. The PRC has experienced economic ups and downs, high inflation, deflation, recessions, uneven development of its regions, and a widening gap between rich and poor and between urban and rural citizens—the characteristics associated with capitalism. At certain times official policies have favored villages, and at others cities. While China's Communist leaders have used the familiar fiscal and monetary tools like adjusting interest rates and money supply, they have achieved desired results faster than their capitalist counterparts. This is so primarily because of the state-controlled banking system, in which, for instance, government-owned banks act as depositories of the compulsory savings of all employees. In the midst of the worldwide fiscal meltdown of 2008–2009, while U.S. President Barack Obama limited himself to criticizing the "shameful" bonuses at the bailed-out Wall Street financial institutions, the Chinese government compelled top managers at major state-owned companies to slash their salaries by 15 percent to 40 percent before tinkering with the remuneration of their workforce.[6] PRC leaders' actions have highlighted the merits of state-directed capitalism.

Their overarching approach synthesizes the theses of the two important books by Adam Smith (1723–1790): *The Theory of Moral Sentiments* (1759), which emphasizes the need for the visible hand of the government to achieve social equity and harmonious development, and *An Inquiry into the Nature and Causes of the Wealth of Nations* (1776), which underscores the need for the invisible hand of the market.[7]

In an ironic twist, instead of letting globalization establish and consolidate the market economy worldwide, as widely expected by Western economists, the PRC used it to further its version of state capitalism. Furthermore, the near-unanimous prediction by Western analysts that economic reform in

China would lead to political liberalization has not materialized. They had based their forecast on what had happened in South Korea, Taiwan, and Singapore. There, rapid economic progress under one-party autocracy had delivered prosperous multiparty democracy. What they failed to note was that these countries were small in area and population. Created artificially by the British, Singapore is a city-state. Taiwan is a renegade offshore island. And South Korea is only half of the small Korean Peninsula. By comparison, China is as large as America in area but four times more populous. Above all, China is more than a country. It is a civilization with a long, distinguished tradition of striking out on its own.

But it was not the first time that most Western analysts, whether of liberal or orthodox Marxist hue, had proved wrong when dealing with non-Western subjects. Few, if any, Western Marxists could have imagined peasants being mobilized as the vanguard of class revolution, a role assigned by Karl Marx strictly to the industrial proletariat in urban areas. Yet that was what came to pass in a predominantly agrarian China.

Now, at the end of thirty years of economic advance, resulting in thirteen-fold growth in the GDP, the People's Republic of China remains a one-party state. But the Communist Party of China (CPC, also known as Chinese Communist Party) in 2008 was not the same as it was in 1978. In its ideology and the composition of its membership, it has undergone a sea change, reflecting the dynamics of economic liberalization. That has greatly enabled it to retain its monopoly of political power. At the popular level, party leaders have by and large succeeded in tying Chinese nationalism to admiration for the CPC, equating the party with the country.

CPC leaders claim that there has been steady progress toward "democracy"—a term they apply in the context of the Confucian philosophy: It judges the quality of the government by its success in harmonizing the interests of the ruler and the ruled. The concepts of creating harmony in society, where citizens constitute the base, originated with the Chinese sage Confucius (551–479 BCE). It acquired a royal stamp from the second century BCE onward, when the emperors decided to appoint officials who passed exams, open to all, in the canon of thirteen Confucian texts. This system encouraged Confucian officials to safeguard the interests of citizens and obliged the emperor—charged with the task of creating and maintaining harmony, cooperation, and order—to heed criticism from his Confucian mandarins. They maintained their integrity by subjecting themselves to self-criticism and self-discipline. In popular perception, that entitled them to counter the ruler's arbitrary ways. As followers of Confucius, who drew his inspiration from heavenly considerations, these public functionaries remained otherworldly. Consequently, in the increasingly materialist world of the early twentieth century, they felt lost.

It was against this background that the Communist Party of China emerged, clandestinely, in July 1921. Its leaders and ranks were as committed to integrity, service, and social harmony as Confucian officials, but they were down-to-earth and responsive to the needs of the common folk. Emulating Confucian scholars, secular Communists practiced self-discipline and self-criticism to maintain their integrity. It made their promise of equity and honest administration under their rule credible to the masses.

Communists were also conscious of the humiliations China had suffered since the 1840s at the hands of foreigners: ceding Hong Kong to the British in 1841 and Taiwan to Japan in 1895 in the First Sino-Japanese War, giving extraterritorial rights to America in 1907 after doing so to leading European nations, and losing Manchuria and other territories because of Japan's aggressions in 1931 and 1937.

Before World War II, the CPC was foremost in mobilizing the nation against Japanese imperialism. During the war, China and Japan fought on opposite sides. That conflict claimed the lives of some 20 million Chinese, the second highest figure after the Soviets. Following the Allied victory in 1945 came the four-year civil war between the Washington-backed Kuomintang (Guomingdang) National Party, headed by General Chiang Kai-shek (1887–1975), and the People's Liberation Army (PLA) of the CPC, led by Mao Zedong. The PLA won. The defeated forces of Chiang Kai-shek fled to the offshore Chinese island of Taiwan (Formosa) and claimed continuity with the (now defunct) Republic of China (ROC).

MAO'S RULE

At the founding of the People's Republic of China on October 1, 1949, Mao said, "China has always been a great, courageous, and industrious nation; it is only in modern times that it has fallen behind. And that was due entirely to oppression and exploitation by foreign imperialism and domestic reactionary governments."[8]

His government immediately implemented land reform, redistributing nearly half of the arable land to rural committees. Freed from centuries of serfdom, peasants improved agricultural output, pushing the annual GDP growth during the First Five Year Plan (1952–1957) to 9 percent. As part of the monetary reform, a new yuan equal to 10,000 old yuans was introduced to curb inflation. Though the official title of the currency was renminbi, meaning people's currency, the pre-Communist name for the basic unit, yuan, persisted. In the course of the next Five Year Plan, agrarian productivity improved as the first stage agricultural cooperatives graduated to better organized entities.

During the next Plan, the implementation of Mao's "Great Leap Forward" (1958–1961) led to the formation of 26,000 large-scale communes. They started their own light industries. This was a radical departure from the traditional pattern of industrialization in the West, involving the migration of peasants to urban centers to work in factories. The government's compulsory requisition of food from the communes—where an adult survived on a daily food intake of less than a pound—created famine. It claimed an estimated 16 to 27 million lives.

Then followed a period of pragmatism, between 1961 and 1965. It was during this phase that Deng Xiaoping, the party's general secretary and an ally of moderate Prime Minister Zhou Enlai, made his widely cited statement: "It doesn't matter if it is a black cat or a white cat. As long as it can catch mice, it is a good cat."[9]

Next came the Cultural Revolution, led by young Red Guards in urban areas, professing to herald "people's democracy," with its main emphasis on egalitarianism and class conflict. Its active phase lasted two years, during which its violent implementation caused an estimated 500,000 deaths. But its consequences persisted until Mao's death in September 1976. During its virulent period, Deng was denounced as "Number Two capitalist-roader" after Liu Shaoqi. He was exiled to Nanchang to work in a tractor repair plant. After the Cultural Revolution had subsided, Mao recalled Deng in 1973 to work with Zhou Enlai and take charge of the People's Liberation Army to "stabilize it." Deng became deputy prime minister and chief of staff of the Central Military Commission in charge of the PLA, only to lose these posts when Zhou died in January 1976.

Despite the turmoil caused by the formation of agricultural cooperatives and communes in villages, and the Cultural Revolution in towns, Mao left behind a China that had advanced economically. Irrigated land grew from 20 percent of the total to 50 percent, reducing rural poverty. A thirteenfold increase in industrial output pushed its share of the GDP from one-eighth of the total to a half. Literacy for males shot up to 81 percent and for females to 45 percent.[10] Also, despite his policy lurches in the economic sphere, Mao stuck to decentralizing political power, which, with a vastly expanded economy that materialized during the post-Mao decades, would provide provincial party leaders enhanced scope for corruption and abuse of office.

After Mao

At the Eleventh CPC National Congress in August 1977, convened inter alia to elect the Central Committee, Deng was reinstated to his earlier high positions, thus becoming number two under Hua Guofeng, who had succeeded Mao as party chairman and prime minister. While suppressing dissent openly critical of Mao, led by the university student–inspired Democracy Wall movement, Deng eased up on state control of the economy. During the summer of 1978, he promoted Four Modernizations, proposed earlier by Zhou—in agriculture, industry, defense, and science.

It was at the Central Committee's Third Plenum in mid-December that Deng unveiled his program of "reform and opening up" (*gaige kaifang* in Chinese) after overcoming stiff opposition by Chen Yun, Li Xiannian, and Deng Liqun in the twelve-member Politburo. The delegates modified the party's main aim of constructing socialism to creating a "planned socialist commodity economy" and building "socialist modernization." This was to be achieved by raising rural income and incentives, experimenting in enterprise autonomy, reducing central planning, and attracting foreign direct investment (FDI) into China.

Cognizant of the resistance to new ideas by the conservative members of the Politburo, Deng opted for graduated change, all the while reiterating his allegiance to Marxism-Leninism–Mao Zedong Thought and invoking Mao in letter and spirit to contextualize his proposed policies. He refrained from talking about the final destination, merely invoking Mao's thought that "practice has to be the judge of theory."

Deng's program allowed large-scale imports of foreign machines and technology, mainly Western and Japanese. To accelerate industrialization as well as adoption of modern marketing strategies and exports, his government required that a foreign company must have a Chinese partner. In return, it permitted the companies in the newly established Special Economic Zones (SEZs) to import goods free of tariffs and taxes, pay only half the local taxes, and operate outside the official rules and regulations applicable to the private sector in China. The SEZ was yet another Chinese innovation, which would be adopted by 120 countries over the next three decades.[11] The Deng administration depoliticized the People's Liberation Army and curtailed its budget by a quarter. It set up a network of high-tech research centers.

Deng disengaged party functionaries from running communes, state enterprises, education, and agriculture, and let professionally qualified managers do the job with a free hand to offer material incentives to improve productivity and expansion. But by having a party functionary shadow every important official, the state authorities maintained the symbiotic relationship between the CPC and the government. (This practice continues.) To motivate officials and the rank and file alike to raise output, he said, "There is no Communist virtue in being poor; on the contrary it is glorious to be rich."[12] The fact that glorifying riches was un-Marxist did not bother Deng. Nonetheless, to soften the shock of his statement, he added, "In a race for riches, some people will emerge as winners before others."

Unlike the demolition job done on Joseph Stalin after his death by his successor, Nikita Khrushchev, the magic of Mao, a towering personality, held. It was not until a generation later that the CPC's gradual drift away from the basics of Marxism culminated in its break with Marxism-Leninism–Mao Zedong Thought. Yet Mao remains the founding pillar of the People's Republic—with his portrait on every bank note stressing the point. After all, it was Mao who recovered every square inch of Chinese territory lost to Japan, unified China, and expelled all foreign influences from the mainland.

An original and self-confident theoretician and strategist, Mao ignored the instructions of the Stalin-directed Comintern (Communist International) and forged the Chinese peasant mass into a revolutionary ramrod that smashed the old order.[13] His rallying of the rural rather than the urban proletariat, from 1927 onward, to carry out a class revolution set Mao apart from orthodox, European Marxist-Leninists. This was the first salient example of China furrowing an independent path in modern history.

Neither the French nor the Bolshevik revolution was anti-imperialist, whereas the anti-imperialist American revolution did not upend class relations. By blending anti-imperialism with socialism, a powerful combination, Mao made an unparalleled contribution to history. Later, China would continue to confound most conventional thinkers in the West.

Summarizing an overarching view of the "Great Helmsman," therefore, Deng concluded five years after Mao's death that he was 70 percent right and 30 percent wrong. That remains the official assessment.

Instead of a headlong lurch into across-the-board denationalization and wholesale lifting of price controls that Russia's Boris Yeltsin would later embark on, Deng followed a gradualist path, justifying every step away from the rigid centralized planning with Mao's aphorism "Make practice the sole criterion for the truth." To convey this message in simple yet graphic terms, Deng said, "We will cross the river by feeling the stones under our feet, one by one."[14] He synthesized socialism and market and came up with the concept of "socialist market" as against "capitalist market."

For instance, in 1984 Deng adopted a dual-track pricing system proposed by Zhang Weiying, director of the Institute of Business Research of Beijing University. Zhang argued that it would enable the government to shift from the state-controlled pricing system to market-determined prices without casting off its commitment to socialism or arousing opposition from those with a vested interest in central planning. The final aim of letting the market decide all prices was to be achieved gradually.

Also Deng got his priorities right—the economy first, then politics. Even in the economic field, he did not jump in. He tried the Special Economic Zones on a small scale from 1980 in the fishing village of Shenzhen near Hong Kong,[15] limiting them to a total of four until 1987, before adopting them on a wider scale. He stuck to the gospel of learning from practice.

During its First Stage, economic reform consisted of contracts between the government and peasants, price liberalization, and allowing markets at the margin of the Five Year Plan. But since private property remained banned and state banks were barred from lending to private enterprises, any protest by the traditionalists within the CPC was muted. On the other hand, because of political decentralization, a legacy of Mao, the reversal of state planning and agricultural collectives was achieved more smoothly than in the highly centralized Soviet Union.

The harsh "one couple, one child" law, enacted in 1980 to control China's exploding population, and the decline in social support for employees in state-owned enterprises, including agricultural cooperatives and communes, compelled parents to save. An earlier incentive to accumulate cash had come in the wake of the government's discontinuation of universal health care in 1979. As a result, Chinese citizens could not be certain of being cared for in their declining years. The increased savings filled the coffers of nationalized banks. They poured loans into state-owned enterprises and infrastructure, thus boosting the rate of economic growth.

In early 1978, eighteen farmers in Xiaogang village in east Anhui Province signed a secret agreement to divide communally owned farmland into individual pieces called household contracts, thus inadvertently initiating a rural revolution. When their initiative became known, it was lauded by Deng, who adopted it as a national policy.[16] Thus a household responsibility system came to replace agricultural cooperatives and communes.

The local CPC committees allocated plots of the hitherto collectively owned land to individual families for up to thirty years, with the ownership rights resting with the state. The peasant families were free to grow what they wanted, sell it in the open market, and retain profits. Deng urged the privately managed Town and Village Enterprises (TVEs) to hire the workers displaced by the improved productivity of land. (In the PRC's administrative system, the smallest unit is a group of villages named after the largest member and titled "town.") As a result, between 1978 and 1988, rural incomes rose annually by 12.2 percent—that is, they doubled every six years.[17]

With the "retirement" of Hua Guofeng in 1981, Deng became the paramount leader under whose rule China adopted a new constitution in 1982.

DENG'S GUIDELINES FOR GOVERNANCE

At the Twelfth CPC National Congress in 1982—a decade after the groundbreaking meeting of President Richard Nixon and Chairman Mao in Beijing—Deng led the delegates to adopt the policy of opening to the outside world. He wrapped his argument in the popular concepts of challenging the hegemony of America, advancing the goal of uniting Taiwan with its motherland, and accelerating China's capacity to achieve its vastly untapped potential. Confident that engagement with foreign multinationals and technology would not alter Chinese identity and culture, he saw merit in China adopting the Western form of economic modernization.

The increased emphasis on growth led the Chinese government to put the border disputes with its neighbors—Vietnam, India, and the Soviet Union—

on the back burner. This was also the reaction to the major losses that the PLA suffered in its poorly planned incursion into Vietnam in 1979.

Over the years, Deng's guidelines on running China crystallized and became the official mantra. The multipoint instruction could be summarized thus: Observe and analyze developments calmly; handle changes patiently and confidently; make your own position secure; hide brilliance, cherish obscurity; yield on small issues with the long-term interest in mind; mask your capabilities by cultivating obscurity; adopt a low profile; refrain from practicing power politics and threatening neighbors or global peace; and avoid becoming a leader while striving to achieve results. In short, avoid conflict, and build the economy rapidly.

Adoption of Deng's set of policies meant jettisoning the Maoist doctrine of friendship with only socialist states and embracing any country that could assist China in its search for markets, natural resources, and diplomatic backing. Thus, within three decades of Mao's demise, China became the globe's most commerce-oriented country, forging ahead of Japan, and the planet's largest receiver of foreign direct investment (FDI) at $92.4 billion in 2008. By 2002, the opening out had progressed so far that 92 percent of Chinese thought their children needed to learn English "to succeed in the world."[18]

Deng's successors have shown flexibility and adroitness in successfully meeting the challenges of the fast-changing scene at home and abroad, while maintaining the CPC's monopoly on power. These characteristics can be attributed to the faithful implementation of Deng's guidelines, part of the overarching Deng Xiaoping Theory. To his credit, the first leader to follow the Deng guidelines was its author himself. He was a calm observer and analyst of the developments at home and abroad, and he had become a past master in patiently and confidently dealing with changes.

His instruction on maintaining a low profile and concealing your capabilities applied to Beijing's diplomats. While Americans never missed a chance to hold forth, the Chinese diplomats rarely, if ever, held press conferences. So the PRC's behavior at the UN Security Council contrasted sharply with America's. Since taking up its seat at the Security Council as a permanent member in 1971, the PRC has exercised its veto only six times, whereas the United States has done so eighty-one times.[19] Chinese diplomats also held fast to Deng's instructions to respect national sovereignty at all costs, strive patiently to resolve disputes peacefully, and resist Western attempts to interfere in the internal affairs of UN members under the rubric of protecting minority rights—well aware of China's problems in Tibet and Xinjiang—or human rights.

An early sign of China's strife-free approach to foreign affairs came in 1982, when it initiated talks with British Prime Minister Margaret Thatcher on a peaceful restitution of Hong Kong to the PRC in 1997. Another outstanding example was Beijing's abstention on the UN Security Council Resolution 678 of November 1990, which authorized member-states to "use all necessary means" to expel the occupying Iraqis from Kuwait. In April 1991, China threatened to veto the U.S.-sponsored draft of Security Council Resolution 688 concerning the Kurdish minority in Iraq if its reference to Chapter VII, which authorizes member-states to use force to implement a resolution, remained in place. Washington agreed to drop this reference if China agreed to abstain. It did.

China stuck to the policy of nonbelligerence on the issue of Iraq, which remained on the active agenda of the Security Council for the next twelve years. Its policy of noninterference in the internal affairs of a sovereign state brought it in conflict with the doctrine of "liberal intervention" that Washington tried to foist on the UN Security Council after the collapse of the Soviet Union in 1991. As a result, the PRC's stance differed from America's in the cases of Burma, North Korea, Sudan, and Zimbabwe.

At home, guided by Deng, the Central Military Commission changed its doctrine in 1985. So far, the PLA had been a mass army trained to wage wars of attrition on its territory and been ready to "hit early, strike hard" at the enemy—a task it performed well in India in 1962 but failed to accomplish in Vietnam in 1979. Now it was to be transformed into a force capable of winning short-duration, high-intensity wars along China's periphery against high-tech enemies. The stress shifted from quantity to quality. The decision to reduce the PLA by 1 million to 2.77 million was implemented in two years, and the officer corps was reduced by half.

Deng felt confident enough to invite a foreigner—albeit an ethnic Chinese—Goh Keng Swee, former deputy minister of Singapore, in 1985 to act as an economic adviser to China's State Council (that is, Cabinet), led since 1980 by Zhao Ziyang. An economic reformer with a rural background, Zhao reduced bureaucratic overstaffing and corruption.[20]

On being promoted to the CPC's general secretary at the Thirteenth National Congress in October 1987 to succeed the aging Hua Yaobang, Zhao was candid enough to acknowledge differences within society. "Different people have different interests and views," he said. "They need opportunities for exchange of views."[21]

This was an official admission that social protest was brewing under the surface. The final demise of communes in 1983, and the latitude given to farmers to grow what they wished, bolstered cash crops at the expense of food grains. That raised food prices. With meals accounting for one-third to one-half of the average family budget, the consumer price index jumped by 19 percent in 1988. Many cities witnessed panic purchase of food and consumer goods. That only worsened the situation. The authorities' anti-inflationary measures caused recession and job losses, with some street protests turning violent. Though this was a typical trajectory of a market economy, it was the first time PRC rulers had to face it. They were lost.

This was the preamble to the Tiananmen (literally "Gate of Heavenly Peace") Square demonstrations in Beijing that gripped the outside world.

THE TIANANMEN SQUARE TURMOIL

Following the death of Hua Yaobang, later viewed as a liberal, on April 15, 1989, his supporters camped at Tiananmen Square ahead of his memorial service on April 23. Instead of dispersing later on, they attracted more protestors demanding democratic reform and greater economic liberalization.

Initially the authorities did not feel disconcerted. Later, as jobless workers, victims of the deepening downturn—which would slash the GDP growth from 11 percent in 1988 to 4 percent a year later—swelled the protestors' ranks, senior officials were alarmed. But differences between hard-line Prime Minister Li Peng and moderate Zhao left the government paralyzed. That increased support for the demonstrators.

Because the impending visit of Mikhail Gorbachev in mid-May to seal the Soviet Union's normalization of relations with the PRC after nearly thirty years was attracting the limelight of international media, the five-man Standing Committee of the Politburo found its options constricted. It could not declare martial law in Beijing and use force to disperse some 50,000 protestors assembled at the vast historic square.

Only after Gorbachev's departure did the Committee of the Elders, led by Deng,[22] call on the PLA to restore order. Even though martial law followed on May 20, the demonstrators refused to disperse.

For the authorities, the last straw was the protestors' installation in their midst of a Styrofoam model of the Statue of Liberty as the goddess of democracy—an image flashed around the world. After the army troops had emptied the surrounding streets on June 3, tanks rolled in the next day to end the protest. The troops fired at the protestors to disperse them. The figure of 200–300 deaths caused by the troops, as claimed by the Chinese authorities, was later found to be roughly in line with the estimate of 180 to 500 in a declassified document of the U.S. National Security Agency.[23]

By June 4, the Committee of the Elders had replaced Zhao, who had apologized to students for the imposition of martial law, as the party's general secretary with Jiang Zemin, a Politburo member and mayor of Shanghai. Jiang's elevation to the top post signaled a break in the party's history. Since he was only twenty-three when the PRC was founded, he lacked a career in the PLA and was therefore not seen wearing the military tunic, as was the case with the older CPC leaders, all of them PLA veterans. As a trained engineer, he blended industrial management with political navigation skills. He had succeeded in peacefully dispersing the student protest in Shanghai that followed Hua's death. He thus unveiled a new chapter in the CPC's history, with comparatively young technocrats in Western business suits competing for influence based on their capacity for adaptation, reflection, and open-mindedness, albeit within certain parameters—in an environment of more accountability than previously.

For now, the bloody suppression of the Tiananmen Square demonstration elicited widespread condemnation abroad, leading to weapons sales sanctions by the European Union and the United States.

Deng was unrepentant. So far, through a skillful blend of gradualism and opportunism, he had preserved the vanguard role of the CPC. He had no intention of letting outsiders set the pace of political reform. His current uncompromising stance on political protest was a harsher reprise of his suppression of the 1977 Democracy Wall movement. Yet the government could not just write off the Tiananmen Square turmoil. It was particularly sensitive to workers' grievances. Responding to their discontent, it slowed down economic reform, clamping down on private enterprises and barring their owners from party membership.

Overall, by 1990, the configuration of the economy had changed as a result of the twelve-year-old reform. The contribution of agriculture to the GDP fell from 42 percent to 30 percent, whereas that of industry rose from 38 percent to 45 percent, and that of services from 20 percent to 25 percent.[24] By 1991, though, it became clear that the economy had reached a plateau. The average annual FDI, almost wholly from Hong Kong and Taiwan Chinese, was only about $2 billion, even though the average tariffs had been reduced to 43 percent. Deng felt the need for further liberalization.

PHASE II OF THE ECONOMIC ADVANCE

During the Chinese New Year holiday in January 1992, the eighty-eight-year-old Deng toured the south, including the Shenzhen SEZ, arguing that private investment, whether foreign or domestic, furthered not only development but also research and education. As an incentive to investors, the government granted the opening of the PRC's first stock exchange in Guangzhao, former Canton.

Later that year, the Fourteenth CPC National Congress, led by Jiang, declared that during the next eight years, the party should focus on building a "socialist market economy" by synthesizing the global market economy with China's "social practice."

To achieve that aim, Jiang and Prime Minister Zhu Rongji, also from Shanghai, unveiled a program of rapid urbanization and industrialization. It involved moving 500 million underemployed peasants gradually to work on countless building sites on the east coast or perform low-skilled jobs in massive state-owned enterprises as well as factories of foreign multinationals in the 2,000 SEZs that would spring up.

This policy, fueled by the soaring FDI—which reached $34 billion in 1994, second only to the United States—coupled with a virtual decontrol of prices, pushed inflation to 24 percent. It set alarm bells ringing. The government raised interests rates, controlled food prices, reexamined investment plans, recalled dodgy loans, and reinforced control over banks. The expansion rate slowed to 9.5 percent, and inflation fell to 8 percent in early 1996.

By 1997 economic reform and industrial advancement had acquired a momentum of their own. They were untouched by Deng's demise in February— as well as the retiring of six of the seven members of the Politburo's Standing Committee, according to the seventy-year retirement age rule, at the CPC's Fifteenth National Congress in October.

At this Congress, Jiang summarized the new policy of rationalizing state-owned enterprises (SOEs) thus: "Hold on to the Big, but let go the Small." It involved selling, merging, or closing SOEs, with the aim of making the majority of the existing or resulting large SOEs profitable by the end of the decade. Nevertheless, the private—officially called "nonstate"—owners of small or medium SOEs remained dependent on the loans from state-owned banks, and senior jobs in these enterprises were filled by local CPC leaders. (Jiang did not spare the government bureaucracy and came up with a plan to cut its strength by half by 2001.) On the other hand, the size and scope of the private sector grew. This in turn would bring about a radical change in the CPC leaders' policy on the party's membership—sooner than most had expected.

To withstand the impact of the 1997–1998 Asian financial crisis, the PRC increased its expenditure on building infrastructure. Nonetheless, China's growth slowed to 7.8 percent in 1998, while inflation dropped sharply. China refused to devalue its currency, the yuan, which was not freely convertible. That reassured foreign investors and attracted more FDI, which, as before, was for the long term. Also the successful reversion of Hong Kong from Britain to the PRC in July 1997 bolstered the confidence of outside investors. The renamed Hong Kong Special Administrative Region was allowed to retain its own old laws, currency, and border controls, as well as a multiparty democratic system, with Beijing taking charge only of its foreign policy and defense.

Few would have guessed that the upholding of the "one country, two systems" doctrine in Hong Kong had within it the seed for turning the "two systems" into "one-and-a-half systems."

DISCARDING THE MARXIST CORE

In September 1999, on the eve of the fortieth anniversary of the PRC, the Communist Party of China dropped its core belief. At its Central Committee's Fourth Plenum, led by Jiang, it took the first step to change its raison d'être. It amended its constitution and declared that "private and individual business" forms an "important component" of the PRC's future. The party discarded its historic creed: It is the broad, toiling masses who create wealth, based on Marx's theory that ultimately all wealth originates in labor. On that foundation rests the concept of collective ownership and planning, and Marxist socialism. Now the CPC conceded that capital owners also created wealth.

Influenced by the clique from the affluent coastal regions that surrounded him, Jiang argued that the party should represent "economic production as well as social and cultural forces," and called on entrepreneurs to join the CPC. By the time the party celebrated its eightieth birthday in July 2001, nearly 100,000 had done so.

This was the culmination of the process of deviation from Marxism-Leninism–Mao Zedong Thought, which had started with the hesitant steps taken by Deng a little over two decades earlier. Reviled by his critics during the Cultural Revolution as "Number Two capitalist-roader," Deng was now praised by his admirers as an original thinker who offered China "socialism with Chinese characteristics." All that remained now was the Leninist structure of the CPC based on the principle of "democratic centralism." It allowed debate within the confines of the party and required its members to implement the decisions taken by the central leadership.

In their defense, Jiang's followers referred to social reality. During the last two decades of the twentieth century, the percentage of workers and peasants in the National People's Congress (i.e., Parliament) had fallen from 27 to 11 and from 21 to 8, respectively—the two groups together accounting for less than one-fifth of the total.[25] This was at odds with the increased proportion of industrial and construction workers in society, resulting from the large-scale migration of peasants to urban centers.

Further changes in the country's class composition would occur after it had joined the six-year-old World Trade Organization (WTO)—once the tension created by the midair collision between an American spy plane and a Chinese fighter in the South China Sea in April 2001 had subsided, and 9/11 had engendered international sympathy for the Bush administration.

As the PRC prepared to join the WTO in November, its rulers could marshal some impressive statistics. Since 1978 the number of Chinese living below the poverty line—defined by the World Bank as those surviving on two-thirds of a U.S. dollar a day—had fallen from 260 million to 42 million in a country of 1.3 billion. Villagers had migrated to urban centers at the annual rate of 12 million, thereby reducing the rural-urban ratio from 80:20 to 60:40.[26] On the other hand, the gap between the affluent and the indigent had widened dramatically, while the social welfare system had all but vanished. Geographically, the economic development was uneven, with the south and east benefiting most.

AFTER WTO MEMBERSHIP

As a prerequisite to its admission to the WTO, the PRC reduced its average tariffs to 15 percent, and the quotas and licenses on imports became almost nonexistent. Western corporations rushed in. Within four years, almost 50,000 U.S. companies began operating in China. They included 400 of America's top 500 corporations.[27] Between 2001 and 2007, the PRC's annual GDP growth rate rose from 8 percent to 12 percent.[28]

Foreign firms' modus operandi was this: Establish a plant in a Chinese SEZ, hire skilled locals at a fraction of the wages at home, manage the assembly line using the latest information and communication technology techniques, ship the final product to the nearest seaport onward to the company's Western home base, and sell it at an enormous profit. The "China Price" became the standard benchmark by which all manufactured goods in the world came to be judged.

Despite the high markups, during a period when gasoline prices in America doubled, China-made computers fell in price by half. Overall, 80 percent of electronic and telecom exports, 70 percent of plastics, and 60 percent of electrical goods came to be manufactured in China by foreign firms. American and other Western consumers benefited with clothes, shoes, and electrical appliances becoming cheaper by 42 percent, 31 percent, and 63 percent, respectively, during 2001–2004.[29]

China's imports jumped too, benefiting such neighbors as Japan and South Korea. Its soaring trade with Japan helped the latter to crawl out of its decade-long recession of the 1990s. Relations between the two traditional rivals improved to the extent that in 2008 they resolved their long-running dispute over offshore gas fields in the East China Sea by opting for joint exploration.

The fast-paced industrialization, urbanization, and construction—funded partly by taxing the neglected countryside—encroached upon agricultural land, displacing peasants, who took to staging large protests more often than before. Each year over 2 million farmers lost their land to new factories, roads, airports, dams, and private land acquisitions for building apartments, shops, and offices.

Taking note of the rising tensions, Jiang declared in 2001 that the Communist Party must "pay close attention to the relationship between the party and the masses, and the feelings of the people," adding, "Whether the people are for or against it is the basic factor deciding the rise and fall of a political party or a political power."[30] This was the first public acknowledgment of the concept of popular accountability in the PRC. However, it was too late for Jiang, more at ease with affluent men of Shanghai and Beijing than common folk, to change his distant governing style.

Before stepping down as the party's general secretary in 2002, the seventy-six-year-old Jiang offered his concept of "three represents" to define the party's role. Addressing the Sixteenth CPC National Congress in November, he fleshed out his concept: The CPC should represent the development of the nation's advanced productive forces and its progressing culture as well as the basic interests of most of its people. He thus put a final stamp on the changed role of the CPC from being a vanguard revolutionary party of the toiling masses to a governing party representing the interests of all classes in society, including capitalists, thus jettisoning the concept of class conflict that forms the core of Marxism. By now 98 percent of the Central Committee members were college graduates, up from 55 percent in 1982.[31]

Hu Puts "People First"

Jiang's job went to Hu Jintao. A hydraulic engineer by training, Hu joined the CPC in 1964 and went on to become director of the All China Youth Federation in the 1980s. Unlike the Shanghai clique surrounding Jiang, Hu built up his career as a party functionary in the deprived hinterland, including Tibet. Succeeding Jiang also as president in March 2003, Hu continued his predecessor's policies. These included providing better protection to private ownership and private property, and giving "nonstate" (meaning private) enterprises more opportunities.

The number of private enterprises and the proportion of registered entrepreneurs who had joined the CPC had soared by 2005. One out of five entrepreneurs had become a CPC member, whereas the proportion for the population at large was one out of twenty. Of the 6 million owners of private enterprises, 4 million were former government officials.[32] They used their party and government connections to the benefit of their companies. Given the Maoist decentralization of power, the state banks, based in provincial capitals, and the provincial development banks followed the instructions of the local party leaders. This became a major source of corruption, poor investment, and nonperforming loans. It was estimated that as a result of bribes, tax evasion, pilfering, and arbitrary local levies, one-seventh of the GDP was lost.[33]

As a result of the rising corruption and the relentless loss of land by peasants, the number of protests in 2005 rose to 87,000—a tenfold increase in twelve years—the average size of a demonstration being fifty.[34] To eliminate corruption, all officials were ordered to attend annual training sessions to raise their competence and promote accountability. This helped—up to a point.

To counter the rising tensions in society and rectify the excess stress on urban development during the Jiang presidency, Hu quietly veered away from his predecessor's policies. But disappointingly for him and his followers, by then Jiang Zemin's worldview had been incorporated into history textbooks, an important tool to shape popular perceptions of the rising generation. The world history books focused on economic growth, innovation, foreign trade, political stability, respect for diverse cultures, and social harmony. They highlighted John Pierpont Morgan (1837–1913), Bill Gates, the New York Stock Exchange, the U.S. space shuttles, and Japan's bullet trains. Instead of wars, dynasties, and Communist revolutions, they offered colorful descriptions on economics, technology, social customs, and globalization. Socialism was relegated to a short chapter in the senior high school history course, with pre-1978 Chinese Communism mentioned in a single sentence. Mao was relegated to one reference in a chapter on etiquette.[35]

Hu focused on developing the hinterland and expanded his power base by turning away from the Shanghai clique to the leaders of the Youth League. He disparaged avaricious, individualistic values linked to a market economy by invoking Mao and the selfless collectivism of his times. To strike a balance between a market economy and the socialist past of China, Hu came up with the concepts of "scientific development" with a Marxist ring and "harmonious society" advocated by Confucius.

Before finalizing the eleventh Five Year Plan (2006–2011), a blueprint for a harmonious society, the government dispatched CPC teams to study social policies in the United States, the European Union, East Asia, Latin America, and Africa. Launched under the title of "Put People First," it aimed to increase the state's role in education, health, and social security. In a sense, Hu Jintao reverted to Deng's edict: "Grasp with two hands, and make sure both hold tight." That is, stress both economic growth and socialist culture.

Both Hu and Prime Minister Wen Jiabao were intent on repairing the attenuated social safety net and reversing neglect of the countryside—the legacies of Jiang's rule, when the growth in rural incomes during 1989–2001 plummeted to 3.8 percent. By rectifying Jiang's excessively pro-urban policies, Hu and Wen raised village incomes to 5.5 percent during 2002–2007.

Yet much lost ground remained to be recovered. In 2007 urban Chinese earned 3.3 times as much as rural Chinese, up from 1.9 times in 1985. When inequality in access to basic public services was factored in, the advantage of town Chinese over village folks rose to between 5 and 6.[36] Between 1978 and 2005, China's GINI coefficient had risen from 0.30 to 0.45.[37] In 2007, there were 414,900 dollar millionaires in the PRC.[38] Little wonder that a poll in 2008 showed that 89 percent were concerned about inequality, 11 percent more than those concerned about corrupt officials.[39]

In contrast to Jiang's leadership style, Hu and Wen listened to the grievances of peasants, workers, and the underprivileged, and tried to build up support for their "people first" policies. As in the past, reversal or modification of past policies or thinking met with resistance in the Politburo's Standing Committee. This was reflected in the pro- and anti-Hu factions securing an equal number of seats in the Standing Committee at the 2007 National Congress. Hu was on firmer ground when stressing harmonization of society or supremacy of the law, or even encouraging gradual political liberalization within the CPC.

The Sixteenth Central Committee's Plenum in October 2006 fleshed out the main aims and tasks for building a harmonious socialist society by 2020: improving "the socialist democratic and legal system" and ruling China according to law in a comprehensive way with "people's rights and interests enjoying respect and guarantees." The publication of a white paper on democracy by the official Institute of Politics of the Chinese Academy of Social Sciences in 2005 had broken new ground. What was discussed, however, was "socialist democracy," dealing with the CPC and the public at large.

Keen to avoid the fate of the Communist Party of the Soviet Union, which ossified during the 1970s under the leadership of Leonid Brezhnev because of overcentralization and one-way traffic emanating from the top, PRC leaders gave the ranks increased opportunities to have their say in policy formation and share their opinions and comments with fellow members. This infused a new life into local PRC committees.

To encourage competition within the party, provincial CPC Congresses began offering electoral lists with 15 to 30 percent more candidates than positions. And for the first time, at the Seventeenth CPC National Congress in

October 2007 there were 5 percent more candidates than the 356 seats on the decision-making Central Committee.

Hu's policy of harmonization was three-pronged. It applied to economic development at home, where the share of the state sector had dwindled to 35 percent, limited mostly to strategic industries and public services, from 80 percent a decade earlier;[40] links with the outside world; and relations with Taiwan.

COMMERCE ROUNDS ROUGH EDGES

The PRC's vigorous mercantilism has helped temper its historic animosity toward Japan, which colonized parts of China. By now the economies of the PRC, Japan, and South Korea have become so interlinked that they have struck deals on joint hydrocarbon exploration and production in the East China Sea. South Korea's booming trade with China, which has made the latter its number one trading partner, has given its government confidence to demand a reduction in the American troops stationed on its soil.

Rapid GDP growth, fueled partly by large Taiwanese investment, helped to calm Beijing's relations with the offshore island, which had ranged between tense to belligerent since the founding of the PRC in 1949.

It was Washington's refusal to recognize the PRC as the legitimate successor to the Republic of China (ROC) that denied Beijing its seat at the UN. Not until 1971 did America relent and let the PRC take its seat at the UN Security Council as a permanent member. Following the historic Nixon-Mao meeting the next year, the Nixon administration opened a U.S. Liaison Office in Beijing on a reciprocal basis. In the 1972 U.S.-PRC communiqué, Washington acknowledged the "One China" policy claimed by both the PRC and Taiwan as the ROC's rump. The 1979 U.S.-PRC communiqué, which led to the establishment of full diplomatic relations between the two nations, reiterated Washington's earlier position on "One China."

Though Washington does not recognize Taiwan as a sovereign state, it maintains close trade and defense links with it. It is committed to protecting Taiwan from PRC attack—but not if Taiwan were to declare formal independence first. While America wants to maintain Taiwan in a twilight zone, Beijing is determined to reclaim the rebel province by any means.

Over the decades there have been several episodes of high drama between the mainland and the offshore island. But following Deng's "peaceful rise" doctrine, Beijing has supplemented its policy of pointing hundreds of missiles at Taiwan with a drive to integrate the rebel province economically. All along, the PRC has refused to have trade or diplomatic links with any country that recognizes Taiwan as the sovereign Republic of China.

Beijing allowed Taiwanese entrepreneurs to invest in the mainland's mushrooming SEZs. They did so in droves. By 2007, over 50,000 Taiwanese companies, with an investment of $150 billion, manufactured electronics, toys, and textiles, and built hotels and apartment blocks. The two-way commerce between the mainland and Taiwan exceeded $100 billion, with China becoming Taiwan's biggest trading partner. An estimated 1 million Taiwanese lived and worked on the mainland.

By then, the Hong Kong Special Administrative Region had been functioning as a semiautonomous region for a decade. That underscored Beijing's continued commitment to uphold the doctrine of "one country, two systems."

In 2008, Washington sided with Beijing to subdue Taiwan's aspirations of international recognition. It became a burning issue when the government of President Chen Shui-bian, leader of the pro-independence Democratic Progressive Party, decided to hold a referendum on Taiwan's application for UN membership along with the presidential poll in March. Sticking to its "three harmonies" doctrine, the Hu government refrained from issuing threats while anticipating a compensatory move by the Bush administration. It came. The White House described the referendum as "provocative" and a danger to stability in East Asia. The referendum failed.

Since Taiwan's economy was lagging behind the mainland's, National Party (Kuomintang) candidate Ma Ying-jeou promised stronger commercial ties with the PRC. That appealed to electors. He defeated Chen Shui-bian, who was seeking reelection.

Relations across the Taiwan Strait improved. Ma dispatched National Party chairman Wu Poh-Hsiung to Beijing to meet Hu. Within months the weekend chartered flights across the Strait trebled to 108, circumventing Hong Kong, as had been the case so far. And arrangements were agreed on for maritime shipping between sixty-three Chinese ports and eleven Taiwan ports.[41]

HUGGING THE RUSSIAN BEAR

After the founding of the PRC, Mao forged a close alliance with the Soviet Union, which helped the new republic to industrialize. But the alliance collapsed in 1960 because of irreconcilable ideological differences, with Soviet leader Nikita Khrushchev criticizing Mao as "an ultraleftist" for his policy of further collectivization of peasants into people's communes and the organ of the CPC, *People's Daily*, denouncing Khrushchev as a "bourgeois revisionist." The split lasted until 1989, when Gorbachev normalized relations with Beijing.

The PRC started purchasing Russian warplanes, submarines, destroyers, and missiles. The Beijing-Moscow military links tightened as a result of the European Union's continued ban on the sale of sophisticated weapons to the PRC following its violent repression of the Tiananmen Square protest.

The PLA lost little time in copying the Russian-designed PT-76 tank, calling it T-62, and manufacturing it domestically. It did the same with several versions of MiG fighter jets, giving them different names. Then it assembled 120 Russian Su-27SK fighter jets and stopped importing them. Overall Beijing-Moscow relations had become so cordial that the Kremlin made allowances for the PLA's ongoing efforts to become self-reliant. By 2005, the Chinese had produced their own independently designed, third-generation fighter jet, J-10, which was on a par with the U.S.-made F-16 and Mirage 2000 of France. China's procurement of supercomputers aided research and design in military and civilian sectors. Among the five hundred fastest computers, used mostly for research, China had fifteen—the largest total outside America, Western Europe, and Japan. Some of the PRC's supercomputers were assembled by a Chinese company.[42]

In diplomacy, China worked closely with Russia at the UN Security Council to counter the Clinton administration's belligerent policy toward President Saddam Hussein of Iraq. To dissuade Washington from resorting to force on the issue of unconditional access to UN inspectors investigating Iraq's WMD program, in February 1998 Beijing sided with Paris and Moscow, which threatened to veto a Security Council resolution authorizing use of force against Iraq. The nonviolent resolution of the Washington-Baghdad standoff was welcomed by Beijing, which was committed to settling disputes peacefully.

Earlier, nearer home, President Jiang sponsored the Shanghai Forum (later renamed the Shanghai Cooperation Organization, SCO), in 1996 to include four adjoining countries: Russia, Kazakhstan, Kyrgyzstan, and Tajikistan. Based in Beijing, its task was to delineate disputed boundaries.[43]

The interests of Beijing and Moscow converged in Central Asia. They shared the common aims of curbing Islamist extremism and drug smuggling, maintaining and improving their commercial interests, and frustrating Washington's agenda to dominate the region.

The United States disapproved of the way Beijing had begun bolstering the SCO, which at its August 1999 summit set up a joint anti-terrorism center in Bishkek. At the PRC's behest, the SCO added Uzbekistan to its ranks even though it does not share borders with all other SCO members, the founding requirement.

In July 2001, during his visit to Moscow, Jiang signed the Sino-Russian Friendship Treaty with President Vladimir Putin. Commerce between the two neighbors thrived. With China emerging as the workshop of the world, and Russia as a preeminent supplier of hydrocarbons, the economies of the two neighbors were complementary, not competitive.

From the modest imports of 50,000 bpd of Russian oil in 2002, shipments from Russia climbed to 300,000 bpd in three years. A fifth of this oil was delivered by rail. Such a large volume made feasible the project of building a Russia-China pipeline 1,500 miles (2,400 kilometers) long, costing $2 billion. It was expected to carry double the current amount. Later, in early 2009, China, flush with cash, would strike a mutually beneficial bargain with Russia. In exchange for a $25 billion loan from China Development Bank, Rosneft and Transneft, the pipeline operator, agreed to provide 300,000 bpd additional oil to China over twenty-five years through a trans-Siberian pipeline to be finished in 2010.[44]

The new charter adopted by the SCO in 2003 specified "noninterference and nonalignment" in international affairs while aiming to create "a new international political and economic order"—implying thereby to end the role of the United States as the sole superpower, an aim first expressed by China and Russia four years earlier.

After Uzbek President Islam Karimov had been condemned by the Western media and governments for the massacre of 167 to 500 unarmed protestors by the security forces in Andijan in May 2005, the Chinese government greeted him with a twenty-one-gun salute during his visit to Beijing in July. He departed with a joint venture in oil worth $600 million. Later that month, at the SCO summit, China and Russia called on the United States to specify the withdrawal date of its soldiers and military hardware from Uzbekistan's Qarshi-Khanabad and Kyrgyzstan's Manas bases it had leased on the eve of the Afghanistan War in October 2001. Karimov canceled the Pentagon's lease of Qarshi-Khanabad.

To widen its influence, the SCO granted observer status not only to Iran but also to India, Pakistan, and Mongolia. In contrast, the SCO rejected

Washington's application for observer status, an embarrassing setback: The United States enjoyed such a status at the Association of South-East Asian Nations (ASEAN).[45]

The weeklong joint Sino-Russian military exercises conducted on China's Shandong Peninsula in August 2005—meant to test the capability of the two armed forces in jointly striking forces of international terrorism, extremism, or separatism—were the first of their kind. (The deployment of fighter aircraft and heavy weaponry militated against the claim of fighting terrorism.) The maneuvers involved 8,000 Chinese and 2,000 Russian troops equipped with a Russian navy squadron and seventeen long-haul aircraft plus nonnuclear-powered submarines, and included amphibious and paratroop landings on the Shandong Peninsula in the Yellow Sea. The exercises were the latest twist in the "Great Game" of major powers in the post-Soviet era in hydrocarbon-rich Central Asia, where there was mounting resistance to the post-9/11 U.S. military presence.

Admiral Gary Roughead, commander of the U.S. Pacific Fleet, told the Associated Press that he was "curious" to know how the two navies would operate and how they would command and control their forces, and how they would integrate in a combined way. He had noticed that since 1993 Chinese submarines and surface ships had been pushing beyond their earlier areas of operation near the PRC's eastern coast.[46] After more than six decades the Pentagon's near-total dominance of the Pacific was being challenged by the increased presence of the Chinese and Russian navies.

In 2005–2006, the PLA's production and acquisition of submarines was five times the Pentagon's. Its strategic aim was to keep U.S. aircraft carriers away from the Asian shoreline if and when necessary. It therefore focused on acquiring sea mines and ballistic missiles that target moving objects at sea and technology that can block U.S.-controlled GPS satellites. This was to be the high end of an asymmetrical warfare, favored by China's Central Military Commission, whose low end, widely practiced in Iraq, was the improvised explosive device (IED).

On the SCO's tenth anniversary in June 2006, Hu chaired the first summit of the organization's six members, along with high representatives of the four observer nations—India, Iran, Pakistan, and Mongolia. Altogether these nations accounted for almost half of the human race. What alarmed Washington was Putin's proposal that the SCO should form an "energy club," which was backed by Iranian President Mahmoud Ahmadinejad's offer to host a meeting of SCO members and observers to discuss energy issues in the region.

Hu's statement that the SCO was not directed at "third parties" failed to reassure Washington—and its closest Asian ally, Japan. "The SCO is becoming a rival block to the U.S. alliance," noted a senior Japanese official. "It does not share our values. We are watching it very closely."[47] Japan was hardly being paranoid. In August 2007, the SCO conducted its first joint military exercises in the Russian Ural region of Chelyabinsk. These were watched by Putin and Hu. The message was not lost on Tokyo or Washington.

During the visit of Putin's successor, Dmitry Medvedev, to Beijing in May 2008, he and Hu condemned the Bush administration's project for an antimissile shield in Eastern Europe. They argued that it would upset the balance of power. If the succeeding Barack Obama administration persists in implementing this plan, and also succeeds in getting Ukraine and Georgia admitted into NATO, then China, equipped almost exclusively with advanced Russian-made or -designed weapons, will most probably attempt to restore the balance of power by upgrading the SCO into a NATO-style military alliance. This is all the more likely if the United States refuses to enter into an international agreement to ban space weaponry and—as expected—starts deploying such weapons. Moscow and Beijing will then most likely pool their resources to enter this expensive arms race.

GLOBAL HUNT FOR OIL AND METALS

Once the PRC became an oil importer in 1993, its imports rose by an annual average of 24 percent, doubling every three years. This made China vulnerable to the vagaries of the international oil market. That in turn resulted in the State Council incorporating energy security into its foreign policy. It decided to participate in hydrocarbon prospecting and production projects abroad as well as in transnational pipeline construction. Diversification of the sources of oil and gas and their transportation became its leading credo. Its domestic drive pushed oil output from 2.89 million bpd in 1993 to 3.74 million bpd in 2007.

Conscious of the volatile environment of the Middle East, China explored Africa, Australia, and Latin America. The PRC's inroads into Africa caught the world's eye when it hosted the first China-Africa Forum in Beijing in November 2006. Attended by the leaders of all forty-eight African nations that recognize the PRC, Beijing left Washington woefully behind in the diplomatic race for Africa and its hydrocarbon and other resources.[48]

An underdeveloped continent three times the size of China, Africa was rich in natural resources. The continent contained one-third of the globe's uranium, half of its gold, two-thirds of its manganese, nine-tenths of its platinum and cobalt, and almost all of its chromium. The PRC was eager to gain access to these minerals to feed its fast-growing industry. By 2003, China's rapid industrialization had made it consume 25 percent of the world's aluminum, steel, and copper, thereby outstripping America. For hydrocarbons, the PRC focused on Angola, Gabon, Nigeria, Somalia, and Sudan.[49] Its copper supplies came from Zambia, iron ore from South Africa, platinum from Zimbabwe, and tropical timber from Congo Brazzaville. Little wonder that China's trade with Africa had almost quadrupled to $48 billion in the six years before the 2006 China-Africa Forum, and that nearly five hundred Chinese companies were active in Africa on their own or in partnership with local firms.

In return for Africa's oil and minerals, China sold low-priced goods to its inhabitants and assisted African countries in building or improving roads, railways, ports, power plants, hydroelectric dams, telecommunications systems, and schools. Chinese workers and executives became as much of a common sight in Africa as they had in the Persian Gulf region earlier. Unlike the United States and the World Bank, China did not prescribe the Western economic or political model for the African countries it assisted. Beijing's aid to African states also far exceeded the World Bank's. The weakening of the World Bank and the IMF in the wake of the 2008–2009 fiscal crisis assisted China in realizing its foreign policy aim of seeing developing countries released from the vagaries of Western capital and Washington's dominance. This was to be the first essential step—in Beijing's international scenario—to restore to sovereign nation-states control of the economy and the profile of domestic politics reflecting local history and culture. For the future, there was the (unspoken) prospect of a large number of skilled and/or entrepreneurial Chinese settling down in some of the sparsely populated but resource-rich African countries, thus helping to invigorate the local economy while relieving demographic pressure in China.

The PRC had targeted Africa before—in the 1960s to help national liberation movements in the colonized parts of the continent through its Communist cadres. In a much changed world, this time it was the China National

Petroleum Corporation (CNPC)—not CPC—which worked hard to gain a foothold in Africa. It was not until 1995 that the CNPC won an oil exploitation contract in Sudan. Two years later it got a further break. Washington banned U.S. trade with Sudan after listing it as a country that supported state terrorism, resulting in Occidental Petroleum withdrawing its oil and pipeline contracts. The Chinese firms quickly filled the gap. Within three months of the Chinese building an oil terminal at Suakin on the Red Sea in May 1999, the first oil supertanker sailed off to China.

By 2005, Sudan, an oil importer before the CNPC's arrival, earned $2 billion a year in oil exports, half of which went to China.

What made the CNPC attractive to the rulers of Sudan and other African states was Beijing's willingness and ability to provide its economic partners political-diplomatic cover when necessary. This unstated understanding became manifest in 2004. When the issue of the massacres in the troubled Sudanese western region of Darfur was debated at the UN Security Council in September, Washington wanted to impose economic sanctions against Sudan. Beijing threatened to veto such a resolution. So the Security Council passed a watered-down resolution on Darfur.

The PRC's relentless quest for hydrocarbons and metals led it to tap sources in Australia and Latin America. By 2006, the China National Offshore Oil Company (Cnooc) had invested in oil and gas exploration rights in Australia, Azerbaijan, Bangladesh, Indonesia, Thailand, and Vietnam. During his visit to Nigeria in April, Chinese President Hu received a standing ovation at the National Assembly when he described China as "a developing country." His statement was at odds with the fact that Beijing had promised $4 billion of infrastructure investment—railways, power plants, and telephones—in the oil-bearing area in return for preferential treatment in the allocation of upcoming exploration and production rights in the oil acreage.

By 2006–2007, the PRC had become the number one buyer of Australian iron ore, manganese, and uranium. The contract for the supply of Australian liquefied natural gas (LNG) between North West Shelf Australia LNG and Guangdong Dapeng LNG in 2004 became the largest single Australian export contract in history.

A diplomatic payoff followed. One of only three countries to commit combat troops for the 2003 U.S.-led invasion of Iraq, Australia said that Washington should not assume its automatic backing for any military assistance the United States might offer against a PRC attack on Taiwan.[50]

While the PRC vigorously pursued its policy of investment and trade in East Asia and the Pacific, as a prelude to challenging U.S. primacy in the Asia-Pacific in the future, the Pentagon prepared for the day when its land bases would be reduced to the minimum. It began fortifying its bases in Palau, Guam, Okinawa, and Hawaii, to fashion an entirely sea-based network of logistics and access channels to enable it to function militarily in a region where America was losing popularity. Washington's influence in Latin America and the Caribbean was also waning.

In 2004, Hu became the first Chinese president to visit Argentina, Brazil, Chile, and Cuba. With the PRC offering lucrative prices for iron ore and soybeans—the export commodities fueling the GDP growth in Argentina and Brazil—relations with these leading Latin American countries had strengthened. Five years later, China Development Bank would agree to loan Brazil's oil company $10 billion to lock up supply of 160,000 bpd in the coming years.[51]

After the Panama Canal was handed over to Panama in 1997, the Hong Kong–based Hutchinson Whampoa company, with a global reputation for managing ports, won the contract to manage ports on both sides of the Canal and handle cargo as well. Though this was a deal with a private firm, it gave the PRC a strategic footing in Central America.[52] It provided an incentive for the upgrading of Central American ports by Chinese firms to expedite the delivery of the PRC's goods to U.S. destinations.

By the time Hu undertook his second tour of Latin America in 2008, fifteen countries in the region had accorded the PRC "market economy status," thereby accelerating trade. The two-way trade at $150 billion was twelve times the figure for 2000. Moreover, the election of leftist leaders in Bolivia, Brazil, Chile, Ecuador, Paraguay, and Venezuela strengthened diplomatic ties, with the international department of the Communist Party of China maintaining fraternal relations with the leftist parties in these countries. This disconcerted Washington.

But what aroused alarm at the State Department was the trips that four members of China's Central Military Commission made to Latin America in 2006–2007. The PRC had become a growing source of weapons supplies to the countries in the region, and it had been training their military officers.[53] Even in the commercial sphere, Washington kept a wary eye on Beijing, uneasy about the way the state-owned Chinese oil corporations were cornering hydrocarbon reserves globally—from Kazakhstan to Australia, and from Angola to Peru.

THE DRAGON AND UNCLE SAM

The simmering tensions between America and the PRC came to the fore in June 2005. Cnooc outbid Chevron for the ownership of Unocal, an American oil corporation, producing less than 1 percent of U.S. crude oil. It aroused harsh political reaction in America, where the president is authorized to bar a takeover on national security grounds.

Reflecting the Bush administration's hostility toward Cnooc, Unocal share-holders rejected its $1.5 billion higher bid. Bush's stance was criticized by many in the United States. Among them was David Goldwyn, former assistant energy secretary under Clinton: "What this misguided policy did was to say that the U.S. will not advocate fair trade when it comes to American assets."[54] The Bush White House was unmoved.

On the eve of Hu's visit to Washington in April 2006, U.S. officials briefed the media to the effect that the Chinese oil companies should not "lock up" energy supplies and should "open" them up. Such homilies were delivered by Washington, which since the early 1990s had been actively guiding Big Oil on how it should bolster its share of the oil acreage outside the Middle East, particularly in Central Asia and Azerbaijan, and implement the State Department's policy of excluding Iran from the region's hydrocarbon industry.

Overall, relations between Beijing and Washington remained equivocal. Trade between the two nations was thriving, with Chinese exports to America in 2007 at $321.5 billion and imports from the United States only $65 billion. The respective figures for 2000, when the PRC was not a WTO member, were $100 billion and $16 billion.[55] In 2004, China's exports of information and communication technology at $180 billion surpassed America's at $149 billion.

In July 2005, the People's Bank of China, the PRC's central bank, broke the peg of 8.28 yuans to 1 U.S. dollar with the ultimate aim of having a market-based, floating rate. It allowed the yuan to appreciate gradually, thus making Chinese exports more expensive. Nonetheless, because of the imbalance in Chinese-American trade, Beijing's foreign exchange reserves soared from $167 million in 1978 to $854 billion by March 2006, a shade higher than Japan's, which had been built up over four decades of rising exports. China invested these funds mostly in U.S. Treasury and Government Sponsored Enterprises—such as Fannie Mae and Freddie Mac—and a variety of other financial instruments that earned a meager return. But they provided the PRC a political lever to be used in the future, if necessary.

In 2006, China overtook Japan to become the holder of the largest foreign reserves in the world, well past $1 trillion. The following year, the PRC's exports at $1.22 trillion surpassed America's, to reach number two in the international league after Germany. At home the PRC's budget surplus had been rising since 2003 and was more than 1 trillion yuan (or $140 billion) in 2007. Given its bulging public treasury, it followed that the PRC would devote part of it to modernize its armed forces. But that aroused Washington's ire.

During his June 2005 visit to Singapore, an important naval base, U.S. Defense Secretary Donald Rumsfeld said, "China's defense expenditures are much higher than Chinese officials have published. Since no nation threatens China, why these continuing large and expanding arms purchases?" Beijing retorted that there was no hidden military budget. Rumsfeld conveniently overlooked the fact that the Pentagon's 281 ships and half a million members in the navy exceeded the total of the next seventeen naval nations.[56] The PRC's declared budget of $45 billion was a tiny fraction of the Pentagon's $459 billion. Even if the undeclared budget were as large as the official one, the total would still be about one-fifth of Washington's annual defense outlay.

MODERNIZING MILITARY AND INNOVATING WAR STRATEGY

Policymakers in Beijing realized that China's economic interests had galloped at a faster rate than its military capacity to safeguard them, and decided to narrow the gap.

Priority was given to safeguarding the sea lanes for oil tankers. Beijing gave Pakistan $200 million to construct a deepwater port in Gwadar, only 390 nautical miles from the Straits of Hormuz, one of the three choke points of global trade, others being Bab al Mandeb leading to the Red Sea and the Malacca Strait in Southeast Asia. China began negotiating to upgrade the Bangladeshi deepwater port of Chittagong, which would enable the Chinese navy to safeguard the sea lane leading to Burma's deepwater port in Sittwe, where an oil pipeline was being built to take the imported crude to China overland. Once these facilities are in place, the PRC will project its naval power toward the Middle East and Indian Ocean, dominated so far by the Pentagon.[57]

Chinese leaders' military doctrine consisted of do's and don'ts. They did not want to replicate the Soviet Union's blunder of entering into a one-on-one arms race with the Pentagon, raising its cumulative total of nuclear arms to a staggering 50,000 at its peak and going bankrupt in the process. Since its testing of an atom bomb in 1964, China's nuclear arsenal has increased slowly, reaching 240 weapons by the end of 2007. By then, Russia had 5,200 nuclear weapons deployed, and the United States had almost 5,400 deployed.[58] The PRC's modernization program launched much later, focused as much on upgrading the old bombs as on developing and deploying mobile, land-based missiles—FD-31 and DF-31A—capable of reaching targets anywhere in the United States. Being mobile they were almost immune to attacks by the Pentagon. The plan was to point 75 to 100 FD-31s and DF-31As, armed with nuclear weapons, at the United States as a deterrent.[59]

That neatly circumvented the declaration in *The National Security Strategy of the United States*, issued by the Bush administration in September 2001: "Our forces will be strong enough to dissuade potential adversaries from pursuing a military buildup in hopes of surpassing, or equaling, the power of the United States." What the PRC's policymakers were interested in was to devise innovative ways of defeating "a technologically superior opponent"—a coded phrase for America.[60]

Though the PLA's modernization had progressed as planned, its means to sustain fighting away from the Chinese border remained limited. Nevertheless, it was developing "disruptive military technologies"—to quote Washington's 2006 Quadrennial Defense Review Report—to offset the superiority of the Pentagon. While, so far, the PRC has lacked strong motivation to challenge the United States in any conflict over natural resources or disputed territories, it is steadily building up the ability to do so.

Taiwan remains a potential flashpoint. The plan to fire its nine hundred short-range and medium-range ballistic missiles to overwhelm Taiwan's air defenses and offensive missile capacity has been in place for many years. The PLA aims to deprive the Pentagon of its crucial intelligence by targeting its satellites either to destroy them or to blind them by using lasers. The test-firing of the PLA's first anti-satellite missile, which successfully destroyed an obsolete Chinese weather satellite in January 2007, demonstrated its growing technological prowess.

China has been upgrading its ballistic and cruise missile systems to improve the range, accuracy, and survivability of these weapons. Its specific aim is to accurately target U.S. aircraft carrier groups at sea as they sail toward Taiwan—to gain time for PLA ground forces to occupy the offshore island.

To locate U.S. aircraft carriers precisely and quickly, China has upgraded the range of its satellites. It continues to enhance the constellation of its orbiting rockets and satellites; it added fifteen rockets and seventeen satellites in 2008 alone.[61] The PRC is forging ahead with its project to build a Beidou 2 global satellite system while participating in Europe's Galileo commercial satellite navigation system.

In doctrinal terms, China's military strategists derive their inspiration from *The Art of War*, attributed to an outstanding general, Sun Zi (Sun-Tzi), a contemporary of Confucius. One verse says, "To defeat the enemy without fighting is the epitome of skill." Sun Zi's overall message is "Attack the enemy's strategy first, his troops second." The ancient general seems to have inspired two young PLA army colonels, Qiao Liang and Wang Xiang-Sui, to write *Unrestricted Warfare*. It was published by the PLA Literature and Arts Publishing House in 1999.[62]

Using a very elastic definition of "warfare," they came up with a comprehensive list of military, trans-military, and nonmilitary ways of defeating the enemy. Under military, they listed atomic, conventional, biochemical, ecological, space, electronic, guerrilla, and terrorist warfare. Their trans-military list consisted of diplomatic, network, intelligence, psychological, tactical, smuggling, drug, and virtual deterrence means. And the nonmilitary category included financial, trade, resources, economic aid, sanctions, the media, and ideological.

The last classification was basically a description of the Cold War that the United States and the Soviet Union waged. In the post–Cold War era, the shattering of the economies of the Asian tigers in 1997 caused by such nonstate actors as George Soros, an international currency speculator, was illustrative. As for the intermediate "trans-military" category, such practices are not limited to nations that are unfriendly or hostile to one another. For instance, Israel is known to collect intelligence in the United States. Equally, while China and America have thriving commercial links, they also steal each other's intelligence—commercial, diplomatic, and military.

With an uncanny prescience Qiao and Wang predicted that "a technologically superior power" would overreact to an attack of "super terrorism." In such an attack, they wrote, "an adversary which uses conventional forces and measures as its main combat strength looks like a big elephant charging into a china shop." This turned out to be an apt description of what the Bush administration did after 9/11.

They raised and answered the age-old, key question: How can a militarily inferior country defeat a superior one? By blending nonmilitary and trans-military means, applying them preferably in an obfuscated manner, and making a skillful use of multinational, supranational, and nonstate institutions.

Through an adroit mix of economic aid, weapons sales, and diplomacy, the PRC succeeded in diluting the impact of economic and other sanctions by America and its Western allies against Burma, Iran, North Korea, Sudan, and Uzbekistan while advancing its own interests.

Beijing's short- and long-term strategies gelled with the edicts of Deng. As for tactics, it was best to look for weaknesses in the armory of the adversary, present or potential. The Chinese noted the heavy dependence on computers of most militaries and saw it as a chink in the armor to be exploited. The goal was to extract intelligence and/or disrupt communications and signals processing. But to the chagrin of the Chinese, the Pentagon had reached a similar conclusion earlier and had targeted the PRC's networks. In the course of defending itself, China seems to have trained cyber warriors so well that they developed an offensive strategy.

Cyber Warfare

The Chinese cyber warriors deployed computer-developed tools as part of the PLA's "pressure point warfare," attacking specific nodes to leave the adversary paralyzed. Their attacks involved using viruses, giving false information, and installing spying software. By so doing, they partially offset the considerable edge that the United States had in technology and firepower. An advanced technique in cyber warfare involved hackers turning thousands of computers into "zombies" under their control and linking them into a botnet, which overwhelmed the targeted internet service provider with simultaneous traffic until the ISP crashed.

In their 2002 cyber attack—code-named "Titan Rain" by the Pentagon—China's hackers downloaded up to twenty tetrabytes of data, twice the amount in the printed collection of the Library of Congress. Since then, the cost of high-tech strikes on government communications has fallen, while the amount of damage they inflict has risen. In June 2007, one or more hackers originating from China reportedly hacked into the Pentagon's military network, penetrating the e-mail system of Defense Secretary Robert Gates.[63]

According to a congressional report published in November 2008, the 43,880 cyber attacks in 2007 were a third higher than those in the previous year. The targets were the U.S. government, defense companies, and businesses. It alleged that China "tolerated" about 250 hacker groups, which stole vast amounts of sensitive U.S. information. While denying the allegation, the PRC described hacking as "criminal" and said that it was "a frequent victim" of hacking.[64] By now cyber warfare has reached such proportions that NATO commanders have bracketed it with missile defense and energy security.

What started as probing on an experimental basis has escalated into a well-financed and organized operation to gain diplomatic, military, economic, and technical information, with espionage agencies worldwide constantly checking foreign governments' networks for their strengths and weaknesses and developing new ways of stealing intelligence. In a wider sense, this was the downside of globalization—in communications, industry, and financial services. That was why and how the fiscal meltdown in Wall Street went global, affecting the developing economies of China and India—which was not the case with the Great Crash of 1929.

At the first sign of the fiscal crisis on Wall Street, China tried to plug the hole in the dam. Its sovereign wealth fund, China Investment Corporation, with capital of $200 billion, bought a 10 percent interest in the ailing Morgan Stanley, an investment bank. Morgan Stanley survived the meltdown.

Urged by Paulson, the People's Bank bought $280 billion worth of U.S. Treasury and state and municipal bonds. That raised its foreign reserves to $1.9 trillion.[65] With an appreciating yuan, which rose above the psychologically important 7 yuans to the dollar level in April 2008, and high Chinese inflation, the People's Bank was losing 10 percent a year on dollar holdings while earning only 3 percent interest on U.S. Treasuries.[66] Because of shrinking demand from American consumers, import orders from the United States fell, hurting the Chinese industry. But the PRC was better equipped to weather the storm than America or any other Western nation. Indeed, it provided an added opportunity to the Hu government to rectify the imbalances created during Jiang's presidency.

An Opportunity for Domestic Reconfiguration

Chinese leaders viewed the havoc the U.S. shadow banking system caused globally with a mixture of schadenfreude, self-congratulation, and concern.

The events had vindicated their policies of controlling the banking sector and disregarding Washington's criticism that their banks were shoveling money to the companies favored by the CPC in order to limit joblessness and social instability. Now they found Paulson shoving cash down the pillars of Wall Street to spare America massive layoffs.

In his speech at the World Economic Forum in Davos in January 2009, Chinese Prime Minister Wen blamed "inappropriate macroeconomic policies of some economies and their unsustainable models of development characterized by low savings and high consumption" and "an excessive expansion of financial instruments in blind pursuit of profit, lack of self-discipline among financial institutions and ratings agencies." For once, it was China admonishing Western leaders, not the other way around. Wen added that the direct impact of the crisis on China was "limited because of our banking system."[67]

In November 2008, the People's Bank lowered the interest rate to 5.58 percent and reduced the reserves requirement for the banking sector by 1 percent to 15.5 percent (large banks) and 14.5 percent (small banks). By international standards, the reserves figure was almost twice as large, indicating a healthier state of the Chinese banking industry than elsewhere. To recapitalize the state-owned commercial banks, the government rapidly injected funds from its $1.9 trillion foreign reserves to cover the banks' bad loans.

Among the financial world's big players, China's national debt at 18.4 percent of the GDP was almost a quarter of the statistic for America.

Equally impressive was the stimulus package that Beijing offered. At $586 billion to be spent over two years, it amounted to 13.8 percent of GDP—and was well ahead of Washington's 4.5 percent for one year. Its plan included a wide range of infrastructure and social welfare projects, including new highways, railroads, and airports, and rebuilding the earthquake-stricken areas in the Sichuan province—as well as low-cost housing, rural electrification, and subsidies for the purchase of cell phones, washing machines, and flat-screen TVs. Coupled with the package was a program to spend $123 billion in three years to provide some form of health insurance to 90 percent of the population.

Besides raising wages for public sector employees, the Hu government's steps included discouraging saving and thus increasing consumption, regaining Beijing's control over major investment decisions by state-owned companies and provincial governments, and improving farm price support and rural infrastructure.

These policies dovetailed with the overall stress that the Hu presidency had been placing on improving the lot of peasants and workers. It was keen to redress the glaring imbalance between rural and urban incomes, the former having been reduced to a third of the latter.

Visiting the village of Xiaogang in Anhui province in September 2008, which pioneered private agriculture in 1978, Hu announced that farmers would be allowed to transfer their land contracts and management rights to others offering better terms. The next month the plenum of the CPC's Central Committee decided to extend the land lease from thirty to seventy years and establish markets where farmers can subcontract, lease, exchange, or swap land-use rights, or join agricultural cooperatives. It was expected that selling the contracts would lead to large-scale farms. The end purpose was to double per capita rural income by 2020 by achieving "economies of scale" through the creation of "big agricultural conglomerates," to improve productivity to increase food supplies needed for higher living standards, to help families save enough to gain access to cities for work, and "to set up a modern rural financial network and a system to balance the development between rural and urban areas, and improve rural democracy."[68]

The Chinese government mandated that all five hundred top foreign companies should unionize and pay 2 percent of the payroll as union dues. This was part of the labor law passed a year earlier to benefit all workers. Initially, there was resistance to this measure by foreign firms, which had been pampered by Chinese authorities during the Jiang presidency. But they fell in line when they realized that Hu's government was serious about tackling the problems of widening inequalities and labor abuse, which were commonplace during his predecessor's rule.

In the face of the global downturn, PRC leaders resolved to prevent GDP growth in 2009 from falling below 8 percent. They perceived an opportunity to lift the PRC up the value chain from small-margin manufacturers on a high volume to service and knowledge-based industries. That meant not only retraining the laid-off workers as Western nations had done earlier but also loosening control of universities, laboratories, and enterprises to encourage innovation through experimentation and incentives.

With its traditional Western lenders mired in a slump, the IMF appealed to China and oil-rich Gulf monarchies for $150 billion it needed to help poor developing countries overcome the fiscal crisis. Reflecting the general sentiment in the non-Western world, China's official *People's Daily* published a call by Shi Jianxun, a prominent Chinese economist, for "a diversified financial order that is not dependent on the United States." In a similar vein, Dominique Strauss-Kahn, the IMF's managing director, said that the organization should be more relevant to the rising economic powers like Brazil, Russia, India, and China—often grouped together as BRIC—and that necessitated a reallocation of votes. In demographic terms, China and India stand out, being the first and second most populous nations on earth. Both are also old civilizations. They interacted with each other in ancient times, when Buddhism, originating in India, spread to the Middle Kingdom. In the modern era, the (English) East India Company became the link between them. Emulating the growth of tea on a large scale in China, it set up tea plantations in northeast India in 1837.

CHAPTER 6

INDIA STRIVES

The republic of India was carved out of the Indian subcontinent colonized by Britain for almost two centuries. A grasp of the history of pre-independent India is, therefore, essential to understanding that complex, multiethnic republic. It is also important to comprehend how and why India differs widely from the People's Republic of China—and why it has fallen far behind the PRC economically even when the Communist Party of China inherited a country ravaged by eighteen years of Japanese aggression, World War II, and a civil war.

It was the disintegrating Mughal Empire in the eighteenth century that allowed the (English) East India Company—a commercial entity with its own army and navy—to conquer the subcontinent. It did so in stages by exploiting rivalries between the competing indigenous rulers and financing its battles with the land taxes it collected.

As it happens, the East India Company provides an illustrious example of how trading and political interests overlap, with the subsequent political hegemony incorporating the initial commercial thrust. It is also the earliest case of a failing business turning to the government for a bailout and accepting the state's supervisory role—a scenario being repeated today, worldwide.

Established by Queen Elizabeth I's royal charter in 1600, the privately owned "Honorable Company of Merchants of London Trading into the East Indies"—later East India Company—started trading in Indian cotton, yarn and fabrics, indigo, rock salt, spices, molasses, and saltpeter. Over the next two centuries it evolved into a mighty commercial-political-military entity, with its own army, navy, and civil service, and its activities spreading to China and beyond.

It was in the Indian subcontinent, however, that the East India Company acquired its elevated status of a "delegation of the whole power and sovereignty of the United Kingdom sent into the East"—to quote Edmund Burke (1729–1797), an eminent British politician.

Having fortified its trading stations in Calcutta (Kolkata), Madras (Chennai), and Bombay (Mumbai) by 1700, it went on to defeat the local ruler at Plassey near Calcutta in 1757 and become the dominant political power in eastern India. It then succeeded in relegating the Mughal ruler in Delhi to a pensioner. Financially weakened by its newly acquired administrative tasks, in 1773 it applied for and secured a loan from the British government, subject to its accepting parliamentary supervision. In 1784, while the India Act invested the British government with ultimate power over the East India Company, the Commutation Act set the scene for its increased trade with China. Integral to this was the practice of using opium, grown in India, as a barter for tea and other Chinese goods. Indeed the opium trade proved so lucrative that it became a powerful argument for maintaining British hegemony in India. It led to the Opium Wars of the early 1840s, when the Chinese emperor tried to end the nefarious commerce.

In their Great Uprising of 1857–1858, involving civilians and soldiers, the Indians tried to throw off the foreign yoke. They failed. The British government dispensed with the intermediary, the East India Company, and imposed direct rule. The independence that came in 1947 along with the partition of the subcontinent into India and Pakistan was the result of a long, mostly nonviolent struggle against British rule, waged chiefly by the Indian National Congress, popularly called the Congress Party. Indian nationalism originated in and grew in contradiction to British imperial rule.

Since London's control of India provided the British industry at home with cheap raw materials and a large market for its manufactured goods, and gave preferred treatment to the British investors in India, it was opposed by the fledgling Indian capitalists. Foreign rule had proved harmful to the economic interest of Indians. The annual GDP growth rate during the last three decades of the British raj was 0.7 percent, a fraction of the annual rise in the population, with real incomes declining overall by 10 percent.[1] The literacy rate was 18 percent, and life expectancy thirty-two years.

During its first six decades of independence, India not only reversed the economic stagnation it suffered under the British, it forged ahead in industry (manufacturing and knowledge), more than doubled life expectancy, raised the literacy rate to 66 percent, and enhanced its military might, joining the exclusive club of the nuclear-armed nations.

Yet India still faces daunting problems. Nearly three-quarters of its citizens continue to live in villages that often lack basic amenities. According to the 2006 United Nations Human Development Report, India ranked 128 in the Human Development Index among 177 countries, compared to China's ranking of 81, Brazil's 70, and Mexico's 52.[2] Sixty-five percent of Indians depend on agriculture—10 percent more than in China—which contributes only 17 percent of the GDP. About a quarter of its 1.2 billion people, living below the poverty line—existing on less than a dollar a day, as defined by the government—are unable to afford an adequate diet.[3] With half of its children being underweight, the figure is almost twice that for sub-Saharan Africa. Although a vigorously implemented family planning program has brought the annual population growth to below 2 percent, the current density of 962 persons per square mile (337 per square kilometer)—two and a half times the figure for China—remains too high for a developing economy.[4] Socially, caste consciousness among rural Hindus remains strong. And violence between majority Hindus and minority Muslims erupts periodically.

INDIA UNDER NEHRU

Within a few years of independence, Jawaharlal Nehru, a leading light of the Congress Party, became India's sole surviving founding father. He had the charisma to hold together a polyglot republic of sixteen major languages during its fledgling years and governed it as the executive prime minister for seventeen years.

The masses revered him because he was a fair-skinned Brahmin, while the middle classes admired him for his Cambridge University education, his honesty and integrity, and his socially progressive views. Nehru's insistence on retaining English as one of the two official languages—as well as the medium of instruction in higher education and a language for international communication—would prove a valuable asset in the age of information technology (IT) followed by information and communications technology (ICT). Equally important, his decision to emulate the Soviet Union's policy of setting up research institutes in physical sciences and top-grade engineering colleges would pay handsome dividends in the years to come.[5]

Nehru had a free hand to forge the key characteristics of the Republic of India: Western-style democracy and secularism at home, and a foreign policy of nonalignment with either the Washington-led capitalist bloc or the Moscow-led socialist bloc. While launching the first Five Year Plan in 1951, he described it as a unique combination of economic planning—a concept commonly associated with Marxist-socialist regimes—and Western-style democracy.

During his tour of China in 1954, Nehru was impressed by the discipline and enthusiasm with which the Chinese, led by the newly triumphant Communist Party of China, were building their economy. Under his guidance, the Congress Party resolved to create "a socialistic pattern of society" in India. The Industrial Policy Resolution adopted by Parliament in 1956 aimed at rapid industrialization. It stated that industries of basic and strategic importance should be in the public sector, which should also include industries requiring large-scale investment: coal, iron and steel, aircraft manufacturing, ship-building, and oil extraction and other mining. Industries like machine tools, heavy chemicals, and fertilizers were assigned to the mixed public-private sector, and the rest to the private sector. The overarching strategy was to lay a solid foundation of basic industries for the next stage of industrialization: consumer goods and light industry.

The Nehru government set out to protect nascent Indian industries from the cold wind of Western competition from abroad and guard against over-production at home, while making optimum use of the available resources in a planned fashion. The overall aim was to supplement political independence with economic self-reliance achieved through an import substitution drive. But given the propensity of the slow-moving Indian bureaucracy to corruption and negativity, the true intent of the official policy got distorted.

A licensing system to rationally regulate imports, output, and investment to make the maximum use of the country's limited resources ended up as a corrupt "license-permit-quota" regime—or the License Raj, as it was commonly known—run by a nexus of senior bureaucrats, elected politicians, and a handful of influential capitalists. Nonetheless, during the last decade of Nehru's rule, industrial output more than doubled.[6] This happened in a political system of multiparty democracy with a free press and an independent judiciary. The electoral politics in a poor country like India precluded the chance of a political party espousing the cause of landowners and capitalists and expecting to win. To garner votes in elections, political parties vied with one another in proposing quick-fix solutions to the monumental tasks of lifting hundreds of millions of people from poverty through sustained industrialization and productivity gains in agriculture.

The democratic setup also encouraged a major party to criticize the governing party's policies when in opposition, only to adopt them if returned to power. This became the pattern from the 1990s onward, with the right-wing Bhartiya Janata Party (BJP, meaning Indian People's Party) emerging as a viable alternative to the centrist Congress Party nationally and in many provinces (states) in northern India. The result was weak governments in Delhi and state capitals. They could not implement development and other programs with the efficiency and single-mindedness of the regime in Beijing.

Given the hold landowners had over the ruling Congress Party since the pre-independence days, the halfhearted land reform laws passed by state governments were poorly implemented. So the growth in food grains hardly kept up with the rise in the population. The second Five Year Plan (1957–1962) made family planning one of its major objectives. This would be achieved with the halving of the annual birthrate, to 2.2 percent.

THE POST-NEHRU ERA

Following Nehru's death in 1964, the Congress Party's dominance in Parliament waned, with the regional parties gaining ground first at the state level and then at the center at its expense. During the premiership of his daughter, Indira Gandhi (1966–1977), the party split into right- and left-wing factions. To establish her left-leaning credentials she nationalized fourteen leading commercial banks. The law required the state-run banks to provide 40 percent of their net credit to priority sectors like agriculture, small-scale industry, retail trade, and small businesses to make the banking sector fulfill its social and developmental tasks. When business leaders protested, she assured them that the measure was not directed against them and instructed the state-controlled financial institutions—Life Insurance Corporation, Industrial Development Bank of India, and the Industrial Finance Corporation—to help them with any difficulty they might encounter because of bank nationalization.

By so doing, Indira Gandhi followed a well-established pattern. During its unbroken power for thirty years, the Congress Party perfected the art of speaking with a forked tongue. During the election campaign, it committed itself vociferously to improving the fate of the poor masses while receiving funds covertly from businessmen and industrialists. The party candidates circumvented the electoral law capping election expenses by publishing "souvenirs," where businessmen paid huge sums for advertising their enterprises and products. Later, the rival BJP would emulate the Congress Party in this regard.

Following the October 1973 Arab-Israeli War, there was a fourfold increase in petroleum prices. The dramatic hike in oil prices fed into the Indian economy, causing high inflation while wages and salaries remained static. The resulting popular discontent took the form of mass demonstrations. They emboldened the opposition to challenge the Indira Gandhi government. This was the backdrop against which, in June 1975, Indira Gandhi was found guilty of electoral malpractices by the court and disqualified from holding public office. That proved the independence of the judiciary. But the verdict in this case pertained to the election that had taken place more than *four years* earlier![7]

Instead of stepping down from high office, Gandhi had the Indian president, F. A. Ahmad, suspend the constitution and impose an emergency. She acquired dictatorial powers. This lasted until early 1977, when her Congress Party was defeated in the parliamentary poll by the Janata Party, a coalition of opposition groups, cobbled together on the basis of simply being anti-Congress.

India's manageable trade deficit in the 1970s worsened from the second oil shock of 1979–1980, caused by the Islamic revolution in Iran. While it pushed up the cost of imports, the higher prices of India's exports eroded its competitiveness. During the brief life of the Janata government, its industries minister, George Fernandes, reiterated Nehru's commitment to economic independence. He expelled such multinational corporations as IBM and Coca-Cola. IBM's expulsion led to a rapid development of the local computer production and maintenance industry, and laid the foundation for its exponential growth in later years. Infosys, established in 1981, went on to become an international player in IT software and consultancy.

On her return to power in 1980, Indira Gandhi nationalized six more banks. Because of the nationalization of twenty leading banks since 1969, bank branches increased tenfold, to nearly 99,000 by 2003, with a branch serving 15,000 people, down from almost 64,000. But while half of the branches were in rural areas, only 6 percent of the 500,000 villages was served by a registered bank.[8]

Contrary to the popular belief in the West that economic liberalization started in 1991, its origins lay with the last administration of Indira Gandhi in the early

1980s. It was as if, anticipating a heart problem, Mother India took preventive measures in 1980 and 1985 to reduce fat, but it was only after a heart attack in 1991 that she changed her lifestyle and subjected herself to a rigorous regime.

Slow motion economic reform continued during the government of Indira Gandhi's son, Rajiv, following her assassination in 1984. It gathered pace after 1988, as the public sector began shrinking. Market reform turned the Bombay Stock Exchange bullish. Annual inflation dropped to single digits, and Western multinationals, so far kept out of India, started moving in.

The GDP growth in the 1980s was 5.9 percent a year, with a population increase of 2.2 percent, and the per capita income rose annually at 3.8 percent.[9] But the growth stemmed chiefly from the decline in the exchange value of the currency, the rupee, and further borrowings at home and abroad.

The defeat of Rajiv Gandhi's Congress Party by the United Front coalition of opposition groups in 1989 led to two prime ministers in as many years. By the end of the decade, repayments of the IMF and commercial loans became strenuous.

In January 1991, when the retreating Iraqi occupation forces in Kuwait set ablaze Kuwaiti oil wells, little did they realize that their destructive action would, by a bizarre turn of events, result in the loosening up of the rigid "license, permit" protocol that had hobbled India's industrialization.

The Kuwait crisis caused by Saddam's invasion of the emirate in August 1990 led to the doubling of India's oil payments and a sharp reduction in the remittances of the Indians working in the Gulf region. On the eve of the next general election in May 1991, India's foreign loans of $70 billion, a third of them from commercial lenders, became an albatross. It managed not to default on its repayments by selling its gold stock to buy foreign exchange, diverting the emergency aid provided by Japan and Germany, and using the IMF's special facilities.

After Rajiv Gandhi's assassination during the election campaign, the party leadership passed to P. V. Narasimha Rao. Though his party won only 244 seats out of 542, he managed to rule for a full five years with the help of small factions not included in his cabinet.

His government inherited a dire situation. India's foreign reserves, down to less than $1 billion, were barely enough to pay for a month's imports. Normally, such reserves should cover a minimum of six months' imports. In return for the IMF's emergency aid, Delhi agreed to devalue its currency by 22 percent and reform its economy at a faster pace.

ECONOMIC LIBERALIZATION AT FULL TILT

The New Industrial Policy, announced by the finance minister, Manmohan Singh, in July 1991 drastically reduced the license-permit-quota regime. It abolished import quotas, slashed tariffs from over 100 percent to 25–36 percent, and ended industrial licensing except for enterprises in defense and national strategy. It limited public-sector monopoly only to security, national strategy, nuclear power, and railways. In the service sector, it allowed private companies in banking, insurance, telecommunications, and air travel. Foreign companies were allowed equity up to 51 percent, up from 40 percent, in thirty-four industries.

To encourage exports, Singh announced the establishment of Export Processing Zones (EPZs), where companies were exempted from government rules and regulations and given tax concessions. Despite the economic reform and efforts to boost exports, India's share of world trade inched from 0.57 percent in 1980 to 0.71 percent in 2000.[10]

During the 1990s, coalition politics, well established in the states, became the norm in Delhi, thus depriving India of strong governments.

During that decade, the GDP growth of 6.7 percent in the first half dipped to 5.4 percent in the second half—despite the greater opportunities for international trade offered by the transformation of the General Agreement on Trade and Tariffs (GATT), of which India was a founder member, into the WTO in 1995.[11]

Though in the 1996 general election, the BJP, which stressed *swadeshi* (meaning "made domestically" in Hindi), or self-reliance, won the most seats, it failed to form a coalition government, and the subsequent United Front cabinets proved too incoherent to survive for long.

Once in power in 1998, the BJP, leading a multiparty coalition, cut tariffs further, lowered barriers to foreign direct investment (FDI), and redefined *swadeshi* as "competing effectively in the global economy." It went on to adopt the Special Economic Zones (SEZ) policy, declaring them to be foreign territory for the purposes of trade, duties, and tariffs, in 2000—twenty years after China had done so. Some of the EPZs were upgraded to SEZs. But by the time the Indian parliament passed the Special Economic Zones Act in 2005, there were only nine functioning SEZs and eight EPZs. The new projects faced intense protests from the farming community. It accused the government of forcibly snatching fertile land from them at heavily discounted prices. This was a stark contrast from what happened in China, where SEZs were welcomed widely.

RIDING THE ICT TIGER

The scare in America and elsewhere in the West that most computers with the built-in time notation until 1999 would crash after midnight on January 1, 2000, proved a once-in-a-millennium opportunity for ICT firms in India to mint money. At a fraction of the fee charged by U.S.-based companies for immunization against "the millennium bug"—Y2K—Indian firms offered to do the job. They got overwhelmed with orders and worked round the clock until the zero hour on the first day of the twenty-first century. The bursting of the dot-com bubble in America that occurred later, in July, would leave the Indian ICT companies virtually unaffected because only a few were listed on U.S. stock exchanges.

The dramatic Y2K opening paved the way for Indian ICT companies to multiply their business in the United States. What aided India-based firms further was the drastic decline in global telecom charges. The companies were staffed by educated, English-speaking employees ready to work at a fraction of the wages paid in developed economies. These factors converged once the widespread use of the Internet enabled people from all over the globe to compete, and trade, with one another in real time. Another innovation that helped economic expansion in India was the cell phone. It was estimated that an extra 10 percent in cell phone penetration in India led to an increase of 0.44 percent growth in the GDP.

Such ICT pioneers as Infosys experienced meteoric growth, to over 50,000 employees, two-thirds of them posted outside its headquarters in Bangalore. A former British military cantonment city with a salubrious climate, Bangalore became the home to 1,700 software companies. Altogether, they accounted for two-fifths of India's ICT services and outsourcing revenue.[12]

According to the National Association of Software and Service Companies (Nasscom) of India, by 2005, the country had acquired two-thirds of the global Information Technology Enabled Services (ITES), also known as offshore IT, and nearly half of the Business Processing Outsourcing (BPO). The BPO involves Western companies outsourcing call-center operations, accounting, payroll processing, and primary research, as well as data analysis and data mining.

The reason for outsourcing was simple: cost cutting. An employee doing an ITES job in the United States earned seven times more than one in India. The savings accruing to an American company from outsourcing turned into profit. The downside was the loss of jobs in the United States, which, in 2002, amounted to 800,000 and continued at a lower rate thereafter. In order to reenter the job market those Americans who were laid off often needed to retrain and acquire higher skills—not an easy task for those in the middle of their working lives. Meanwhile, digital and broadband revolutions boosted offshoring ICT business. With the time-zone difference, companies in India offered twenty-four-hour service seven days a week to their clients in America.

With the aggregate outsourcing and ITES business expected to soar to $110 billion globally by 2010, and India garnering more than half of it,[13] the prospects for its ICT companies looked promising. They were expected to retain the preeminent position they had carved out for themselves in the Indian economy. Between 1992, when economic liberalization really got going, and 2006, the list of the top ten corporations at the Mumbai Stock Exchange underwent a radical change. The leaders in the traditional sectors of banking, cement, oil, steel, tea, and textiles yielded to such ICT-related services stalwarts as Tata Consultancy, Infosys, Wipro, and Bharati Airtel.

"Twenty years ago, India was known [in America] as a country of snake charmers, poor people, and Mother Teresa," noted Thomas Friedman in his book *The Earth Is Flat: A Brief History of the Twenty-first Century.* "Now it is also seen as a country of brainy people and computer wizards."[14]

These "computer wizards" were the graduates of the institutes of technology in India, which were established at the insistence of Nehru, now widely dismissed in the West as a misguided socialist. The first of the seven institutes of technology (IIT) to impart higher education in engineering, science, and technology was inaugurated in 1951 at Kharagpur, northwest of Calcutta. The chance of passing the IIT Joint Entrance Examination is 2 percent. The corresponding figures for Harvard University and the Massachusetts Institute of Technology are 11 percent and 16 percent respectively.[15]

Little wonder that during the heyday of the IT revolution in the 1990s and at the turn of the twenty-first century, a third of the engineers in Silicon Valley in northern California were Indians, and two out of five IT startups were by Indian entrepreneurs.[16] These achievements boosted the cultural and intellectual morale of a people who had been under the yoke of Britain for nearly two centuries.

India's involvement in the ICT business provided glittering material for glossy newsmagazines in the United States keen to applaud the rise of the world's largest democracy as it accelerated its drive into market economy and globalization. At home, the (minority) English-language newspapers and magazines went into overdrive, declaring India to be an "Information Superpower," deserving a global status of a kind. Such claims flew in the face of the following facts: The ICT business provided direct and indirect employment to less than 1 percent of the national workforce of 400 million in a country where half the households lacked electricity and only 5 percent had a landline telephone connection.

The ICT business had a far more beneficial impact on India's exports. As a result of the boost in foreign orders in the aftermath of the Y2K bonanza, India's current trade account went into surplus in the first three years of the twenty-first century. But the GDP growth rates varied between a modest 5 percent to 6 percent. The following year, 2004, held a promise of exceeding the 5–6 percent range.

THE POOR WIELD THE BALLOT WEAPON

The rosy prospect of a rising GDP made BJP leaders confident of being returned to power in the May 2004 general election. But they were not. Why? Because the benefits of the improved growth rates were being skimmed off by the top 5 percent of the population, leaving 70 percent of the populace, surviving on less than $2 a day, stagnating. The election gave them a chance to register their protest, and they did. They favored the opposition Congress Party, which emerged as the largest group but lacked a majority. Backed by sixty Communist MPs (members of Parliament), who forwent cabinet posts, the Congress Party led a coalition government.

Yet the gulf between the indigent and the affluent continued to widen. Between 2004 and 2006, the number of dollar billionaires in India rose from thirteen to thirty-six, surpassing twenty-four in Japan, the globe's second largest economy. This was a reflection of the steep rise in stock market values.

In the last five months of 2005, the Bombay Stock Exchange's Sensex index jumped from 7,000 to 9,000.

The 2004 poll result thus highlighted a salient fact overlooked by most Western experts and journalists: The benefits of deregulation and globalization have been skimmed off by the already well-off in India. Also unnoticed was the fact that after more than a quarter century of economic liberalization, the actual number of Indians below the poverty line *rose* by 5 percent. During that period the number of those existing below the poverty line in China declined by 70 percent. While India accounted for one-sixth of the human race, it was home to a quarter of the world's poor.[17]

Even if we leave aside the differences between the GDP growths in these mega-nations, the 1 percent expansion rate in India reduced poverty by much less than in China. This was due to inequalities mainly in land and education. The GINI coefficients of land distribution in rural India and China in 2003 were 0.74 and 0.49 respectively. According to the World Bank, the GINI coefficient of the distribution of adult schooling years in India and China in 2000 was respectively 0.56 and 0.37.[18]

Between the tip of the social pyramid and its vast base of the rural population lies the middle class, with its three tiers—upper, middle, and lower—the focus of local and foreign companies for their durable consumer goods and appliances. Most of the villagers do not figure in the calculations of these firms, and rightly so: They do not have the cash to buy their products.

Most village Indians have to struggle to be able to eat three meals a day throughout the year. The size and frequency of meals varies between twice-a-year harvests, with their full bellies near the harvesting season shrinking steadily. During the half century of India's independence, the per capita annual grain production rose 60 percent to 430 pounds (191 kilograms). But because of gross inequality and poor distribution, hunger and malnutrition prevailed frequently in parts of the country. To counter the prospect of destitution, the authorities stored 40 to 50 million tons of food grains in warehouses. They also set up a Public Distribution System, but its proper functioning was limited to urban areas, accounting for a quarter of the national population. The corruption was so rife that only about a fifth of the food meant for the countryside reached the needy, the bulk being siphoned off to the black market.[19]

In 2006, India was as corrupt as China, as reflected by the Corruption Perception Index compiled by the Berlin-based Transparency International.[20]

Both mega-nations suffered equally from uneven development of their regions. Among the Indian states, the five richest were Punjab, Haryana, Gujarat, Maharashtra, and Tamil Nadu. The four middle-income regions were the three remaining southern states (Andhra Pradesh, Karnataka, and Kerala) plus West Bengal. The states of Bihar and Uttar Pradesh, accounting for a quarter of the national population, were the poorest.

With the GDP growth rate rising to 9 percent in 2007, the year became India's best. Its nominal GDP crossed the $1 trillion mark. But the figure was only two-fifths of China's, while the populations of the two Asian giants are roughly equal. The proportion was the same when measured by the Purchasing Power Parity.[21] It then began declining even before the global meltdown, which did less damage to India than to North America and the European Union.

In mid-2008, with nearly $300 billon in its foreign exchange reserves, India was number five in the league table—after China, Japan, Russia, and the Eurozone. At home, 70 percent of its banking sector was nationalized. The banks' nonperforming loans amounted to 1 percent. Capital ratios in banks were 12 to 13 percent.[22] While the banking shares in America were in freefall in 2008–2009, those in India were holding up so well that in February 2009, the market value of the State Bank of India exceeded that of Citigroup, the largest bank of the United States![23] The growth in 2009 was expected to be around 7 percent.

Most of the growth in India was fueled by domestic demand. In 2007, India's exports amounted to 14.6 percent of the GDP, whereas the figure for China was 37.1 percent.[24] Significantly, while 60 percent of Chinese children in primary schools were learning English, no such program was on the horizon in India. Only 11 percent of the students in Indian schools enroll at universities, half the figure for China.

India's industrialization has proceeded at a far slower pace than China's. Only one out of eight Indians is employed in industry, whereas the figure for China is twice as much. In services, 23 percent of the Indian workforce produces 55 percent of the GDP; in China 28 percent employed in that sector generate 40 percent of the GDP. That means India's services sector is more efficient than China's.

The wide differences in living standards, education, and the extent of industrialization preclude the idea of a race between India and China. Yet it is worth recalling that after the India-China War in 1962, this concept became embedded in the White House as well as the Kremlin.

INDIA'S TRIANGULATION

The bonhomie between India under Nehru and China under Mao in the early and mid-1950s dissipated as the decade unrolled. The preamble to the Delhi-Beijing agreement on "Trade and Intercourse Between the Tibet Region of China and India" signed in 1954 included the seminal *Panchsheel* (Sanskrit, meaning "Five Principles") of foreign policy: "Mutual respect for each other's territorial integrity and sovereignty; mutual nonaggression; mutual noninterference in each other's internal affairs; equality and mutual benefit; and peaceful coexistence."

But that did not stop Nehru from lending support to the Tibetan refugees in and around the border town of Kalimpong in their insurgency plans against Beijing. They were being encouraged by the CIA and the Taiwanese intelligence agency. Starting modestly in eastern Tibet in 1956–1957, the rebellion spread to the west. In the fighting that erupted in the Tibetan capital of Lhasa in early 1959, the Dalai Lama sided with the rebels. When the Beijing authorities reestablished control, the Dalai Lama fled and secured asylum in India.

The soured relations between India and China became strained on the issue of border demarcation, which the British raj had not carried out properly. In August and October 1959 there were armed skirmishes along the disputed frontiers. The growing animosity between Delhi and Beijing pleased not only America but also the Soviet Union, which was developing its own border dispute with China. The split between the Soviet Union and the People's Republic of China in 1960 coincided with the Kremlin shipping military hardware to India. Over the next two decades, these supplies would escalate, with Moscow then allowing the Indians to assemble its MiG warplanes at home and later produce them under license—an arrangement American and British arms manufacturers had pointedly refused to make for their warplanes.

In August–September 1962, India moved its troops to forward positions along the disputed borders. That triggered a war. Within a month, the Chinese overran the Indian border posts and in the east marched into the plains of Assam. But just as Nehru made a secret appeal to Washington for military intervention, Beijing declared a unilateral cease-fire and withdrew its forces to the frontier. Nonetheless, India received a squadron of large transport planes from the Pentagon. Special American and British military missions laid the groundwork for military assistance to India worth $120 million over the next three years. Thus, Nehru, the apostle of nonalignment, ended up aligning with Moscow *and* Washington. This unique triangulation during the Cold War went largely unnoticed by Western analysts, who continued to describe Nehru as "nonaligned" with an undisguised tilt toward Moscow.

The war pushed India and China onto the world stage, with Delhi backed by both superpowers and Beijing strictly on its own. That led Mao to accelerate the nuclear weapons program. China's testing of an atom bomb near Lop Nor, Kansu, in October 1964 led the two superpowers to pursue complementary, rather than competitive, policies toward India. They boosted it economically and militarily as a counterforce to China. India desperately needed the aid: Its GDP growth during 1965–1979 was a dismal 2 percent, whereas its population was rising by more than 4 percent a year.

By the mid-1960s, India owed America $2.32 billion, or more than half of the total money in circulation, as a result of purchasing American food grains at concession rates since the mid-1950s. The prime reason for Washington's largesse was its desire to see India win the economic race against Communist China and establish the superiority of Western-style democracy to Communism to the rest of the Afro-Asian world.

Later, Moscow increased its military and economic aid to India. By the late 1960s, it became India's largest supplier of arms. In 1970–1971 the Soviet Union became the biggest single buyer of Indian goods, a shade ahead of America. During 1966–1968, when India faced an acute food shortage, the Lyndon Johnson administration supplied it with the bulk of the 20 million tons of food grains needed at a discount.

India's brief war with Pakistan in December 1971, which turned East Pakistan into independent Bangladesh, made India the strongest military power in south Asia, from Iran to Indochina. Any strain in Delhi-Washington relations caused by the 1971 war proved transient. The second Nixon administration, inaugurated in January 1973, decided to write off $2.2 billion out of the $3.2 billion worth of rupees that Washington then held in India and leave the rest to cover the expenses of maintaining its embassies, consulates, and information centers in India and Nepal.

During his visit to India in November, Soviet leader Leonid Brezhnev signed a fifteen-year agreement on "further development of economic and trade cooperation" between the two countries, which was publicly welcomed by Washington. The Kremlin went on to "loan" India 2 million tons of wheat.

Not to be left behind, the World Bank put its oar in. So too did the Aid-India Consortium, consisting of Western nations and Japan. Many of its members overcame their feeling of unease at India's extravagance in developing and exploding in May 1974 a "nuclear device" in the Rajasthan desert at the staggering cost of $1.5 billion, spent over a decade, and went on to sanction, at their meeting in June, a loan of $1.4 billion—the largest sum ever—to Delhi.

As a nuclear power, India caught up with the PRC after a decade. It thus remained in a race with the PRC but only at the cost of distorting its economy by spending four times as much on military as on development. Yet in the defense sector too India fell behind China.

DELHI'S MILITARY POWER

While China was swift in copying the Russian-made weapons and producing its own versions, the Indians were slow and bureaucratic. A joint Indo-Russian BrahMos project to produce a supersonic antiship missile, started in 1999, had not been completed five years later. It was a similar story with Delhi's attempt to produce its own main battle tank, Arjun, to rival Russia's T-90. In 2004 it was in "the process of development." So too was India's Nishant Unmanned Aerial Vehicle project. In the words of a Western expert attending the DefExpo exhibition in Delhi in 2004, the problem was "too much red tape."[25]

By then backhanders on weapons contracts had sullied Indian politics. The image of Rajiv Gandhi as "Mr. Clean" was tarnished when a scandal broke in 1986. It was alleged that he was implicated in kickbacks from India's purchase of self-propelled Bofors artillery guns from their Swedish manufacturer. The scandal snowballed and led to the defeat of his party in the 1989 general election.

Twelve years later, reporters from an online magazine, *Tehelka*, posing as arms salesmen videotaped senior politicians and defense officials taking bribes. Little wonder that in the Transparency International's Corruption Perception Index in 2005, India's ranking at 88 was on a par with Benin, Bosnia, Gabon, Iran, Mali, and Tanzania.

By virtue of the size of its area, population, economy, and military muscle at 1.2 million troops, India is the strongest power in south Asia. Yet its ambition of exercising hegemony over the region has been frustrated by its rival, Pakistan. Although no match for India in any meaningful way, Pakistan has the ability to act as an effective spoiler, an enterprise in which it has been actively encouraged by China, which provided Islamabad inter alia with the basic design of an atom bomb. That enabled Pakistan to test its nuclear bombs within days of India doing so in May 1998. Pakistan thus became the eighth nation to possess the nuclear bomb—after the United States, Russia, Britain, France, China, Israel, and India. By possessing an arsenal of atom bombs, the less powerful Pakistan acquired parity with India, which far outweighs Pakistan in conventional forces and hardware.

THE LARGEST HUGS THE MOST POWERFUL

With the collapse of the Soviet Union, Delhi lost the second pole in its "alignment" policy. That improved relations between the world's largest democracy and the most powerful one. In that context, the sanctions against India that followed its testing of nuclear bombs in 1998—as required by U.S. law—were ultimately a minor irritant.

President Clinton's five-day India visit in March 2000, covering not only Delhi but also an IT hub of Hyderabad and a village in Rajasthan, implied that much. The two sides signed agreements on science, technology, and commerce. And Clinton spoke of institutionalizing India-U.S. dialogue up to the highest level and of continuing talks on the nuclear issue.

Continuing its economic liberalization in 2001, India opened its defense industry to private companies. But a foreign supplier selling weapons above $70 million was required to invest 30 percent in Indian goods and services. The intent was to create a bridge between the Indian defense industry and potential vendors, both foreign and Indian, to help private industry to obtain industrial licenses for the manufacture of defense products.

The George W. Bush administration tightened its embrace with India. In June 2005 the two countries signed a "New Framework for the U.S.-India Defense Relationship" as part of their ongoing strategic cooperation. It provided for the establishment of a bilateral "Defense Procurement and Production Group" to supervise the defense trade and prospects for coproduction and technology collaboration. The pact stated that the two sides "will work to conclude Defense transactions . . . as a means to . . . reinforce our strategic partnership."

This group had noted that Delhi had earlier spent $3 billion on 140 Russian-made Su-30s to be delivered during 2007–2017. It had also decided to purchase the Russian modified Kiev class aircraft carrier *Admiral Gorshkov*, after it had been refitted and upgraded following a boiler room explosion, at the cost of $3.4 billion.[26] New Delhi thus underscored its determination to safeguard the sea lanes carrying oil and liquefied natural gas from the Gulf region to India.

Like China, India is modernizing its arsenal of ballistic and cruise missiles to improve the range, accuracy, and survivability of weapons in Asia. Its most advanced ICBM, Agni-3, with a range of 2,200 miles (3500 kilometers), can reach Beijing.[27]

During the Bush–Manmohan Singh summit in Washington in July 2005, the two leaders agreed on civilian nuclear cooperation. And in the course of Bush's visit to New Delhi in March 2006, they signed a Civil Nuclear Cooperation Agreement. The deal was disapproved by both the right-of-center BJP and the Left Front. The BJP opposed it because in its view it circumscribed India's nuclear weapons program and virtually banned nuclear arms testing, even though India was not a signatory to the Comprehensive Test Ban Treaty. The anti-American Left Front opposed the deal because it was hostile to growing links between India and imperialist United States.

In July 2008, the Singh government faced its first no-confidence vote in its four years in office in the lower house of Parliament after the Left Front withdrew its support for ratifying the agreement with Washington. It survived by 275 votes to 256. The U.S. Congress gave its approval to the United States–India Nuclear Cooperation Approval and Non-proliferation Enhancement Act in October. At Washington's instigation, the forty-five-strong Nuclear Supply Group agreed to sell civilian technology and equipment to India, even though it has not signed the nuclear Non-Proliferation Treaty.

The decision of the Nuclear Supply Group, which included China, had to be unanimous. The PRC was opposed to the idea of giving a pass to New Delhi but, sticking to Deng's guidelines—"yield on small issues with the long-term interest in mind; and adopt a low profile"—refrained from becoming the odd man out. China did so even when it knew that the United States perceived

India as a viable counterweight to its rising influence in Asia and was bolstering Delhi's power.

But India suffers from certain built-in weaknesses it cannot escape or overcome. Being a polyglot nation, it lacks the unity and strength of China, which, excepting the small Tibetan and Uighur minorities, is ethnically homogeneous. Also, the increasingly corrupt democratic politics of India, where the standards of public life have declined sharply over the decades, make it less equipped to march to an economic goal with the single-mindedness of a popular, authoritarian regime as in China.

Certain inherent weaknesses also apply to the European Union—a conglomerate of many languages and nations—which so far has remained a common market rather than a single political-administrative entity.

CHAPTER 7

THE EUROPEAN UNION, WORK IN PROGRESS . . .

In the twentieth century Europe suffered the worst excesses of violence arising from imperialism, militant nationalism, fascism, Nazism, and Communism. In World War II, waged primarily in Europe, 23 million Soviets perished, as did 7.2 million Germans, 5.6 million Poles, and 6 million Jews—among others. Having endured the fires of Mars, Europeans opted for Venus in the postwar period.

If a new era of reconciliation was to be inaugurated, the starting point had to be Franco-German relations. But given their age-old rivalry, the beginning could only be modest, with a narrow yet pragmatic focus: Five years after World War II came a proposal to jointly manage the nationalized coal and steel industries of France and West Germany.

Over the next six decades, that small seed blossomed into a complex tree called the European Union headquartered in Brussels, Belgium, with twenty-seven branches, varying in size enormously—from the tiny Malta (124 square miles/320 square kilometers; population 403,000) to Germany (137,800 square miles/357,020 square kilometers; population 82.5 million)—with a total population of 491 million.

A uniquely multilayered governance system, the European Union involves not only national governments but also supranational institutions—the European Commission, European Parliament, European Court of Justice, and European Central Bank—and transnational interest groups, with a mechanism for regular interaction among them. Besides administering the European Monetary Union, the Common Agricultural Policy, and the Social

Charter, the European Union deliberates on environmental issues—as well as defense and security to a limited scale. With its member countries' aggregate defense budgets of €160 billion ($250 billion), more than half of the Pentagon's in 2008, the European Union ranks—in theory—as the second most powerful bloc militarily.

The European Union is unique. It is neither a federation—which results when its constituents transfer their sovereignty fully to a union—nor a confederation, where sovereignty lies with the constituents who agree to pool it at the confederate level. At the same time, following the 1992 Maastricht Treaty, its constituents decided to achieve a common foreign and security policy, an aim yet to be realized fully. Therefore, while the European Union is more than an economic alliance, it is less than a political-administrative federation or confederation.

Were it to turn itself into a federation or confederation, it would become removed from rural and small-town Europeans. It would also lose twenty-six votes at the United Nations. Since it has grown slowly and organically, it remains strong at its core. The downside is that the European Union's structure is so bafflingly complex that even seasoned journalists have to struggle to comprehend it fully. While European politicians pat themselves on the back for devising a sophisticated international organization that has managed to satisfy an array of competing interests, they have failed to present it in easily understood terms to their citizens. Their move to consolidate the series of treaties signed since 1950—on which the European Union rests—into a comprehensive constitution failed when the document was put to referendums in France and the Netherlands in 2004.

The scenario of creating the United States of Europe in the future seems to many European politicians as logical and attractive. But it has yet to grip the imagination of the majority of European voters. Nor is there a chance of overcoming the resistance of a wide variety of vested interests that will lose out with the total disappearance of national sovereignty.

The 2007 Lisbon/Reform Treaty streamlining the European Union's institutions has yet to be ratified by all EU members. It was assailed by Vaclav Klaus, president of the Czech Republic, which assumed the bloc's rotating presidency in January 2009. Addressing the European Parliament in February, he called the European Union an undemocratic and elitist project comparable to a Soviet-era dictatorship that forbade free thought, and added that the Lisbon Treaty would only make the situation worse.[1] As a dissident during the Communist era in Czechoslovakia, a role that won him kudos in the West, Klaus seemed incapable of shedding his contrariness despite the changed circumstances, which had catapulted him to presidency of a part of the old Czechoslovakia. He appeared untutored in recent European history. It was the collapse of the Soviet Union in 1991—preceded by the disbanding of the Moscow-led Warsaw Pact and followed by the unraveling of the Socialist Federal Republic of Yugoslavia—that provided the small European Community with the previously unimagined scope for expansion.

Now, as a common market, the European Union vies with America. In 2007, with its two-way commerce with China soaring to $347 billion, it surpassed the United States (at $301 billion) as Beijing's foremost trading partner.[2] In March 2008, against the background of a weakening U.S. dollar, the 2007 GDP of the fifteen countries of the Eurozone, with a population of 320 million, exceeded America's.[3] Since then the greenback has strengthened against the euro, reversing the positions of the United States and the Eurozone, which gained another member, Slovakia, on January 1, 2009. Nonetheless, the euro competes with the U.S. dollar as a reserve currency.

The European Union's broad aims are to promote economic expansion in Europe, participate actively in global trade, and lobby for European interests in the international arena. Its membership is open only to those European countries that are democratic and abide by the rule of law and human rights—and have a market economy capable of withstanding competition within the bloc.

A more demanding task for an established or a fresh EU constituent, though, is to reorient the perception of its history by its citizens. In the past, much stress has been placed on how European nations differ in order to devise and strengthen the identity of a nation. Now, as members of the EU family, they are required to emphasize what is common among them. This challenge can be met successfully only over generations.

The contrast between postwar West Germany and France was particularly striking. As a defeated nation, West Germans had to start building afresh all their institutions, including political parties, under the supervision of the occupying Allied powers. In this environment only conservative Christian Democrats and left-of-center Social Democrats had a chance to strike roots and grow. Being hostile to Communist East Germany, both parties were anti-Communist. The political scene in France was altogether different. There Communists had played an important role in the resistance against the Nazi occupiers during World War II and had therefore emerged as a solid political force, with a majority following among workers. Washington was keen to weaken French Communists as were the non-Communists in France.

This was the background to the proposal to place the state-owned coal and steel industries of France and West Germany under joint management to improve their productivity and resolve prewar disputes about coal mining across national borders. The proposal was made in 1950 by France's foreign minister Robert Schumann and economist Jean Monet.

THE HUMBLE SEED

Schumann and Monet's idea was accepted by the French and West German governments. The proposal, codified in April 1951, was implemented in August 1952 under the European Coal and Steel Community (ECSC), the first of a series of multilateral organizations based on the concept of supranationalism.

The ECSC's success encouraged its chief executive to lobby neighboring European governments to expand cooperation in commerce and economy. This led to the signing of the Treaty of Rome in 1954. It expanded ECSC membership to six. In 1958, Belgium, France, Italy, Luxembourg, the Netherlands, and West Germany established a customs union—the European Economic Community (EEC)—and the European Atomic Energy Committee (EAEC, popularly known as Euratom) for cooperation in developing nuclear energy.

The EEC's primary aims were to develop a common market and a customs union between member-states. A common market necessitated free circulation of goods, capital, services, and people. And a customs union meant applying common external tariffs on all goods entering the single market. Free movement of persons enabled citizens to move freely between member-states to live, work, study, or retire in another country. But member-states were permitted to limit the exercise of these freedoms in accordance with the criteria stated in the 1958 EEC Treaty.

The Merger Treaty, signed in Brussels and enforced in July 1967, amalgamated the ECSC, EEC, and Euratom and called the new entity the European Communities. Out of this came the European Community (EC),[4] the result of the Treaty establishing the European Community (TEC). The Soviet Union's military intervention in Czechoslovakia in 1968 created a fissure between Moscow and the Italian Communist Party, the largest in the Western world, which would adopt its own brand of ideology called Euro-communism. This development encouraged a move toward integration within the EC, which resolved to create a single European currency in 1969.

In the mid-1970s—when Britain was one of the bloc's leading members—the EC began to impinge on international relations. It started signing Trade and Cooperation agreements with other countries. Internally, it began a democratization process by giving a nominated Consultative Assembly powers over its budget. In 1979 a directly elected 410-member European Parliament (785-member in 2008) came into being with wider authority. Two years later, the president of the European Commission, the executive arm of the EC, started attending the summits of G7, which was established to tackle common economic problems of the most industrialized nations—four of which belonged to the EC.

The 1980s was the decade of further expansion (to twelve members) and consolidation. Following the adoption of a common flag and the Single European Act in 1986, the EC established a framework for the Single European Market. Its adoption of a Social Charter—equivalent to the U.S. Bill of Rights—in 1989, outlining certain human and social rights acceptable to all EC members, was its first important move outside the economy. Among the countries that did not sign the social charter initially was Britain, then ruled by conservative Prime Minister Margaret Thatcher.

In that year the EC also made its first significant foreign policy decision. In the wake of China's crackdown on protesters in Tiananmen Square, it banned advanced weapons sale to Beijing.[5] When Brussels inclined to lift its arms embargo, Washington threatened to ban the export of U.S.-made high-tech parts used by European weapons manufacturers. The European Union relented.

POST-COMMUNIST EUROPE

The dissolution of the Warsaw Pact and the Soviet Union led the EC to accelerate economic integration of its constituents and encourage former Communist states to seek its membership. Its leaders codified the prerequisites for membership—the foremost specifying a representative government chosen in free and fair elections based on adult suffrage. This marked the formal burial of the original ideological underpinning of anti-Communism for the European project.

The adoption of the Treaty on European Union, signed in the Dutch town of Maastricht in 1992, paved the way for creating a regional body, called the European Union, with such trappings of sovereignty as its own legislative, executive, and judicial organs. Besides incorporating the European Monetary Union into the Treaty of Rome, the Maastricht Treaty listed the following objectives: a common foreign and security policy and common standards in justice and home affairs.[6] It came into force in November 1993. With Austria, Sweden, and Finland joining the European Union in 1995, its strength rose to fifteen, with all of them becoming founder-members of the World Trade Organization. As a customs union, the European Union negotiated with others as a single unit.

Altogether the European Union's enhanced goals included unveiling a common currency by January 1, 1999, promoting social progress such as health care and labor rights, protecting the environment, guaranteeing civil and human rights, ensuring justice, and making Europe secure. To achieve these additional aims, the European Union set up an intergovernmental body called the Council of the European Union. It was composed of the executive leaders of member states—and the nominated president of the European Commission, the European Union's executive arm, who was charged with initiating legislation, conducting day-to-day administration, and acting in the interest of the European Union as a whole.[7] The EU Council was to be chaired by rotating presidency, lasting six months, and its secretariat run by the secretary-general.

The EU Council's frequently changing presidency was a prime reason for the bloc's failure to exercise political influence proportionate to its enormous economic clout. Sometimes the switch-over of the presidency occurred at awkward moments. While Europe, along with America and other continents, struggled to mitigate the fiscal meltdown, the EU Council presidency changed. It shifted from France, led by a high-profile, hyperactive President Nicolas Sarkozy, to Mirek Topolanek, the executive prime minister of the Czech Republic, whose parliament had not yet ratified the 2007 Reform/Lisbon Treaty. To the embarrassment of many, Czech President Klaus refused to fly the EU flag over his official seat at the Prague Castle, arguing that the Czech Republic was not an EU province.

The European Parliament was granted sovereignty by member states to legislate on the agreed subjects. But the implementation of EU policies was left to individual nations. Likewise, member-states recognized the jurisdiction of the Court of Justice to varying degrees. Given the vastly varied histories of EU members, the task of aligning their foreign and security perspectives, assigned to the high representative for the Common Foreign and Security Policy, proved formidable. The challenge became all the more demanding with the intake of ten countries in 2004, raising the total to twenty-five.[8]

Eight of the new entrants were former members of the Soviet Union, the Socialist Federal Republic of Yugoslavia, or the Warsaw Pact. The perspective with which their leaders viewed the world, particularly Russia, was at variance with that of their counterparts from the older members of the European Union. Little wonder that the differences among the bloc's nations regarding the European Union's policy toward Russia in general, and the Kremlin's war with Georgia in particular, would prove unbridgeable and make news headlines worldwide. Nonetheless, within two years of the WTO's inception, the European Union flexed its economic muscle—against the United States.

THE EUROPEAN UNION FORGES ITS IDENTITY—IN STAGES

In 1997, an oil consortium led by Total SA of France, and including Gazprom of Russia and Petronas of Malaysia, signed a $2 billion contract with the National Iranian Oil Company to develop its vast offshore South Pars gas field. Washington declared that as these corporations had violated its Iraq-Libya Sanctions Act (ILSA) of 1995 by investing more than $40 million in Iran's gas industry, it would impose sanctions against them.

Arguing that these sanctions violated international trading laws, and that an American law could not be applied extraterritorially, the European Union threatened retaliatory action if President Clinton took action under ILSA. It was backed by Japan. Tokyo said that it would lodge a complaint with the WTO, since ILSA violated WTO rules. Faced with such serious threats, Clinton backed off.[9]

The next year the EU Council took its first hesitant step in the security field. It created a military task force of 60,000 reserve troops and invited member-states to contribute troops on a case-by-case basis for humanitarian aid and rescue, peacekeeping, and crisis management. The European Union undertook a police mission in Bosnia and Herzegovina in January

2003 to help establish a professional, multiethnic police force there and as-sist it in fighting large-scale organized crime. Its military operation in Mace-donia in March offset the need for NATO intervention.

These EU initiatives were viewed benignly by the Bush administration in Washington. But when the EU Council decided the next year to establish the European Defense Agency (EDA) to lobby for more collective expenditure and research by EU defense ministries and industries, the United States saw red. Its officials fretted that an enhanced focus on the European Union's de-fense capabilities would erode resources for NATO.

A serious trans-Atlantic discord arose in 2006 when the EDA published its paper on the next two decades of conflict: *An Initial Long-Term Vision for Eu-ropean Defense Capability and Capacity Needs*. As a result of declining fertility rates, the defense ministries would struggle to attract recruits of fighting age at a time when the needs of graying populations would strain national budgets, it said. Also, increasingly circumspect taxpayers and politicians would be reluctant to contemplate casualties and/or potentially controversial interventions abroad—particularly in those regions, such as the Middle East and Afghanistan, where large numbers of immigrants have come from. In addition, European voters would insist on UN backing for military operations, assembling of a wide coalition of EU nations, and an involvement of NGOs. Therefore, future Euro-pean defense and security operations would be "expeditionary, multinational and multi-dimensional," aimed at achieving "security and stability" more than "victory" as defined by the military, the paper concluded.[10]

The tone and thrust of the EDA paper were sharply different from the re-peated assertions of the Bush White House to keep fighting for clear victory in a global war on terror. Washington had a good reason to frown. But to the disappointment of the Bush administration—as well as the Obama team—the EDA's forecast had come to pass. An examination of NATO's involvement in Afghanistan provided the evidence. Sensitive to public opinion at home, Ger-many refused to let its troops in Afghanistan engage in combat with the local insurgents active in the east and south, thus deviating sharply from Canada and Britain. Moreover, despite repeated calls by U.S. Defense Secretary Robert Gates for additional troops in Afghanistan, the Netherlands government planned to reduce the size of its contingent there.

By launching its own currency, the euro, in 1999, the European Union had started a process with the potential to rival the greenback as a reserve currency.

Indeed, within a decade of its launch, as the single currency of sixteen countries with €751 billion in circulation (equivalent to $953 billion), the euro acquired the distinction of having the highest combined value of cash in circulation in the world, surpassing the U.S. dollar. By then, the euro had become the currency favored by the radical oil states of Venezuela and Iran. And Russia's central bank, possessing the third largest foreign reserves, had pegged the ruble's exchange rate to a basket that was 55 percent euro and 45 percent U.S. dollar.

Initially, there were doubts about the soundness of the euro. Between January 1999—when the euro was launched as an electronic currency to be used by banks, foreign exchange dealers, big companies, and stock markets—and December 2001, its exchange rate fell from the initial $1.18 to $0.90. But once euro notes and coins began circulating and replacing the national currencies, from January 1, 2002 onward, its value rose steadily to a peak of $1.60 in July 2008. By then, 25 percent of all reserves in the world were held in euros, whereas the proportion of dollars was down to 65 percent.

The size of the Eurozone steadily expanded from the original eleven nations, with five additions (the latest one in January 2009)—all of them subject to strict fiscal conditions, supervised by the European Central Bank in Frankfurt, which vied with the Federal Reserve Bank in Washington. The only major European nation to stay out of the Eurozone was Britain. Such an impressive economic integration occurred against the background of an intense debate about the political identity of the European Union.

The Pitfalls of a Unique Identity

At the turn of the century, whereas Chancellor Gerhard Schroeder of Germany advocated a push toward a federalist model, he was opposed by French President Jacques Chirac and British Prime Minister Tony Blair. They insisted that the European Union must remain an organization of "states united," not a "united states."

In the end the European Council decided in 2001 to form a constitutional convention, chaired by Valéry Giscard d'Estaing, former president of France, to review its institutions in order to make the European Union more efficient, democratic, and comprehensible to the average citizen.

Giscard d'Estaing's report in 2003 led to the drafting of the document "Treaty Establishing a Constitution for Europe" in 2004. It was both a constitutional treaty and a constitution. The first sentence of its first article read: "This Constitution establishes the European Union, on which the Member States confer competences to attain objectives they have in common."

Among other things, the 2004 constitution replaced the rotating presidency of the European Council with a president elected for two and a half years (and renewable once) by the heads of government, thus giving the bloc's supreme office a lasting image it sorely lacked. Equally important for world diplomacy, it stipulated the replacement of the current high representative for the Common Foreign and Security Policy with a union minister for foreign affairs. Together these provisions would have enabled the European Union to transform its gigantic economic power into an equivalent diplomatic clout.

But this was not to be. The constitution was put to vote in each member-state before either the national parliament or the electorate. It was rejected in referendums in France and the Netherlands. Apparently, there was disjunction between the aspirations of the political class and the feelings of ordinary Europeans, who saw the continental constitution as an underhand method of imposing a distant, inaccessible authority, wrapped in excessive red tape, on top of the local, provincial, and national governments. Nevertheless, the setback in France and the Netherlands failed to dissuade European politicians from finding a way to achieve the aim of a unified political façade for the European Union without arousing popular suspicions about the eventual rise of the United States of Europe.

Meanwhile, as a result of the earlier agreements, the European Union's expansion went ahead in January 2004. The new members were Cyprus, the Czech Republic, Estonia, Hungary, Latvia, Lithuania, Malta, Poland, Slovakia, and Slovenia. Three years later Bulgaria and Romania followed.

To reassure the electorate that the idea of a common European constitution had been discarded, the EU Council decided to amend extensively the existing Treaty on European Union (Maastricht) and the TEC. Out of that emerged the Reform Treaty, popularly known as the Treaty of Lisbon, where it was signed by the EU Council in December 2007.

By describing the new document as a mere amendment to the already existing treaties, the EU Council gave its members a rationale to present it to their respective parliaments rather than the electorate. That ploy worked—the exception being Ireland. The dissenting Irish prime minister called a referendum in June 2008. Voters rejected the Lisbon/Reform Treaty by a large margin. So the plan to hold 2009 European Parliament elections under the latest treaty rules fell apart.

Throughout 2008, acute differences between leading EU nations surfaced not only on foreign affairs but also on tackling the financial meltdown. While Britain, France, and most other EU nations followed the Keynesian formula of raising demand by pumping money into the system, Germany, the European Union's largest economy, refused to do so. Its policymakers were haunted by the hyperinflation of the Weimar Republic in the 1920s in the same way that their American counterparts were scarred by the Great Crash of 1929. Later, some EU members began to advocate restricting commercial freedoms within the bloc that have been its bedrock since its inception, in order to save jobs at home.

The unprecedented worldwide economic contraction in 2008–2009 exposed the fault lines in the European Union. Its members lacked a common financial or tax policy or even agreed-to criteria for subsidizing a failing industry. However, the sums invested by many EU governments to recapitalize banks totaled $380 billion, with a further underwriting of banks' $3.17 trillion loans to thaw the frozen credit channels.[11]

Within the Eurozone, Greece, Ireland, Italy, and Spain suffered particularly badly because of the collapse of the housing market and construction and/or excessively large public debt. The Eurozone's comparatively better-off members were keen to help their struggling fellow-members rather than the non-Eurozone countries within the European Union.

A division developed between the old EU members and the fresh ones from the Eastern and Central European countries, once part of the Soviet bloc. The latter found themselves in a pitiable state. They had embraced the Washington Consensus with the zeal of new converts only to find the liberal, capitalist model flawed. On the eve of the EU emergency summit in Brussels on March 1, 2009, held to review the grim economic scene, Poland convened a parallel summit of nine Central and Eastern European countries. Their plea in Brussels for a faster integration into the Eurozone by loosening its strict qualifying rules was rejected. The EU summit ended with the bland reaffirmation of its commitment to a single market and rejection of protectionism.

Earlier, even on such a European issue as recognizing the breakaway region of Kosovo as an independent state, there was no unanimity among EU nations. While France confirmed that it would recognize Kosovo's independence, declared in February 2008, several EU member-states led by Spain made clear their legal concerns.[12] That encouraged Russia to reiterate its backing of Serbia's refusal to recognize Kosovo's secession.

Further differences surfaced when a brief war broke out between Georgia and Russia in August. Italy sided with Moscow, whereas Britain lined up with Georgia, and France took a midway position. Germany and Spain refused to condemn the Kremlin.

The admission of the Baltic States and Poland into the European Union had sharpened discord within the bloc on foreign and security policy toward Moscow. Nursing long-held grudges against Russia, the Polish leaders had blocked or slowed the European Union's policy of forging cordial relations with the Kremlin—much to the irritation of Germany, where strengthening ties with Moscow transcended party differences.

The concept of a bipartisan foreign policy—a norm in well-established democracies like America, Britain, and Germany—was alien in such Eastern European states as Poland. What all post-Communist countries in Europe had warmly embraced, though, was the commitment to the separation of powers, around which revolves the rule of law and independent media, which together constitute the Western model of democracy.

CHAPTER 8

DEMOCRACY

ONE SIZE DOESN'T FIT ALL

The American version of democracy specifies sharp divisions between the executive, legislative, and judicial organs of the state. But in the British model, the executive and legislative arms are combined, with the leader of the largest party or a coalition of parties in Parliament forming the cabinet, the highest executive authority, with the monarch as the head of state. The Republic of India has followed the British model, except that its indirectly elected president is the head of state. There is also a major difference between the systems in which elections are held at fixed intervals—as in the United States—and where the chief executive has leeway to call an early election if it suits his or her party or coalition of parties, as is the case in Britain and India.

The American president's authority to appoint Supreme Court judges enhances his or her constitutional status. He or she is also empowered to grant pardons and commute sentences in the case of convicted criminals, thus overriding the judicial system. And the president is authorized to write signing statements in congressional bills, challenging certain sections. President George W. Bush used 1,200 signing statements to amend or cancel as many sections in new bills—*almost twice the number challenged by all the previous forty-two presidents combined.*[1] Thus the chief executive in the United States stands above the Congress and the Supreme Court. In short, the three state organs in the United States are separate but far from equal. Bush's presidency highlighted that fact in no uncertain terms.

"MANAGED" DEMOCRACY

Yet when Russian President Vladimir Putin exercised his power with firmness, he faced strong criticism by most American analysts, accusing him of

turning authoritarian. They conspicuously avoided using that term for President Boris Yeltsin even though he governed largely by decree, centralized
power in the Kremlin, and single-handedly wrote a constitution, which was
weighted heavily in favor of the executive president at the expense of the parliament.[2] It is worth noting that this constitution won the approval of three
out of five Russian voters.

The system that evolved during Yeltsin's presidency, and was consolidated
by Putin, is often described in the West as a "managed democracy." With a
strong executive at its core, it offers a nominally multiparty system, where citizens' rights of free expression and association are curtailed and the opposition factions are allowed to function in a restricted fashion.

Citizens of a country should be the ultimate judges of the suitability or
otherwise of a social system. Only their opinions should count, no one else's.
In 2006, the much-respected Yuri-Levada Institute gauged popular attitudes
on this subject in Russia for the independent EU-Russia Center in Brussels. Its
wide-scale opinion survey showed that 35 percent wanted to return to the
Soviet system, 26 percent thought that Putin's quasi-authoritarian system was
more suitable for Russia, and only 16 percent wanted Western-style democracy. Almost two-thirds preferred a strong state assuring security to citizens
to a liberal state committed to upholding liberties. Instead of favoring separation of executive, legislative, and judicial powers, the respondents wanted an
overarching state authority to coordinate the institutions of national power.
(In a nationwide poll on the greatest Russian in history by the leading TV
channel in 2008, Joseph Stalin got 519,071 votes against 524,575 for the winner
Alexander Nevsky, a medieval warrior prince.) When choosing their priorities,
68 percent ticked "security," 64 percent "housing," and only 18 percent "free expression," with a puny 4 percent "free association."[3]

With his approval rating never falling below 70 percent, Putin was apparently in tune with popular opinion in the Russian Federation. That, and the
soaring revenue from oil and gas exports, emboldened him to respond forcefully to the West's criticism of his governance, which was coupled with homilies on democracy. He did so on the eve of the G8 summit in St. Petersburg
in 2006.[4] He would go on to disappoint those in the West who had wagered
that he would maneuver to latch on to the presidency beyond 2008. And, to
the puzzlement of most Western analysts of Russia, as the prime minister
Putin scored an approval rating of over 80 percent.[5]

In the pre-Bolshevik Revolution era, Russia experimented with democracy properly only after the abdication of the authoritarian Tsar Nicholas II in February 1917 in the midst of World War I. After four months Alexander Kerensky replaced Prince Gregory Lvov as executive prime minister. So the Bolsheviks, led by Vladimir Lenin, who overthrew the Kerensky government in October, did not encounter much resistance to establishing their dictatorship.

Sharing the same history as Russia, the Central Asian republics of Kazakhstan, Kyrgyzstan, Tajikistan, Turkmenistan, and Uzbekistan too have adopted the Russian model of democracy. After finding that the price, political and economic, for being in the good books of Uncle Sam was too high, the Central Asian leaders—all of them more fluent in Russian than their native tongues—returned to the bosom of the familiar Mother Russia. They completed their reversion with Kyrgyzstan ordering the United States in February 2009 to quit the Manas air base it had leased to the Pentagon in 2001 during the Afghanistan War, the president of Uzbekistan having acted in the same way in the case of the Qarshi-Khanabad air base four years earlier.

Unlike tsarist Russia, Czechoslovakia had a tradition of democracy before World War II. Therefore a return of Communist Czechoslovakia to Western-style democracy after the collapse of the Soviet bloc in 1990 was fairly smooth.

Following the switch-over from Communist authoritarianism to capitalist democracy in Eastern Europe, there was an expectation in Western capitals that the democratic tide would next reach the Arab world, the last bastion of autocratic rule. That did not happen. Why? The Eastern European regimes had a coherent ideology of Marxism-Leninism they shared with the Soviet Union. In contrast, there was no common ideological thread running through the Middle East, divided between monarchies and republics. They drew their legitimacy from different sources: some from orthodox Islam, others from mere republicanism, and still others from pan-Arabism.

THE OTTOMANS' ARAB COLONIES

Overall, the Arab bloc stands apart from the Afro-Asian colonies of the European powers, most of which achieved independence during the first two and a half decades of the post–World War II era.

While Britain, France, and the Netherlands ruled their colonies in Asia and Africa during the nineteenth and the first half of the twentieth centuries, they experienced steady expansion of the political and economic rights of ordinary citizens at home—with the franchise extended from men with property to those with education and then to women only after World War I, in phases—and the founding and consolidation of democratic institutions and practices. This had an impact on the fate of those inhabiting their colonies. For instance, imperial Britain gave the voting right first to a select few in British India in 1892. It expanded the franchise, albeit at a snail's pace. By the time it quit India more than half a century later, only about one Indian out of five had the right to vote.

Nonetheless, the basic elements of democratic development in the imperial country rubbed off on the elite in the non-European colonies as the latter imbibed higher education in the metropolitan countries. This in turn laid a foundation on which the freshly independent states could build their domestic politics. India did so successfully, Pakistan and Nigeria, fitfully.

In the case of the Arab lands, the imperial power was Ottoman Turkey. As the Royal Court in Istanbul monopolized all political space, the dialectic of the government and opposition was absent. By deploying different mechanisms the authorities controlled and co-opted citizenry at large.

The first written constitution, containing a bill of rights and a provision for an elected chamber, promulgated by Sultan Abdul Hamid (ruled 1876–1909) in December 1876, lasted a little over a year. It was not until 1908 that a powerful group of young intellectuals, called the "Young Turks," compelled the sultan to reinstate the constitution. They then overthrew Abdul Hamid, who was succeeded by Sultan Muhammad VI (1909–1923). He was the ruler during World War I, which ended in 1918 with the disintegration of the Ottoman Empire. Its Arab colonies fell into the hands of Britain and France.

As there was no democratic evolution in Ottoman Turkey, the nucleus of the empire, there was none in the colonies. Among other things, there was an almost total absence of secular, voluntary associations, the precursors of the present-day nongovernmental organizations (NGOs).

Britain and France, the new imperial masters in the Middle East, acted differently. Republican France opted for republics in both Syria and Lebanon. In contrast, monarchical Britain founded monarchies in Iraq and Jordan—and kept Palestine under its direct control—while sustaining the already existing hereditary rulers in the sparsely populated Arabian Peninsula steeped in traditional tribalism and Islam.

ISLAM AND DEMOCRACY

Contrary to popular belief in the West, democracy is sanctified in Islam. "Take counsel with them [the believers] in the affairs," states the Quran (3:154). "Those who answer their Lord, and perform the prayer, their affairs being counsel between them" (42:36).[6]

Citing these Quranic injunctions, Article VII of the Constitution of the Islamic Republic of Iran states that "Councils and Consultative Bodies are the main decision-making and administrative organs of the country." Since the Islamic revolution in 1979, Iran has held three referendums; eight elections for Parliament; ten for the presidency; five for the Assembly of Experts, a constitutional body that inter alia elects the supreme leader for an eight-year tenure; and three for local governments. In every case voters had multiple choices, though not based on political parties. National elections were held on time even when Iran was at war with Iraq from 1980 to 1988—a contrast to the postponing of the general election by the British government during World War II.

The official title of the country is not Islamic Emirate (as was the case with the Taliban-ruled Afghanistan) of Iran, or Islamic State, but Islamic Republic, which means that power lies with the public, and all Iranians aged fifteen or more are entitled to vote. And its political, social, and economic affairs are conducted according to the tenets of Islam.

The constitution, drafted by the popularly elected First Assembly of Experts, makes a clear distinction between the executive, legislative, and judicial organs of the government. Where it differs from the secular Western versions is in its provision for an outstanding Islamic jurisprudent to be the supreme leader[7] chosen by the directly elected Assembly of Experts for an eight-year term.

Standing above the executive, legislative, and judicial branches of the state, the supreme leader exercises extensive powers, including the right to declare war or peace on the recommendation of the Supreme Defense Council, some of its members being his nominees. He appoints the supreme judge, the chief of the general staff, and half of the twelve members of the Guardian Council, authorized to interpret the Constitution and vet candidates for public office.[8]

The president is the chief executive and is elected directly for a four-year term. If the Supreme Court finds him derelict in his duties or if Parliament declares him incompetent, he can be dismissed by the supreme leader. Legislative authority rests with Parliament, which is elected for a four-year term. Bills passed by Parliament are vetted by the Guardian Council to ensure that they are in line with the constitution and Islamic precepts.

Of the fifty-seven members of the intergovernmental Islamic Conference Organization, Iran is one of only four where Shiites are in the majority, the others being Azerbaijan, Bahrain, and Iraq. So Iran's constitution makers incorporated the concept of an Islamic jurisprudent acting as the supreme leader until the arrival of the Mahdi, the Rightly Guided One, who will end injustice on earth before the Day of Judgment while claiming divine sanction. The Shiites of Iran believe that their last, infallible twelfth Imam, Muhammad al Qasim, went into occultation in 873 CE, and that he will reappear as the Mahdi. In the interim, Iran's constitution provides for the supreme leader to act as the ultimate ruler.[9] Such a provision in the constitution of a Sunni-majority state is unthinkable.

The record of popular elections in Iran, whether at the local or national level, shows intense competition for public office in an environment where voter turnout remains open to speculation. In 1997, the candidate backed by the religious establishment—Ali Akbar Nateq-Nouri—was decisively defeated by an outsider, Muhammad Khatami. In another instance, the mayor of Iran, Mahmoud Ahmadinejad, a pious layman, soundly defeated Ali Akbar Hashemi Rafsanjani, an affluent former president who was also one of the founder-leaders of the Islamic Republic. Most Iranians maintain that their country provides a successful example of representative government and Islam working in tandem over the past three decades.

Who the final victors in Iran's electoral contests will be remains unpredictable, as does the turnout of electors. In the general elections for president or Parliament the voter turnout is rarely below 60 percent, which is regarded as exceptional in U.S. presidential races. In 2008, despite the massive use of the Internet, cell phones, text messages, and YouTube videos; the unprecedented enthusiasm of young citizens for the first African-American candidate, Barack Obama; and the staggering amounts of money he spent on the party primaries and the presidential campaign, voter turnout only inched upwards to 63 percent.[10] Unsurprisingly, the comparative lack of civic sense among Americans leaves unimpressed not only Europeans, whose average turnout in general elections hovers around 80 percent, but also Iranians and Indians.

THE ARAB WORLD

In the Arab world, of the democratic constitutions promulgated by France in Lebanon (1927) and Syria (1930), the one in Lebanon has endured in a modified form, with elections held regularly except during the 1975–1990 civil war. But the democratic regime in Syria proved short-lived.

In March 1949, the U.S. Central Intelligence Agency helped Brigadier General Hosni Zaim to stage a military coup against a democratically elected government, after he had promised to make peace with Israel following the 1948 Arab-Israeli War. Following his signing of the armistice with Israel in mid-July, and giving up the small enclave Syria held inside Palestine, Zaim tried to negotiate peace with Israel through Washington. But a month later he was ousted by a group of nationalist military officers and executed.[11]

Thus the United States acquired the distinction of engineering the first military coup against a democratic government in the Middle East. This unsavory piece of history goes conveniently unnoticed and unmentioned not only by American policymakers but also by most academics and experts.

It is hard to reconcile Washington's actions with the assertions made by President George W. Bush. Taking his cue from Natan Sharansky's book *The Case for Democracy* (2004), Bush argued that since democracies do not attack one another, he had invaded Iraq, governed by a dictator, to implant democracy there, thus making Iraq peaceful.

This idea, originally aired in 1996 by Israeli Prime Minister Binyamin Netanyahu, does not stand up to scrutiny. In 1974, the democratically elected Turkish Prime Minister Ecevit Bulent invaded Cyprus ruled by a popularly elected president, Archbishop Makarios (aka Michael Mouskos). A more recent example was Pakistan's popularly elected government of Nawaz Sharif staging a large-scale attack on the Kargil region of Indian-administered Kashmir in 1999. This led to the massing of one million soldiers on both sides of the international line, arrayed in an offensive position. Following President Clinton's intervention, Nawaz Sharif withdrew his troops.

History shows that that whenever there has been conflict between securing Israel's recognition by an Arab state and advancing democracy in that country, Washington has always scuttled the democratic mission. Egypt under President Anwar Sadat (ruled 1970–1981), who signed a peace treaty with Israel in

1979, provided a stark example. He rammed its approval through an unrepresentative parliament. Then he put the issue before the electorate, not by itself but along with a string of such disparate subjects as having a Bill of Rights, in a referendum. The participants were required to answer all these questions with a single yes or no. The result was that 99.1 percent said yes![12] Sadat's successor, Hosni Mubarak, closely allied with Washington, has continued to preside over a secular regime that can at best be described as a quasi-dictatorship.

Most people in the non-Western world viewed the Bush administration's democracy crusade skeptically. A survey of forty-seven countries, involving 45,000 respondents, by the Washington-based Pew Research Center in April–May 2007 showed that majorities in all but one country believed that the United States promoted democracy "mostly where it served American interests."[13]

Because of their hydrocarbon riches and geostrategic importance as a crossroads of Asia, Africa, and Europe, the Arab Middle East and Iran have drawn a great deal of attention and energy of Western politicians and think tanks. These intellectuals and public figures often extrapolate their analyses of this region to the Muslim world at large.

But Arabs and Iranians are only about a third of the global Muslim population of 1.3 billion. By and large, the Muslims living in south and Southeast Asia—Pakistan to Indonesia via Malaysia—twice as many as Arab and Iranian Muslims, have had no problem harmonizing Islam with democracy. In these regions there is a common understanding and acceptance of the essential tenets of a representative government: fair elections, separation of the three organs of the state, and an independent press. But outside this part of the globe, there is one mega-nation—China—whose leaders offer an altogether different definition of democracy, derived from the recorded thoughts of Confucius.

DEMOCRACY WITH CHINESE CHARACTERISTICS

From Liang Qichao (died 1885) to Deng Xiaoping, China's reformists have viewed democracy within the context of Confucian philosophy. Confucius based his thinking on the axioms that human nature is essentially benign, that an individual is educable, and that a good government results when there is harmony of interests between the ruler and the ruled, with both sides striving for prosperity and with strong security forces to ensure peace and order while avoiding disorder at all costs. Such an environment enables every law-abiding citizen to contribute his or her best to the communal good. When an individual fits into such a system and performs to the best of his or her ability, that is "democracy" in action.

Subscribing to this thesis, Mao Zedong, leader of the Communist Party of China (CPC), concluded that anti-social, anti-collectivist behavior by a citizen put him or her beyond the pale of "the people." Such an individual had no legitimate place in the *People's* Republic of China.

So long as Mao was alive, his word prevailed. After his death in 1976 and the arrest of his radical wife, Jiang Qing, soon after, a movement for Western-style democracy built up gradually to an apex in June 1989 in Beijing's Tiananmen Square. After the crackdown on that movement, the official Propaganda Department outlawed the demand for separating the CPC from the government as well as such terms as "freedom."

The earlier Cultural Revolution, launched by the Maoist wing within the CPC under the guise of "people's democracy," had shown the pitfalls of letting loose ill-disciplined mobs. That chaotic episode encouraged CPC leaders to stick to the tried-and-tested strategy of calibrated reform from the top. At the same time they blamed Western democracy for engendering a distinct Taiwanese identity in the rebel province, which fueled demand for Taiwan's independence.

All the same, democracy has been one of the important subjects under study at the Chinese Academy of Social Sciences (CASS) in Beijing. With 4,000 researchers and scholars—four-fifths of them foreign-returned—at its fifty research centers, it is the largest think tank in the world. It is a hothouse of ideas, conventional and unconventional, covering domestic as well as international issues in their complexities.

In the absence of opposition parties, open disagreements between leaders, and independent trade unions, and with the media more interested in promoting social harmony than political accountability, intellectual debate became a surrogate for politics. It also furnished decision makers with a variety of options. But there are lines scholars were not allowed to cross. Marking thirty years of economic reform in December 2008, President Hu Jintao said, "We must draw on the benefits of humankind's political civilization. But we will never copy the model of the Western political system."[14]

The government remained alert to those elements, local or foreign, that strove to erode the power of the CPC. Following the color revolutions between November 2003 and March 2005 in Georgia, Ukraine, and Kyrgyzstan,

the authorities established a special task force to examine the role of the foreign NGOs. Working with a state-backed think tank, it sent research teams
not only to the affected countries but also to adjoining Belarus and Uzbekistan. Based on their findings, the PRC severely restricted foreign NGOs' activities. It loaned its crowd control experts to the Central Asian republics to
impart their security agencies' appropriate skills.[15]

The CASS's Institute of Politics was the source of white papers on democracy published for public discussion. The first one appeared in 2005. While
accepting the overarching thesis that democracy was a necessary condition
for economic and political progress, Chinese leaders viewed it pragmatically—
as an instrument to achieve the Confucian aims of political stability and economic well-being. In other words, they strove to devise "democracy with
Chinese characteristics" following their earlier presentation of "socialism with
Chinese characteristics."

As a rule, the annual session of the National People's Congress (i.e., Parliament) is accompanied by a session of the Chinese People's Political Consultative Congress (CPPCC), an advisory body. The CPPCC has a longer history
than the National People's Congress, with its delegates coming from both the
Communist Party of China and the smaller political entities allied to it. It was
the CPPCC that approved the state's name, the People's Republic of China, in
1949 as well as the national flag and anthem, and elected the first government.
It acted as a de facto parliament until the promulgation of the new constitution five years later, which established the National People's Congress. By that
time the eight non-CPC groups were collectively called the United Front Democratic Parties.[16] Now, dominated by the CPC, the CPPCC consists of delegates from these parties and mass organizations as well as independents. At
present two of the twenty-eight cabinet ministers are not CPC members.

The principle of "consultative democracy" has been applied to the CPC
as well as non-CPC groups. The CPC's Organization Department gives six
weeks to party members and the public to comment on a proposed candidate's suitability for a CPC position. If the comments are unfavorable, then
the Organization Department withdraws its proposal.[17] At the National
People's Congress, its Standing Committee has enlarged public participation
in the drafting of laws and regulations. On important property legislation in
March 2007, it convened half a dozen sessions and examined more than
10,000 comments.

In short, participatory democracy has emerged as a salient feature of the Chinese model. By getting citizens involved in formal debates and voting on important issues, the authorities have found a way to realize major democratic tenets of deliberation and political equality while bypassing the partisan rivalry and point-scoring characteristic of Western democracy without diluting the CPC's hold on power.

According to Fang Ning, deputy director of the Institute of Politics and a coauthor of the 2005 official "White Paper on Democracy," "Western democracy is like going to a restaurant and choosing whether you want a French, Italian or German chef who will decide on your behalf what is on the menu. With Chinese democracy we always have the same chef—the Communist Party—but we will increasingly get to choose which dishes he cooks."[18]

In purely practical terms, economic reform could not be accomplished without associated administrative reform, and that in turn brought about political changes, albeit inadvertently. In the PRC, the authorities started to involve citizens in major policy making through consultations, meetings with experts, opinion surveys, and even referendums. Open hearings on the economics of public services proved particularly popular.

For instance, in the southwestern megalopolis of Chongqing (population 30 million), the local government's legal department had held six hundred public hearings on such issues as compensation to peasants whose lands were taken over, minimum wages, and charges for utilities. To bypass the vociferous minority dominating such exercises, the local authority resorted to lottery. In one instance, it selected 275 residents by lottery to confer with experts for a whole day to pare down thirty proposed building projects to twelve. Their decision was forwarded to the city's People's Congress, which endorsed it.[19]

China's long-established practices of competitive examinations for official posts open to all, promotion based on merit, and the resulting social mobility provided a strong base for a steady progression of Chinese-style democracy. Yet the basic concept of political democracy—giving citizens the option to choose their political leaders—needed to be addressed. While party leaders showed no intention of abandoning the CPC's monopoly over politics, or the cardinal principle of party-government symbiosis, they compromised—to a certain extent.

Four years after the formal dissolution of communes and agricultural cooperatives in 1983, the government introduced elections in rural areas. During the next decade almost half of China's 700,000 villages went through the exercise as the central government extended the experiment on a province-by-province basis. In 1998 it mandated by law that such polls should be held every three years by secret ballot in private booths, and it authorized the elected local councils to have an input in such issues as taxes, investment of collective funds, land acquisitions, and family planning.

But village council members remained subordinate to the local CPC secretary. Moreover, a village council was not part of the official power structure, since its lowest tier was the unelected township council, representing either a large town or a collective of small villages led by a town. Therefore elected village councils had to bow to nominated township councils.

In 1998, the local party leaders of Buyun township in Sichuan province held a direct election for mayor—normally chosen by the members of the town's people's congress—and allowed non-CPC members to contest. After initially condemning the poll as a "violation of the constitution," the authorities in Beijing described it as reflective of "a positive direction of rural democracy." Since then several townships in Sichuan and other provinces have held direct elections for mayors without the formal consent of CPC leaders. Yet their results get published even in official newspapers like the *China Daily*.[20] The attitude of top CPC leaders has been "Wait and watch." They have noted the disputes between elected village chiefs and township mayors with their corresponding party secretaries, who shadow government officials to ensure that the officeholders stick to the party line. They have yet to devise a formal procedure to resolve such differences.

Overall, CPC leaders weigh the issue of holding elections at the town level and upwards in pragmatic terms. Will such an exercise help tackle the challenges of escalating public protest, widening inequality, corruption of the political elite, the weakness of the domestic market, and the poor state of the rural economy? The answers to these questions, as provided by the researchers at the Institute of Politics, seem to be in the negative. Those opposed to competitive electoral politics argue that in such races the rich in urban centers will get their proxies elected, and they will thus further their narrow interests at the expense of public welfare. In rural areas the emerging middle class will prevail at the cost of the struggling peasantry.

Their prediction is borne out by the state of electoral democracy in India. The cost of running for Parliament in Delhi is enormous. The average income and wealth of an Indian member MP is in the topmost bracket, even though most of the voters in his or her constituency fall in the lowest bracket. Yet in order to recoup the vast sums spent on electioneering, successful candidates sell their political influence for money. According to Transparency International, electoral and political processes are the primary sources of corruption in India. Another example is the astronomical costs of presidential and congressional elections in America. The successful Democratic presidential candidate, Barack Obama, spent $1 billion on his twenty-one-month-long campaign. That amounted to shelling out $14 for *each* vote he won in the final race.

Irrespective of a country's political system—multiparty or single party, parliamentary or presidential—it is governed by laws. Following the making of laws—done by vigorous or rubber-stamp parliaments—comes law enforcement, accomplished by civil servants, police, and judges who are selected on the basis of examinations and performance reviews. Under the guidance of Hu Jintao, the party began reiterating the importance of the rule of law. The Sixth Plenum of the Sixteenth CPC Central Committee resolved in 2006 to improve further "the socialist democratic and legal system" and ensure that the country was governed "according to law . . . in an all-round way," with people's rights and interests respected.

That process had in fact started a year after the 1989 Tiananmen Square protest, with the Administrative Litigation Act. It entitled citizens to legal recourse in the event of the government's abuse of power. In 1991, for the first time, China recognized the concept of human rights when it published a white paper titled "The Situation of Human Rights in China." Three years later came the State Indemnity Law, which entitled a citizen to seek compensation in case of loss resulting from a government agency invading his or her legitimate rights and interests. In 1999, the Law on Administrative Punishment provided for punishing criminal offenses committed not only by the state's administrative, economic, and judicial agencies but also by those in the CPC's leadership organs.[21]

Between 1996 and 2001, cases against the government rose tenfold, to nearly 100,000. And with qualified lawyers increasingly becoming judges, the chance of winning against the government grew to 40 percent.[22] The PRC was pursuing the idea of setting up a Sino-European law school with the assistance of the European Commission to improve its legal system.

In 1999, the PRC started responding to the U.S. State Department's annual report on China's human rights practices, with its own *The Human Rights Record of the United States*. Its first report, published in March 2005, catalogued statistics on crime, violent death, imprisonment, poverty, rape, child abuse, and racial and sexual discrimination. Its report in March 2007 was wide-ranging and backed its statements with evidence. It pointed out that the FBI had held 6,742 individuals since 9/11 without charge, and that three-quarters of them were released because of a lack of evidence. It referred to violations of citizens' privacy by the federal government as sanctioned by the 2001 USA PATRIOT Act. A survey published in the *Washington Post* on December 13, 2006, showed that two-thirds of Americans believed that the FBI and other federal agencies were infringing on their privacy rights. Moreover, the ongoing use of capital punishment in the United States contravened the right to life as stated in Article 3 of the Universal Declaration of Human Rights. And unlike other governments, the Bush administration had violated human rights abroad on a wide scale. In gross violation of the Geneva Conventions, it had systematically abused prisoners of war in Iraq and Afghanistan. The report alluded to the survey of the Bloomberg School of Public Health at Johns Hopkins University published in October 2006. It estimated that more than 655,000 Iraqis had died in Iraq since the start of the war in March 2003.

The purpose of publishing such reports, explained the PRC government, was to help the people of the world to have "a better understanding of the situation in the United States" and thus "promote the international cause of human rights." To achieve that aim, it swiftly posted the English translation of its reports on the Internet.

THE ERA OF THE INTERNET

The Internet and cell phones have opened up immense opportunities for democratization of society everywhere. China is no exception. Increasingly, ordinary people feel they are entitled to express their views and monitor others', while expecting a response from the authorities.

In January 2009, according to official figures, the number of Internet users in China approached 300 million, an exponential growth from 20 million in 2000—well ahead of the 253 million Web users in America. In the wider context, however, the 23 percent penetration of the Internet in the PRC in early

2009 matched the level for the world at large—which was only a third of the figure for the United States.[23] What was remarkable, though, was the figure for bloggers in China: 70 million.[24] So too was the statistic of 624 million cell phone subscribers, amounting to half the population.

Chinese citizens' increased use of the Internet to access news and share views and videos revealed abuses of power. The subsequent airing of complaints led the authorities to respond quickly and honestly through action or explanation. In May 2008 the government ordered its agencies to counter false information with accurate disclosures or clarifications. It reduced the list of subjects considered taboo. But the blocking of Web sites dealing with Tibetan independence, Taiwan, the Tiananmen Square protest, and the religious sect Falun Gong remained. The official censors swiftly located and deleted "objectionable" content. Cyber cafés were required to install filtering software, record the names of users, and monitor their usage of the Internet.

At the same time, the authorities became proactive, using the Web to circulate their news and views. They decided to set the agenda by disseminating "authoritative information" early and taking the initiative in news propaganda. To that end, they set up Internet Propaganda Leading Groups to offer online comments on articles, news threads, and blogs as well as refute rumors.

When the authorities found themselves proved wrong by bloggers with their evidence on display, they tried to make amends quickly. For example, in response to riots in the southwestern province of Guizhou in June 2008 against the cover-up of a teenage girl's death, the authorities at first dismissed the protestors as "criminals." The images posted on the Web by bloggers challenged this claim. Faced with this evidence, the government relented. It sacked the police officers responsible for roughing up the demonstrators. And the provincial CPC leader offered a public apology.[25]

Five months later, the officials in Chongqing took an unprecedented step. They posted the video of a three-hour meeting between striking taxi drivers and the local CPC chief online to let the public know what transpired during the closed-door talks.

Critics argue that by providing citizens with a safety valve to air their grievances and see them redressed, without permitting meaningful change in the authoritarian system, the CPC government had found a means of retaining power for much longer than would have been the case otherwise. All the same, with the advent of the Internet and cell phones, such terms as "openness," "transparency," and "accountability," which Mikhail Gorbachev first introduced in the Communist world, began finding their way into the CPC's statements. And rising official transparency whetted the public's appetite for scrutiny.

As with democracy, so with freedom.

PRIORITIZING OF FREEDOMS

There are several categories of freedom, and which one precedes which varies from country to country. Indisputably, however, the primal need of humans is survival, which depends on sustenance. So they aspire first and foremost to be free from hunger.

Freedom from want should therefore top the list of freedoms. Yet there is continued insistence by America and other Western nations—all of them rich and industrialized—that socioeconomic rights be separated from civic and political rights and that they should be assigned a secondary status.

The debate has a long history. It became heated when the number of freshly independent countries in Asia and Africa rose sharply in the 1960s. The following decade saw the emergence of a civil liberties movement in many Third World countries, and in the 1980s activists advocated group rights and people's rights over their natural resources.

On the eve of the Vienna Summit on Human Rights in 1993, the debate was finely balanced. The summit ended with a declaration incorporating both sides of the argument. While stating that all human rights were "universal, indivisible and interdependent and interrelated," the Vienna Declaration recognized that "the significance of national and regional peculiarities and various historical, cultural and religious backgrounds must be borne in mind." That helped upgrade economic, cultural, and social rights, which were adopted by many development agencies.

By then, however, the world's largest democracy, India, had already taken an important stride in that direction. It came in the wake of a judgment by Supreme Court Justice V. R. Krishna Iyer concerning article 21 of the Indian constitution, which guarantees "right to life." He ruled that "life" meant a life of dignity and not mere animal survival. And that included right to shelter, education, privacy, and foreign travel.[26]

To deliver freedom from hunger to a citizen by enabling him or her to win the struggle for survival emerges as the noblest and most humane achievement of any government. By lifting one-third of China's 1.3 billion people out of poverty in a quarter century, the PRC quantitatively advanced economic freedom like no other country in history so far. This dovetailed with the important sayings of Mencius (372–289 BCE), who developed the ideas of Confucius. He stated that the government was responsible for the general welfare of its citizens and that denying them the right to food and welfare was worse than violating their political rights.[27]

Little wonder that in its 2007 report on human rights in the United States, the PRC assailed the U.S. government for the lack of proper guarantees for its citizens' economic, social, and cultural rights. It pointed out that one out of eight Americans was living in poverty in 2006, and that white Americans' incomes were 64 percent higher than blacks' and 40 percent higher than Hispanics'. Moreover, American women were not paid equally for doing the same work as men.[28]

Assuring security of life, limb, and property for its population is the second most important freedom that a state can offer. With the ravages of the 1966–1968 Cultural Revolution now confined to history books, the current Chinese government scored well on this count. A complementary part of personal and property security is freedom from arbitrary arrest, which translates as the rule of law. There China remains deficient. For all practical purposes, the Communist Party of China is above the law.

An important part of economic freedom is the right to choose one's occupation, which is linked with freedom to travel. Industrialization and urbanization at a breakneck speed gave this freedom to more than 100 million rural Chinese, who migrated to urban centers during 2000–2005 without any hindrance.

With restrictions on foreign travel eased, the number of Chinese going abroad rocketed from 3 million in 1992 to nearly 40 million in 2008. An estimated 350,000 Western residents in China interacted freely with the local people. Between 1978 and 2005, the number of publications shot up from a few dozen state-controlled newspapers to more than 2,000 newspapers and 9,000 magazines. "A large and growing variety of news sources and a new generation of journalists have steadily expanded the boundaries of the permissible," noted Howard D. French in the *International Herald Tribune*. On the other hand, only Xinhua, the *People's Daily*, the CCTV, and China Radio International were allowed to have foreign correspondents and bureaus.[29]

Restrictions on the freedom to think were getting eroded by the Internet and cell phones. Within official institutions such as the CASS, debate was encouraged so that more options could become available to policymakers. Outside these organizations, bookstores in large cities stocked books by practically all important Western intellectuals translated into Chinese. Nevertheless, freedom of expression remained restricted. And the Internet was policed, with teams of computer scientists quickly erecting a firewall with a minimum of four filters.

Finally, the freedom to choose leaders and make them accountable to voters remained restricted to the village level. Though forming a majority of the national population, rural Chinese lacked power beyond the narrow confines of a village.

The contrasting views of China and America can best be understood within their respective sets of values. At one end of the spectrum stands individualism, cutthroat competition, and partisan politics, and at the other, collectivism, consensus, and united leadership—labeled by some as Asian values. A striking element of Asian societies is the centrality of the family, which dates back to the days of Confucius. He was the original advocate of family values, placing filial loyalty and respect for elders at the core of his philosophy. Nothing illustrates this better than the Chinese custom of stating the family name first and then the given name.

It is worth noting that having gained independence from European domination, the peoples in East and Southeast Asia have tended to opt for a middle way between liberal Western democracy and authoritarian rule—that is, a managed or guided democracy, a term also applied to the political system in Russia, a Eurasian continent.

In sum, be it democracy or freedoms, the United States faces viable alternatives. This is equally true of the soft power it exercises.

CHAPTER 9

SOFT POWER CHALLENGES TO AMERICA

Though Joseph Nye of Harvard University is credited with coining the term "soft power" in the early 1990s, its origins go far back—to the second Roosevelt administration (1937–1941). Franklin D. Roosevelt realized that only by communicating with and winning popular backing in foreign lands could America feel truly secure. That led to the establishment of the United States Information Agency and the Voice of America, and later the Peace Corps during the presidency of John F. Kennedy in 1962.

Earlier, U.S. soft power had manifested itself in the form of such goods and services as Coca-Cola, Cadillac, Hoovers, and Hollywood movies, which subtly but effectively underlined the virtues of beneficial American enterprise and culture. In more recent times, rock music, McDonald's fast food, Levi's jeans, Starbucks coffee shops, and CNN have carried a similar message to the world beyond U.S. shores. The cumulative effect of this ongoing phenomenon has been to raise the American government's legitimacy internationally and enable it to continue its role as the rule-setter in multilateral organizations.

According to Nye, soft power—defined as the ability to influence and shape the preferences of others—is a derivative of a nation's culture, values, and achievements. This definition held universally for a little over a decade—until a much wider interpretation was offered by the Chinese Academy of Social Sciences (CASS).

It offered a list of sixty-four indexes and subindexes constituting comprehensive national power (CNP; *zonghe guoli* in Chinese). Its major constituents

are defense capability, economic strength, scientific and technological capabilities, population, human development, the media, and arts and culture. In
all these areas, numerical indexes and subindexes either exist or can be devised. Once these are averaged and suitably weighted for a country, its CNP
is computed as a number.

Using its extensive criteria, the CASS concluded that in 2006, the CNP score
of the United States was 90.62 out of 100. China's score of 59.10 put it in almost
the same league as Russia (63.03), France (62.0), and Germany (61.93)—
marginally surpassing Japan (57.84) but well ahead of India at 50.43.[1]

Though China is way behind America, its policymakers are keen to narrow the gap. A study of the latest batch of one hundred articles by important
CASS scholars in 2008 showed that nearly eighty of them focused on the
United States. They either explained how the United States functioned politically, economically, militarily, or culturally, or outlined means to deploy to
block, sidestep, curtail, or limit Washington's towering power and influence.[2]

Later the National Security Council Secretariat in Delhi used a CASS
methodology to compute the National Security Index of thirty countries. It
took into account the Human Development Index, Research and Development Index, GDP Performance Index (GDPPI), Defense Expenditure Index,
and Population Index. Each of these indexes was a composite, with different
elements weighted differently. For instance, the GDPPI was computed by giving the GDP Index four times more weight than the GDP Growth Index.[3]

Soft power is part of the CNP. But being hydra-headed, it is easier to describe it in negative terms rather than in positive ones. It consists of everything
that is *not* the hard power of the military. Therefore, striving for a high rate
of economic growth, improving human development, enhancing research and
development, advancing science and technology, maintaining national sovereignty, and operating within international law are part of soft power. So too
are the cultural and sports achievements of a nation.

The hosting of the 29th Olympiad in Beijing in 2008 seemed a most op-
portune task for the People's Republic of China to project its soft power.

THE SPECTACLE OF THE OLYMPIAD

The Olympiad offered the PRC a golden chance to show how it viewed itself—modern, energetic, disciplined, economically powerful—and wished to

be seen by others. Its opening ceremony at the specially constructed bird's nest–shaped National Stadium in Beijing made the point in a spectacular, yet strictly nonpolitical, style. The date was 08.08.08, and the time 8 PM. Here in a row were four eights, number eight signifying prosperity and confidence according to Confucius.

The spellbinding four-hour ceremony had a cast of 15,000 performers. It opened with a roll of Fou drums, with 2,008 drummers from the People's Liberation Army beating the drums with glowing red drumsticks. They were followed by 3,000 men in robes, chanting a line of Confucius, "Friends have come from afar; how happy we are." A giant scroll was then unrolled to offer a stunning taste of China's history and culture as the centerpiece of the show.

First came a gripping presentation of the outstanding Chinese inventions: paper (105 CE; with hemp, linen, and tree bark in common use by the second century), printing (868 CE), gunpowder (1040), and the magnetic compass (1088). Then followed an illustration of the Silk Road with a train of camels. Next arose a deep-throated recitation of another saying of Confucius, "We are all brothers in this world."[4]

The scale, synchronization, and ingenuity of the performances and presentations were breathtaking. The 91,000 spectators in the stadium included more than 100 heads of state or government. And the global TV audience was estimated at 4 billion, nearly two-thirds of the human race.

"The Power and the Glory," ran the headline on the front page of *The Times* of London on August 9, 2008. "China salutes the awestruck world."

What went unnoticed by the international media was the fact that 94 percent of the 120,000 volunteers for the Olympiad were younger than thirty-five. That fact highlighted the overwhelming support the regime had among those born long after the Communist victory in 1949. Equally remarkable had been the number of young volunteers pouring in from all over the country to help the victims of the earthquake that rocked the Sichuan province in May 2008, killing more than 80,000 people and leaving nearly 10 million people homeless.[5] The images of the speedy and efficient handling of the Sichuan disaster by China's soldiers and civilians compared sharply with the shambolic performance of the Bush administration in August 2005 in tackling Hurricane Katrina, which flooded New Orleans.

By the time the 2008 Olympiad closed, China had won forty-nine gold medals—a substantial improvement on the 2004 score—well ahead of America's thirty-four. The $100 million cost of the opening and closing ceremonies was a fraction of the total budget of $43 billion. No other country could expect, or even aspire, to beat the PRC's Olympics performance or expense.

But then few countries can claim an unbroken civilization of five millennia, as China does. For long periods it has existed as a political-cultural entity that did not need the outside world. It thus came to acquire literature and modes of thinking, as well as medicine, that have remained uniquely its own. Unlike India, another ancient civilization, China did not become a full-fledged colony of a foreign power. Therefore its intellectuals maintained an independence and originality of thought that their Indian counterparts lost during their long servitude under the British.

So when the PRC's leaders opened its doors and windows to the outside world, they were confident that the basic Chinese identity would remain intact while their compatriots acquired the advanced technology and business management skills of the West. At the same time, they endeavored to project China's cultural profile and language abroad. By the time the Olympic Games opened in Beijing, its government had tripled the branches of the Confucius Institutes—established in 2004 and modeled on the British Council and Goethe Institute to promote English and German languages and literatures respectively—to 260 in seventy-five countries, often locating them at leading universities.[6] By 2010, these institutes will raise the number of foreigners learning Chinese fourfold, to 10 million.

THE ZHENG HE REVIVAL

While the ancient sage Confucius remains a lodestar in the firmament of Chinese culture, the PRC's leaders have resuscitated a towering figure of a more recent age to project within the Afro-Asian world—to remarkably good effect—China's history of peaceful exploration of the outside world. The figure is Zheng He (1371–1433), an explorer, diplomat, and admiral whose explorations of the Indian and Pacific Oceans made the likes of Christopher Columbus and Vasco de Gama appear amateur.

A native of the Muslim-majority province of Yunnan, ten-year-old Zheng He—formerly Ma He (the Chinese version of Muhammad)—was captured by the army of the Ming Dynasty sent to crush a rebellion. He was castrated and drafted as an orderly. At the age of twenty, he fell under the command of Zhu

Di, a royal prince. He assisted the prince in defeating Emperor Jianwen in a civil war in 1403. Acquiring the title of Yongle ("Great Joy"), the new emperor promoted Zheng He first as the grand eunuch and then the admiral of the imperial fleet. It consisted of 317 ships of various sizes—62 of them treasure ships loaded with precious goods, as presents for foreign rulers or trading items—and employed nearly 28,000 men.

Between 1405 and 1433, Zheng undertook seven expeditions. They covered not only Timor, Java, Sumatra, Thailand, Malaysia, and Sri Lanka, but also southern India, southern Iran, the Arabian Peninsula, and East Africa. He implanted many groups of Chinese Muslims in the ports of present-day Malaysia and Indonesia, and turned Malacca into an important international Islamic trade center. His actions and intentions were mostly peaceable.

In contemporary PRC, Zheng has been presented as the Chinese admiral who encountered many kingdoms in Southeast and Southwest Asia, the Arabian Peninsula, and East Africa, but never conquered any. He was therefore an early apostle of peaceful relations between different countries and cultures. To celebrate the sexcentennial anniversary of Zheng's voyages in 2005, the PRC organized exhibitions and seminars not only in the major cities of China but also in Singapore, Malaysia, the Philippines, and Indonesia to perpetuate what the official literature described as "Zheng's spirit of loving peace and diligence." In other words, when the Chinese explored foreign lands, they did not colonize them or their people, or strip them of their natural resources. Thus, instead of being expedient or ad hoc, China's present policy of peaceful development and respect for the sovereignty of other nations was deeply rooted.

Above and beyond these symbolic gestures, the PRC has been overly active in the diplomatic arena. The policy of retiring older diplomats introduced in the early 1990s had brought to the fore the Chinese diplomatic corps that was young, flexible, and fluent in English and other foreign languages. Emulating America, the PRC has started its own Peace Corps–style organization to send skilled volunteers abroad. While China continued to send tens of thousands of its students to the United States and the European Union for further studies, it has welcomed foreign students, mainly Asian and African. Its intake of Indonesian students, for instance, was twice as high as America's.

Beijing's aid to the Asian states has grown rapidly. By 2003, its financial assistance to Indonesia was twice as much as Washington's, and to the Philippines about four times higher.[7] Having concluded a free trade agreement with the ten-nation Association of South-East Asian Nations (ASEAN), with whom it runs trade deficits, China began negotiating a similar deal with fifteen other countries. It removed all tariffs on commerce with forty-five poor countries.

Addressing the Africa summit in Beijing in 2006, Chinese President Hu Jintao announced the doubling of development aid to African states, running at $2.7 billion in 2004, along with $5 billion in soft loans and credits by 2009 as well as a special $5 billion fund to encourage Chinese businesses to invest in the continent. He announced further debt cancellation initiatives and the extension of duty-free market access to more products from Africa's least-developed countries. He also unveiled plans to train 15,000 African professionals. The summit decided to double trade between Africa and China to $100 billion by 2010 from $50 billion in 2006, which was nearly five times higher than in 2001.[8]

The PRC's plans to create a metal hub in Zambia to import its copper, cobalt, diamonds, tin, and uranium by setting up a Special Economic Zone there, and construct railway, road, and shipping links with it, are being implemented. Next in line is Mauritius, to be transformed into the PRC's trading hub, with many Chinese companies getting preferential access to the twenty-strong Common Market of East and South Africa. To complement these two development projects will be the shipping hub in Dar Es Salaam in Tanzania. The focus in West Africa will be on Liberia and oil-rich Nigeria.[9] With the PRC unveiling and implementing such ambitious plans in the continent, fewer African states were turning for financial aid to the World Bank and the IMF, with their stringent U.S.-directed conditions.

China perceived the release of developing nations from the clutches of international capital dominated by the United States as part of its long-term policy: to bring about the replacement of the present Washington-dominated economic order with one in which nominally independent nations become truly sovereign and manage their economic and political system without kowtowing to America.

Through its meteoric yet peaceful rise the PRC offered an alternative scenario to the developing world of Asia, Africa, and Latin America. It showcased the "Chinese Dream"—achieving rapid economic growth while maintaining national sovereignty and operating within international law—at a time of America's plunging popularity during the Bush presidency. Its strategy worked. In 2006 leaders of nearly a hundred countries visited Beijing to get a taste of the Chinese Dream. The stark difference between it and the American Dream was that the latter applied to individuals, who prosper by working diligently, whereas the former was pertinent to a country as a whole. The luminaries of such diverse nations as Vietnam, Algeria, and Nigeria admired the Chinese model of prioritizing economic progress and alleviation of poverty over political reform and building a harmonious society.

According to a 2005 BBC survey, in fourteen out of twenty-three countries a majority or plurality saw China's influence as benign. Overall, 48 percent saw China positively, 10 percent more than America.[10] The Pew Research Center's survey of forty-seven countries in 2007 showed that China was viewed favorably in Russia (62 percent, 26 percent unfavorably) and most African countries, with favorable ratings upward of 70 percent and negative ratings between 7 percent and 11 percent. The survey's director concluded that China's influence in the world was growing faster than America's and was seen as having a more beneficial impact on African countries than America had.[11] Even in India, a perceived rival of China, a favorable view of China trumped an unfavorable view.

Most people in all these countries apparently formed their views on China—or America—on the basis of news reports. And given the ubiquity of television, it meant news provided by local channels or global satellite channels.

THE UBIQUITY OF TV NEWS

In TV news, Ted Turner, an American media entrepreneur, broke new ground in 1980. He introduced a twenty-four-hour roll-on satellite television news channel called Cable News Network (CNN) with the memorable line, "We won't be signing off until the world ends . . . and we will cover the end of the world, live." His was an expensive enterprise that lost money—until the 1991 Gulf War.

During that conflict only the correspondents of CNN and the BBC (established in 1928) were allowed to stay in Baghdad and report the events. Because of its American origins, CNN became compulsory watching even for the leading combatants, U.S. President George H. W. Bush and Iraqi President Saddam Hussein. They ended up using it as an instant diplomatic channel.

So the international TV audience, irrespective of their location, saw the 1991 Gulf War through the lenses of the BBC and CNN. That underlined the monopoly enjoyed by the English language and the Anglo-American TV networks.

Though, in theory, the subsequent growth of cable television worldwide raised the prospect of ending the Anglo-American duopoly in twenty-four-hour TV news, not much happened because of the exorbitant cost of gathering and editing TV news. That changed with the arrival in 1996 of Al Jazeera (meaning "Gulf") satellite TV funded, but not controlled, by the hydrocarbon-rich Qatar. Staffed largely by BBC-trained journalists who had worked earlier for its Arabic language TV channel, Al Jazeera's declared policy was to offer a global perspective from an Arab and Muslim angle.

Other Arab language channels followed, but none came near the 35-million-member audience that Al Jazeera built up by the turn of the century by offering fearless reports and controversial discussion programs that got it banned from almost all the Arab states at one time or another. Being the only TV channel operating in the Taliban-administered Afghanistan, Al Jazeera had the opportunity to transmit the visual consequences of the Pentagon's relentless bombing in October 2001, and it did so. As a result, in its last air raid on Kabul on November 14, the Pentagon hit its bureau, located in a residential neighborhood next to a mosque.[12]

To leave nothing to chance in news dissemination, the Pentagon embedded correspondents with the combat units of CENTCOM (Central Command) when it led an invasion of Iraq in March 2003. Its "shock and awe" strategy—relentless, saturated bombing with cruise missiles, rockets, and gravity bombs—aimed to demoralize the Iraqi forces into paralysis and enable its troops to reach Baghdad from the Kuwaiti border in three to four days. That did not happen. The presence of Arab and Iranian TV networks, particularly Al Jazeera, which also had a reporter embedded with the CENTCOM troops, undermined the Pentagon's plans.

Al Jazeera and other Arab channels offered balanced fare. They complemented the briefings and sound bites by Bush and British Prime Minister Blair, and the advances made by the Anglo-American forces, with the devastation caused by the shining missiles fired from warships: the gory images of charred Iraqi bodies next to wrecked vehicles, grievously wounded civilians, dead American and British troops and injured Iraqi soldiers, hospitals choked with wounded and burned Iraqi civilians. This was a stark contrast to the

Anglo-American networks' offerings: the Anglo-American medics treating injured Iraqi civilians tenderly as their armed colleagues handed out drinking water cans to thirsty Iraqi prisoners of war.

Al Jazeera relayed images—and facts—that contradicted the Pentagon's claims that its troops had captured Umm Qasr port and later Basra after claiming that the (fictitious) Iraqi 51st Division had surrendered wholesale. The total collapse of the Iraqi forces envisioned by the Pentagon planners failed to materialize.

So credible was the Al Jazeera Arabic version that many television companies outside the Arabic-speaking world—in Europe, Asia, and Latin America—showed its clips. Overall, Al Jazeera provided a unique service: presentation of both sides of the hot war in real time, which had never happened before in history.

The Pentagon hit back. On April 8, 2003, a warplane fired two missiles at the Al Jazeera office in Baghdad, killing its chief correspondent, Tariq Ayoub, while he was describing a pitched battle between the Iraqis and the Americans. Washington's act was counterproductive. It underscored Al Jazeera's fierce independence and gained it further popularity.

In the global context, with the sharply rising literacy rates in Asia, Africa, and Latin America, the number of well-informed, discriminating citizens has grown exponentially. That has strengthened local and national identities at the expense of the overarching popularity of American goods and services, dating back to the 1950s and 1960s.

More recently, the ever-growing use of cell phones with cameras and of laptop computers meant that in the future it would be almost impossible for the military of the United States or any other country to censor war news. This became apparent during the five-week war between Israel and Hizbullah in Lebanon in July–August 2006. The deployment of mobile phones with cameras and laptops disseminated images that would have been unthinkable a decade earlier.

In November 2006, on the tenth anniversary of Al Jazeera Arabic, its management launched Al Jazeera English, thus breaking the duopoly of the BBC and CNN in the international arena. Belying early expectations, Al Jazeera English stuck too closely to the format and approach of the BBC and CNN. That, and the failure to deliver a sharp presentation of an Arab and Muslim perspective on news, meant that the expected breakthrough by 2009 eluded

Al Jazeera English. Even after broadcasting for two years, it had not released audience figures. It also found itself locked out of the United States, with cable outlets only in Washington, DC; Burlington, Vermont; and Toledo, Ohio. That indicated the success the Bush administration had in associating Al Jazeera with Al Qaida simply because it continued to air newsworthy excerpts of periodic videotapes and audiotapes of Osama bin Laden's statements.

By 2009, however, France 24 had gone on the air, broadcasting in English and French from a French viewpoint, followed by the English-language Press TV, which aimed to provide an Iranian perspective. Then came Russia with its own twenty-four-hour TV news in English for the global audience.

In 2005, the government of Venezuela in association with those in Argentina, Bolivia, Cuba, and Uruguay launched a Spanish-language terrestrial and satellite TV network called teleSUR (officially titled La Nueva Televisora del Sur, "The New TV of the South") in Caracas, to compete with CNN (Spanish) and Univision, a Spanish TV channel based in the United States. Within a year it became accessible in seventeen Latin American countries and signed a cooperation agreement with Al Jazeera. In 2008, it started airing some news programs in Portuguese through many community stations in Brazil.

Not to be left behind, China's state-run CCTV9 expanded its international broadcasting to rival CNN. The state-run Xinhua news agency also vastly upgraded its service and increased its output in languages other than Chinese and English.[13]

As expected, on September 27, 2008, Xinhua's English-language section and CCTV9 led their broadcasts with the Chinese astronaut Zhai Zhigang floating out of the spaceship for twenty minutes and saying, "I greet the Chinese people and the people of the world."[14] This was the culmination of the PRC's space program, launched in 1999 with Shenzhou (meaning "Divine Vessel"), followed after several intermediate steps with its first manned launch of Shen-5 in 2003. China was now the third country to stage such a launch after the Soviet Union (in 1961) and America. Beijing planned to put two astronauts on the moon—preferably by 2010.[15]

Following the launch of the lunar explorer Chang'e-1 in October 2007, Prime Minister Wen Jiabao said, "This achievement is a major manifestation of the increase in our Comprehensive National Power, and the ceaseless enhancement of our innovative ability." In this endeavor the PRC faced a direct challenge by India, the other Asian mega-nation. Delhi too wanted to put an astronaut on the moon—by 2015. At $2.45 billion, the cost of the project was astronomical.[16] The economic payback of the venture for China or India was minimal. Rather, the goal was to garner the respect of Asians and others that came with spectacular success.

In the Indian broadcasting sector, when the government ended its monopoly in the mid-1990s, new TV channels proliferated in all the eighteen major Indian languages, including English. Of nearly seventy such channels—either specializing in news, business, sports, and movies or offering a well-rounded menu—about a score, focusing on news and comment, became economically viable, providing audiences a wide variety of perspectives depending on the viewers' mother tongue. In multilingual India, language matters. With the exception of Hindi, it is the language that decides the boundaries of the states of India.

The proliferation of broadcasting media, made possible by the telecom industry's giant strides in technology along with a steep fall in costs, have diluted the impact of the soft power wielded in the past by America and its traditional ally, Britain, with its prestigious public-service BBC.

BOLLYWOOD ASCENDANT

The Indian film industry, established in 1913 with the making of *Raja Harishchandra*, has carved out a special place for itself in South Asia and elsewhere. In India movies remain the most popular form of mass entertainment. More important, from the perspective of soft power projection, Indian films, dubbed in foreign languages, travel well abroad—all the way from Indonesia to Algeria via Uzbekistan and East Africa. After visiting the Soviet Union, an Indian film critic remarked that the Soviets had three Indian heroes: "Jawaharlal Nehru, Indira Gandhi, and Raj Kapoor, although not necessarily in that order—probably the reverse." Kapoor was one of India's greatest film stars as well as directors. The scripts of his movies were penned mostly by Khwaja Ahmad Abbas, a left-wing writer and journalist. During Kapoor's heyday, lasting a quarter century after Indian independence in 1947, Soviet audiences, particularly in Central Asia and the Caucasus, embraced the color and melodious music of his well-crafted films—a refreshing contrast to the drab works of socialist realism produced by Mosfilm.[17]

In volume, the Indian movie industry surpassed Hollywood in 1980. Of the 1,000-plus movies produced annually in India, less than half originate in the studios of Bombay, yet Bombay is the heart of the Hindi film industry, known by its global brand name "Bollywood." The term has been in vogue internationally since the early 1990s as a synonym for the Indian movie industry as a whole. But in reality, Bollywood has a serious rival in Kollywood, a portmanteau of Kodambakkam—the Madras (aka Chennai) neighborhood housing film studios—and Hollywood. Movies made in Tamil in Kollywood travel well in southeast Asia because of the Tamil diaspora there.

While the appeal and influence of Hollywood movies, dubbed in major European languages, in Europe and Latin America have been widely recognized, the films had a minimum impact on the average filmgoer in independent India. English is the language of an urban-dwelling minority. Because of the paucity of foreign exchange, the government of independent India did not allow Hollywood producers to repatriate profits. So there was no incentive for American moviemakers to dub their films into Hindi for an Indian audience. In any case, producers in India were so addicted to plagiarizing ideas from popular Hollywood movies that they lost little time in reproducing the original in a decidedly Indian mold.

More important, the racial and cultural divide between America and the typical Indian moviegoer is unbridgeable. That is precisely why Indian films have tremendous appeal to ordinary people in Southeast Asia, Southwest Asia, Central Asia, the Middle East, and North and East Africa. The audiences identify with the actors racially and culturally in a way they can never do with white (or even black) Americans. Also, the social mores presented in Indian movies, particularly relations between genders, and between parents and children, approximate their own. Small wonder that, at 3.6 billion a year, the global audience for Bollywood and Kollywood films in 2003 was well ahead of Hollywood's 2.6 billion.[18] By now, Indian superstars like Amitabh Bachchan and Shahrukh Khan have acquired sufficiently high profiles internationally to have their models in Madame Tussaud's Wax Museum in London.

Since most of the Afro-Asian world is unlikely to transform itself to resemble the liberal, capitalist society of America, or even Britain, the soft power projection of Hollywood will remain stunted in that universe. Given the healthy state of Indian cinema, the country's seventh largest industry, which employs over 6 million people, and free flow of capital in a globalizing world, Indian billionaire Anil Ambani of Reliance ADA Group—the owner of UTV, a major film producer in Bollywood—succeeded in muscling into Hollywood.

He signed a deal with the DreamWorks SKG studio of the legendary Steven Spielberg in 2008 to establish a new $1.2 billion film company, a pioneering Hollywood-Bollywood partnership. Nevertheless, the deal is unlikely to result in India's social-cultural values being marketed through Hollywood movies, since artistic control will remain firmly with Spielberg.

While continuing diversification of soft power and its rising importance augur well for enhanced understanding between different nations, the term "soft power" is defined ultimately by its adjective. Decidedly inferior to hard power, it is incapable of preventing the planet's hot spots from bursting into flames.

While stressing and restressing the peaceful rise of China, its leaders can ill afford to overlook precedence. History shows that there are always tensions between the established great power and an emergent power and that behind diplomatic smiles and handshakes, these rivals hold sharp knives to be wielded when simmering tensions boil over.

PRC leaders also understand that it is the distribution of Comprehensive National Power among the leading players on the world stage that will decide the weighty issue of war and peace. Despite the immense strides China has made in barely three decades, its policymakers are anything but complacent. "Hostile foreign powers have not abandoned their conspiracy and tactics to westernize China and to divide the country," warned Hu in late 2008.[19]

CHAPTER 10

FUTURE FLASH POINTS

The future flash points between America, China, and Russia fall into four categories: perceived threats to national security, gaining control of disputed territories, competition for vital resources such as oil and natural gas, and currency and trade. There are also Washington's tensions with Venezuela and Iran, as they provide viable, alternative sociopolitical models to what the United States has been exporting over the past few generations. Since Israel is resolved to preserve its monopoly of a nuclear arsenal in the region, it views Tehran's nuclear program with undisguised hostility. It strives to keep the issue alive by periodic leaks that its special air force unit is ready to strike the Iranian sites at a moment's notice.

In the global context, Russia provides the prime example of a perceived threat to its national security as it faces the prospect of the Pentagon establishing a missile shield in Eastern Europe and NATO extending its membership to Ukraine and Georgia.

Mistakenly equating his obduracy with strong leadership, President George W. Bush remained inflexible on these issues. In contrast, President Vladimir Putin offered viable alternatives to address the possibility of missile attacks on Europe from the Middle East. He proposed that an anti-missile defense system be set up in Turkey, a NATO member, or Azerbaijan, where a former Soviet base could easily be upgraded. Bush rejected the idea. Then, in April 2008, Putin proposed a joint U.S.-Russian anti-missile defense with the necessary equipment installed at two military bases in southern Russia. But Bush remained locked into his original "Take it or leave it" mode.

Unsurprisingly, therefore, in his first address to the nation in November 2008, Russian President Dmitry Medvedev said that if the Pentagon's missile system went ahead, then Russia would deploy mobile, truck-based Iskander missiles in its Kaliningrad exclave and point them at Poland. Situated between Poland and Lithuania, Kaliningrad (formerly the German city of Koenigsberg, birthplace of philosopher Immanuel Kant) is Russia's only Baltic port not icebound during winter and is therefore crucial for the maintenance of its Baltic Fleet. Such a move would be made within the ongoing program of modernizing Russia's military hardware, including its nuclear arsenal.

Washington's behavior fit the pattern that had emerged since the disintegration of the Soviet Union. As the sole superpower, the United States took initiatives in security matters globally without due consideration to their wider implications. In the absence of any protest, it got its way unchallenged. But if it encountered protest, then it said, "The matter is strictly between the United States and Poland or the Czech Republic. Who are you to say what the United States can or cannot do?" Washington thus turned the issue into a battle of wills. If it decided to take into account the other (weaker) side's genuine concerns, that would be tantamount to a climb-down and would make the protesting side bolder the next time around, so the reasoning went at the White House.

In this psychological tug-of-war, basic facts got overlooked. In this case, the key point was the feasibility of the anti-missile defense system. Its origins lay in President Ronald Reagan's Strategic Defense Initiative of 1983—to use ground- and space-based systems to protect America from attack by strategic ballistic missiles. After a quarter century and an expense of $120 billion to $150 billion, the first question was: "Has the system been developed sufficiently to work?" The short answer was: "Not yet."

Second, can the present system be fooled by the enemy launching a lot of dummy missiles with the same radar and infrared signatures as the real one—or by bits of metal foil or by the 90 percent reduction of the real missile's susceptibility to laser penetration by painting it white? The answer in each case is yes.[1]

Regarding NATO's extension, Ukraine's membership was controversial at home and in the region for political and cultural reasons. Russia has deep cultural-religious links with Ukraine. Since its inception in 988 CE, the Russian Orthodox Church had its patriarchate in Kiev for six centuries. It was only then moved to Moscow.[2] Almost as many Ukrainian nationals speak Russian as speak the Ukrainian language, both of which are written in the Cyrillic script.

The eastern and southern parts of Ukraine tilted toward Russia while the western and northern regions looked westward. Its president, Viktor Yushchenko, who assumed power in the wake of the Orange Revolution of November 2004–January 2005, was pro-West. But under a long-term leasing agreement with the Kremlin, Russia's Black Sea Fleet was based at the Ukrainian port of Sevastopol in a region populated by ethnic Russians. Ukraine is thus best suited to act as a buffer—physical and diplomatic—between Russia and the West. Its inclusion in NATO will sharpen tensions between Moscow and the Pentagon-led NATO.

In Georgia, President Mikheil Saakashvili overplayed his hand by mounting an offensive against the pro-Russian breakaway region of South Ossetia in August 2008. By so doing he provided a legitimate ground to the Kremlin to flex its military muscle. It did, and it went on to recognize South Ossetia and Abkhazia as sovereign states, citing Washington's recognition of independence for Kosovo, wrested from Serbia militarily by NATO without a United Nations Security Council resolution. In early 2009, it started building military bases for the governments of South Ossetia and Abkhazia.

Saakashvili's misadventure reduced the chance of Georgia being admitted to NATO as a full member in the near future, which neither Germany nor France envisaged or wanted. The extension of NATO to Georgia, abutting Armenia and Azerbaijan in the Caucasian region, alarmed Iran as well. Long before the Kremlin argued that the American plan to install an anti-missile shield in Eastern Europe threatened its security, Tehran had offered the same argument in the context of the Persian Gulf region.

As a forerunner of Putin's proposal of establishing a single security and defense space in Europe, Iran had called for the formation of a body to ensure security for all the states in the Gulf area without the involvement of an outside power. This could be done by expanding the Gulf Cooperation Council (GCC), established in 1981 by Bahrain, Kuwait, Oman, Qatar, Saudi Arabia, and the United Arab Emirates.

Its proposal fell on stony ground as far as other governments were concerned. The popular opinion on this subject in the Gulf monarchies did not count. On several important subjects, including Iran, there was disjunction between the ruler and the ruled in the Arab Middle East. The 2008 Annual Arab Public Opinion Poll by the University of Maryland and Zogby International, involving 4,000 respondents from Egypt, Jordan, Lebanon, Morocco, Saudi Arabia, and the United Arab Emirates, showed that most Arabs did not see Iran as a threat and did not support international pressure on Iran to curtail its nuclear program.[3] The monarchical GCC, beholden to the West for protection, was ill-prepared to consider an independent regional body to assure security to its members as proposed by Tehran. And Iraqi President Saddam Hussein was pathologically anti-Iranian.

But by 2004 Saddam was gone. The subsequent Shiite-led government in Baghdad began forging cordial relations with Tehran. The regional monarchies took note. As a result they invited Iran's president, Mahmoud Ahmadinejad, to attend their annual GCC summit in December 2007 as an observer. He did so.

RUSSIA-IRAN-U.S. TRIANGULATION

By then, however, Iran's nuclear program had been on the UN Security Council's agenda for more than two years, with the Council's five permanent members and Germany coordinating their stance toward Iran. The process started in 2004 with negotiations between Tehran and the European Union, represented by Britain, France, and Germany, collectively called EU3. The "Grand Bargain" being considered between the two sides was the European Union's concessions to Iran in technology transfers, trade and cooperation, and security and political issues in return for its voluntary surrender of its right to produce nuclear fuel to run its reactors for civilian purposes.

The EU3 soon realized that, given America's occupation of Afghanistan and Iraq, which increased Tehran's feeling of insecurity, their discussion of Iran's security was meaningless without Washington's direct or indirect participation. When the matter came up for discussion at the White House in January 2005 after Bush's reelection, he opted for surgical strikes on Iran to destroy its nuclear sites. Those advocating this strategy believed that such limited military action would show the Iranian people that their ruling mullahs were incapable of protecting the republic and trigger a popular uprising against them. That is, surgical strikes would bring about a regime change in a country forming part of the "Axis of Evil." Bush's adoption of this option killed the EU3's diplomatic enterprise about a "Grand Bargain" with Iran.

When it came to implementing the surgical strikes plan, the Pentagon faced a serious problem. Washington's human intelligence on Iran had dried up—as a result of the blunder made by a CIA officer in Langley, Virginia, in early 2004. He mistakenly sent information to an Iranian agent, who also worked for the Iranian intelligence, according to James Risen, the Pulitzer prize–winning *New York Times* reporter on national security, in his book *State of War: The Secret History of the CIA and the Bush Administration*.[4] That mistake resulted in the Tehran government uprooting the CIA espionage network in Iran.

Revelations in the *New Yorker* and the *Washington Post* in January–February 2005 showed that the Pentagon began flying drones over Iran beginning in April 2004 to compensate for the loss of human intelligence. They used radar, video, still photography, and air filters to test Iranian defenses and seek traces of nuclear activity. Iranians noticed drones in the Caspian region; Natanz, the known site of the uranium enrichment; Isfahan; and along the Iraq border. The local press ran stories about UFOs. An unnamed Iranian security official told the *Washington Post* that the security chiefs decided not to engage the drones because to do so would give information about the country's air defense capabilities. Iran protested through the Swiss embassy, which maintained an American Interests Section.[5]

America's aerial reconnaissance was complemented by ground action. In his mid-January article in the *New Yorker*, Seymour Hersh revealed that undercover American commando groups and other Special Forces units had been conducting clandestine reconnaissance missions inside Iran since at least July 2004. One such task force was working closely with those Pakistani scientists and technicians who had dealt with their Iranian counterparts in the past.[6]

None of this surprised Iran's leaders. They had seen the United States repeatedly violating President Ronald Reagan's promise of noninterference in Iran's internal affairs. These violations went beyond the beaming into Iran of hostile radio and television programs, produced by U.S.-financed channels, and Washington's assistance to dissident groups among Iran's ethnic Kurds, Baluchis, and Arabs to destabilize the regime.

Along with covert operations went overt attempts to intimidate Iran. Having posted two aircraft carrier groups in the Persian Gulf in 2007, the Bush White House dispatched its hawkish vice president, Dick Cheney, to issue a dire warning to Tehran from the deck of an aircraft carrier.

According to the revelations made by Risen in his book *State of War*, even the preceding administration of President Bill Clinton was far from reconciled with the continued existence of the Islamic Republic. The Clinton White House authorized the CIA to mount its audacious Operation Merlin in February 2000. The CIA dispatched a Soviet-era defector, a former Soviet nuclear weapons engineer, to Vienna, where, posing as an unemployed scientist selling nuclear secrets, he was instructed to contact the Iranian representatives dealing with the International Atomic Energy Agency (IAEA). He was carrying doctored Soviet blueprints, leaked to the CIA by another Soviet defector, for a triggering device for an atom bomb. Had the Iranians used these blueprints to build a trigger over the next many years, they would have ended up with "disappointing fizzle" instead of a mushroom cloud. The Russian scientist spotted the defect in the design and told his CIA handlers, but they advised him to go ahead with the plan. Once in Vienna, afraid that the Iranians would detect the flaw, he opened his sealed document and inserted a note, pointing out the errors. He then delivered the package to the apartment of the Iranian representative without meeting anybody. In the past the CIA had played such tricks on adversaries regarding conventional arms, but it was the first time it extended this tactic to an unconventional weapon once it had secured authorization at the highest level.[7]

Such CIA activities would have reminded Putin of his days as a KGB colonel. Now, as Russia's president, he was committed to nonproliferation of nuclear weapons. Like the IAEA, his foreign intelligence agency had not discovered evidence that Tehran was engaged in a nuclear arms program. His government's bottom line was that Iran must not quit the Non-Proliferation Treaty as North Korea did in 2003 in response to Bush's hard line. (North Korea then accelerated its nuclear program and exploded an atom bomb in October 2006.)

The Kremlin was dead set against the Pentagon's military action against Iran. Putin empathized with Tehran's anxiety about the Islamic Republic's security: He had similar concerns about the impact on Russia of Bush's anti-missile defense system in Eastern Europe. During the six-party talks in May 2008 to update the 2006 package for Iran if it shelved uranium enrichment, Russia proposed that the six nations, including the United States, give Iran security guarantees to relieve tensions in the region. Within hours, the spokesman for Bush said, "Security guarantees [for Iran] are not something we are looking into at the moment."[8] This left Iran's leaders with no doubt about the Bush White House's malevolent intent toward their republic.

The Kremlin noted Washington's instant rejection of its suggestion with a certain apprehension. It knew that Tehran's response would be fierce. Its military commanders had warned that, irrespective of who attacked Iran—America or Israel—Iran would respond by launching missiles not only against Israel but also against U.S. targets in the region. The Pentagon had thirty-two military bases in Iraq that fell within Iran's short-range missiles' range. This would be followed by asymmetrical warfare in the region, which would be equally lethal.

As the first Shiite Islamic state in the world, Iran enjoyed the loyalty of the Shiites in the region and in Afghanistan in the same way as the Soviet Union did among Communists and their sympathizers in Europe for three and a half decades. Given its network among the Shiites in the Gulf monarchies, Iran would activate its sleeper cells and cause considerable damage to American interests and the local oil industry. The Saudi Shiite minority was concentrated in the kingdom's oil-rich Al Hasa area. Shiites comprised nearly 65 percent of the population of Bahrain—the headquarters of the U.S. Navy's Fifth Fleet. A quarter of Kuwait's population was Shiite.

The government in Tehran remained alert, its military conducting a series of combined exercises on land, air, and sea, culminating in six-day-long naval and air force exercises involving sixty warships and covering 50,000 square miles in December 2008.

The replacement of Donald Rumsfeld with Robert Gates in November 2006 injected a healthy dose of realism into the Pentagon. At his confirmation hearings he said, "We have seen, in Iraq, that once war is unleashed, it becomes unpredictable. And I think the consequences of a military conflict with Iran could be quite dramatic." Later he argued publicly that a military attack would lead Iran to withdraw from the nuclear Non-Proliferation Treaty and expel IAEA inspectors, and "could ignite a broad Middle East war in which 140,000 U.S. troops in Iraq would inevitably get involved."[9]

Such realism had yet to enter the thinking of Israel's leaders. It kept leaking information as to how its special air force unit was geared up to go. But it needed Washington's assistance for its aircraft to overfly Iraq unscathed. Bush denied it this passage in May 2008. But the possibility remained—particularly under the premiership of the hawkish Netanyahu.

While Israel was capable of starting the air campaign, it would not be able to accomplish the task fully. As a senior Defense Intelligence Agency official told David E. Sanger of the *New York Times*, it would take about 1,000 striking sorties—air, cruise missiles, multiple restrikes—to ensure total destruction of the targets. Each strike would be followed by satellite imaging to determine how deep the bombs or missiles had gone. After the initial, surprise run, later strikes would encounter robust defense by the Iranians.[10]

Since analyzing satellite images would take time, each subsequent strike could only be launched after an interval of one to two weeks. In the interim public opinion in the region and the rest of the Muslim world, and elsewhere, would be inflamed, with the pro-American Arab regimes feeling the popular heat. Military activity in the Gulf would also remove Iran's oil output of 4 million bpd from global supplies. That would push up petroleum prices despite the recession. In addition, there was the prospect of blocking the narrow Hormuz Strait, through which two-fifths of all seaborne oil trade passed.

In 2009 Washington's refrain that "the military option remained on the table" had not altered despite the change in the occupancy of the White House. Neither President Barack Obama nor Secretary of State Hillary Rodham Clinton had withdrawn the statement about a military option. Addressing the Forty-fifth Munich Trans-Atlantic conference on security policy in February 2009, Vice President Joseph Biden basically repeated what the previous administration had said: "Stop uranium enrichment; stop supporting terrorism."[11] What would signify real change in Washington's strategy toward Tehran is to accept the proposal Iran had offered to Bush in May 2003: talks on all contentious issues *without any preconditions*. Such a prospect does not seem to be on the horizon as yet. Therefore, the tense relations between Tehran and Washington have the potential of escalating into a military conflict—with consequences that would be more disastrous than was the case with Bush's invasion of Iraq.

As for Russia, whose relations with Iran span centuries, its present policymakers are clear-eyed. The last thing they want is a destabilized Iran next door, which would result if the Pentagon targeted Iran—or allowed Israel to do so—when Afghanistan remained to be pacified after eight years of warfare. If the alternative was a nuclear-armed Iran, so be it. Its arsenal would be a fraction of the fifty-five atom bombs Pakistan has fabricated since 1998.

Unlike Pakistan, a heavily populated country with scant natural resources, Iran is underpopulated and endowed with enormous reserves of oil and natural gas. As the world enters the next decade, the importance of access to oil and gas deposits will soar.

Resources War

Most experts predict that oil output will reach its apex by 2017, then decline inexorably until the end of the century. The latest to join their ranks was the Paris-based International Energy Agency. In December 2008, it upped the annual rate of the decline of the globe's existing oil fields from 3.7 percent to 6.7 percent. That is, in the absence of new finds, petroleum reserves would be exhausted in fifteen years.[12]

However, since three-quarters of all known deposits lie in the member-states of the Organization of Oil Exporting Countries (OPEC), where most of the forty largest oil fields are located, the world should be divided into OPEC and non-OPEC regions. The output in the latter category has already reached a peak and is declining. So the non-OPEC world, which includes America, China, and India, will become increasingly dependent on oil imports from OPEC.[13]

The policymakers in Washington, Beijing, and Delhi have been well aware of the centrality of oil and gas to the living standards of their citizens—and thus to the price of hydrocarbons.

In recent times, a dramatic evidence of this came when Iraq, led by Saddam Hussein, invaded and occupied Kuwait in August 1990. President George H. W. Bush, a former oilman, realized instantly that by taking over Kuwait, Saddam would double the oil reserves under his control to 20 percent of the global total. By so doing, he would challenge the supremacy of Saudi Arabia, an ally of Washington for half a century. Possessing 25 percent of world reserves, the Saudi kingdom had become the swing producer and largely determined oil prices to the benefit of the West, the globe's largest consumer.[14] The speed with which Bush assembled a coalition of more than two dozen nations and expelled the occupying Iraqi forces from Kuwait reaffirmed the vital importance of petroleum. By ordering his forces to set ablaze Kuwaiti oil wells as they retreated to the Iraqi borders, Saddam too emphasized the salient nature of the most versatile mineral.

During the buildup to the invasion of Iraq in March 2003, however, President George W. Bush raised the slogans of destroying Saddam's weapons of mass destruction and ushering in democracy. If he had publicly, or even privately, conceded that gaining access to Iraq's hydrocarbon riches was on his agenda, he would have undermined his high-minded claims. It transpired later that the Bush White House changed the code for the Iraq War from the initial Operation Iraqi Liberation to Operation Iraqi Freedom as soon as it realized that Operation Iraqi Liberation yielded the acronym OIL.

Paul O'Neill, the first Treasury secretary under George Bush, provided evidence in his memoirs that Iraqi oil had figured at the first meeting of the National Security Council meeting on January 30, 2001.[15] And, according to Falah al Jibury, an Iraqi-American oil consultant who had acted as Reagan's back channel to Saddam in the 1980s, the U.S. administration began making plans for Iraq's oil industry "within weeks" of Bush taking office.[16] During the chaos in the wake of the fall of Baghdad in April 2003, it was only the oil ministry that the Pentagon's forces guarded diligently. If, in the end, nothing came of Washington's oil ambitions in Iraq, it was because of the mayhem and violence that followed the Pentagon's swift military victory and the intense Iraqi nationalism that holds the country's oil dear.

A decade earlier, China had become an oil importer. The rapid rise in petroleum imports led the State Council to integrate energy security into its foreign policy. Diversification of the sources and transportation of oil and gas went hand in hand with erecting refineries capable of handling heavy oil and vigorously developing the natural gas industry.

To enable the state-owned China National Petroleum Corporation (CNPC) to invest abroad, the government allowed it to raise prices. The CNPC's profits surged from $6 billion in 1993 to $21 billion in 1997. By then oil and gas produced 20 percent of the country's energy, twenty times higher than was the case at the founding of the People's Republic of China in 1949. In line with official doctrine, the state-owned petroleum companies considered the PRC's energy security as their prime concern, with their own commercial interest of making profit being secondary. Their modus operandi was thus the reverse of the Western oil corporations'.

By 2002, China was importing a third of its oil consumption of 5.29 million bpd. That was the case with America in 1983 in percentage terms. Between then and 2007, oil imports in the United States rose to 67 percent of the demand of 20.7 million bpd, while its reserves dwindled to 2.4 percent of the global total. The White House's aim of achieving oil independence by 1979 turned out to be a fantasy. Moreover, America's debilitating dependency on oil imports occurred just as the major Western oil companies—the so-called Seven Sisters—were weakening. While they controlled nearly four-fifths of petroleum output worldwide in 1968, their global reserves fell to one-eighth of the total in 2007, mostly in North America and Western Europe.

That is, seven-eighths of the world's oil reserves belonged to the state-owned companies in oil-bearing countries. This suited the PRC, a champion of the public ownership of a country's natural resources. What caused it concern was that 70 percent of its oil imports, originating in the Middle East or Sudan, passed in tankers through the narrow, crowded, accident-prone five-hundred-mile-long Malacca Strait between Malaysia and Indonesia, barely two miles wide at its narrowest point. This strategic strait fell under the jurisdiction of the Pentagon's PACOM (Pacific Command), charged with patrolling the Indian Ocean, South China Sea, and western Pacific. In 2004, Singapore gave the U.S. Navy access to its freshly opened, automated naval base at its artificial island of Changi, with large enough berthing to accommodate an American aircraft carrier.

The PRC noted the latest development with trepidation. It noted too that India was busily upgrading its military facilities on Andaman and Nicobar Islands to the north of the Malacca Strait. An aggrieved Chinese President Hu Jintao complained that "certain powers" attempted all along to "control the navigation" through the Malacca Strait.[17]

China realized that in the absence of enough naval power of its own, it could not protect the oil lanes used by its tankers. It therefore focused on building overland pipelines from neighboring Russia and Central Asian republics as well as Burma, thus reducing its dependence on ocean routes. Its State Council set up a special State Energy Office in May 2005 under its direct control. General Xiong Guangkai, the deputy chief of China's general staff, stressed the military aspects of oil and gas by pointing out that the competition for them had become more intense. The inference was clear: China must expand its navy to safeguard the tankers carrying oil to the mainland.

In December 2008, for the first time since 1433, China decided to deploy three naval ships off the coast of Somalia, where increased piracy had severely endangered shipping lanes. It also announced that it was seriously considering building an aircraft carrier.[18] If China builds an aircraft carrier and deploys it away from its shores to safeguard its expanded international interests, it would merely be doing what the leading Western nations have done over the past two centuries.

So far, following its own dictum of "peaceful rise," Beijing has stuck to obtaining hydrocarbons and other commodities peacefully, and kept any rivalry with the United States within commercial boundaries. Yet China's hot pursuit of oil and gas abroad has led it into conflict with the United States in Burma (Myanmar) and Sudan. It has successfully blocked economic sanctions against Burma at the UN Security Council, arguing that the violations of human rights by the ruling army junta did not threaten international peace and security. It has protected Sudan's government from harsh international measures for its failure to stop ethnic cleansing in its Darfur region, while stressing the need for a solution to the problem through the African Union.

The PRC has been assiduously extending its influence overland. Following Washington's ban on U.S. investments in Burma because of its military rulers' human rights abuses, American petroleum companies pulled out. The opposite case was post-Soviet Kazakhstan. Western oil companies rushed to sign up lucrative contracts there. Their spirits soared as Kazakhstan's proven reserves rose steadily from 5.2 billion to 9 billion barrels during 1993–2002, and then jumped to 36 billion barrels in 2003.

By then, CNPC had also arrived in Kazakhstan with a bang. In September 1997 it signed a contract involving oil fields east of the Caspian Sea and in the northwestern region of the republic. In what was hailed as "the deal of the century," the CNPC agreed to pay $4.7 billion for exploration and production rights and promised to invest a further $10 billion in the infrastructure. By bringing the Kazakh oil to its underdeveloped border province of Xinjiang, simmering with the discontent of the native Uighurs, China wished to solve its own economic and political problems as well as Kazakhstan's. And, impressed by the PRC's dazzling economic growth, Kazakh officials saw it as a source of enormous commercial opportunity.

Pursuing an aggressive acquisitive drive, the CNPC and its subsidiaries acquired stakes in forty-four countries, from Angola to Azerbaijan, Myanmar to Mauritania, and Sudan to Saudi Arabia, during the decade of 1993–2002. In purely economic terms, it made sense for the Chinese companies to acquire oil and gas acreage abroad, as their production costs were a fraction of the international market price.

The CPNC and its subsidiaries garnered all these contracts by beating off competition from such long-established stalwarts as Amoco, Texaco, and Unocal of America. This disconcerted Washington. Worse was to follow. In 2005 the CNPC acquired the Canadian-registered PetroKazakhstan, which owned oil fields in southern Kazakhstan, for $4.2 billion. The arrival of a major Chinese oil corporation in Canada, the "front yard" of the United States, alarmed the White House.

Its alarm turned into panic when the China National Offshore Oil Company (Cnooc) attempted to buy Unocal, an American oil corporation, by offering a higher price for its shares than the competing Chevron. Cnooc's attempt caused a hostile political reaction in the United States, whose president is authorized to bar a takeover on national security grounds. So far this power had been used only once before—by George H. W. Bush in 1990, when he blocked the sale of Mamco Manufacturing, an airplane parts maker, to a military-related agency of the Chinese government.[19] His son did not have to invoke presidential power, however, as Unocal's shareholders rejected Cnooc's offer.

The spat between Uzbek President Islam Karimov and Washington after the massacre of unarmed protestors in Andijan in May 2005 facilitated the PRC's deal for a joint venture in oil exploration in Uzbekistan during Karimov's visit to Beijing.

The Bush administration's nadir came in November 2008 in—of all places—Iraq, occupied by American troops. It witnessed the Iraqi government awarding its first oil contract to develop the Ahdab oil field to a Chinese corporation.

In the coming decades, hydrocarbon supplies will dwindle. And Beijing's dependence on trade with Washington will decline as its commercial links with the European Union as well as African, Asian, and Latin American countries are strengthened. The subsequent weakening of economic ties with the United States, the key incentive for the PRC's restraint, will occur as competition between America and China—number one and two oil consumers—intensifies. That will raise the chance of an armed conflict between them. After all, it was the escalation in the American-Japanese tension over oil supplies that led to Japan's preemptive strike on the U.S. Navy at Pearl Harbor in December 1941.

When it comes to natural resources other than hydrocarbons, Africa looms large. Envious of the commercial and diplomatic strides China has made on that continent, the Pentagon decided to set up the Africa Command, only to drop the idea—for now—when no African country agreed to host it. But the proposal is not dead. After all, Central Command (CENTCOM) is based not in the Middle East but in Tampa, Florida.

According to Washington's 2006 Quadrennial Defense Review Report, a study of the PRC's arms procurement and strategic thinking shows that it was developing capabilities for use in conflicts over resources. The report added, ominously, that lack of transparency in China's defense and security affairs increased the possibility of "misunderstanding and miscalculation."[20]

A follow-up Pentagon report in May 2007 noted China's rapid rise as "a regional and economic power with global aspirations" and warned that it was planning to project its military further afield from the Taiwan Strait into the Asia-Pacific region in preparation for possible conflicts over territory or resources. The territorial flash points are chiefly in Asia, pointedly in Taiwan, a hundred nautical miles from the mainland.

TAIWAN, OR "REPUBLIC OF CHINA ON TAIWAN"

Following its defeat by Japan in the First Sino-Japanese War of 1894–1895, China ceded Taiwan (Formosa). Its status as a Japanese colony ended in 1945 with the defeat of Japan in World War II.

Two months after the founding of the PRC in October 1949, the defeated Chiang Kai-shek escaped by air to Taiwan and declared its capital of Taipei to be the capital of the Republic of China (ROC). Washington managed to deny the PRC its seat at the UN for twenty-two years. When the Nixon administration opened a U.S. Liaison Office in Beijing on a reciprocal basis, it did so on the basis of the principle of "One China"—to which both Mao Zedong and Chiang Kai-shek subscribed, albeit applying their mutually exclusive interpretations.

Chiang ruled Taiwan as a military dictator until his death in 1975. It was not until 1986 that gradual democratization led to the formation of the opposition Democratic Progressive Party (DPP). It advocated independence for Taiwan, thus scuttling the idea of One China, which the National Party held to. A decade later a constitutional amendment replaced the indirect election of executive president by Parliament with direct election.

When the incumbent Lee Teng-hui of the ruling National Party found himself facing a serious challenge by his pro-independence DPP rival, the PRC carried out military exercises on its eastern seaboard to warn of dire consequences if Taiwan declared independence. The Clinton administration dispatched two aircraft carrier groups to patrol the Taiwan Strait. Lee retained the presidency. The crisis passed.

In 2000, DPP candidate Chen Shi-bian won, ending the National Party's monopoly of power. But he triumphed only by promising *not* to declare independence so long as the PRC did not attack Taiwan. He thus appealed to moderate voters. He also placated Washington, whose commitment to protect Taiwan from a PRC attack was predicated on the island refraining from declaring independence.

It has been the PRC's cardinal tenet that Taiwan is an integral part of China and must return to the Motherland, just as Hong Kong did in 1997 and Macao, a Portuguese colony, two years later. It worked assiduously to get Taiwan de-recognized in the international community. It succeeded: By 2009, of the 192 UN members, only 23 recognized Taiwan as the Republic of China. They were all small countries in the Pacific Ocean, Central America, and Africa, which depended on Taiwan's hefty financial aid.

On the other hand, the United States has continued to sell advanced weapons to Taiwan in accordance with the Taiwan Relations Act of 1979, requiring Washington to furnish Taiwan with arms to defend itself, and senior PACOM (Pacific Command) officers have started observing Taiwan's annual Han Kuang armed forces exercises to judge the island's military preparedness. The sale of $6.5 billion worth of advanced weaponry to Taiwan in October 2008 prompted a strong denunciation by Beijing, which suspended the annual meetings between top Chinese and American military officers. A year earlier, the PRC announced that a seamless network of all-weather air defense had been installed to cover all of China, complementing its surface-to-air missiles force and jet fighter interceptors.[21]

Taiwan was more than a matter of territory for the PRC. Military strategy and geopolitics were involved. A highly militarized island of 23 million people, Taiwan had a reserve armed force of 3.87 million. According to General Wen Zongren, chairman of the Political Committee of China's Military Science Institute, Taiwan was a leading player in creating a maritime stranglehold on the PRC's natural place across the oceans. "Only when we break this blockade shall we be able to talk about China's rise," he said. "To rise suddenly, China must pass through oceans and go out of the oceans in its future development."[22]

Taiwan's continued existence as a prospering democratic, capitalist, autonomous entity with per capita GDP seven times China's—calling itself Republic of China on Taiwan—was repellent to PRC leaders. It reminded them of the humiliation inflicted upon China by Japan more than a century ago; it also provided the mainland's democratic opposition with a functioning, alternative social system.

Also, with the passage of time, more and more of the islanders were identifying themselves as Taiwanese. In 2003, almost 43 percent did so.[23] The courses for the Taiwanese civil service examinations excluded history and geography of China. After his reelection in 2004, Chen proposed referendums on reinforcing Taiwan's defenses and opening negotiations with Beijing as a prelude to holding a plebiscite on Taiwan's independence.

The PRC responded by adopting an anti-secession law in 2005, warning Taiwan that it would consider the island's claim to a sovereign state as secession—an eventuality it would counter by all means, including force. Significantly, while reasserting China's claim to Taiwan, the anti-secession law requires that any military action must be approved by both the Central Military Commission and the civilian State Council. The 2005 law affected the referendum held in Taiwan in 2006. Because of the National Party's boycott, the necessary quorum of 50 percent did not materialize.

Since 2001, the PRC has held combined military exercises twice a year aimed at capturing Taiwan. It has put in place a coordinated network of short- and medium-range ballistic missiles, mobile and stationary, to overpower Taiwan's air defenses and missiles network. Given its nearly 150 U.S.-made F-16s and more than 50 French-made Mirages, Taiwan is expected to perform well against the PRC's air force with a smaller number of advanced warplanes.

To overpower Taiwan's 300,000 army troops, the PRC would have to transport 30 infantry divisions across the Strait in 1,000-plus landing craft, facing Taiwan's supersonic antiship missiles—a task likely to take a fortnight. While Taiwan's defense minister claimed that the island had enough equipment and supplies to sustain the war for two weeks, most neutral experts believed it would be one week—the time needed for the Pentagon to intervene, provided that its aircraft carrier groups sailed smoothly.

To counter this strategy, Beijing decided to increase its submarine force with Russian Kilo class craft equipped with antiship SS-N-22 cruise missiles. That led to a warning in Washington's 2006 Quadrennial Defense Review Report that the PRC had "the greatest potential to . . . field disruptive military technologies that could over time offset traditional U.S. military advantages."[24] Implementing this complex strategy in a hot war, however, would present immense logistical challenges for the PRC.

All the same, the pace of the PRC's modernization of its military aroused concern in Washington. "The pace and scope of China's military buildup are, already, such as to put regional military balances at risk," stated the Pentagon's *Annual Report to Congress: The Military Power of the People's Republic of China* in 2005. "Current trends in China's military modernization could provide China with a force of prosecuting a range of military options in Asia—well beyond Taiwan—potentially posing a credible threat to modern militaries operating in the region."[25]

So the stakes were high as far as the status of Taiwan was concerned not only in terms of enhancing the Communist regime's mandate at home but also externally—enabling the PRC to extend its influence abroad as never before. Moreover, the fiscal meltdown provided unexpected opportunities for the PRC to extend and consolidate its influence externally while locking up supplies of hydrocarbons and other commodities for the future. Flush with funds in the PRC's foreign exchange portfolio, Hu undertook another tour of Africa just as the new Obama administration was settling down in Washington.

At his confirmation hearings the freshly appointed U.S. Treasury Secretary Timothy Geithner told a Senate committee that Obama believed that China was "manipulating" its currency. This incensed the Chinese government. What China has been doing is to "manage" its currency within a fixed range, not manipulate it. Managing a currency is by its definition a defensive act, whereas manipulating involves a deliberate, preplanned activity and is therefore an offensive move.

If the United States officially declares that the PRC is manipulating its currency, then that raises the specter of Washington imposing penalty tariffs on Chinese imports, which would lead China to react with its own retaliatory measures. Geithner's statement showed that a deadly dispute between Washington and Beijing on currency and commerce could not be ruled out.

It is salutary to note that it was economic pressure on Iraq that led to its invasion of Kuwait in August 1990. Early in the year, Kuwait deliberately flooded the oil market, which lowered prices and hurt Iraq as it struggled to recover from a debilitating eight-year war with Iran. Kuwait also demanded the immediate return of $14 billion loaned to Baghdad during the long conflict in the form of oil delivered by Kuwait to Iraq's customers. And the 1991 Gulf War sowed the seed of the Pentagon-led invasion of Iraq twelve years later.

CHINA AND THE UNITED STATES: CURRENCY AND COMMERCE CONFLICT

A hysterical response to rising imports from Japan into America in the 1980s led to the passage of the Omnibus Trade and Competitiveness Act of 1988. It empowered the administration to initiate alone, or in tandem with the International Monetary Fund, action to force a country to readjust its currency if it had been manipulated to produce a material trade imbalance. It was not surprising, therefore, to hear persistent voices of alarm in the United States about burgeoning imports from China and Beijing's mountain of foreign exchange (largely dollar) reserves.

On July 21, 2005, the People's Bank of China unpegged the yuan from the U.S. dollar and revalued it by 2 percent, fixing the exchange rate at 8.11 yuan to a dollar. In theory it switched to a floating rate; in practice it meant keeping the exchange rate within a narrow range. This did not satisfy Washington.

The annual reports of the United States–China Economic and Security Review Commission—formed as a prelude to the PRC joining the World Trade Organization in 2001—said as much. Its 2005 report claimed that the PRC was using trade as an instrument to bolster its military prowess. It achieved this goal by upgrading its high-tech industry through huge public sector investment and by subsidizing foreign direct investment as well as export growth. The root cause of this accomplishment was an undervalued yuan, which fueled exports. The benefits accruing to the PRC came at the cost of a loss of 1.6 million jobs in America during 1989–2003 because of cheap Chinese imports.[26] It concluded that "on balance the trends in the U.S.-China relationship have negative implications for our long term national economic and security interests."[27]

The report warned against Chinese corporations acquiring American companies, but there was no need for it. There was a prevalent feeling among politicians in the United States that the nominally commercial entities in the PRC were in the final analysis directed by the Communist Party of China, and that set them apart from companies in the European Union and Japan. Even when a Hong Kong–based company, Hutchinson Whampoa, won the contract for managing the Panama Canal and its ports after the canal was returned to Panama by the United States in 1997 (see Chapter 5), American lawmakers raised the alarm. So the barriers to Chinese companies buying up large-size American corporations were already high. This was not the case with Japanese or EU firms. From the early 1990s to 2004, foreigners had invested $1.5 trillion in America, purchasing companies, stocks, and property.[28] But by 2005, the total purchases of American companies by their Chinese counterparts amounted to a mere $3.5 billion, including China's Lenovo Group buying IBM's personal computer section for $1.75 billion.

Responding to the Commission's reports, the Bush administration set up a special enforcement task force within the U.S. Trade Representative's Office to monitor the growth of Chinese imports. And in response to repeated calls for action, it granted special protection to American companies producing color televisions, garments, semiconductors, textiles, and wooden furniture.

But there was no letup by the Commission. Its December 2007 report accused the PRC of such trading malpractices as "unfair industrial subsidies" and restricting workers' rights. It called on Congress to define currency manipulation as "an illegal export subsidy" and allow the subsidy to be taken into account when determining penalty tariffs.[29]

In April 2008, the slowly appreciating yuan passed the psychologically important 7 yuans to the dollar level. The PRC continued to resist calls for a single major reevaluation of 25 to 30 percent. Such a drastic step would have a serious negative impact on China, economically and socially, Beijing declared. It argued that most of its exports originated with Western companies operating in China and that they were the ultimate beneficiaries of the boom in China-made exports. It pointed out that cheap Chinese imports led to higher consumer spending in the United States, which was bolstered by the rise in the service and knowledge sectors.

Furthermore, if America or any other World Trade Organization member presented a case to the WTO that the PRC was violating WTO rules by subsidizing state-owned companies through its state-controlled banking system, it would be hard for the PRC to prove the negative. The accounting system in the Chinese companies and banks lacked the degree of transparency that existed in the West and some Asian countries.

During the 2008 U.S. presidential election campaign both candidates, Obama and Senator John McCain, repeatedly accused the PRC of unfair trade practices and currency manipulation, with Obama, articulating American workers' views, being more vociferous than his rival. The day after Obama's inauguration as president in January 2009, the exchange rate was 6.8415 yuans to a dollar, amounting to 21 percent appreciation of the Chinese currency since its unpegging in July 2005.

To slow the plunge in its exports, the PRC had started giving exporters a larger tax rebate. That could incite the strong protectionist lobby in the Democratic Party to pressure the Obama administration to declare that China was manipulating the yuan. China could retaliate by selling its U.S. Treasury bonds as well as Fannie Mae and Freddie Mac bonds.

Already, mutual distrust between the two nations is rising. There is a growing feeling among many Chinese people and officials that America deliberately triggered a global meltdown to slow down China's peaceful rise.[30] A misunderstanding of such magnitude, if not dispelled by vigorous effort from both sides, would be a preamble to a trade and fiscal war between the two economic giants, the consequences of which would be earth-shattering, no matter what the general state of the global economy.

CHAPTER 11

CONCLUSIONS

The fall of the Berlin Wall in November 1989 turned out to be a preamble to the disintegration of the Soviet Union two years later. The Washington-led alliance felt elated, and rightly so. A new world order had arrived, declared President George H. W. Bush, in which "the nations of the world, East and West, North and South, can prosper and live in peace."

There was not much of peace, however. Between the collapse of the Berlin Wall and President George W. Bush's invasion of Iraq in 2003, the unrivaled United States mounted ten large-scale military interventions—one every fifteen months—a world record.[1] Of these, only two involved reversing aggression, as in Iraqi-occupied Kuwait in 1991, or self-defense, as with the Taliban-administered Afghanistan a decade later.

Most of the Pentagon's campaigns—ranging from Iraqi Kurdistan, Somalia, and Haiti to Bosnia and Serbia—occurred under the rubric of "humanitarian intervention," sanctified by the United Nations Security Council. The sole superpower had acquired such a halo that it encountered little resistance in turning the UN Security Council into a virtual extension of its State Department.

And when, in the case of Iraq, the Bush administration failed in early 2003 to bend the Security Council to its will, it went ahead with its invasion nevertheless. Its swift victory added to its hubris while the majority of the Security Council's permanent as well as nonpermanent members watched, aghast, from the sidelines.

But the wheel turned when the Pentagon found itself in a quagmire in Iraq. France's president, Jacques Chirac, loudly trumpeted that he stood vindicated. The leader of the hitherto squeamish Russia, President Vladimir Putin, issued a document asserting that "the myth about the uni-polar world fell apart once and for all in Iraq."

In Chirac's and Putin's behavior, historians recognized echoes of the non-French European leaders after the fall of Napoleon I in 1815. The monarchs of Britain, Austria, Russia, and Prussia formed the Concert of Europe to ensure that no single European country became as powerful as France had under Napoleon I.

Out of this concert was born the doctrine of the balance of power, which became the guiding principle of international relations. Along with this emerged the concept of competitive coexistence. That is, big powers learned to coexist peacefully while competing with one another commercially and po-litically. As an increasing number of intellectuals in America and elsewhere began to grasp this trajectory of history, the initial euphoria in the West—aptly captured in the title of Francis Fukuyama's *The End of History and the Last Man* (1992)—began to evaporate. They started realizing that the uncon-tested supremacy of the United States in all important aspects of civilization—economics, politics, military, and culture—was not destined to last for an eon.

For instance, as the 1990s gave way to the twenty-first century, it became ap-parent that there was no evidence to support the thesis that a majority of those living in nondemocratic countries viewed liberal, Western democracy as the apogee of governance. When given an option to choose their ruling repre-sentatives, voters in the Middle East almost invariably chose Islamists who were committed to marrying representative government with the edicts of Islam.

History had not ended, argued the pugnacious school in America, a neo-conservative ideology best represented by Robert Kagan. It offered the sce-nario of sharpening great power rivalry between democracies led by Washington and autocracies, represented in the main by Russia and the People's Republic of China. It was to be a return to the Cold War under dif-ferent labels.

Kagan's binary thesis (black/white, with nothing in between) was a reprise of Bush's "You're with us, or you're with terrorists." It was equally simplistic.

His argument that when push comes to shove, Saudi Arabia "may see virtue in drawing closer to fellow autocrats in Moscow and Beijing"[2] defies history and facts on the ground. The seventy-seven-year old monarchical autocracy of Saudi Arabia has been closely tied to the United States since 1943, when President Franklin D. Roosevelt was beating the drum of "Four Freedoms," including the freedom of citizens to choose their rulers. The ultimate guarantor of the Saudi kingdom has been, and remains, the United States. It is the U.S. Fifth Fleet that is based in the adjoining Bahrain run by an autocratic hereditary ruler; there are no Russian or Chinese aircraft carriers floating in the Gulf region.

On the other side of the globe is Venezuela, which has been democratic, by Western standards, since 1959. That system has continued under the presidency of Hugo Chavez since 1999. Indeed, Venezuela has had more referendums, and general elections for president and Parliament, under Chavez than during any previous decade. Where would Venezuela be placed in Kagan's binary world?

Attempting to put America at the head of a newly minted column of committed democracies stems from a failure to acknowledge a cold fact: The United States is on a downward slide. It is not just the habitual Cassandras and diehard detractors of the United States who are relishing the prospect of America's inexorably declining power and influence. Such a judgment has been made by the official documents published by the U.S. government.

The global trends review, produced by the National Intelligence Council (NIC) every four years for the upcoming administration, is a case in point. Its report, published in December 2004, for the second Bush administration forecast "continued U.S. dominance" and declared that oil and gas supplies were "sufficient to meet global demands." The subsequent NIC report, released nearly four years later, said, "Owing to the relative decline of its economic, and to a lesser extent, military power, the U.S. will no longer have the same flexibility in choosing among as many options [as it has now]." The relative strength and potential leverage of the United States were in decline in an increasingly multipolar world, it concluded.[3] The NIC confirmed the view that had gained currency earlier among intellectuals in America and elsewhere in the West. Some reacted to this prospect with alarm and others with a calming reassurance.

Alarmists visualized the United States being replaced by the People's Republic of China as the dominant superpower. They saw red in Beijing stacking up U.S. Treasury bonds with the malevolent intent of twisting Uncle Sam's arm in the none-too-distant future. They pointed out that in a reconfigured East Asia, with one-third of the global population, the PRC had become not just the economic fountainhead, surpassing Japan, but also the leader in all nonmilitary fields, pushing America off its perch. They failed to note that by overreacting to the 9/11 attacks and mounting two major wars while *reducing* taxes at home, it was Bush who had bolstered—albeit inadvertently—the power and glory of the Middle Kingdom.

The other school of thought tried to calm popular nerves. It assailed the concept of the zero-sum game: the gain of non-American powers becoming the automatic loss of America and vice versa. It asserted that given the multifarious strengths of the United States, it was quite capable of accommodating the newly empowered countries—particularly China, with its core philosophy of governance being diametrically opposed to America's—into the evolving new world order. The bottom line was that the United States must retain the power to set the international agenda, to decide which simmering problem had turned into a crisis to be tackled headlong.

What both schools of thought had in common was their emotional ties with America and their undying wish to see it remain number one even in radically changed times, while they kept the American audience and policymakers in the foreground. This approach left untapped an intellectual field that did not revolve around the United States and was not dialectical—America versus China, the West against Asia, or democracies versus autocracies. And that is the area this book has tried to cover by offering a clear-eyed assessment of the major powers, setting out their respective strengths and weaknesses, and future trends.

Furthermore, noting the contemporary world's heavy dependence on hydrocarbons to sustain or raise living standards, this volume has also dealt with Venezuela and Iran. Endowed with vast quantities of oil and gas, these two countries provide political and economic models that are at variance with what the United States has to offer in South America and the hydrocarbon-rich Gulf region.

The multipolar world sketched in the preceding chapters consists of several major players—America, the European Union, China, Russia, and India. Since power is multidimensional, no single country will continue to be dominant in *all* fields. The modus operandi of the future is accommodation between leading powers at certain times and deterrence at others—a flexible combination of the main actors emerging to thwart the excessive ambitions of one of them. In other words, an international setup in which great powers will be able to thwart the unbridled aims of an aspiring superpower. Back to the age-old balance of power at work.

Chinese leaders were probably the first to imagine a world along these lines. They were certainly the first to call on the scholars at the Chinese Academy of Social Sciences (CASS) to quantify comprehensive national power (CNP). Now, thanks to the Academy's pioneering work, a scientific formula exists to measure a country's CNP—a realistic evaluation, shorn of ideology.

CHINA'S HARD-NOSED REALISM

In 2006 the United States scored 90.62 out of 100 on the CNP scale, whereas the PRC got only 59.10.

So the alarmists in America can rest assured that China's leaders are by no means thinking of catching up with America, much less overtaking it. They subscribe to the dictum of Sun Zi, the ancient author of *The Art of War*: "To defeat the enemy without fighting is the epitome of skill." Unsurprisingly, therefore, most of the recent CASS articles offer either analyses of the salient features of U.S. power and influence or outline tactics to block, side-step, curtail, or limit them.

The latest insight into the thinking of CASS scholars and Chinese leaders was given by an editorial in the official *China Daily*. Commenting on the inauguration of Barack Obama as president in January 2009, it said, "U.S. leaders have never been shy about talking about their country's ambition. For them, it is divinely granted destiny no matter what other nations think." It then predicted that "Obama's defense of U.S. interests will inevitably clash with those of other nations."[4]

The general strategy for circumventing America or molding it to constrain its foreign policy, however, was laid out a decade earlier by Qiao Liang and Wang Xiang-Sui in their book *Unrestricted Warfare*. Combine nonmilitary and trans-military means; apply them in an obfuscated fashion wherever you can; and use multinational, supranational, and nonstate institutions to defeat a militarily superior adversary, they recommended. Using an amalgam of these methods, Beijing has succeeded in blunting Washington's measures against Iran, North Korea, Myanmar, Sudan, and Uzbekistan while furthering its economic and diplomatic interests.[5]

The PRC's drive to strengthen its commercial ties with America has not stopped it from consistently opposing Washington's attempts to meddle in the internal affairs of other nations under the garb of United Nations Security Council resolutions. It persisted in opposing the United States at the UN Security Council even when it was the only permanent member of the Council to do so—as in the case of Iraq's Kurds in 1991.

It was much later, in 1998, that the Russian foreign ministry, led by Yevgeny Primakov, mustered enough courage to spike the Clinton administration's plan to foist its unilateral interpretation of an earlier resolution on Iraq. The United States tried to gain UN authorization for military action against Saddam Hussein's regime after the repeated failures of CIA-engineered coups to overthrow it. When Russia, backed by China, threatened to veto Washington's draft resolution, Clinton retreated.

With the collaboration of China and Russia—still economically dependent on America and the U.S.-influenced International Monetary Fund—the international community received its first glimpse of the workings of a multipolar world. It was an early example of the pattern likely to become established in the coming decades, with several major powers—America, the European Union, China, Russia, India, and Brazil—active on the world stage.

In August 2008, as the Russian Federation hit Georgia hard after Georgian Mikheil Saakashvili ordered the shelling of Tskhinvali, the capital of the breakaway region of South Ossetia, all President Bush did was to verbally condemn the Kremlin's military onslaught.

The Russian-Georgian spat signaled the end of the United States acting as the sole superpower militarily. By happenstance, America's military hegemony lasted as many years—1991 to 2008—as did the supremacy of the Allies after World War I, from the 1919 Versailles Treaty to the remilitarization of the Rhineland by resurgent Germany in 1936 in violation of the treaty. If those who rushed to announce the everlasting hegemony of the United States in 1991 had pondered the words of Sir Winston Churchill—"The longer you look back, the further you can look forward"—they would not have been caught short as they were.

RUSSIA-CHINA RELATIONS:
LESS THAN MARRIAGE

The other issue where the PRC and the Kremlin have moved in step is Iran. They noted, disapprovingly, that the United States, backed by Britain, had tried to misuse earlier UN resolutions on Iraq passed under Chapter VII of the UN Charter ("Action with respect to threats to the peace, breaches of the peace and acts of aggression"). So when it came to the draft resolutions presented to the UN Security Council on Iran's nuclear program under Chapter VII, they successfully insisted on stipulating Article 41 (which specifies "measures not involving the use of armed force") of Chapter VII.

As Iran's neighbor sharing the Caspian Sea, Russia has critical interest in its stability and security, no matter who rules in Tehran. Moreover, it empathizes with Iran on the latter's feeling of insecurity, since Washington has yet to disown publicly covert plans to overthrow the Iranian regime or to scuttle its clandestine project to sabotage Iran's nuclear facility for uranium enrichment at Natanz. The Kremlin sees Russia's security threatened by the Pentagon's plan to build anti-missile defense facilities in Eastern Europe.

By constructing and equipping Iran's first nuclear power plant, Moscow has shown its confidence in the regime's peaceful intentions. Energy-hungry China has its eyes set on the vast deposits of oil and gas in the soil and territorial waters of Iran. Sinopec's inking of a $2 billion contract to develop an oil field in southwest Iran in December 2007 highlighted Beijing's interest. Chinese companies have filled the vacuum in other areas of Iran's industry left by their German counterparts, who departed under American pressure.

While China and Russia are committed to nonproliferation of nuclear arms, they cannot ignore Washington's willful refusal to foreswear the option of toppling the Islamic regime as a first step to recognizing Iran's critical role as a regional power.

Global history since World War II shows that for countries—small, middling, or great—acquiring nuclear weapons is about the most basic requirement: the survival of the regime or the nation. Joining the nuclear club has proved an effective strategy for survival. The possession of the city-busting weaponry and means to deliver it has the potential for causing Mutually Assured Destruction (MAD) and acts as a uniquely powerful deterrent. While the madness of this strategy is recognized universally, the salient point that goes virtually unmentioned is that acquiring nuclear arms has proved an effective step for a regime to take when its survival is at stake.

The latest example is North Korea. Bush's belligerent policy toward it drove its leader, Kim Jong Il, to accelerate the nuclear arms program and test a bomb in October 2006. He thus improved his bargaining power. In the end he succeeded in getting North Korea removed from the list of states that support international terrorism, and it ceased to be a member of the "Axis of Evil."

It was four decades earlier that Israel fabricated its first atom bomb. Even though, in the mid-1950s, Israel was militarily superior to the combined strength of its Arab neighbors, its leaders pondered the prospect when that would cease to be the case. And they could not be 100 percent certain that the Western powers would come to their rescue in case of war. Therefore they decided to produce their own atom bomb—to ensure the nation's survival.

As yet there is no hard evidence that Iran has actually started a nuclear weapons program. (That Iran's engineers and scientists, at a certain point, most probably worked on schematic designs for an atom bomb and a missile head does not amount to actual work being undertaken.) But if its leaders were to give up the legitimate right to enrich uranium per se, they would forfeit the option of producing a nuclear bomb in the future—if the changed circumstances demanded it—as part of their defensive strategy. That option would be unacceptable to them or the leaders of any other nation that feels threatened by the United States—as North Korea did, until recently—or its closest regional ally, Israel.

The challenge for the Obama administration is to devise a policy that accepts, discreetly, Iran's right to consider a nuclear weapons option while U.S. negotiators try to convince it that its security would be best served by not following that path. The Obama White House's offer of a nonaggression pact with Tehran would go a long way in that direction.

What is lacking in Washington's approach to both Iran and Russia is empathy with the other party, to ask and understand what is driving it to behave the way it does, regard its fears and concerns as genuine, and address them. That is the real test of fruitful diplomacy.

COOPERATION AND COMPETITION

The growing Chinese-Russian cooperation—in military (as in the Shanghai Cooperation Organization), commerce, and diplomacy—is not without its strains. Holding fast to its tenet of respecting the territorial integrity of the UN

member-states, the PRC refused to support the Kremlin's recognition of South
Ossetia and Abkhazia as independent states.

Cooperation and competition is, in fact, the template of several relation-
ships among the major powers. While strengthening its ties with America,
commercial and military, Delhi has conducted joint military exercises with
China, which is its number one trading partner. At the same time, India is
purchasing advanced fighter jets from Russia and a refitted, modern aircraft
carrier, the first to be owned by a non-Western nation.

The sharpest example of engagement and containment is the relationship
between Beijing and Washington. While busily buying U.S. Treasury bonds,
the PRC was finessing its strategy of developing area-denial weapons and anti-
satellite and cyber warfare capabilities to be used against the Pentagon. On its
part, the Pentagon's reconnaissance planes and ships aggressively gathered
military intelligence, the latest example being the U.S. Navy's surveillance ship
Impeccable tracking Chinese submarines near China's offshore island of
Hainan, the base of the PRC's ballistic missile submarine fleet.[6]

Taking a long-term view, PRC leaders have concluded that the United States
will turn its attention eastward to try to recover the ground it lost during the
two-term Bush presidency, and that will bring it into conflict with China.

But for the 9/11 attacks, the first Bush administration would have confronted the PRC already. That was what Paul Wolfowitz, the number two official at the Defense Department, was preparing to do. As a doctoral student
at the University of Chicago in the late 1960s, he came under the influence of
Professor Albert Wohlstetter, a military strategist. The guru of the Cold War
hawks, Wohlstetter believed that détente with the Soviet Union verged on trea-
son. He argued that if you forecast conflict with China two decades in the future, you fight it in the present and remove that danger to U.S. supremacy.
The terrorist attacks in September 2001 diverted Wolfowitz from his China
agenda and gave him a second chance to sell his preemptive strike doctrine
that Bush Senior had rejected nine years earlier.[7]

For now, American policymakers have abandoned their stale theory that
globalization and China's breakneck economic growth would lead to meaningful political reform culminating in Chinese citizens electing their own
rulers in free and fair elections. There is no prospect of Chinese voters being
given the right to choose their governing councils above the village level.

Elsewhere, a gradual move toward a representative government in the Middle East is likely, with a free choice favoring Islamists.

Most Likely Scenario of the Future

Contrary to the predictions of many American pundits that globalization and free markets will transform nation-states into market-states, there will be a strong revival of the inviolability of national sovereignty. This was well illustrated by the way the Burmese military rulers spurned offers of foreign aid in the aftermath of the cyclone in 2008 and got away with it.

The fiscal tempest caused by the reckless policies of Washington, originating in Ronald Reagan's presidency in the 1980s, along with the crash in the value of wide-ranging assets in North America and the European Union, has made the Chinese model of the state-guided economic development attractive to developing nations, particularly in Africa and Latin America.

Over the next few decades, with dwindling reserves of oil and gas, the importance of hydrocarbons will rise dramatically. Three-fifths of oil and two-fifths of natural gas reserves are in the Gulf region. So it will be vitally important for the world at large to note how well, or badly, the present authoritarian and semiauthoritarian rulers of the hydrocarbon-rich Gulf countries, currently deriving their legitimacy from a mix of tribalism and Islam, succeed in blending representative democracy with Islam.

The transfer of power from hereditary ruler to popularly elected representatives will almost certainly lead the democratic governments in these Gulf states to distance themselves from the United States. One of the main reasons why these royal autocrats have aligned themselves with Washington is their belief that, in the final analysis, only the Pentagon can provide them with a security umbrella. But their popularly elected governments will realize that they can protect their countries from foreign aggression by expanding the twenty-eight-year-old Gulf Cooperation Council to include Iran and Iraq, now that these two neighbors have left their past rivalry behind. That would make the Pentagon's presence in the Gulf redundant and remove a major source of tension in this vital region.

One of the major benefits arising from a multipolar world will be the fillip it will give to the regional organizations. The ten-member Association of South-East Asian Nations (ASEAN), now focused on economic cooperation, will be emboldened to expand its remit to defense. This is already happening elsewhere.

In 2008, the summit of the twelve-nation Union of South American Nations, meeting in Brasilia, decided to create a military coordinating component to be called *Conselho Sul-Americano de Defensa* (Council of South American Defense) with an increasingly NATO-like structure, although without an operating field capability.

In the economic field, the expanding GDPs of mega-nations like India are providing opportunities to highly educated and skilled persons at home as never before. This has reduced the brain drain to a trickle. In the early 1980s, 75 percent of the graduates of the high-caliber Indian Institutes of Technology migrated to North America. Now the figure is down to 5 percent.

Attracting the best minds from the Third World has been very beneficial to the United States. But with expanding economies, improving educational systems, and better job opportunities at home, the flow of scholars from the non-Western world will slacken. The case of India indicates that the United States will lose this valuable asset in the coming decades.

Overall, with rising literacy in Latin America, Africa, and Asia, the number of literate non-Western people is growing fast. So too is the size of the opinion formers in these continents. Given the ubiquity of television, the bulk of the world's population is getting informed about the events in their countries and abroad by television news in their own languages and increasingly from their own perspective rather than an American or British one.

All these developments will cumulatively reduce the power and influence of the United States, which enjoyed the status of the sole superpower for almost two decades, and help level the playing field for China, the European Union, Russia, India, and Brazil.

EPILOGUE

The swearing in of Barack Obama as president in January 2009 improved America's image abroad, mostly in Europe and South America. But it made only a marginal difference in the Muslim world because Obama's policy follow-up did not meet the expectations raised by his soaring oratory. At home, his swift and strong stimulus package, funded by taxpayers and foreign borrowing, arrested the decline in the GDP. But it did little to pull the world economy out of the doldrums. That task fell willy-nilly to the People's Republic of China.

China thus had an opportunity to demonstrate the superiority of its state-directed capitalism to the free-market variety. It would do so by maintaining an impressive GDP growth in 2009. It is worth noting that earlier, instead of letting globalization establish and consolidate a capitalist market economy worldwide, China had used globalization to advance its state capitalism.

Now, owning over $2 trillion in foreign exchange reserves and maintaining a healthy budget surplus at home, China exploited the downturn in the Western economies to achieve multiple aims. Its state-owned corporations accelerated their acquisition of foreign energy and raw materials companies. It launched an ambitious program to spread its soft power abroad. It expanded the foreign-language news broadcasts of its government-owned CCTV, and its Xinhua agency started making short news programs to be shown on third-generation (3G) mobile phones. It decided to restructure its media, entertainment, and culture industries to make them market-oriented and compete with the likes of Time Warner, Walt Disney, Viacom, and News Corporation. To counter the fall in its exports, it encouraged consumption at home and acted to reduce the income gap between rural and urban dwellers by inter alia restoring the welfare safety net that had virtually disappeared in the course of economic liberalization.

By managing to keep its GDP growth at 8.5 percent a year while most other economies contracted, China acquired a higher economic profile in the international arena. In contrast, Japan, with its GDP shrinking by 5.4 percent in 2009, will yield its status as the world's second largest economy to China in 2010.[1] So according to Deng Xiaoping's leading guideline—"Hide your capability, and bide your time"—the moment had come for China to show its cards. As it was, the rest of the international community looked to Beijing to pull the world out of the Great Recession—a role played so far by the United States.

To their credit, the leaders of the West and China had realized the increased interdependence of the world's economies as a result of growing globalization. So on April 2, 2009, when the heads of G20 member-states assembled for their second summit in London, they were keen to act unanimously to diffuse the fiscal crisis.

The general strategy for overcoming the malaise, they agreed, centered on pumping huge sums of public funds to stop the Great Recession turning into the Great Depression and on reforming the fiscal system in the leading Western nations as well as the international financial institutions they controlled.

Belying the official title of "G20," the ultimate power rested with the elite G7—now compelled to co-opt the cash-rich China. Before the summit, G7 leaders had failed to bridge their differences on the size of domestic stimulus packages and the extent of reform in financial markets. Obama and British Prime Minister Gordon Brown stood on one side, with French President Nicolas Sarkozy and German Chancellor Angela Merkel on the other. Obama and Brown urged their French and German counterparts to commit more to fiscal stimulus at home, but failed. Sarkozy and Merkel argued that they had done enough and that the welfare safety net for the unemployed and the underprivileged in their countries was far more robust than in the United States. They would be vindicated when statistics released later showed French and German economies registering growth in the second quarter, whereas those in America and Britain remained negative.

While all leaders agreed that it was the slide toward deregulation on Wall Street and the City of London that had pushed the world to the edge of an economic abyss, Obama and Brown were not prepared to accept the strict regulation of financial markets proposed by Sarkozy and Merkel. They relented only when Sarkozy threatened to walk out. The reform of the global banking system—said the G20's final communiqué—will consist of controls on hedge funds, tighter rules for credit rating agencies, and immediate naming and shaming of tax havens that failed to share information.

Hedge funds will be required to disclose their indebtedness to enable regulators to assess their risk taking. Since more than three-fifths of 8,000 hedge funds worldwide, with nearly four-fifths of the aggregate capital of $1.4 trillion, are based in America, if this measure is promulgated there, it will effectively rewrite the way hedge funds have been managed so far.

The Basel-based Financial Stability Forum, established in 1999 as an informal network of central banks, financial ministries, and market regulators, was to be rebranded the Financial Stability Board and accorded sweeping new authority to oversee banks and international markets.

G20 leaders decided to provide an additional $1.1 trillion to the International Monetary Fund, World Bank, and other multilateral financial institutions to increase their lending to vulnerable countries, thus expanding the global stimulus package.

Brown, the host, was satisfied at the unanimous adoption of the final communiqué, which inter alia agreed on a global approach to deal with toxic assets. But it was Sarkozy who stole the limelight by revealing that there were "tensions, wrestling matches and vested interests," during the day-long conference. "Since Bretton Woods [in 1944], the world has been living on the Anglo-Saxon [financial] model," he said. "It has its advantages [but] clearly today a page has been turned."[2]

Another sign of "a page being turned" was the prominence given to the Chinese leader Hu Jintao. Alone among G20 leaders, it was Hu, on the eve of the London summit, who said, "Despite its severe impact on China's economy, the current financial crisis also creates opportunity for the country."[3]

CHINA LEADS THE WAY

For China, the potential for growth lay both at home and abroad. Its companies increased their stakes in the hydrocarbon industries of not only neighboring Russia and Kazakhstan but also Africa and Latin America. Moreover, instead of limiting themselves to securing licenses for unexplored blocks, they started bidding for the blocks that either were producing oil or were about to—a sector that had so far been the monopoly of Western corporations.

In August 2009, China National Offshore Oil Company (CNOOC) moved to acquire one-sixth of Nigeria's proven oil reserves of 36 billion barrels by bidding for stakes in those oil blocks that until the end of 2008 were operated by Western corporations. Its cumulative offer, believed to be several times the figure the current Western producers in Nigeria were pledging, was in the range of $30 billion to $50 billion.[4] If successful, the contract for 6 billion barrels of oil will exceed the 4.7 billion barrels that China's oil companies had acquired cumulatively in Angola, Gabon, Somalia, and Sudan.

The state-controlled China Development Bank offered a $25 billion loan to Russia's leading oil company and pipeline operator to provide 300,000 barrels per day (bpd) in additional oil to China over twenty-five years. And a subsidiary of the China National Petroleum Corporation contracted to lend Kazakhstan $10 billion as part of a joint venture to develop its hydrocarbon reserves.

During Chinese Vice President Xi Jinping's tour of South America in January 2009, China Development Bank agreed to loan Venezuela's PdVSA $6 billion for oil to be supplied to China over the next twenty years. Three months later, Beijing doubled the fund in return for Venezuela increasing its oil shipments from the present 380,000 bpd to 1 million bpd. The China Development Bank lent Brazil's oil company, Petrobras, $10 billion in exchange for a supply of 160,000 bpd in the coming years.[5] This figure was close to the $11.2 billion that the Inter-American Development Bank lent to various South American countries in 2008. Earlier China had established its commercial presence in Brazil by offering lucrative prices for iron ore and soybeans, the export commodities fueling Brazil's recent economic growth.

At home, the Chinese government's $585 billion stimulus package combined heavy investment in major infrastructure projects with rebuilding its neglected social safety net, its health care system, and its long overlooked rural development schemes.

China's banking system—state-controlled and flush with cash and a rich supply of labor—opened its lending spigots to the full. As a result, consumer spending and capital investment in China rose sharply.

When the credit crash in the West caused a substantial drop in China's exports—depriving 20 million migrant workers in the industrialized coastal cities of their livelihood—the authorities facilitated the return of many to their home villages and encouraged others to enroll in state-sponsored retraining programs to acquire higher skills for better jobs in the future.

Whereas Western leaders could do no more than castigate bankers filling their pockets with bonuses as the balance sheets of their corporations turned red, the Chinese government compelled top managers at major state-owned companies to cut their salaries by 15 percent to 40 percent before tinkering with the remuneration of their workforce.

China contributed to the debate on the global fiscal meltdown and ways of avoiding a recurrence. In his online article posted on the eve of the London G20 summit, Zhou Xiaochuan, governor of China's central bank, referred to the increasingly frequent financial crises that had embroiled the world.[6] They had resulted when the domestic needs of the country issuing the primary reserve currency clashed with international fiscal requirements. For instance, responding to the demoralization caused by the 9/11 attacks, the U.S. Federal Reserve Board drastically reduced interest rates to an almost-record low of 1 percent to boost domestic consumption at a time when rapidly expanding economies outside America needed higher interest rates to cool their growth rates. The solution, said Zhou, lay in devising a supersovereign reserve currency managed by a global institution that could be used to both create and control global liquidity. Referring to the International Monetary Fund's Special Drawing Rights (SDR)—a virtual currency whose value is set by a basket of the U.S. dollar, the euro, the British pound, and the Japanese yen—he noted that the SDR had not been allowed to play its full role so far. If its role is enhanced, it might someday become the global reserve currency.

Zhou's article created a flutter in financial markets. They surmised that the dollar was on the verge of losing its status as the foremost reserve currency. Obama intervened. "I don't think there is need for a global currency," he asserted. "The dollar is extraordinarily strong right now."[7]

UNCERTAIN FUTURE OF THE U.S. DOLLAR

That was the case in late March 2009, when most currencies were weak. The fiscal hurricane triggered by the Lehman Brothers's bankruptcy six months earlier had led currency investors worldwide to seek shelter under the U.S. dollar, the safest currency. But as the hurricane subsided and non-American currencies recovered, and the total cost of the massive U.S. federal intervention in the economy was calculated, doubts arose about the medium-term strength of the greenback.

The potential commitments of the U.S. government as an investor, lender, insurer, and buyer of last resort had skyrocketed to a staggering $9.8 trillion, 70 percent of the GDP.[8]

Little wonder that barely six months later Robert Zoellick, the American president of the World Bank, warned that "the future for the United States will depend on whether and how it will address large deficits, recover without inflation that could undermine its credit and currency, and overhaul its financial system." He predicted that the euro's acceptability could grow.[9] Indeed Iran, the second highest exporter in OPEC, had already started pricing its oil exports in euros. With Ireland's approval of the Lisbon Treaty in October, the scene was set for the European Union to secure the bigger global role commensurate with its economic might.

Zoellick also predicted that "over 10 to 20 years," the yuan will evolve into "a force in financial markets." Beijing had already moved to make yuan an international currency. In March 2009 it gave Argentina access to more than $10 billion in yuans. It then extended this facility to Belarus, Indonesia, Malaysia, and South Korea. In September, China used yuans to purchase the equivalent of $50 billion of the first bond sale by the IMF to help raise $500 billion to finance lending to struggling economies. By lending these yuans to developing countries, the IMF will help internationalize the Chinese currency.[10] Soon after, China decided to issue 6 billion yuan worth of government bonds in Hong Kong, which has its own currency, the Hong Kong dollar. As Hong Kong is one of the world's freest financial markets, the Chinese bond issue will aid internationalization of the yuan.

Meanwhile, in the United States the $787 billion stimulus package authorized by Congress in February 2009 was working its way through the economic system. A little over a third involved tax cuts, which benefited 95 percent of Americans. A little less than a third provided relief to state governments and individuals, which saved jobs. The remainder was for building infrastructure, involving nearly 30,000 projects, including renewable energy.[11]

On the negative side, the staggering losses in credit card debt, student loans, and commercial property and car loans were still gradually working their way through the system, inhibiting any sustained return to growth. During the first eight months of 2009, over 450 banks and mortgage lenders failed, and a further 416 were on a regulatory watch list of troubled firms. At 9.7 percent, unemployment was the highest since 1983 and set to rise even further, and the GDP was expected to shrink by 2.6 percent in 2009.

Yet the voluntary action taken by bankers in America and elsewhere to counter the fiscal meltdown was niggardly. A poll in G20 member-states for the BBC World Service found that less than a third of the respondents were satisfied with the bankers' actions to address the financial crisis.[12]

In the United States, the eight-month-old Obama administration had failed to take adequate steps to restrict financial institutions' size, their risk taking, and their interconnectedness, and to stem the flow of profligate executive bonuses. Worse, it had allowed the surviving big banks to become even bigger in the aftermath of the collapse of the three gargantuan investment banks on Wall Street. Goldman Sachs set aside $11.4 billion for bonuses.

On the eve of the first anniversary of Lehman Brothers's fall, Obama was reduced to appealing to bankers not to wait for the law requiring them to translate financial products into plain language, put executive pay up for shareholder votes, and alter the bonus culture by focusing on long-term performance.[13]

With the Dow Jones Industrial Average Index in mid-September closing 47 percent above its lowest point of 6,547 on March 9, the bankers were in no mood to listen to such homilies. They saw no need for reform. The government's strategy to defuse the crisis—letting bankers garner gains while taxpayers bore losses—suited the fiscal industry. With its lobbyists working overtime at Capitol Hill, the industry had cooled the lawmakers' initial enthusiasm for recasting the financial system.

It is worth recalling that it was Lehman Brothers's collapse and the subsequent seizure of credit circulation globally, coupled with Senator John McCain's inane remark that the economy was on a firm footing, that had tipped the balance in the presidential election campaign in Obama's favor and given substance to his slogan "Change we can have."

OBAMA'S ERSATZ CHANGE

But once in power, Obama delayed his promised schedule of military withdrawal from Iraq and adopted what George W. Bush had planned. He ended torture of prisoners and decided to close the Guantánamo detention center, but he retained key provisions about extraordinary renditions.

Change was most noticeable in the tone and the language he used. Absent was the bombast and bullying of Bush. That difference endeared him to Europeans. A survey of America and twelve European nations by the German

Marshall Fund of the United States showed that about 77 percent in the European Union backed Obama's handling of international affairs, while only 19 percent in a similar survey a year earlier supported Bush's handling of them.[14] Europeans' admiring fascination with Obama reached an apogee in the decision by the Oslo-based Nobel Committee to award him the 2009 Peace Prize. By so doing, the committee buried its long-established convention of honoring actual achievement, not potential for it. But this left intact Europeans' views on the war in Afghanistan. They were opposed to the increased military involvement there, as urged by Obama, with European governments by and large reflecting popular opinion.

A worldwide poll by the Washington-based Pew Research Center showed that the image of America had risen sharply in Europe, Mexico, Brazil, and Argentina. But the rise was small in India and China. It was marginal in the Arab Middle East and nonexistent in Russia, Pakistan, and Turkey.[15]

This was the case despite Obama's groundbreaking speech to the Turkish parliament in Ankara in April. "The United States is not and will never be at war with Islam," he said. "America's relationship with the Muslim community, the Muslim world, cannot be based just on the opposition to terrorism. We seek broader engagement based on mutual trust and mutual respect."[16]

The main reason for failing to make a dent in America's continuing unpopularity in the Muslim world was rooted in the Israeli-Palestinian conflict. Obama fell into the trap of the wily prime minister of Israel, Benjamin Netanyahu, when he agreed to link progress in the Israeli-Palestinian peace talks with success in spiking Iran's nuclear program and set an arbitrary deadline of December 2009 for Iran. By letting the Israeli leader decide Washington's agenda for Tehran, Obama failed to break with the long-established pattern of the tail wagging the dog. Having made a weighty diplomatic gain unilaterally, Netanyahu refused to freeze Jewish settlements on the West Bank and East Jerusalem permanently, as demanded by Obama. And Arab leaders refused to make any concessions to Israel until it agreed to the freeze.

Elsewhere, North Korea tested a nuclear bomb under Obama's watch. And his offer of direct talks with Iran without preconditions did not soften Tehran's stance on the nuclear issue.

In mid-September, while canceling Bush's anti-missile defense project in Poland and the Czech Republic, Obama reiterated his predecessor's claim that the threat of missile attacks came from Iran. His decision, he argued, was based on "the new assessments" of the nature of that menace. With their range of 1,200 miles, Tehran's missiles could target parts of Europe but not eastern America. He therefore opted for deploying, by 2011, existing ship-based weapons to launch SM-3 interceptor missiles from the Mediterranean to intercept and destroy medium-range missiles targeting Israel. By 2015, the Obama Plan will include three ground-based sites, most likely in eastern and southern Europe.[17]

By discarding the Bush Plan—involving the installation of an X-band advanced radar system in the Czech Republic capable of seeing deep into the European sector of Russia with its many missile sites—Obama removed the Kremlin's main fear. "I very much hope this correct and brave decision will be followed by others," said Russian Prime Minister Vladimir Putin.[18]

RUSSIA'S STRENGTHENING ENERGY CARD

The Kremlin's national security strategy adopted in May 2009 described the Pentagon's acquisition of a nuclear first-strike capability as the foremost threat to Russia. During their summit in Moscow two months later, President Dmitry Medvedev explained to Obama that Russia's opposition to the missile shield stemmed from the risk it posed to the doctrine of nuclear deterrence. (It is worth noting that in 1962, it was Washington's fear of a Soviet nuclear first-strike capability that led to President John Kennedy's uncompromising response to Moscow's plan to base its missiles in Cuba, barely ninety miles from American shores, and that caused the Cuban missile crisis.) Unlike in the Soviet era, the Kremlin's conventional forces were now so run-down that it had to depend on its nuclear umbrella, with ballistic missiles being the key.

The state-guided media in Russia described Obama's trip to Moscow as a "working visit," with TV giving it low priority. This was in line with popular opinion. Only 6 percent of Russians viewed the United States positively.[19] And according to the University of Maryland's WorldPublicOpinion.org, only 15 percent of Russians agreed that America was playing a positive role in world affairs, with most saying that it abused its power and forced Russia to do what it wanted.[20]

The national mood in Russia had lifted in line with rising oil prices, which nearly doubled within six months of sinking to $33 a barrel in December 2008. For each $1 rise in the price of petroleum, the government earned $1.7 billion a year. The Micex index of major Russian companies more than doubled in 2009 after hitting a record low in late October 2008.

In the second quarter of 2009, the GDP grew by 7.5 percent compared to the first quarter, indicating that Russia was turning the economic corner. Moreover, during that period, at 7.4 million bpd, Russia's exports of crude oil exceeded Saudi Arabia's 7.0 million bpd. It thus became the world's number one exporter of petroleum, having been the leading exporter of natural gas for several years.[21] This news was received with some trepidation in Washington.

While the tone of the Obama administration was different from that of its predecessor, and some of its foreign policies diverged from Bush's, both subscribed to the same doctrine: Whatever the White House perceives as a threat—North Korea, Iran, proliferation of nuclear arms—must be seen the same way by Moscow and Beijing.

IRAN AT THE CENTER

Having conceded, rightly, that the diplomatic process with Tehran would not be advanced by threats, Obama reversed his stance by raising the prospect of "much stronger international sanctions" if Iran did not suspend uranium enrichment. In his *Newsweek* interview in May, he alluded to "all options being on the table," a favorite phrase of Bush. Two months later, neither the Pentagon nor the Israel Defense Force tried to conceal the conducting of a joint exercise at Nellis Air Force base in Nevada, code-named Red Flag, that featured in-flight refueling of Israeli jets by U.S. military planes.

When Obama offered to deal with Tehran on the basis of mutual interest in an atmosphere of mutual respect, he did not cancel or repudiate the ongoing covert U.S. program of destabilizing Iran, with a budget of $400 million.

He took the welcome initiative of addressing a confidential letter to Iran's supreme leader, Ayatollah Ali Khamanei. But there was no hint—official or otherwise—that he mentioned the groundbreaking offer Iran had made to the State Department in May 2003, through the Swiss embassy in Tehran, for direct talks on all subjects, including the nuclear program, without preconditions.[22] Had he done so, he would have practiced what he preached in his Ankara speech: Security requires peace, and peace begins by "learning to stand in somebody else's shoes to see through their eyes."[23]

Soon after, Obama and his team reverted to the old strategy of sticks and carrots. Following in the footsteps of the Bush administration, they took to pressuring Russia and China to fall in line with their tough stance. They ignored Medvedev's description of Iran as Russia's "major partner" on the eve of Obama's visit to Moscow. Moreover, they ignored salient facts. As littoral states of the Caspian Sea, Iran and Russia are neighbors. The Russian-built civilian nuclear plant in Bushehr is set to be commissioned in 2010. And the Kremlin is more concerned about the potential nuclear threat from Pakistan, which could fall into militant Islamist hands, than the theoretical one from Tehran.

They also turned a blind eye to Beijing's thriving commercial ties with Tehran. Between 1994 and 2008 the two-way trade between them ballooned seventy-four-fold, to $29 billion. China was buying 15 percent of its oil imports from Iran. Its commitments to develop Iran's hydrocarbon industry were estimated at a hefty $120 billion. Between June and August 2009, Chinese oil corporations signed $8 billion worth of contracts with Iran to develop the gigantic South Pars gas field and help expand two existing Iranian oil refineries. And Iran's oil corporation invited Chinese companies to participate in a $42.8 billion project to construct seven oil refineries and a 1,000-mile trans-Iran pipeline.[24] Tehran's scheme dovetailed with Beijing's strategic plan to import Iran's petroleum and natural gas by pipelines across Central Asia, thus avoiding the sea routes vulnerable to U.S. naval interdiction. This was part of China's long-term aim of circumventing, curtailing, or limiting America's power and influence[25]—an objective it shared with Iran.

Whereas America and its close allies at the UN Security Council threatened "punishing sanctions"—including cutting off gasoline supplies in which Iran is deficient—on the Islamic Republic if it did not stop its uranium enrichment program, China's foreign affairs vice minister, He Yafei, said, "I don't like the word punishment. I think all issues can be solved through dialogue and negotiations."[26] It transpired that the Chinese oil corporations had started supplying gasoline to Iran as British and Indian companies stopped doing so.

Beijing has consistently backed diplomacy. For instance, following Iraq's invasion of Kuwait in August 1991, Beijing advocated negotiations with Baghdad and subsequently abstained on the vote at the UN Security Council authorizing military action.

Unlike ham-handed Iraqi dictator Saddam Hussein, Iran's leaders had shown some diplomatic finesse. They preempted the surprise move that America, Britain, and France (aka P3, three permanent members of the UN Security Council) had planned at the October 1 meeting in Geneva of Iran with Six Powers (P3 plus China, Russia, and Germany) for confronting Iran with the evidence of a clandestine nuclear facility near Qom. Ten days before the Geneva meeting, the leaders informed the International Atomic Energy Agency (IAEA) that Iran was constructing "a pilot scale enrichment plant" to produce low-enriched uranium (LEU) and that no uranium had been processed. During IAEA chief Muhammad ElBaradei's subsequent trip to Tehran, his hosts settled the date for the IAEA's inspection of the Qom site.

At the one-day Geneva conference Iran agreed to ship a significant proportion of its 1,600 kilograms of LEU to Russia and France for enriching to 20 percent. It would then be used in Iran's existing nuclear reactors to produce medical isotopes.

If the next meeting of Iran and Six Powers focuses on "freeze for freeze"— Iran to suspend its enrichment program in exchange for the UN Security Council not raising the present nominal economic sanctions—then it is unlikely to be as fruitful as the one on October 1.

It is unrealistic to expect Iran to suspend its uranium enrichment program, which it is entitled to under the Nuclear Non-Proliferation Treaty it has signed. The issue is linked to national security. Acquiring nuclear weapons is about a sovereign state's most basic requirement: the survival of the regime or nation. Joining the nuclear club has proved to be an effective strategy for survival. Israel and North Korea provide glaring examples.

Unsure of Western military assistance in a conventional war with Arab nations and of its ability to maintain, alone, armed superiority over Arab adversaries, Israel's leaders embarked on a nuclear weapons program in the mid-1950s and succeeded a decade later. Since then Israel has acquired an arsenal of some two hundred atom bombs.

So long as the Iranian regime has not secured unconditional diplomatic recognition and acceptance from Washington in the way it has from Moscow, Beijing, Brussels, and Delhi, it will feel insecure. So the solution lies in direct Iran-America talks with an agenda laid out in Tehran's recent five-page document titled, "Cooperation for Peace, Justice and Progress"—a rehash of its May 2003 proposal. The subjects include frozen Iranian assets in America, Hizbullah and Hamas, Afghanistan and Iraq, and most importantly regional security arrangements.

An examination of the talks on a nuclear-free North Korea is instructive. It shows two offers that have not yet cropped up in the contacts with the Iranians: a guarantee against attack or subversion of North Korea by America and the readiness of Washington and Tokyo for full diplomatic relations.

Iran has been frozen out of the pro-Western six-member Gulf Cooperation Council, to which it belongs by virtue of geography.[27] So having secured an observer status at the six-member Shanghai Cooperation Organization (SCO, consisting of four Central Asian republics, China, and Russia), Iran has been assiduously seeking full membership.

Interestingly, when Mahmoud Ahmadinejad attended the annual SCO summit in Dushanbe, Tajikistan, in August 2009, he was officially hailed as the reelected president of Iran.

Iran Stumbles, Chavez Flaunts the Democracy Flag

During the widespread protests following the controversial presidential election in Iran in mid-June, none of the SCO member-states commented on the widely suspected poll-rigging in favor of Ahmadinejad, or the violence with which the security forces quashed the nationwide peaceful protest, killing sixty-nine people. This was in contrast to the critical statements made by Obama and other Western leaders.

Traditionally, the Iranian regime loosens up during the presidential election campaign. Judges treat dissident journalists lightly, and the police refrain from confiscating TV satellite dishes, which are officially banned. This is done to encourage citizens to vote. Voter turnout is perceived, rightly, as a measure of the regime's popularity.

Overconfident of the hard-line incumbent's public standing, the government allowed three ninety-minute TV debates between him and each of his three challengers. This gave an unprecedented opportunity for opposition views to be aired before an audience of 50 million. It dramatically enhanced the chances of reformist Mir Hussein Mousavi, a former prime minister during the 1980–1988 Iran-Iraq War.

At 84 percent, voter participation was the second highest in the Republic's history. It meant that more upper-middle-class and upper-class Iranians—often secular—voted than before. This favored Mousavi. So the official result, announced posthaste, which gave nearly 63 percent of the ballots to Ahmadinejad versus Mousavi's 34 percent, stunned most Iranians and foreign analysts.

Until this election—despite evidence of modest tinkering with the first round of the 2005 presidential poll—post-shah Iran had demonstrated that Islam and democracy could work in harmony. The postelection events showed that when strains between the two concepts developed, it was democracy that got short shrift.

None of this bothered the leaders of Iran's neighboring Muslim nations. Nor did it matter to the top officials in Moscow or Beijing.

Undoubtedly, democracy as a concept has great appeal, but what it means in practice varies vastly. For instance, the Asian Barometer of Political Attitudes recorded in 2009 showed that 53.8 percent in China believed that a democratic system was preferable. But when asked how democratic China was on a scale of 1 to 10, the Chinese placed their nation at 7.22—third in Asia—well ahead of Japan, the Philippines, and South Korea.[28]

Much to the embarrassment of the Obama administration, when it came to upholding Western-style democracy in Latin America, it was Hugo Chavez who led the campaign. He did so in June 2009, when Honduran generals ousted the democratically elected president, Manuel Zelaya, on the spurious basis that by holding a nonbinding referendum on the constitution he was planning a second term of office for himself. Chavez's lead was followed by Brazilian President Luyiz Inacio Lula da Silva, with the dithering Obama administration giving mixed signals.

On September 20, it was a Venezuelan aircraft that collected the exiled Zelaya in Managua, Nicaragua, touched down briefly in El Salvador, and then took off for an unknown destination. Zelaya and his four companions crossed into Honduras clandestinely and found refuge in the Brazilian embassy in Tegucigalpa, thereby forcing the usurper government to negotiate a compromise. Regardless of the final outcome of this saga, the presence of Zelaya inside Honduras changed the balance of power.

During that week in September, there was a formal recognition of the change in the balance of global economic power. The leaders of the G20 member-states meeting in Pittsburgh, Pennsylvania, declared: "We designate the G20 to be the main forum for our international economic cooperation."

A MULTIPOLAR WORLD TAKING SHAPE

So the quarter-century-old elite G7, made up of the industrialized West, gave way to G20, whose members accounted for two-thirds of the planet's population, four-fifths of world trade, and nine-tenths of the global economy. In per capita GDP, it covered a wide spectrum—from the lowly figure of $1,122 for India to the highest, for Australia, at $50,000.

The third G20 summit required that each of its members submit its economic policies to "a peer review" from other governments and the IMF. This decision applied to all, including the United States.

At its annual meeting in October, the IMF decided to transfer 5 percent of its voting rights from the industrialized countries to emerging economies by January 2011. It is about time. Whereas Belgium's GDP is half of South Korea's, it has 50 percent more votes at the IMF.

Then there is the stipulation that all major decisions at the IMF must secure a minimum of 85 percent of the vote. Since the United States has a 17 percent voting share, it has a veto. It is now up to BRIC nations—Brazil, Russia, India, and China—which take up four of the twelve top positions in the GDP league table, to get the voting requirement for major decisions reduced by 3 percent.

In the diplomatic arena, the pattern of cooperation and competition between major powers—an important feature of a multipolar world—is emerging. An example is the way Moscow and Washington worked together during September 2009 to devise a plan for Iran to ship its LEU to Russia and France for enriching to 20 percent. This happened only after the Obama administration had dropped Bush's missile defense plan in Eastern Europe.

China too has been engaged in the "cooperate and compete" mode with America. In the economic field it has bought staggering amounts of U.S. Treasury bonds to help cover Washington's yawning deficits. At the same time, by strictly regulating the appreciation of the yuan against the dollar, it continues to sell its products at prices lower than those of American-made products.

In the confrontation between Pyongyang and Washington on the nuclear issue, China has also practiced cooperation and competition. Without China's hefty economic support, the North Korean regime would not be able to survive. And Beijing has cooperated with Washington to bring North Korea to the negotiating table with three other concerned parties—South Korea, Russia, and Japan—as well as prepared the ground for bilateral talks between the two adversaries.

Finally, China and Russia are set to prevent UN-authorized military action against Iran, no matter what it does to its nuclear program. At their insistence all Security Council resolutions on Iran so far have been under Section 41 of Chapter VII of the UN Charter—instead of merely Chapter VII, which was the case with resolutions on Iraq. Article 41 says that "measures not involving the use of armed forces are to be employed."[29] Any stiffening of present economic sanctions will be minimal and will basically leave Iran unaffected.

That marks the end of the era of the American Empire.

NOTES

Notes to Chapter 1

1. Cited in Odd Arne Westad, *The Global Cold War: Third World Interventions and the Making of Our Times* (Cambridge: Cambridge University Press, 2007), pp. 111, 166.

2. During the interwar period, direct U.S. investment in Europe more than doubled, and nearly 1,300 American companies began operating in Europe. George C. Herring, *From Colony to Superpower: U.S. Foreign Relations Since 1776* (New York: Oxford University Press, 2008).

3. It was not until November 1954 that the Dow Jones Industrial Average surpassed its September 3, 1929, peak of 381.7. *Guardian (London)*, October 4 and 15, 2008.

4. Clive Webb, "Haunted by History," *Guardian Review (London)*, October 3, 2008; N. Gregory Mankiw, "Can We Avoid a Depression?" *New York Times*, October 26, 2008.

5. George Walden, "Into the Arms of Uncle Joe," *Observer (London)*, August 3, 2008.

6. Paul Krugman, "The Obama Agenda," *New York Times,* November 7, 2008.

7. Michael C. C. Adams, *The Best War Ever: America and World War II* (Baltimore: Johns Hopkins University Press, 1993), p. 114.

8. Paul Kennedy, *The Rise and Fall of the Great Powers* (New York: Random House, 1987), p. 358.

9. Fareed Zakaria, *The Post-American World* (New York: W. W. Norton; London: Allen Lane, 2008), pp. 34–35.

10. Cited in Westad, *The Global Cold War*, p. 93.

Notes to Chapter 2

1. Abdel Bari Atwan, *The Secret History of Al-Qaida* (London: Abacus, 2007), p. 162.

2. Dilip Hiro, *Neighbors, Not Friends: Iraq and Iran after the Gulf Wars* (New York: Routledge, 2001), p. 40.

3. Ibid., pp. 66–67.

4. Gunnysack was the name given to a mythological Haitian character who snatched children staying out too late at night and pushed them inside his gunnysack—a fate that would befall anybody who spoke ill of Papa Doc.

5. The constitution did not allow Jean Bertrand Aristide to serve consecutive terms.

6. Cited in Stephen F. Cohen, *Failed Crusade: America and the Tragedy of Post-Communist Russia* (New York: W. W. Norton, 2001), p. 8.

7. Zbigniew Brzezinski, "The Cold War and Its Aftermath," *Foreign Affairs* (Fall 1992): p. 33.

8. *New Times* (Moscow), no. 23, 1993.

9. Cohen, *Failed Crusade*, p. 96. The U.S. Freedom Support Act of 1992 provided only $400 million for the former Soviet states. Timothy Colton, *Yeltsin: A Life* (New York: Basic Books, 2008), p. 268.

10. Ruslan Khasbulatov and Alexander Rutskoi would be pardoned by the newly elected Duma in 1994.

11. Colton, *Yeltsin*, p. 291; Cohen, *Failed Crusade*, pp. 149–150.

12. Colton, *Yeltsin*, p. 353.

13. Stephen F. Cohen, "American Journalism and Russia's Tragedy," *Nation*, October 2, 2000.

14. Cohen, *Failed Crusade*, p. 12.

15. "International Response to the Second Chechen War," Wikipedia, en.wikipedia.org/wiki/International_response_to_the_Second_Chechen_War.

16. Cited in Andrew Bacevich, *The Limits of Power: The End of American Exceptionalism* (New York: Metropolitan Books, 2008), pp. 58–59.

17. Jonathan Stein, "Bush Pep Talk to Generals: 'Stay Strong! Stay the Course! Kill Them!'" In the Blogs, MotherJones.com, www.motherjones.com/mojo/2008/06/bush-pep-talk-generals-stay-strong-stay-course-kill-them.

18. Roger Dobson, "Bush IQ Low on Presidential League," *Sunday Times* (London), September 10, 2006.

19. Richard Perle was recruited to coach George W. Bush on the Middle East during his presidential campaign in 2000.

20. Ron Suskind, *The Price of Loyalty: George W. Bush, the White House, and the Education of Paul O'Neill* (New York: Simon & Schuster, 2004), p. 85.

21. Dilip Hiro, *Secrets and Lies: The True Story of the Iraq War* (London: Politico's Publishing, 2005), p. 537. Hereafter *Secrets and Lies* (U.K. edition).

22. Gardiner Harris and William J. Broad, "Smiles Return to US Scientists' Faces," *New York Times*, January 22, 2009.

23. Dilip Hiro, *Secrets and Lies* (New York: Nation Books, 2004; London: Politico's Publishing, 2005), pp. 75–76. Hereafter *Secrets and Lies*.

24. Preventive war is different from preemptive war. When two opposing sides are clearly lined up in an offensive mode, one can mount a preemptive strike against the other. But in a preventive war, the self-proclaimed threatened state invades a country that *might* attack it to eliminate such an eventuality.

25. Hiro, *Secrets and Lies*, pp. 7–8.

26. I deal with these questions later in this chapter and in Chapter 8.

27. See Dilip Hiro, *The Essential Middle East: A Comprehensive Guide* (New York: Carroll & Graf, 2003), p. 104.

28. *Guardian (London)*, September 25, October 3 and 7, 2003.

29. Cited in Dilip Hiro, *Secrets and Lies* (U.K. edition), p. 547. Lord Bingham, former law lord of Britain, called the invasion of Iraq "a serious violation of international law" and

accused Britain and America of acting like a "world vigilante." Richard Norton-Taylor, "Top Judge: US and UK Acted as 'Vigilantes' in Iraq Invasion," *Guardian (London)*, November 18, 2008.

30. See Hiro, *The Essential Middle East*, pp. 165, 170, and Dilip Hiro, "Iraq Reckoning," *Nation*, September 12, 2005, www.thenation.com/doc/20050912/infact.

31. Nicholas D. Kristof, "US Spending $5,000/Second in Iraq," *New York Times*, March 22, 2008.

32. Public buildings were looted and burned in all the capitals of Iraq's remaining seventeen provinces.

33. Hiro, *Secrets and Lies* (U.K. edition), pp. 542–543.

34. Ibid., pp. 547–548.

35. All told there were some 1,800 such photographs and video clips. This exposé came on the heels of the leaking of a legal brief prepared for Rumsfeld in March 2003 arguing that, since the president safeguarded national security, any ban on torture, even under American law, could not be applied to "interrogation undertaken pursuant to the President's commander-in-chief authority."

36. Jonathan Freedland, "Seasonal Forgiveness Has a Limit." *Guardian (London)*, December 24, 2008. According to a *New York Times* editorial on December 18, 2008, the Senate Armed Services Committee had made a strong case for bringing criminal charges against Donald Rumsfeld and his legal counsel, and potentially other officials, including White House counsel and Dick Cheney's former chief of staff.

37. Hiro, *Secrets and Lies* (U.K. edition), p. 548.

38. Paul Harris and Peter Beaumont, "Iraq Created a Terrorist Flood, American Spymasters Warn Bush," *Observer* (London), September 24, 2006; Dan Glaister, "Campaign in Iraq Has Increased Terrorism Threat, Says American Intelligence Report," *Guardian (London)*, September 25, 2006.

39. Julian Glover, "British Believe Bush Is More Dangerous Than Kim Jong-Il," *Guardian (London)*, November 3, 2006.

40. Rami Khouri, "America Through Arab Eyes," *International Herald Tribune*, April 22, 2008.

41. Suzanne Goldenberg, "New Chapter Begins with End to Secret Prisons and Torture," *Guardian (London)*, January 23, 2009.

42. Ewen MacAskill, "Findings Also Show Fall in Support for War on Terror," *Guardian (London)*, June 15, 2006.

43. George Monbiot, "How These Gibbering Numbskulls Came to Dominate Washington," *Guardian (London)*, October 28, 2008.

44. Meg Bortin, "Distrust of US Gets Deeper but Not Wider," *International Herald Tribune*, June 28, 2007; Albert R. Hunt, "'My Way or the Highway' No Longer Works for US," *International Herald Tribune*, August 6, 2007.

45. Mark Leonard, *What Does China Think?* (New York: Public Affairs, 2008), p. 130.

46. In 2008, IED explosions in Iraq fell to 9,000-plus. Thom Shanker, "US Relies on Technology to Counter Afghan Terrorism," *New York Times*, February 26, 2009.

47. Vikas Bajaj, "Despite Big Rally, Grim Outlook on Profits and Jobs," *New York Times*, October 14, 2008.

48. Stephen Mihm, "The Seer Who Saw It Coming," *New York Times*, August 18, 2008.

49. Bloomberg News, "US Banks 'Effectively Insolvent,'" *International Herald Tribune*, January 26, 2009.

50. The term "securitization" stems from the fact that it is the securities that are sold to investors to obtain funds.

51. Alan S. Blinder, "Six Bad Moves that Led US into Crisis," *International Herald Tribune*, January 26, 2009.

52. A third of U.S. hedge funds that made a profit in 2008 did so largely by short-selling. Among the four fund managers who earned more than $1 billion was George Soros. "He Makes $1.7b amid Credit Crisis," *Electric New Paper* (Singapore), March 28, 2009, newpaper.asia1.com.sg/printfriendly/0,4139,197155,00.html.

53. Alan Rappeport, "A Short History of Hedge Funds," CFO.com, March 27, 2007, www.cfo.com/article.cfm/8914091.

54. Money market funds are mutual funds—professionally managed investment schemes that pool cash from many investors and invest in stocks and bonds—that invest in highest rated debt maturing in less than thirteen months.

55. Peter S. Goodman, "Taking Hard New Look at a Greenspan Legacy," *New York Times*, October 8, 2008.

56. David Segal, "Buffett Takes Blame for 'Dumb Things' in '08," *New York Times*, March 1, 2009.

57. Charles R. Morris, *The Trillion Dollar Meltdown: Easy Money, High Rollers, and the Great Credit Crash* (New York: PublicAffairs, 2008), p. 78; Christopher Cox, chairman of U.S. Securities and Exchange Commission, "Swapping Secrecy for Transparency," *New York Times*, October 20, 2008.

58. Morris, *Meltdown*, p. 77.

59. David Segal, "Buffet's Silence on Moody's Is Loud," *New York Times*, March 1, 2009.

60. "Road to Ruin," *Guardian (London)*, January 16, 2009.

61. Gretchen Morgenson, "Did Rating Watchdog Become Lapdog?" *International Herald Tribune*, December 8, 2008.

62. Michael M. Grynbaum, "U.S. Finds Questionable Practices by Ratings Agencies," *New York Times*, July 9, 2008.

63. Joe Nocera, "Tough Rules Kept Indian Banks Sound," *New York Times*, December 20, 2008.

64. Morris, *Meltdown*, p. 70.

65. Ibid., p. 54.

66. Stephen Mihm, "The Seer Who Saw It Coming," *New York Times*, August 18, 2008.

67. There had been notable exceptions to the post–World War II policy of letting un-economic companies fail. In 1979 there was a bailout of Chrysler by President Jimmy Carter, and a decade later, Bush Senior rescued Savings and Loan banks with $110 billion of public money.

68. Heather Timmons and Julia Werdigier, "U.S. Bonds Facing Global Test of Faith," *New York Times*, July 21, 2008.

69. "Commercial Paper," Wikipedia, en.wikipedia.org/wiki/Commercial_paper.

70. The U.S. Treasury intervened to guarantee par value for money markets. "The Price of Failure," *Economist*, October 4, 2008, p. 99.

71. Within a week of this massive bailout, some AIG executives and sales representatives spent $440,000 on a retreat at an exclusive resort.

72. Following the state takeover, Sir Fred Goodwin, the chief executive of Royal Bank of Scotland, was forced to resign, and given the nickname of "Fred the Shred."

73. Becky Barrow, "Mortgages Were Crazy, Says Bank," *Daily Mail* (London), December 21, 2008.

74. Brian Knowlton and Michael M. Grynbaum, "Two Lions Face a Reckoning: Greenspan Acknowledges Fallibility," *International Herald Tribune*, October 24, 2008; Andrew Clark and Jill Treanor, "Greenspan—I Was Wrong About the Economy. Sort Of," *Guardian (London)*, October 24, 2008.

75. Bonuses are awarded to top officials and lower ranks of a company when it makes unexpectedly large profits. To award bonuses to those working for the financial institutions that had failed or were about to go bankrupt defied logic as well as morality.

76. Among his many admirers was journalist and author Bob Woodward, whose book on Alan Greenspan, published in 2000, was titled *Maestro: Greenspan's Fed and the American Boom.*

77. Oliver Burkeman, "Look Out for Number One," *Guardian (London)*, March 10, 2009.

78. "Savings and Loan Crisis," Wikipedia, en.wikipedia.org/wiki/Savings_and _Loan_crisis.

79. Joe Nocera, "Chorus Grows: Nationalize the Banks," *New York Times*, February 14, 2009.

80. Madeleine Bunting, "Faith. Belief. Trust. This Economic Orthodoxy Was Built on Superstition," Comment Is Free, *Guardian (London)*, October 6, 2008, www.guardian .co.uk/commentisfree/2008/oct/06/economics.economy.

81. "Lessons from a Crisis," *Economist*, October 4, 2008, p. 45; Alex Berenson, "Free Market's Demise? Don't Bet on It," *New York Times*, October 7, 2008.

82. Sheryl Gay Stolberg, "Bush Risks Being Sidelined at International Finance Meeting," *New York Times*, November 14, 2008.

83. Eric Lichtblau, "Policing of Stock Fraud Falls in the US," *New York Times*, December 26, 2008.

84. Mark Landler, "Sarkozy Puts Paris Accent on Summitry," *New York Times*, November 19, 2008.

85. David Stout, "'Old Sage' Bush Muses on His Years in Office," *New York Times*, December 20, 2008.

86. Sarah Baxter, "Bush's $300m Library in Danger of Becoming White Elephant," *Sunday Times* (London), December 28, 2008.

87. For theological differences between Sunnis and Shiites, see Hiro, *The Essential Middle East*, pp. 485–86, 502.

88. Ian Black, "Iraqi Shoe-Thrower Was Beaten by Security, Says Judge," *Guardian (London)*, December 20, 2008.

89. Michael Cooper, "Palin Weighs Down Ticket," *New York Times*, October 31, 2008.

90. Terence Hunt, "Bush Accuses Russia of 'Bullying and Intimidation,'" Fox News, August 15, 2008, www.foxnews.com/wires/2008Aug15/0,4670,Bush,00.html.

91. Mary Dejevsky, "Vladimir Putin: 'Georgia? We Couldn't Just Let Russia Get a Bloody Nose,'" *Independent* (London), September 12, 2008, www.independent.co.uk/news/world/europe/vladimir-putin-georgia-we-couldnt-just-let-russia-get-a-bloody-nose-927110.html.

NOTES TO CHAPTER 3

1. Timothy Colton, *Yeltsin: A Life* (New York: Basic Books, 2008), p. 230.

2. Cited in *Edward Lucas, The New Cold War: The Future of Putin's Russia and the Threat to the West* (New York: Palgrave Macmillan; London: Bloomsbury, 2008), p. 43.

3. "Privatization in Russia," *Business Forum* (Winter–Spring 1994), www.entrepreneur.com/tradejournals/article/16110623.html.

4. In 1996, Roman Abramovich and Boris Berezovsky acquired controlling interest in Sibneft for a mere $100 million as a result of the 1995 loans-for-shares program.

5. Dilip Hiro, *Neighbors, Not Friends: Iraq and Iran after the Gulf Wars* (New York: Routledge, 2001), pp. 139–140.

6. Michael Wines, "An Ailing Russia Lives a Tough Life That's Getting Shorter," *New York Times,* December 3, 2000.

7. Stephen F. Cohen, "Bombing of Serbia by NATO," *Nation*, May 24, 1999.

8. Stephen F. Cohen, "American Journalism and Russia's Tragedy," *Nation*, October 2, 2000.

9. The Associated Press and Bloomberg News, "Russian Central Bank Loosens Hold on Ruble," November 24, 2008.

10. Simon Tisdall, "West's Missed Opportunity That Led to an Aggressive and Cynical Putin," *Guardian (London)*, September 2, 2008.

11. Lucas, *The New Cold War*, p. 101.

12. See Dilip Hiro, *Inside Central Asia: A Political and Cultural History of Uzbekistan, Turkmenistan, Kazakhstan, Kyrgyzstan, Tajikistan, Turkey and Iran* (New York: Overlook Press, 2009), pp. 304–307.

13. Vladislav Surkov retained his post as first deputy chief of staff under President Dmitry Medvedev.

14. Lucas, *The New Cold War*, p. 156.

15. Sophia Kishkovsky, "New Life for Church Media in Russia," *New York Times*, December 21, 2008.

16. Lucas, *The New Cold War*, p. 155.

17. The Russian Orthodox Church, with its liturgy performed in Old Slavonic, was originally based in Kiev, Ukraine, and moved to Moscow only in 1589.

18. Cited in Lucas, *The New Cold War*, p. 164.

19. Ibid.

20. President Vladimir Putin, "Annual Address to the Federal Assembly of the Russian Federation," April 25, 2005, kremlin.ru/eng/speeches/2005/04/25/2031_type70029type82912_87086.shtml.

21. The Stabilization Fund would mushroom to $100 billion by May 2007.

22. Cited in Howard Zinn, *A People's History of the United States: 1492–Present* (New York: HarperCollins, 2001), p. 413.

23. "Federation Council Approves Atomprom Creation," January 24, 2007, www .kommersant.com/p-9929/r_500/nuclear_civil_reform.

24. "America Withdraws from ABM Treaty," BBC News, December 13, 2001, news.bbc .co.uk/1/hi/world/americas/1707812.stm.

25. In January 2009, Cuba played host to two Russian bombers carrying nuclear arms.

26. The next year's defense budget was to rise by a quarter to $50 billion. Thom Shanker, "Resurgent Russian Military Marches Anew," *New York Times,* October 20, 2008.

27. The leaders of the Czech Republic and Poland protested, arguing that the U.S. missile defense system concerned them and Washington, and was outside the jurisdiction of the EU president.

28. Ian Traynor and Luke Harding, "Sarkozy Backs Russian Calls for Pan-European Security Pact," *Guardian (London),* November 15, 2008.

29. Tom Parfitt and Julian Borger, "Russia to Raise Nuclear Missile Output Fourfold," *Guardian (London),* December 24, 2008.

30. Luke Harding, "Russia Challenges with Nuclear Overhaul," *Guardian (London),* September 27, 2008.

31. Simon Tisdall, "Banning the Bomb," *Guardian (London),* January 23, 2009.

32. Graham Bowley and Michael Schwirtz, "Russia Ties Itself Even Closer to Chavez's Venezuela," *New York Times,* September 27, 2008.

33. Marianna Belenkaya, "Putin's Visit to the Middle East Will Not Be a Mere Formality," RIA Novsoti, February 7, 2007, www.cdi.org/russia/johnson/2007–30–35.cfm.

34. President Vladimir Putin, "Responses to Questions from Russian Journalists," December 6, 2004, kremlin.ru/eng/speeches/2004/12/06/1232_type82915_80868.shtml.

35. Philippe Naughton, "Putin Takes Swipe at Hungry America's 'Comrade Wolf,'" *The Times* (London), May 11, 2006.

36. Steven Lee Myers and Andrew E. Kramer, "Group of 8 Talks, Like So Much These Days, Are All About Energy: Russia's Gas and Oil," *New York Times,* July 12, 2006.

37. Katrin Bennhold, "Faith in West Is at Risk in Crisis," *New York Times,* January 9, 2009.

38. Vladimir Putin, "Unilateral Force Has Nothing to Do with Global Democracy," Comment Is Free, *Guardian (London),* February 13, 2007, www.guardian.co.uk/comment isfree/2007/feb/13/comment.russia.

39. Julian Borger, "Russia's New Doctrine," *Guardian (London),* April 11, 2007.

40. Judy Dempsey, "Berlin Deepens Its Moscow Bonds," *International Herald Tribune,* October 22, 2008.

41. Andrew E. Kramer, "Russia Sees in Credit Crisis the End of US Domination," *New York Times,* October 3, 2008.

42. Brian Whitmore, "Russian Oligarchs Feeling the Heat of Financial Crisis," Radio Free Europe/Radio Liberty, October 20, 2008, www.rferl.org/content/Oleg_Deripaska/1331255.html.

43. John Gray, "The Rush to Control the World's Oil and Water Will Turn Lethal," *Observer* (London), March 30, 2008.

NOTES TO CHAPTER 4

1. The five American oil giants were Esso, Gulf, Socal, Socony, and Texaco. The Seven Sisters' remaining two members were British Petroleum, the renamed Anglo-Iranian Oil Company, and Royal Dutch Shell.

2. The Shah's death in July 1980 eased the crisis but did not dissipate it.

3. Rami Khouri, "America Through Arab Eyes," *International Herald Tribune*, April 28, 2008.

4. Dilip Hiro, *Neighbors, Not Friends: Iraq and Iran after the Gulf Wars* (New York: Routledge, 2001), p. 210.

5. Ibid., p. 257.

6. Dilip Hiro, *War Without End: The Rise of Islamist Terrorism and Global Response*, rev. ed. (New York: Routledge, 2002), p. 311.

7. Ibid., p. 459, note 81.

8. "President Delivers State of the Union Address," Office of the Press Secretary, January 29, 2002, georgewbush-whitehouse.archives.gov/news/releases/2002/01/20020129–11.html.

9. David E. Sanger, *The Inheritance: The World Obama Confronts and the Challenges to American Power* (New York: Harmony Books; London: Bantam, 2009), pp. 47–48.

10. The final, foolproof assurance to Tehran came on October 6, 2004—with the publication of the *Comprehensive Report by the Special Adviser to the DCI on Iraq's WMD*, which concluded that Iraq destroyed stockpiles of illicit weapons within months of the end of the 1991 Gulf War. Dilip Hiro, *Secrets and Lies: The True Story of the Iraq War* (London: Politico's Publishing, 2005), pp. 547–548.

11. Sanger, *The Inheritance*, p. 67.

12. The resulting clash between the pro-Islamist parliament and the pro-Washington ruler led to periodic dissolving of the legislature, the latest dissolution occurring in March 2009. The Associated Press and Reuters, "Emir of Kuwait Dissolves Parliament amid Impasse," March 19, 2009.

13. The Associated Press, "Iran Marks Seizure of US Embassy," November 4, 2008.

14. Anoushirvan Ehteshami, *After Khomeini: The Iranian Second Republic* (New York: Routledge, 1995), pp. 177–178, 195.

15. C. J. Chivers and Brian Knowlton, "Putin Gives His Support to Caspian Neighbors," *International Herald Tribune*, October 17, 2007. Putin became the first Russian leader to visit Tehran since Joseph Stalin in 1943.

16. Esmail Kosari's claim that the S-300 missiles were being delivered was denied by Moscow. *International Herald Tribune*, December 22 and 23, 2008.

17. Andrew Kramer, "As Gas Producers Join Forces, Some Lobby for Cartel," *New York Times*, December 24, 2008.

18. The Associated Press and Bloomberg News, "Sinpec Signs Deal on Iran Oil," December 11, 2007.

19. Dilip Hiro, *The Essential Middle East: A Comprehensive Guide* (New York: Carroll & Graf, 2003), pp. 391–392.

20. These countries are Bolivia, Colombia, Ecuador, Panama, Peru, and Venezuela.

21. Bart Jones, *¡Hugo! The Hugo Chávez Story from Mud Hut to Perpetual Revolution* (Hanover, NH: Steerforth; London: Bodley Head, 2008), p. 281.

22. On the day of the February 1992 failed coup, in his speech to the National Assembly, Rafael Caldera said, "It is difficult to ask people to self-immolate themselves for freedom and democracy when they think freedom and democracy are not capable of feeding them and stopping the exorbitant rise in the cost of living." Cited in ibid., p. 159.

23. The first two republics were formed in 1811 and 1813 during the wars of independence, the third in 1819 with Gran Colombia, and the fourth in 1830.

24. Saddam Hussein sent his deputy to the OPEC summit.

25. Mr. Danger is the blue-eyed Yankee who grabs land from unwary Venezuelan peasants in *Dona Barbara*, a 1929 classic novel by former president Rómulo Gallegos, a writer-politician.

26. Dilip Hiro, *Blood of the Earth: The Battle for the World's Vanishing Oil Resources* (New York: Nation Books, 2007), p. 178.

27. Patrick J. McDonnell and Edwin Chen, "Bush Exits Summit as Trade Talks End in Disagreement," *Los Angeles Times*, November 6, 2005.

28. Mark Weisbrot, "Populists Aid Poor, Spur Growth," *Augusta (GA) Chronicle*, March 23, 2006.

29. Jones, *¡Hugo!* pp. 441, 451.

30. Peter Beaumont, "Chavez's Bolivarian Revolution," *Observer Review* (London), May 7, 2006. The poverty rate dropped to 26 percent at the end of 2008. Simon Romero, "Despite Vote, Chavez Faces Obstacles," *New York Times*, February 17, 2009.

31. Simon Romero, "Venezuela Suspending Heating Aid to US," *New York Times*, January 6, 2008.

32. Hiro, *Blood of the Earth*, p. 181.

33. *Daily Telegraph* (London), January 5, 2006. On May Day 2006, President Evo Morales took control of Bolivia's oil and gas fields and gave foreign energy companies six months to agree to new contracts with his government, thereby fulfilling one of his major promises during the election campaign.

34. The aggregate GDP of Mercosur members in terms of purchasing power parity is the fifth largest in the world.

35. Alexei Barrionuevo, "Latin America Shows Its Collective Strength," *New York Times*, December 18, 2008.

36. Joshua Goodman, "Leader of Brazil Opts for Amazon, Not Alps," Bloomberg News, January 29, 2009.

37. Simon Romero, "Approval of Constitution Helps Bolivian President," *New York Times*, January 27, 2009.

38. David Stout, "Chávez Calls Bush 'the Devil' in U.N. Speech," *New York Times*, September 20, 2006, www.nytimes.com/2006/09/20/world/americas/20cnd-Chavez.html?ex=1158984000&en=aa643a6bdfaf2377&ei=5087%0A.

39. Exxon took its case to a court in London and lost.

40. Rory Carroll, "Chavez Invites in Russian Planes," *Guardian (London)*, March 16, 2009.

41. David Barboza, "China Gets a Warmer Welcome for Its Cash," *New York Times*, February 21, 2009.

NOTES TO CHAPTER 5

1. Isabel Hilton, "Beijing Loved Bush's America," *Guardian (London)*, February 20, 2009.

2. Any sharp movement out of dollars would have caused the greenback to fall even faster and further, hurting dollar holders even more than the United States. So China stayed with its policy of gradual portfolio adjustments at the margin as further dollar surpluses accrued.

3. Will Hutton, *The Writing on the Wall: China and the West in the 21st Century* (London: Abacus, 2008), p. 119.

4. Brian Knowlton, "Chinese Happy at Way Things Going," *International Herald Tribune*, July 22, 2008.

5. Meg Bortin, "Distrust of US Gets Deeper but Not Wider," *International Herald Tribune*, June 28, 2007.

6. Wei Gu, "In Crisis China Shows Its Hand," *International Herald Tribune*, February 26, 2009.

7. Chinese Prime Minister Wen Jiabao is known to travel abroad with both books of Adam Smith in his baggage.

8. Cited in Parag Khanna, *The Second World: Empires and Influence in New Global Order* (New York: Random House; London: Allen Lane, 2008), p. 301.

9. Cited in Fareed Zakaria, *The Post-American World* (New York: W. W. Norton; London: Allen Lane, 2008), p. 89.

10. Chris Bramall, *Sources of Chinese Economic Growth, 1978–1996* (Oxford: Oxford University Press, 2000), pp. 132, 158.

11. Delegations from many nations visited the Chinese Special Economic Zones to learn from their experience.

12. Cited in Hutton, *The Writing on the Wall*, p. 96.

13. In contrast, leaders of the Communist Party of India (CPI), also founded in 1921, meekly followed the instructions of the Comintern conveyed to them through the Communist Party of Great Britain. The CPI failed to produce a leader of the caliber of Mao to feel confident enough to blaze an independent trail appropriate to the specific conditions of Indian society.

14. Gordon Redding, "Feeling the Stones on the River Bed: Prospects and Implications for China's Entry into the World of Global Competition," Ivey Management Services, May/June 2005, www.iveybusinessjournal.com/view_article.asp?intArticle_ID=555.

15. Within two decades, Shenzhen would become a thriving city of over 10 million and absorb the aggregate investment of $30 billion.

16. Edward Wong, "A Bid to Help Poor Rural China to Catch Up," *New York Times*, October 13, 2008.

17. Alan Wheatley, "Darker View of Chinese 'Miracle,'" *International Herald Tribune*, January 6, 2009.

18. Knowlton, "Chinese Happy at Way Things Going." Though the figure declined to 77 percent in 2008, nearly 60 percent of Chinese primary school pupils were learning English.

19. Britain and France used the veto thirty-two and eighteen times respectively. "United Nations Security Council Veto Power," Wikipedia, en.wikipedia.org/wiki/United _Nations_Security_Council_veto_power.

20. Goh Keng Swee held that job for ten years.

21. Cited in Hutton, *The Writing on the Wall*, p. 140.

22. Besides Deng, the Committee of the Elders consisted of Chen Yun, Li Xiannian, and Deng Liqun, who had formally resigned from the Politburo in 1987 but remained influential.

23. "Top Secret/Exdis: Secretary's Morning Summary for June 4, 1989," www.gwu.edu/ ~nsarchiv/NSAEBB/NSAEBB16/documents/13–01.htm.

24. Instituto per Gli Studi di Politica Internazionale, *Report on the State of International System*, Rome, 1992, p. 68.

25. Hutton, *The Writing on the Wall*, p. 140.

26. Dilip Hiro, *Blood of the Earth: The Battle for the World's Vanishing Oil Resources* (New York: Nation Books, 2007), p. 192.

27. Within a few years Wal-Mart, the globe's largest retail outlet, sourced four-fifths of its products worldwide from China.

28. Geoff Dyer, "Growth in China Seen Slowing to 7.5%," *Guardian (London)*, November 26, 2008.

29. Hiro, *Blood of the Earth*, p. 210.

30. Hutton, *The Writing on the Wall*, p. 121.

31. Kishore Mahbubani, *The New Asian Hemisphere: The Irresistible Shift of Global Power to the East* (New York: PublicAffairs, 2008), p. 71.

32. Minxin Pei, *China's Trapped Transition: The Limits of Development Autocracy* (Cambridge, MA: Harvard University Press, 2006), pp. 92–95, 154.

33. Mark Leonard, *What Does China Think?* (New York: PublicAffairs, 2008), p. 37.

34. "China White Paper on Democracy," BBC News, October 19, 2005, news.bbc.co.uk/ 1/hi/world/asia-pacific/4355768.stm.

35. Joseph Kahn, "A Textbook Example of Change in China," *New York Times*, August 31, 2006.

36. Alan Wheatley, "Income Gap Unsettles Chinese," *International Herald Tribune*, December 23, 2008; Wheatley, "Darker View of Chinese 'Miracle.'"

37. The GINI coefficient is a ratio varying between zero and one. Zero means perfect equality, with everyone having exactly the same income, and 1 means perfect inequality, with one person having all the income and others having none. Denmark had the lowest figure of 0.23 and Namibia the highest at 0.70.

38. Joy Dunbar, "China Set to Leapfrog UK in High-net Terms," FTAdviser.com, June 26, 2008, www.ftadviser.com/financialadviser/advisers/news/article/20080626/d49c4eaa-41e8–11dd-a236–0015171400aa/china-set-to-leapfrog-uk-in-highnet-terms.jsp.

39. Knowlton, "Chinese Happy at Way Things Going."

40. Jim Yardley, "China's Communists Resilient," *New York Times*, August 7, 2008.

41. Edward Wong, "With Pacts, Taipei and Beijing Draw Closer," *New York Times*, November 5, 2008.

42. Ashley Vance, "Frontiers Expand for Super-Fast Computers," *New York Times*, November 19, 2008.

43. In 1996, China also signed the Comprehensive Test Ban Treaty.

44. Andrew J. Kramer, "Russia Turns Its Eyes Eastward with LNG Plant," *New York Times*, February 18, 2009.

45. Hiro, *Blood of the Earth*, p. 207.

46. Associated Press, August 18, 2005.

47. Hiro, *Blood of the Earth*, pp. 352–353. India had lobbied hard through Russia to be accorded an observer status at the Shanghai Cooperation Organization.

48. Earlier, Africa's leaders had rebuffed the Pentagon's approach to establish its Africa Command on the continent's soil.

49. In absolute terms, Angola became the second most important oil source for China in 2005 after Saudi Arabia, overtaking Iran.

50. David Zweig and Bi Jianhai, "China's Global Hunt for Energy," *Foreign Affairs* (September–October 2005). In February 2009, Aluminum Corp of China agreed to invest $19.5 billion in cash-hungry Rio Tinto of Australia.

51. David Barboza, "China Gets a Warmer Welcome for Its Cash," *New York Times*, February 21, 2009.

52. "China and the Panama Canal Debate and Poll: Is China in a Position to Take Over the Panama Canal?" Political Debates and Polls Forum, YouDebate.com, www.you debate.com/DEBATES/panama_china.HTM.

53. David Shambaugh, "China's New Foray into Latin America," *YaleGlobal*, November 17, 2008, yaleglobal.yale.edu/display.article?id=11615.

54. Hiro, *Blood of the Earth*, p. 209.

55. "US-China Trade Statistics and China's World Trade Statistics," the US-China Business Council, www.uschina.org/statistics/tradetable.html.

56. Hiro, *Blood of the Earth*, p. 211.

57. Robert D. Kaplan, "Lost in the Pacific," *International Herald Tribune*, September 22–23, 2007.

58. "Russia and Weapons of Mass Destruction," Wikipedia, en.wikipedia.org/wiki/Russia_and_weapons_of_mass_destruction; "United States and Weapons of Mass Destruction," Wikipedia, en.wikipedia.org/wiki/United_States_and_weapons_of_mass_destruction.

59. "China Profile: Nuclear Overview," Nuclear Threat Initiative, March 2009, www.nti.org/e_research/profiles/China/Nuclear/index.html; David E. Sanger, *The Inheritance: The World Obama Confronts and the Challenges to American Power* (New York: Harmony Books; London: Bantam, 2009), p. 383.

60. I discuss this further in Chapter 8.

61. Ed Pilkington, "China Winning Cyber War, Congress Warned," *Guardian (London)*, November 21, 2008.

62. Later that year, the Foreign Broadcasting Information Service of the United States posted the English translation of the book on the Internet.

63. On August 26, 2008, the eve of Chancellor Angela Merkel's three-day visit to China, *Der Spiegel* reported that German officials had detected spying software in the foreign ministry and Merkel's office.

64. Pilkington, "China Winning Cyber War."

65. Of the more than $1 trillion China had in greenbacks, $600 billion were in Treasuries, the rest in Fannie Mae, Freddie Mac, and other GSEs.

66. Keith Bradsher, "Rising Cost of Buying US Debt Puts Strain on China's Economy," *New York Times*, September 3, 2008.

67. Ashley Seager, "Beijing Blames America for the Global Crisis," *Guardian (London)*, January 29, 2009.

68. Wong, "A Bid to Help Poor Rural China."

Notes to Chapter 6

1. David Smith, *The Dragon and the Elephant: China, India, and the New World Order* (London: Profile Books, 2007), p. 76.

2. Country Tables: 2007/2008 Report, Human Development Reports, United Nation Development Programme, hdrstats.undp.org/countries.

3. Randeep Ramesh, "British Minister Defends £825 Million Aid to Help India's Poor," *Guardian (London)*, November 19, 2008. If the poverty level is raised to $2 a day, then seven out of ten Indians exist below that line.

4. The population density of China is 410 persons per square mile.

5. See Chapter 1.

6. Ramchandra Guha, *India After Gandhi: The History of the World's Largest Democracy* (New York: Harper Perennial, 2007), p. 693.

7. In July 2007, there were 41,000 civil and criminal cases pending in the Supreme Court, another 3.6 million in high courts, and a further 25 million in district courts. Kishore Mahbubani, *The New Asian Hemisphere: The Irresistible Shift of Global Power to the East* (New York: PublicAffairs, 2008), p. 89.

8. "Economy of India," Wikipedia, en.wikipedia.org/wiki/Economy_of_India.

9. Smith, *The Dragon and the Elephant*, p. 80.

10. Guha, *India After Gandhi*, p. 699. By 2007, India accounted for only 1 percent of the globe's commerce in goods. Linda Yeuh, "Landfall in Asia," *Guardian (London)*, October 28, 2008.

11. Starting in 1996, India allowed twelve new foreign bank branches a year. Equally, other WTO members allowed Indian banks to open branches in their territories.

12. Smith, *The Dragon and the Elephant*, p. 139; Mahbubani, *The New Asian Hemisphere*, p. 93. By 2006, more than 35,000 Indian expatriates had returned and set up businesses in Bangalore. Another 32,000 returned from the United Kingdom. To encourage the return of expatriates with foreign passports, India gives them Overseas Citizenship Certificates, which provide all the privileges of citizenship.

13. National Association of Software and Service Companies Web site, www.nasscom.in.

14. Thomas L. Friedman, *The Earth Is Flat: A Brief History of the Twenty-first Century* (New York: Farrar, Straus & Giroux, 2005), p. 459.

15. Mahbubani, *The New Asian Hemisphere*, p. 59.

16. Smith, *The Dragon and the Elephant*, p. 137.

17. Ramesh, "British Minister Defends £825 Million Aid"; Somini Sengupta, "India Faces a Paradox in Its Ill-fed Children," *International Herald Tribune*, March 11, 2009.

18. Pranab Bardhan, "Inequality in India and China: Is Globalization to Blame?" *YaleGlobal*, October 15, 2007, yaleglobal.yale.edu/display.article?id=9819.

19. Smith, *The Dragon and the Elephant*, p. 79.

20. The ranking for both countries was 70 in a list of 177 countries. Mahbubani, *The New Asian Hemisphere*, p. 59.

21. "Economy of India"; "Economy of China," Wikipedia, en.wikipedia.org/wiki/Economy_of_China.

22. Joe Nocera, "Tough Rules Kept Indian Banks Sound," *New York Times*, December 20, 2008.

23. Heather Timmins, "In Global Crisis, India Finds Strength and Hope in Weakness," *International Herald Tribune,* February 28–March 1, 2009.

24. Ibid.

25. "Israel Ahead of India," *Times of India* (Mumbai), February 7, 2004, timesofindia.indiatimes.com/India/Why_Israel_is_far_ahead_of_us_in_defence_sector/articleshow/msid-480471,curpg-2.cms.

26. The refurbished aircraft carrier would be named after an ancient Indian emperor, Vikramaditya.

27. Donald Greenlees, "China and India Lead Surge in Missile Development in Asia," *International Herald Tribune*, September 20, 2007.

Notes to Chapter 7

1. The Associated Press, "EU Scolded by Its Chief," February 20, 2009.

2. At 175,000, the number of Chinese students in the EU was almost two and a half times the figure for the United States. Fu Ying, "Post-Olympics China and Its Relations with the West," Ministry of Foreign Affairs of the People's Republic of China, October 20, 2008, www.fmprc.gov.cn/eng/wjb/zwjg/zwbd/t522131.htm; Kishore Mahbubani, *The New Asian Hemisphere: The Irresistible Shift of Global Power to the East* (New York: PublicAffairs, 2008), p. 91.

3. This happened on March 16, 2008, when the euro topped $1.56 and America's 2007 GDP was $13,843 billion. "Weak Dollar Costs U.S. Economy Its No. 1 Spot," Reuters, March 14, 2008, www.reuters.com/article/ousivMolt/idUSL1491971920080314.

4. Britain, Ireland, and Denmark were admitted to the EC only in 1973.

5. The ban remained in place in 2009.

6. The Maastricht Treaty also introduced the concept of Community citizenship.

7. The president of the Commission and all other commissioners are nominated by the EU Council, with each member-state entitled to name one commissioner to take charge of a particular department.

8. The new members were Cyprus, the Czech Republic, Estonia, Hungary, Latvia, Lithuania, Malta, Poland, Slovakia, and Slovenia.

9. To save face, Clinton issued waivers in the case of these three non-American companies, a redundant exercise. Dilip Hiro, *Neighbors, Not Friends: Iraq and Iran After the Gulf Wars* (New York: Routledge, 2001), pp. 220, 229–230.

10. David Rennie, "Defense Strategy Snatches Stability from the Jaws of Victory," *Daily Telegraph* (London), October 3, 2006.

11. Steven Erlanger and Stephen Castle, "EU Chiefs Attempt to Cool Bloc's Crisis," *New York Times*, March 2, 2009.

12. President George W. Bush said that Kosovo's people were "independent," but he withheld formal recognition.

NOTES TO CHAPTER 8

1. Charlie Savage, "Obama Orders Review of Bush Maneuvers," *New York Times*, March 9, 2009.

2. In fact, the Clinton administration welcomed the passing of the 1993 constitution as well as Yeltsin's use of tank fire to terrify his opponents in the popularly elected parliament.

3. William Pfaff, "Russia's Deep Animosity," *International Herald Tribune*, March 6, 2007.

4. See Chapter 3.

5. Cathy Young, "A Brewing Storm," *International Herald Tribune,* January 3–4, 2009.

6. Arthur J. Arberry, *The Koran Interpreted* (Oxford: Oxford University Press, 1964), pp. 65, 502.

7. The actual constitutional term for this office in Persian is *rahbar*, meaning simply "leader [of the revolution]." But using the word "leader" in English causes confusion, as the term applies to official and unofficial positions. Hence the term "supreme leader" has come into vogue outside Iran.

8. The other half of the Guardian Council is elected by the parliament.

9. See further Dilip Hiro, *The Essential Middle East: A Comprehensive Guide* (New York: Carroll & Graf, 2003), p. 310.

10. On the whole Americans hold their politicians in low esteem. The approval rating of the U.S. Congress has plunged from the long-established 18 percent to 10 percent.

11. Hiro, *The Essential Middle East*, p. 586.

12. Ibid., p. 548.

13. Meg Bortin, "Distrust of US Gets Deeper but Not Wider," *International Herald Tribune*, June 28, 2007.

14. Jim Yardley, "After 30 Years, Economic Perils on China's Path," *New York Times*, December 19, 2008.

15. Mark Leonard, *What Does China Think?* (New York: PublicAffairs, 2008), p. 123.

16. The United Front Democratic Parties include the Revolutionary Committee of Kuomintang, China Democratic League, Chinese Peasants' and Workers' Democratic Party, and Taiwan Democratic Self-Government League.

17. David Shambaugh, "Let a Thousand Democracies Bloom," *International Herald Tribune*, July 7–8, 2007.

18. Cited in Leonard, *What Does China Think?* p. 51.

19. Ibid., pp. 68–71.

20. Pallavi Aiyar, "Not Quite Love but China Flirts with Democracy," *Indian Express* (Delhi), January 15, 2005.

21. In reality, only about half of the laws are enforced. Kishore Mahbubani, *The New Asian Hemisphere: The Irresistible Shift of Global Power to the East* (New York: PublicAffairs, 2008), p. 87.

22. Leonard, *What Does China Think?* pp. 73–74.

23. The Associated Press, "Cell Phones Gaining in Poor Areas, Study Finds," March 2, 2009. Internet users in India came to only 52 million.

24. Andrew Jacobs, "China's Web Wild Card," *International Herald Tribune*, February 6, 2009.

25. Dune Lawrence, "For Its Online Critics, China Adapts Response," *International Herald Tribune*, November 19, 2008.

26. The eighty-sixth amendment to the Indian constitution added the right to education to the list of guaranteed rights.

27. "Ancient China's Technology: The Science & Technology Ancient China Taught the West," East West Dialogue, east_west_dialogue.tripod.com/id1.html.

28. "China Issues Human Rights Record of the United States," Embassy of the People's Republic of China in the United States of America, March 8, 2007, www.china-embassy.org/eng/zt/zgrq/t302225.htm.

29. Howard W. French, "Chinese Media See the World with a Blind Eye," *International Herald Tribune*, December 7, 2007.

Notes to Chapter 9

1. "Comprehensive National Power," Wikipedia, en.wikipedia.org/wiki/Comprehensive_national_power.

2. John Lee, "The Danger of an Attractive Obama," *International Herald Tribune*, February 3, 2009.

3. "Evolving a Comprehensive National Security Index," *Financial Express*, February 17, 2003, www.financialexpress.com/news/evolving-a-comprehensive-national-security-index/73228/2.

4. Evidently, Confucius overlooked women of the world.

5. The Chinese government announced a three-year, $150 billion reconstruction program for the province.

6. John Lee, "Why China Wants to Win," *International Herald Tribune*, November 13, 2008.

7. Josh Kurlantzick, "Chinese Soft Power in Southeast Asia (Part I)," *Globalist*, July 2, 2007, www.theglobalist.com/StoryId.aspx?StoryId=6240.

8. "China Vows to Ramp Up Aid, Investment, Trade with Africa," *Bridges Weekly Trade News Digest* 10, no. 37 (November 8, 2006), ictsd.net/i/news/bridgesweekly/6390/.

9. Mark Leonard, *What Does China Think?* (New York: PublicAffairs, 2008), pp. 118–120.

10. BBC, www.bbc.co.uk/.

11. Meg Bortin, "Distrust of US Gets Deeper but Not Wider," *International Herald Tribune*, June 28, 2007.

12. Dilip Hiro, *War Without End: The Rise of Islamist Terrorism and Global Response*, rev. ed. (New York: Routledge, 2002), p. 363.

13. The latest to enter the satellite TV news sector was Japan's NHK World, the country's sole public broadcasting network, in February 2009.

14. David Smith, "One Small Step for Zhai, One Giant Leap into the Space Race for China," *Observer* (London), September 28, 2008.

15. N. Gopal Raj, "China's Manned Space Program Marches Ahead," *Hindu* (Delhi), October 11, 2008.

16. Randeep Ramesh, "India Plans £1.7 Billion Manned Space Mission by 2015," *Guardian (London)*, February 24, 2009.

17. Sanjoy Hazarika, "Raj Kapoor, Top Indian Film Star, Is Dead at 64," *New York Times*, June 3, 1988, www.nytimes.com/1988/06/03/obituaries/raj-kapoor-top-indian-film-star -is-dead-at-64.html.

18. Ramchandra Guha, *India After Gandhi: The History of the World's Largest Democracy* (New York: Ecco; London; Macmillan, 2007), p. 742.

19. Lee, "Why China Wants to Win."

Notes to Chapter 10

1. George Monbiot, "The US Missile Defence System Is the Magic Pudding That Will Never Run Out," Comment Is Free, *Guardian (London)*, August 19, 2008, www.guardian .co.uk/commentisfree/2008/aug/19/usforeignpolicy.russia.

2. See Dilip Hiro, *The Essential Middle East: A Comprehensive Guide* (New York: Carroll & Graf, 2003), p. 449.

3. Rami Khouri, "America Through Arab Eyes," *International Herald Tribune*, April 22, 2008.

4. James Risen, *State of War: The Secret History of the CIA and the Bush Administration* (New York: Free Press, 2006), p. 61.

5. Iran's Intelligence Minister Ali Yunusi said, "Most of the shining objects that our people see in Iran's airspace are American espionage equipments used to spy on Iran's nuclear and military facilities," and added that Iran had shot down some drones and discovered spying devices in them. *Washington Post*, February 13, 2005; Reuters, February 16, 2005.

6. Following Iraq's staging of the "war of cities" in March 1985, involving missile attacks on Iranian cities during the 1980–1988 Iran-Iraq War, Iran's supreme leader, Ayatollah Ruhollah Khomeini, likely lifted his ban on nuclear arms programs that he had imposed in the early days of the conflict. Since nuclear weapons did not distinguish between combatants and noncombatants, they were un-Islamic, he had ruled. Following Khomeini's reversal on the subject, the Iranian officials built up contacts with Pakistan's Dr. A. Q. Khan, later called the "Father of the Atom Bomb." As a result, Pakistan-made centrifuges for enriching uranium arrived in Iran by the end of 1987. Adrian Levy and Catherine Scott-Clark, *Deception: Pakistan, the United States and the Global Nuclear Weapons Conspiracy* (New York: Walker & Company, 2007), p. 172.

7. Risen, *State of War*, p. 194.

8. Reuters, "Security Pledge on Iran Not in Works, Bush Says," May 14, 2008.

9. David E. Sanger, "Israel Asked US for Aid to Hit Iran Atomic Site," *New York Times*, January 12, 2009.

10. David E. Sanger, *The Inheritance: The World Obama Confronts and the Challenges to American Power* (New York: Harmony Books; London: Bantam, 2009), p. 100.

11. Sarah Baxter, "Biden Hangs Tough on Nuclear Issue in Offering Talks with Iran," *Sunday Times* (London), February 8, 2009.

12. Terry Macalister and George Monbiot, "Global Oil Supply Will Peak in 2020, Says Energy Agency," *Guardian (London)*, December 15, 2008.

13. Dilip Hiro, *Blood of the Earth: The Battle for the World's Vanishing Oil Resources* (New York: Nation Books, 2007), p. 60.

14. Dilip Hiro, *Desert Shield to Desert Storm: The Second Gulf War* (New York: Routledge, 1992), p. 108.

15. Ron Suskind, *The Price of Loyalty: George W. Bush, the White House, and the Education of Paul O'Neill* (New York: Simon & Schuster, 2004), p. 85.

16. Hiro, *Blood of the Earth*, pp. 137–138.

17. Will Hutton, *The Writing on the Wall: China and the West in the 21st Century* (London: Abacus, 2008), p. 243.

18. Edward Wong, "China Signals More Interest in Building Aircraft Carrier," *New York Times*, December 23, 2008.

19. The ExonFlorio amendment of the Omnibus Trade and Competitiveness Act of 1988 empowered the president to block foreign takeovers if they threatened national security. During 2003–2006 there were six reviews and five withdrawals under threat of review—more than in the previous decade combined.

20. Executive Summary, *Annual Report to Congress: Military Power of the People's Republic of China, 2008*, Office of the Secretary of Defense, Washington, DC, March 4, 2008, www.asiaing.com/military-power-of-the-people-s-republic-of-china-2008.html.

21. David Lague, "Taiwan and China Flex Muscles," *International Herald Tribune*, October 11, 2007.

22. William R. Hawkins, "JCS Chairman Pace Engages in Wishful Thinking About Beijing's Military Ambitions," AmericanEconomicAlert.org, February 11, 2006, www.americaneconomicalert.org/view_art.asp?Prod_ID=2238.

23. Hutton, *The Writing on the Wall*, p. 248.

24. Executive Summary, *Military Power of the People's Republic of China, 2008*.

25. Cited in Hutton, *The Writing on the Wall*, p. 250.

26. In its reports, the Commission made no mention of the prospects for retraining redundant, low-skilled American workers for high-skilled jobs, which would benefit them and the nation's economy. By contrast, following the downturn in the PRC's exports as a result of the global fiscal meltdown in 2008–2009, the Chinese government introduced retraining programs for laid-off workers.

27. Report to U.S. Congress of the United States–China Economic and Security Review Commission, 2005, pp. 19, 44–45.

28. Edward M. Graham and David M. Marchick, *US National Security and Foreign Direct Investment* (Washington, DC: Peterson Institute of International Economics, 2006), p. 102.

29. James A. Dorn, "Nationalistic Barriers," *South China Morning Post*, December 13, 2007, reprinted on the Web site of the Cato Institute, www.cato.org/pub_display.php?pub_id=8844.

30. Indira A. R. Lakshmanan, "Bush Sets China Course, but Will Obama Follow?" *International Herald Tribune*, December 10, 2008.

NOTES TO CHAPTER 11

1. After the fall of the Berlin Wall in November 1989, the Pentagon staged alone or led major military operations in Panama (December 1989), Iraqi-occupied Kuwait (January 1991), Iraqi Kurdistan (June 1991), Somalia (1992 and 1993), Bosnia (1994), Haiti (1994), Iraq (Operation Desert Fox, December 1998), Serbia (1999), and Afghanistan (2001).

2. Robert Kagan, *The Return of History and the End of Dreams* (New York: Knopf; London: Atlantic Books, 2008), p. 75.

3. Julian Borger, "US Intelligence: 'We Can No Longer Call Shots Alone,'" *Guardian (London)*, November 21, 2008.

4. John Lee, "The Danger of an Attractive Obama," *International Herald Tribune*, February 3, 2009.

5. The latest instance was the PRC blocking America's move at the UN Security Council to condemn Sudan's expulsion of aid workers from Darfur. Simon Tisdall, "Naval Skirmish Shows U.S. and China Are Sailing into Choppy Waters," *Guardian (London)*, March 11, 2009.

6. Mark McDonald, "Beijing Says U.S. Incited Tense Standoff by Navies," *New York Times*, March 11, 2009. It was over Hainan Island that in April 2001 an American reconnaissance plane had a forced landing after its midair collision with a Chinese fighter plane.

7. Dilip Hiro, *Secrets and Lies* (New York: Nation Books, 2004; London: Politico's Publishing, 2005), pp. 5–6, 10.

NOTES TO EPILOGUE

1. Hiroko Tabuchi, "Chinese Economic Juggernaut Is Gaining on Japan," *New York Times*, October 2, 2009, http://www.nytimes.com/2009/10/02/business/economy/02yen.html?_r=1.

2. Patrick Wintour and Larry Elliot, "Brown's New World Order," *Guardian* (London), April 3, 2009, www.guardian.co.uk/world/2009/apr/03/g20-gordon-brown-global-economy.

3. Dilip Hiro, "The World Melts, China Grows," *Asia Times* (Hong Kong), May 6, 2009, www.atimes.com/atimes/China_Business/KE06Cb01.html.

4. Tom Burgis, "Chinese Seek Huge Stake Nigeria Oil," *Financial Times* (London), September 20, 2009, www.ft.com/cms/s/0/5d72e37a-ac90–11de-a754–00144feabdco.html.

5. Simon Romero and Alexei Barrionuevo, "Deals Help China Expand Sway in Latin America," *New York Times*, April 15, 2009, http://www.nytimes.com/2009/04/16/world/16chinaloan.html.

6. During 1994–2000, there were economic crises in nine major countries that affected the global economy: Mexico (1994), Thailand-Indonesia-Malaysia-South Korea-the Philippines (1997–1998), Russia and Brazil (1998), and Argentina (2000).

7. Tom Dispatch, "Defying the Economic Odds, the World Melts Down, China Grows," http://www.tomdispatch.com/post/175067.

8. The breakdown was $1.6 trillion commercial paper; $1.6 trillion, federal home loan bank securities; $0.7 trillion, Troubled Asset-Relief Program for investment in banks and automakers; $0.7 trillion invested to shore up AIG and Bear Stearns; government as

lender: $0.9 trillion, Term Asset-backed Securities Loan Facility; $0.9 trillion, term action facility; $0.5 trillion, other loans; government as insurer: $0.7 trillion, bank debt; $1.0 trillion Citibank and Bank of America; $0.4 trillion, Fannie Mae. Brian Knowlton and Edmund L. Andrews, "US Pitches Assets to Balky Investors," *International Herald Tribune*, March 24, 2009.

9. Heather Stewart, "Economic Crisis Will End the Global Reign of US Dollar, Warns World Bank President," *Guardian* (London), September 29, 2009, www.guardian.co.uk/business/2009/sep/28/us-dollar-usurped-china-euro-world-bank.

10. "China to Buy $50 Billion of IMF's First Bonds," *International Herald Tribune*, September 4, 2009.

11. Joe Biden, "What You Might Not Know About the Recovery," *New York Times*, July 27, 2009, www.nytimes.com/2009/07/26/opinion/26biden.html.

12. Andrew Clark, "'Scrap Bloated Bonuses,'" *Guardian* (London), September 15, 2009, www.guardian.co.uk/business/2009/sep/14/obama-speech-wall-street.

13. Ibid.

14. Peter Baker, "Good Will, but Few Foreign Policy Benefits for Obama," *New York Times*, September 21, 2009, www.nytimes.com/2009/09/20/us/politics/20prexy.html?scp=1&sq=peter baker good will&st=cse.

15. Ibid.

16. Robert Tait, "Obama Woos Muslims from Secular Turkey," *Guardian* (London), April 7, 2009, www.guardian.co.uk/world/2009/apr/07/barack-obama-turkey-islam.

17. The SM-3 missile had undergone eight successful tests since 2007.

18. Clifford J. Levy and Peter Baker, "Russia's Reaction on Missile Plan Leaves Iran Issue Hanging," *New York Times*, September 18, 2009, www.nytimes.com/2009/09/19/world/europe/19shield.html.

19. Ellen Barry, "As Obama Visits, Russian TV Alters Take on U.S.," *New York Times*, July 6, 2009.

20. Luke Harding, "No Fanfare for 'Working Visit,'" *Guardian* (London), July 7, 2009, www.guardian.co.uk/world/2009/jul/06/barack-obama-visit-russia-media.

21. Stephen Bierman, "Russia Raises Oil Production as OPEC Cuts," *International Herald Tribune*, September 9, 2009.

22. See p. 124.

23. Jeremy Ban-Ami, "Tel Aviv, Then and Now," *International Herald Tribune*, April 10, 2009.

24. Michael Wines, "China's Ties with Iran Complicate Diplomacy," *New York Times*, September 30, 2009, www.nytimes.com/2009/09/30/world/asia/30china.html.

25. See p. 238.

26. Tania Branigan, "Can China Help to Defuse the Nuclear Threat from Iran?" *Observer* (London), September 27, 2009, www.guardian.co.uk/world/2009/sep/27/china-iran-nuclear-weapons-threat.

27. See pp. 153–154.

28. Tania Branigan, "Young, Gifted and Red: The Communist Party's Quiet Revolution," *Guardian* (London), May 19, 2009, www.guardian.co.uk/world/2009/may/20/china-changing-communist-party.

29. It is article 42 that provides for military action should measures in Article 41 prove inadequate to dispel threats to international peace.

SELECT BIBLIOGRAPHY

Bacevich, Andrew J. *The Limits of Power: The End of American Exceptionalism*. New York: Metropolitan Books, 2008.

Bennis, Phyllis. *Calling the Shots: How Washington Dominates Today's UN*. Updated ed. New York: Olive Branch Press, 2000; Moreton-in-Marsh, UK: Arris Books, 2004.

Cohen, Stephen F. *Failed Crusade: America and the Tragedy of Post-Communist Russia*. New York: W. W. Norton, 2001.

Colton, Timothy. *Yeltsin: A Life*. New York: Basic Books, 2008.

Darwin, John. *After Tamerlane: The Global History of Empire Since 1405*. London: Allen Lane, 2007; New York: Bloomsbury, 2008.

Emmott, Bill. *Rivals: How the Power Struggle Between China, India and Japan Will Shape Our Next Decade*. Orlando, FL: Harcourt; London: Allen Lane, 2008.

Galbraith, John Kenneth. *The Great Crash, 1929*. Boston: Houghton Mifflin, 1955; London: Penguin, 1992.

Guha, Ramchandra. *India After Gandhi: The History of the World's Largest Democracy*. New York: Ecco; London: Macmillan, 2007.

Hiro, Dilip. *Blood of the Earth: The Battle for the World's Vanishing Oil Resources*. New York: Nation Books, 2007.

——. *Blood of the Earth: The Global Battle for Vanishing Oil Resources*. London: Politico's Publishing, 2008.

——. *The Essential Middle East: A Comprehensive Guide*. New York: Carroll & Graf, 2003.

——. *Neighbors, Not Friends: Iraq and Iran after the Gulf Wars*. New York: Routledge, 2001.

——. *Secrets and Lies: Operation "Iraqi Freedom" and After*. New York: Nation Books, 2004.

——. *Secrets and Lies: The True Story of the Iraq War*. London: Politico's Publishing, 2005.

——. *Timeline History of India*. New York: Barnes and Noble, 2006.

——. *War Without End: The Rise of Islamist Terrorism and Global Response*. Revised edition. New York: Routledge, 2002.

Hutton, Will. *The Writing on the Wall: China and the West in the 21st Century*. New York: Free Press, 2006; London: Abacus, 2008.

Jones, Bart. ¡Hugo! The Hugo Chávez Story from Mud Hut to Perpetual Revolution. Hanover, NH: Steerforth; London: Bodley Head, 2008.

Kagan, Robert. The Return of History and the End of Dreams. New York: Knopf; London: Atlantic Books, 2008.

Khanna, Parag. The Second World: Empires and Influence in New Global Order. New York: Random House; London: Allen Lane, 2008.

Krugman, Paul. The Return of Depression Economics and the Crisis of 2008. New York: W. W. Norton; London: Penguin, 2009.

Leonard, Mark. What Does China Think? New York: PublicAffairs; London: Fourth Estate, 2008.

Lucas, Edward. The New Cold War: How the Kremlin Menaces Both Russia and the West. New York: Palgrave Macmillan; London: Bloomsbury, 2008.

Mahbubani, Kishore. The New Asian Hemisphere: The Irresistible Shift of Global Power to the East. New York: PublicAffairs, 2008.

Mayer, Jane. The Dark Side: The Inside Story of How the War on Terror Turned into a War on American Ideals. New York: Doubleday, 2008.

Morris, Charles. The Trillion Dollar Meltdown: Easy Money, High Rollers, and the Credit Crash. New York: PublicAffairs, 2008.

Risen, James. State of War: The Secret History of the CIA and the Bush Administration. New York: Free Press, 2006.

Sanger, David E. The Inheritance: The World Obama Confronts and the Challenges to American Power. New York: Harmony Books; London: Bantam, 2009.

Smith, David. The Dragon and the Elephant: China, India, and the New World Order. London: Profile Books, 2007.

Soros, George. The New Paradigm for Financial Markets: The Credit Crisis of 2008 and What It Means. New York: PublicAffairs, 2008.

Wallerstein, Immanuel. The Decline of American Power: The U.S. in a Chaotic World. New York: New Press, 2003.

Westad, Odd Arne. The Global Cold War: Third World Interventions and the Making of Our Times. Cambridge: Cambridge University Press, 2007.

Wintle, Justin. China: The Rough Guide Chronicle. London: Rough Guides, 2002.

Zakaria, Fareed. The Post-American World. New York: W. W. Norton; London: Allen Lane, 2008.

INDEX

For a name starting with Al or El, see its second part. A person's religious or secular title has been omitted.

Ho Chi Minh, 9, 18
Ho Chi Minh City, 22
Hollywood, 17, 237, 247, 248–249
Honduras, 140
Hong Kong, 40, 64, 151, 158, 160, 162, 265
Hong Kong Special Administrative Region, 162, 169
Hoover vacuum cleaner, 237
Hormuz Strait, 178, 258
household responsibility system (China), 156
Hua Guofeng. 153, 156, 158, 159
Hu Jintao, 9, 165, 166–167, 172, 173, 176, 177, 182, 183–184, 227, 231, 242, 249, 261, 267
human rights, 232
  civic and political rights, 234, 236
  cultural, economic and social rights, 234–235
  See also Vienna Summit on Human Rights
Hungary, 21, 22, 40, 87, 114, 216
Hurricane Katrina, 83, 239
Hussein (Imam of Shiites), 53
Hussein, Saddam, 25, 28, 50, 58, 92, 124, 125, 136, 243, 254, 259
Hutchinson Whampoa, 176, 269
Hyderabad, 207
Hypo Real Estate, 77

IBM, 192
Ichkeria, 96
Impeccable, 279
Improvised Explosive Devices (IEDs), 61–62, 172
India and Indians, 2, 82, 149, 185, 189, 190, 199, 225, 238, 241, 274, 276, 281

banking system of, 10, 70, 191, 192, 199
and Britain, 10, 187–88, 197, 201, 222
bureaucracy of, 190, 202
and China, 5, 10, 156, 158, 187, 199–201, 199–201, 204–205, 246, 261, 276, 279
corruption and inequality in, 190, 197–198, 202, 205
democracy in, 190–191, 201, 205, 219, 222, 224, 230, 234
economy and economic policy of, 10, 188–189, 190, 192–195, 197, 198, 199, 201, 203–204, 281
electoral politics of, 190–192, 197, 202, 230–231
and English language and media, 189, 195, 197, 199, 247, 248
and global financial crisis, 182
and Germany, 193
history of, 187–188
and Information and Communications Technology, 10, 184, 189, 193, 195–197, 203
and International Monetary Fund, 193
and Japan, 193
judicial system in, 192
and nuclear weapons, 10, 189, 202, 203
land reform in, 191, 198
military of, 200–201, 202–204
oil and gas in, 192, 193
and Pakistan, 201, 203
and Russia, 202, 204
and Shanghai Cooperation Organization, 171, 172
and Soviet Union, 200, 201, 202, 203
and Tibet, 200